THE GREAT TASK
REMAINING BEFORE US

D1596243

The Great Task Remaining Before Us

Reconstruction as America's Continuing Civil War

Edited by
Paul A. Cimbala and
Randall M. Miller

FORDHAM UNIVERSITY PRESS
NEW YORK   2010

Fordham University Press has no responsibility for the persistence or accuracy of URLs for external or third-party Internet websites referred to in this publication and does not guarantee that any content on such websites is, or will remain, accurate or appropriate.

Fordham University Press also publishes its books in a variety of electronic formats. Some content that appears in print may not be available in electronic books.

Library of Congress Cataloging-in-Publication Data

The great task remaining before us : Reconstruction as America's continuing Civil War / edited by Paul A. Cimbala and Randall M. Miller.—1st ed.
    p.   cm.— (Reconstructing America)
   Includes bibliographical references and index.
   ISBN 978-0-8232-3202-4 (cloth : alk. paper)—ISBN 978-0-8232-3203-1 (pbk. : alk. paper)—ISBN 978-0-8232-3204-8 (ebook)
   1. Reconstruction (U.S. history, 1865–1877)   2. Reconstruction (U.S. history, 1865–1877)—Social aspects.   3. United States—Social conditions—1865–1918.   4. Southern States—Social conditions—1865–1945.   5. Memory—Social aspects—United States—History.   6. Memory—Social aspects—Southern States—History.   I. Cimbala, Paul A. (Paul Alan), 1951–   II. Miller, Randall M.
E668.G778   2010
973.8—dc22

                                                                    2010013603

Printed in the United States of America
12 11 10   5 4 3 2 1
First edition

To the librarians at Fordham University and Saint Joseph's University

Contents

Preface   *ix*

Acknowledgments   *xv*

Introduction: An Unfinished War | 1
G. Ward Hubbs

1   A Victory Spoiled: West Tennessee
Unionists during Reconstruction | 9
Derek W. Frisby

2   "I Wanted a Gun": Black Soldiers
and White Violence in Civil War
and Postwar Kentucky
and Missouri | 30
Aaron Astor

3   "The Rebel Spirit in Kentucky": The
Politics of Readjustment in a Border
State, 1865–1868 | 54
Anne E. Marshall

4   The Crucible of Reconstruction:
Unionists and the Struggle for
Alabama's Postwar Home Front | 69
Margaret M. Storey

5   "A New Field of Labor": Antislavery
Women, Freedmen's Aid, and
Political Power | 88
Carol Faulkner

6   "Objects of Humanity": The White
Poor in Civil War and
Reconstruction Georgia | 101
Denise E. Wright

7   Racial Identity and Reconstruction:
     New Orleans's Free People of Color
     and the Dilemma of
     Emancipation | 122
     Justin A. Nystrom

8   "My Children on the Field": Wade
     Hampton, Biography, and the Roots
     of the Lost Cause | 139
     Rod Andrew Jr.

9   Rebels in War and Peace: Their Ethos
     and Its Impact | 154
     Jason K. Phillips

10   Reconstructing Loyalty: Love, Fear,
     and Power in the Postwar South | 173
     Carole Emberton

11   Reconstructing the Nation,
     Reconstructing the Party: Postwar
     Republicans and the Evolution
     of a Party | 183
     Michael Green

Notes   205
List of Contributors   259
Index   261

Preface

This book, through a series of select case studies, proposes to remap considerations of the Civil War and the Reconstruction era by charting the ways that the needs, interests, and experiences of going to war, fighting it, and making sense of it informed and directed Reconstruction politics, public life, social change, and cultural memory. In doing so, it shows that "the war" did not end with Lee's surrender at Appomattox and Lincoln's assassination in Washington. Much unfinished business remained. Both Northerners and Southerners still struggled with what the war demanded of them during "the peace." Frederick Douglass, for one, observed after the passage of the Thirteenth Amendment by which slavery was abolished that the work of liberty continued. So, too, did the work of binding up the nation's wounds. Defining freedom; remaking or at least rebuilding the South; integrating the expanded roles of women and blacks during the war into postwar society, culture, and polities; deciding the place of the military in public life; demobilizing or redeploying soldiers; organizing a new party system; and determining the scope and meanings of "Union," among several vital issues coming from the war—all loomed large during Reconstruction.

Central to the unfinished business of the war was a question the *New York Times*, among many, had posed as early as 1862 and echoed thereafter: "What shall we do with the negro?" With emancipation as policy and then legal reality, Frederick Douglass's answer was to give him rights and leave him alone. Radical Republicans pressed to do just that. But any action for the freedpeople inevitably caused a reaction to it and often against them, for the scale and extent of the adjustments necessary for blacks to function as a "free people" were more than most whites could then accept. Ending slavery called into question all manner of economic, social, cultural, and political arrangements that had operated for generations.

The end of slavery came so suddenly and violently that there were no models for adjusting to it within a democratic polity in which white men ruled, at least by force of numbers alone. White Americans experimented with a variety of ways to make "freedom" for blacks work short of granting full equality in fact as well as law. Those experiments constituted a significant investment in trying to make sense of the war. Blacks, however, did not wait for whites, whether friends in Congress or abolitionists, to act for them. By asserting their own rights as humans to control their own families, find their own work, build their own churches, and make their own way, even to claim political power for themselves, blacks forced the issues everywhere during and after the war. In that regard, the unfinished business of what to "do with the negro" became simultaneously a local question on many fronts wherever blacks and whites met—and often contested with—one another, and a national question that did not go away even with the suppression of black rights.

Of almost equal weight was the question of reuniting the divided Union, now with its "new birth of freedom" and (in many Northerners' eyes at least) its renewed sense of almost millennial purpose. The process required leadership at all levels of government and society. And it required good governments to lead. From the inception of the republic during the Revolutionary era, Americans had sought to realize what Thomas Jefferson had insisted was the test of the Revolution itself: making good government. The coming apart of the Union over slavery had tested the ability of the great experiment in self-government to endure (as Abraham Lincoln reminded Americans in his inaugural addresses and the Gettysburg Address), but patching up that Union demanded more than a return to the federalism and political alignments before the war. The several, and competing, political interests of Republicans and Democrats; Union victors and former Confederates; men already enfranchised and men and women, whites and blacks, wanting that franchise—all struggled with one another and among themselves to make new governments on their terms. Some Radical Republicans wanted the federal government to assume new powers as the "guardian of freedom," while others worried that extensions of federal power threatened democracy itself. Issues of race, local control, physical reconstruction, economic policy, and all manner of self-interest complicated the setting up and management of governments and the "reconstruction" process. They also cast light again on the continuing American problem of balancing local and federal authority and distributing political power among "the people." And all the while, Americans insisted, the world was watching.

One example of the ways the war raised questions about government's place and purpose was the vexing problem of what to do with the military. The war had brought the military into new and larger roles in politics and society. Far from being an apolitical element, as American commonwealthman tradition demanded, the army became an instrument of social and political change during and after the war. For example, the Union Army's policies regarding "contrabands" in not returning fugitive slaves to Southern masters and in putting them to work for the army's interest pushed the government toward "freedom" for slaves during the war, just as the soldier vote in 1864 ensured Lincoln's reelection and a vigorous prosecution of the war to defeat secession and end slavery. The military's role in the physical destruction and then reconstruction of the South, in setting up work policies and managing labor during the war, and, for a time, in representing law and order after the war made it the focus of much concern about the place of the military in society. To be sure, demobilization came rapidly and depleted the ability of Republicans to enforce federal Reconstruction laws and interests in the South, and the reliance of new Republican governments in the South on black soldiers as militia during Reconstruction simultaneously enraged white Southerners and demonstrated the political weakness of those governments, paradoxically making possible some experiments in black freedom while also hastening the fall of those governments.

At the same time, some men found in the military a life and purpose they did not want to give up when the war was over. Some Union and former Confederate soldiers stayed on or joined up, and most of them were deployed to extend the opportunities for postwar "freedom" by "opening" the West for development and settlement. Some Union veterans continued the work the army had begun in getting "freedpeople" to work in the South by serving as Freedmen's Bureau officers, just as Confederate veterans provided the advance guard of the paramilitary groups opposing Reconstruction. And in their veterans' organizations, North and South, former soldiers lobbied their governments for pensions and their society for honorable memory. The military presence in America never fully retreated thereafter.

On a more mundane but fundamental level for most Americans, the unfinished business of the war was returning to some kind of normalcy in their daily lives. Giving meaning to the sacrifices of war meant putting in a crop, reclaiming or finding a job, reuniting with one's family divided by war or abandoned by circumstance, getting fitted with a prosthetic arm or leg and hoping to make one's way in a world that still demanded men use their hands, and, for many soldiers, returning to communities that could never understand what horrors men in battle had witnessed and what new definitions of courage and manhood that war had demanded. At the same time, women and others who had stayed behind sometimes struggled to incorporate veterans back into their lives and communities and did not always, or easily, concede to them fully their former status.

The social adaptations varied from place to place, not only between North and South but also within them. Southern communities often faced a physical reconstruction of places ravaged or savaged by war. The destruction and despoliation of buildings and land served as reminders of defeat, but they also destroyed the older compass of associations. The burnt church no longer stood as the landmark reference for a town, and the breached levees no longer held the river and tidal waters at bay. Re-forming communities in such circumstances thus required psychological as well as physical labor. At the same time, the demography of many places no longer recalled prewar days. People were on the move because of the war, and some people never returned to the old places by reason of death, flight, or a search for new chances elsewhere. After the war many people either kept moving, uprooted, or gave up any prospects in the old places. Some Northerners went south, some Southerners went north, and many Northerners and Southerners alike headed west—all to try their luck in a new land.

Even the definitions of who belonged and who could be trusted to create or re-create "a community" required new calculations based on new understandings of "patriotism" and "loyalty" to one's own family and community. For many Northerners, "the Union" had become less an abstraction and more "a nation." Men from different places had fought together and gained a common vocabulary drawn from battle and camp. Families at home had followed the progress of their men, and thus the nation in action, in newspaper accounts and letters, and they had invested in that progress by buying war bonds and producing for governmental consumption. They also came to see, if sometimes also to worry, that decisions in Chicago grain markets, New York and Philadelphia banking houses, and New England manufactures intertwined to bind together not only a market but also a people. Service to the nation, like one's religion, became a ticket of admission to acceptance in many Northern communities.

For many white Southerners, the Confederacy's failure in creating a nation did not defeat "the South" as an idea and ideal. Indeed, in many ways, the war and its aftermath made white Southerners more "Southern" as they celebrated their armies as men of brave and Christian character—true sons of the South—by making the soldiers' conduct and the collective memory of their sacrifices, rather than the final military outcome, the proof they had fought for—and must continue to honor—a noble cause.

At the same time, the war and then Reconstruction made white Southerners more local in their identities and commitments as they rushed to defend home from real and threatened invasions of "Yankees," whether as "bummers" on the march or "carpetbaggers" on the make. For white Southerners, the war and its aftermath forced new definitions of loyalty because the emancipation of blacks had unhinged all the old verities of white mastery and a unified social order. From the whites' perspective, blacks had "betrayed" them by running to Union lines and taking up arms against them. The war and Reconstruction thus made white Southerners more conscious of their whiteness as the marrow of community. War and Reconstruction also reinforced the small-government ideal among white Southerners while many blacks took a more expansive view of government's possibilities and looked to federal and state governments to defend freedom and expand opportunities. In the South whites became more committed to gaining control of local governments and asserting anew "states rights" as the shibboleth of "democratic" government and the shield for protection of family and community.

In the North and the South alike, the dissenters, malingerers, profiteers, and others who had acted "disloyally" by exploiting the circumstances of war for their own gain or in any way had violated the sanctity of home and hearth—all such were outside the community. One unfinished business of the war was settling old accounts after it. Thus the violence of the war continued in individual and collective acts to pay back grievances, reassert control and impose order, or purge the community of "outsiders." Unsettlements caused by war led to resettlements after it, as communities drove out those who could not be trusted.

In sum, neither victor nor vanquished accepted the war's end as settling all that the war had cost in blood and loss. Nor should we. Indeed, even the supposed reconciliation of veterans beginning in the late 1870s, and the memory of the war as an ennobling experience for white Northerners and Southerners who fought in it, could not erase altogether the fact that many of the physical, social, economic, political, and psychological demands of the war and "reconstruction" remained incomplete as the century closed.

The recent historiography of Reconstruction has followed Eric Foner's call, in his seminal study *Reconstruction: America's Unfinished Revolution 1863–1877* (HarperCollins, 1988), to re-center the story on the struggle for black freedom and to broaden the chronology of Reconstruction by dating it from the decision to make emancipation a policy during the war and extending it to the end of the nineteenth century, by which time white Northerners had abandoned blacks to their fate and white Southerners had "redeemed" the South from Republican rule through intimidation and violence and reasserted white control over blacks in the public sphere. Some scholars have enlarged the compass of inquiry to include North as well as South and, led by Heather Cox Richardson, even have begun to look westward in trying to make sense of what the war wrought. A new generation of scholars has pushed the beginnings of Reconstruction ever backward into the antebellum period. They see Reconstruction as a process on many fronts, working out variously in many places through the war and its aftermath and continuing well into the next century. Then, too, economic, social, and cultural history increasingly informs the approaches of scholars to Reconstruction.

That said, much work on Reconstruction remains locked in limited conceptions of time or space by focusing on a particular moment or by limiting any comparative perspective. This collection of essays makes no assertion of settling accounts or offering a comprehensive sweep of topics, geography, chronology, or historical genres. It does attempt to suggest that the contours of the unfinished business of the war are more malleable and complicated than any single drawing.

If some historians have marked off the mid–nineteenth century into supposedly neat categories of antebellum America, Civil War, and Reconstruction that seemingly had little to do with one another, this book seeks to pull them together. To borrow from Abraham Lincoln's charge to Americans in his Gettysburg Address, "the great task remaining before us" as scholars and students of the Civil War and Reconstruction era, then, is to explore more fully and widely the connections between wartime and postwar worlds in every facet of human life.

Paul A. Cimbala and Randall M. Miller

Acknowledgments

The editors of this volume are indebted to numerous individuals who encouraged them to finish their work and move on to other things. The librarians at Fordham University and Saint Joseph's University deserve our deep appreciation for helping us in this project, as in so many others. The volume is dedicated to them for all that they have done for us and our students and for all that they will continue to do as they strive to make the historian's job a little easier than it otherwise would be. We also acknowledge and thank the librarians at Haverford College, the University of Pennsylvania, the Library Company of Philadelphia, and the Historical Society of Pennsylvania, who smoothed the path of getting hold of the sources for revising essays, fact-checking, and tidying up, when necessary. We also are grateful to our institutions for their continued generous support. This volume is the fourth of our series of collections containing essays about the Civil War and Reconstruction published by Fordham University Press. We thank the Press's staff for encouraging the project and guiding it to completion, and we thank the leadership at the Press for recognizing the opportunities for discovering and publishing new scholarship on the Civil War and Reconstruction and making such concerns a major publishing interest. The editors also wish to thank Linda Patterson Miller and Elizabeth C. Vozzola for tolerating yet another of our joint projects and for being so gracious in accepting the bribes of dinners out as partial compensation for all the intrusions and interruptions our work has made on theirs.

THE GREAT TASK
REMAINING BEFORE US

Introduction: An Unfinished War

G. Ward Hubbs

T he war is over," declared Union General Ulysses S. Grant at Appomattox, Virginia, on April 9, 1865; "the rebels are our countrymen again."[1] Grant's adversary, Confederate General Robert E. Lee, told his men to go home and resume their occupations, obey the laws, and become good citizens. And many did. When they reached home, perhaps unconsciously closing a chapter in their lives, diarists stopped making entries.[2] That spring and summer of 1865 was a time for former soldiers to get on with their lives and to put the past four years behind them. With Richmond burned and occupied, the Rebel government fallen, its armies surrendered and dispersed, most Americans were convinced that their war was surely over.

The Confederacy's collapse has marked a convenient end to the Civil War. And it works, especially given our compulsion for the dramatic. The armies first clashed on Wilmer McLean's farm near Manassas, Virginia. Over the next four years, the future of the Union often hung in the balance until some professor from Maine or hard-drinking tanner from Illinois tipped the scales. Finally, those armies met once again on McLean's new farm near Appomattox. Days later, at the very moment of triumph, an assassin's bullet turned a jubilant nation into a grieving one; Lincoln, Christ-like, had sacrificed his own life for ours. But a two-day Grand Review down Pennsylvania Avenue would end it all in triumph. Irony, symmetry, and providential deliverance—this drama would be the fodder for countless books.

Reconstruction would be fodder for countless other books. Unlike the dramatic clarity of the Civil War, however, the ensuing decade seemed directionless. Its characters often appear to be petty, opportunistic, or unscrupulous, while its plot is vague, confusing, or depressing. When at last the curtain falls, an exhausted audience walks out after the Wormley House Bargain of 1877 puts an end to the confusing morass.

The war *is* over, General Grant had proclaimed. But Ringo, the freedman in William Faulkner's *The Unvanquished*, remained wary. "Naw, suh . . . This war ain't over. Hit just started good."[3]

Why, given the collapse of the Confederate government and the defeat of its armies—as well as the opinions of the participants themselves—would anyone *not* separate the Civil War and Reconstruction at Appomattox (to have a single event serve for several)? The historians in this collection have looked closely at everyday life in the South and, instead of discontinuity, have discovered a remarkable continuity from secession through the 1870s, especially in terms of violence, politics, benevolence, and social identity.[4]

The Civil War was easily the most violent war in our country's history, and in the first essay of this volume Derek Frisby examines the quasi-organized violence in West Tennessee after Lee's surrender. When former Confederates attacked Unionists and freedpeople, the Republican state government there gave freedmen the franchise and established a state guard to corral their belligerent enemies.[5] The state guard eventually imposed martial law on at least thirty counties and faced down the newly organized Ku Klux Klan. The fact that the Klan operated on a local stage, independent of a government, has tended to obscure both the political nature of the violence and its continuity with the four-year contest between the Union and the Confederacy. One West Tennessee Unionist put it plainly when he wrote that claims of Confederate defeat represented "the most gigantic falsehood of the age." Frisby himself could easily have substituted the words of his former professor, George C. Rable: "Peace became war carried on by other means" (an inversion of Clausewitz used so commonly that it escapes attribution).[6]

Aaron Astor, in the second essay of this collection, also sees continuity in the ongoing violence, this time in neighboring Kentucky and Missouri. Unlike West Tennessee, however, conservative whites—both Unionist and former Confederates—in these two border states made common cause to resist black emancipation, blacks in the military, and ultimately black citizenship. For four years, the Confederate and Union armies had battled over these issues. After Appomattox, Astor concludes, "the battle over the place of African Americans in Kentucky and Missouri society merely entered a new phase."

In the third essay, Anne E. Marshall's study of Kentucky underscores Astor's point by extending it to politics. Former antagonists on the battlefield, she writes, "would come together at the polls, making the politics of race common ground." Marshall calls this Kentucky's second civil war, with "all of the vitriolic rhetoric and violent imagery of bloody Civil War engagements." This time, she concludes, the pro-Confederate forces won. Kentucky may not have been typical of former enemies in battle making comrades in peace, but it was typical of one result of the war: a Solid South. That judgment is open to many qualifications; nonetheless, surely most historians would agree that with each passing year Southern politics became more polarized. Dissent was a wedge that Democrats in particular could never tolerate.

The continuation of violence linked to political activity also characterized Alabama, where Unionists found themselves "indelibly marked in a ruined land." According to Margaret M. Storey in the fourth essay, the withdrawal of most federal forces by the summer of 1865 left the Unionists on their own to defend themselves against former—and still formidable—Rebels who went about burning houses and murdering their foes. By 1868 former Unionists were pitted against the Ku Klux Klan, what many have labeled "the terrorist arm of the Democratic Party."[7] Facing local governments unwilling to defend them, Unionists suspected that (as in Anne Marshall's Kentucky) although the Union had been victorious at Appomattox, "they would not be victorious at home."

As an example of this continuing violence and division between Unionists and former Confederates, Storey mentions the Reverend Arad S. Lakin. In the mid-1860s, the national churches reestablished themselves in the former slave states. In Alabama the work of the Methodist Episcopal Church was led by the Reverend Lakin. While his family taught freedpeople in Huntsville, Lakin worked to establish biracial congregations throughout the state. He carried a Navy revolver, especially after he was hunted down by the Klan and threatened with lynching in the most famous political cartoon to emerge from Reconstruction.[8] Lakin's story is one of continuing violence and division between Unionists and former Confederates, certainly; but it also is an instance of Northern benevolence where yet again the Appomattox divide is inappropriate.

In 1964, Willie Lee Rose published her prize-winning *Rehearsal for Reconstruction: The Port Royal Experiment*, which detailed efforts to assist the freedpeople in the Sea Islands of South Carolina. In the introduction, C. Vann Woodward underscored the episode's significance as a "dress rehearsal" for Reconstruction, in part because the experiment started in early 1862.[9] But characterizing Reconstruction as another phase of the war would have made such apologies unnecessary. Carol Faulkner, in the fifth contribution to this collection, rejects the division between war and Reconstruction in her study building upon Rose's *Rehearsal for Reconstruction*. Faulkner focuses on the effects that reform efforts had on the reformers themselves—in this case antislavery women. She observes that many historians use Appomattox as a convenient end not only to the war, but also to women's benevolent efforts. In fact, women's participation in such reform work grew more intense in the shift from sponsorship by the government to sponsorship by voluntary—usually Christian—associations. "Only by extending the boundaries of the war into Reconstruction," she writes, "can we understand the gendered battles over emancipation, charity, and women's work."

The continuity of benevolence, albeit of a different sort, is the subject of the sixth essay, Denise E. Wright's study of welfare in Georgia. In Georgia, poor whites benefited from large aid programs originating first from the Confederate state, then from the Freedmen's Bureau, and finally from charitable associations headquartered in the North. Wright's conclusion that these programs and initiatives cannot be fully understood in isolation could easily be extended to a host of other topics.

Violence, politics, and benevolence were all aspects of the larger process of sorting out race and nationalism that engaged all Americans (not just politicians and soldiers) across the country (not just on the battlefield or in the seats of governments) for far longer than four years. It is hardly coincidental then that all but one of these essays (Mike Green's study of the Republican Party) turn on a crucial point: that life on a small scale warrants close attention. We cannot assume that analyzing Senate voting records would tell us much about what was going on in Gibson County, Tennessee. We cannot assume that Andrew Johnson's speeches would tell us much about what people were saying in Brunswick, Missouri. We cannot assume that closely examining the Great Men or Great Women would tell us much about Everyman and Everywoman.

Justin Nystrom's case studies of the way the Civil War and its aftermath affected free Creoles of color is the focus of the seventh essay. That his subjects were transformed by the war is just such an example of what can be understood by looking through a microscope instead of a telescope. Antebellum New Orleans society was divided broadly into three groups, with Creoles of color forming the vital middle ground between bound black slaves and free whites. Because these Creoles both obscured the relationship between race and freedom and served as a model to those slaves who would be free, white governments passed a series of laws increasingly restricting Creoles' freedoms. The war and early fall of New Orleans changed this three-tiered system in dramatic and unexpected ways. The ensuing end of slavery destroyed Creoles' former racial identity and forced them into a more rigid social structure of white and nonwhite. Many families reacted by taking a series of small steps across several generations to assume a white identity in this new bichromatic society—with varying degrees of success.

The experience of Creoles in New Orleans could be overlooked as peculiar to that city and perhaps a handful of others. But Nystrom's study complements other studies of how the Civil War established new social identities. In the eighth essay, Rod Andrew argues that examining an individual is "essential" to understand fully how the Lost Cause arose out of the experiences of the war years. He looks at Wade Hampton of South Carolina, an archetypical committed Confederate.

Unlike the biographical studies by Andrew and Nystrom, most of the essays in this book look at communities, some very small, where, in Derek Frisby's words, "conflicts devolved into brutal cycles of retaliation and vengeance," this time engaging individuals rather than armies. The hamlets, villages, and towns where these problems had to be confronted represent an extraordinarily rich resource. Small-scale life may appear humdrum from the outside, but can be complex, involved, and energetic on the inside. "Plain folk" often lead vigorous intellectual and civic lives. They may not articulate their ideas well. They may not write treatises. But everyday people can think deeply and believe passionately. Focusing on the nineteenth century's national events to the exclusion of the local ones not only distorts our perspective, but also misses some of the critical developments that were occurring throughout the hinterland. This does not mean that cobbling together hundreds of local histories will result in a great synthesis. It instead suggests that, for all their individual peculiarities, communities exhibit common elements and patterns that reveal the course of Southern history in interesting ways.

My own research into Greensboro, Alabama, may point in this direction.[10] In the early nineteenth century, autonomous individualists flocked to the region to make their fortunes on slaves and cotton. Lacking a community in the traditional sense, they created overlapping voluntary associations founded on self-interest; that is, they created characteristically American communities. Theirs differed little from other towns on both sides of the Mason Dixon line; they were forced to deal with the problems of transience and a lack of traditions. But after Fort Sumter, Greensborians, who had once shared little, began to march together, drink soup from the same pot, and sleep on the same ground. Some even died for each other. For the first time, they no longer identified themselves as Americans, but as Confederates. They shared a common purpose, a common fate, and came home with a common story. What had once been a modern voluntary society was replaced by a traditional Southern community founded on loyalty to each other. The slight threads of a voluntary society had been replaced with steel chains of exclusive devotion to a cause. Where they had once struggled to keep people from leaving, the former Confederates were now proudly committed to keeping other people—at least certain other people—out. Nor did they hesitate to act upon their convictions. During the late 1860s, the Klan drove out the only prominent white Unionist, and an occupying Yankee soldier and a politically prominent freedman were both murdered publicly in separate incidents on Main Street. The scalawag, Yankee, and freedman were targeted as symbols of those who had not supported the Confederate effort—those, in other words, who were outside the community. Once again, the Civil War merely entered a new phase after Appomattox. Thus the war created Southerners. As Jason Phillips explains in the ninth contribution to this volume, an exploration of the unrelenting commitment of die-hard rebels to their cause even in defeat, "shared experiences united a generation of Southern men." Here, on the streets of Greensboro and not in the halls of Congress, the war continued to be waged as blacks and whites, Unionists and former Confederates, acted from incompatible social premises. Because such differences could not be bridged, Reconstruction was doomed and Southern distinctiveness entrenched.

This creation of a separate Southern identity in Greensboro and other Confederate towns is a mirror image of the creation of a separate Unionist identity that Margaret Storey traces in north Alabama. In both cases, the Civil War forced heretofore independent souls into mutual reliance and new identities marked by loyalty—in one case among former Confederates, in another among struggling Unionists. This process only gathered momentum after the armies' defeat and the soldiers moved back home. We can only wish for similar studies of the emergence of black communities or of the effect fighting had on Northern towns.[11]

Carole Emberton has rightly identified loyalty as the "a primary organizing principle" for the South in the tenth essay. For too long, its meaning has been confined to Union patriotism. By contrast, Confederates invested much more in the term. Loyalty meant entering into special relationships of commitment, relationships that transcended the rights and contracts embedded in our legal commercial world. If loyalty meant treating some people specially, it meant treating those who were outside these special relationships quite differently. The loyal Southern community looked back to the Civil War as its defining moment. Rituals—whether in reminiscences published in the newspaper or in the virtually identical speeches given for decades on Confederate Memorial Day—recalled sacrifices and heroic past deeds. Such rituals were significant instruments by which the loyal Southern community marked who was included and who was excluded. Inclusion and exclusion was the dark side of loyalty and Southern distinctiveness.

Not only has the significance of loyalty been downplayed because of its identification with Union patriotism; loyalty also has been slighted because historians too often confuse Confederate nationalism with the Confederate government. We have allowed the fall of Richmond to blind us to the persistence of Dixie. David Potter warned against identifying the state with the nation in his famous essay, "The Historian's Use of Nationalism and Vice Versa." A state, he reminded us, is an objective institution; a nation, on the other hand, is a psychological condition among individuals sharing a common heritage, culture, and corporate personality.[12]

Confusing institutions with *mentalités* distorts the past and permits the easy dichotomies that these essays counter. Nevertheless, institutions can provide a framework for those shared conditions, those shared ideas, as Michael Green illustrates in his exploration of the Republican Party in the last essay. Green draws readers back to the fact that local expressions of the issues of the war and its aftermath at times require reference to the larger national context. Indeed, it was the Republican Party's relentless attention to reconstructing the Union from the very start of the war, even as it evolved as a political party during and after the conflict, that added to and aggravated the local issues that continued through the war and into Reconstruction in places such as Alabama and Kentucky.

The contributors to this volume have dealt strictly with the continuity of the experiences of war and peace during the 1860s and 1870s. But we should not end this consideration in the Wormley House, where American history textbooks have been getting it wrong for decades. The point at which to end the first volume and begin the second is not at the disputed election of 1876, but at Lincoln's election in 1860 or at Fort Sumter in 1861. It was then that those Americans living in seceded states began looking at themselves in a fundamentally different way, and Appomattox did not change that.[13] This feeling of separateness only increased, and any differences wrought by the supposed end of Reconstruction are trivial compared to those created by the war. As Robert Penn Warren famously put it, "only at the moment when Lee handed Grant his sword was the Confederacy born; or to state matters another way, in the moment of death the Confederacy entered upon its immortality."[14] Not just in the South but in the North as well, the war remains unfinished.

On November 19, 1863, the war well past its midpoint, President Lincoln stood before those gathered to dedicate a military cemetery in southern Pennsylvania. The only Confederates there lay buried in the ground, or soon would be. "Four score and seven years ago," he began, a new nation had been created "conceived in liberty, and dedicated to the proposition that all men are created equal." What liberty and equality meant was unclear; indeed, Americans were killing each other over the meaning of these founding principles.

The president spoke of continuing what the war had started, but he did not mean the growing industrial infrastructure, faith in technology, political centralization, or urbanization—the stuff of modern life that we often list as products of the war. (I heard a Southern wit once declare, inaccurately but amusingly, that modern Atlanta was what Southerners went to war to prevent.)

Again, Lincoln did not mention those developments, if indeed he was even aware of them. He had something else in mind.

"It is for us the living," he continued, "to be dedicated here to the unfinished work which they who fought here have thus far so nobly advanced." And what was that work? Yes, it was to defeat the Confederates and reunite the country. But it also was to ensure for all time "that this nation, under God, shall have a new birth of freedom." On the first day of that year, the President had signed the Emancipation Proclamation, which was as much a recommitment to liberty as a limitation of slavery.

Lincoln understood that the struggle that engaged the nation would not end with the defeat of the Confederacy because our greater task could never really end. Freedom, equality, and independence—these would always need defending. Freedom, equality, and independence—these would always need extending if the American mission to the world were to succeed. The war, and with it the destruction of slavery and rebellion, was just the opening phase in a never-ending struggle to expand liberty, our capacity for self-government. This was the new birth of freedom he identified, a sacred commitment to the idea "that government of the people, by the people, for the people, shall not perish from this earth." The war remains unfinished.

1   A Victory Spoiled: West Tennessee Unionists during Reconstruction

Derek W. Frisby

I nopportune military and political conditions had prevented the installation of a civilian government during the three-year federal occupation of Tennessee. Guerrilla violence and Confederate incursions, most notably Nathan Bedford Forrest's raids into West Tennessee, had disrupted the elections of December 1862 and March 1864, creating considerable embarrassment for the region's Unionists, derisively termed "homemade Yankees" by their enemies. These persistent Confederate raids into West Tennessee cast further doubt upon Andrew Johnson's military government's ability to provide security for loyal citizens or restore the stability of civilian government to not just West Tennessee but any other part of the state as well. The cycle of recriminations between Johnson and federal commanders for the failures of the occupation bred disaffection with the mission of restoring the region back to the Union, an attitude that undermined any grassroots effort to bring peace and revive loyal governments to the occupied South's communities. Because of these obstacles and embarrassments in restoring West Tennessee to the Union, state and federal authorities appeared increasingly passive, if not altogether indifferent, about the West Tennesseans' plight over the course of the war.

This unresponsive attitude alienated West Tennessee Unionists from their supposed allies, prevented them from enjoying the spoils of federal victory, and ultimately left them at the mercy of their former enemies. Additionally, the federal government's evolution from a policy of restoration of the Union to that of Reconstruction, with its emphasis on civil rights for freedmen, left Southern Unionists disoriented in the new Southern economic, social, and political landscape and disillusioned with government at all levels. West Tennessee Unionists' experiences are indicative of Reconstruction's failure to appreciate the challenges of Southern Unionism and incorporate these loyal Southerners into a strategy that would positively affect the character of the peace. The struggle of West Tennessee Unionism not only underscores the opportunities squandered during this era, but also provides a chillingly familiar reminder of the challenges and limits of Reconstruction policy amid historical rivalries and prejudices.[1]

With the Confederacy's desperate late-1864 invasion of Tennessee thwarted at Franklin and Nashville, Andrew Johnson and more than five hundred Tennessee Unionist delegates finally gathered in the state capital to form a new civilian government. They undoubtedly basked in the glow of Johnson's recent election to the vice presidency of the United States and the latest Union victories in Middle Tennessee. Additionally, press reports and rumors that Confederate support among Tennesseans was "withering" and that the Confederate cause was "hopeless" buoyed their celebratory spirits. The delegates now believed their state was finally secure enough to begin restoring civil authority. However, the transition from military to civilian government in Tennessee brought to the surface old questions about which of the state's three geographically based "Grand Divisions" (East, Middle, or West Tennessee) would control the new state government. The subsequent struggle for power fractured the Unionist coalition and rekindled the historical sectional animosities that had divided the state since its inception.[2]

East Tennesseans, under Confederate occupation for more than two years, claimed that they had suffered and sacrificed more than any other Unionists and sought to control the convention from the outset. They immediately proposed apportioning representation at the convention on the basis of the results of the June 1861 separation referendum, a secessionist charade intended to legitimize the unconstitutional actions of pro-Confederate Governor Isham Harris. Under this scheme, East Tennessee, which was the only Grand Division to reject secession, would be allocated the largest share of delegates and thereby gain control over the proceedings. This move angered Middle and West Tennessee's delegates, who had divided over the calling of a convention but still overwhelmingly selected Unionist delegates should the state choose to hold a convention to discuss secession. They threatened to withdraw unless representation could be apportioned more fairly. Fearing such a massive defection, the two sides apparently reached an unspecified compromise and settled on a "one delegate, one vote" format for representation. This was a rather hollow victory for the Middle and West Tennesseans, however, because East Tennesseans in attendance outnumbered the delegates from the other two Grand Divisions and thus remained in effective control.[3]

Debate soon shifted away from procedural concerns to more substantive matters, but the sectional disputes continued. Delegates engaged in often rancorous exchanges, arguing whether the meeting would be a "preliminary" step toward a constitutional convention—as advertised and required by the 1834 state constitution—or would simply offer amendments to Tennessee's antebellum constitution to be placed before the voters immediately. Those opposing any delay and favoring the amendments' immediate adoption to establish a new order in Tennessee government were largely delegates from East Tennessee (known as "Radicals"), but about 40 percent of the delegates (termed "Conservatives" and mostly from Middle and West Tennessee) wanted to follow the old constitutional procedures and favored an orderly return to any semblance of antebellum government.

The Conservatives' insistence on following established procedures for constitutional revision stalled the convention's progress. Conservatives warned the Radicals against taking actions that would resemble the extraconstitutional measures undertaken by the state's secessionists in revising the state constitution just four years earlier. After days of fruitless deliberation, some of the more frustrated Conservative delegates walked out. Owing to the dissidents' absence and Governor Johnson's inspirational address advocating immediate constitutional revision and the abolition of slavery, the remaining 230 delegates managed to pass their program during the final two days of the convention. The proposed changes included a "schedule" of revisions to the 1834 constitution repudiating secession, the abrogation of all acts and appointments of the state's Confederate administration, the approval of Johnson's acts and appointments as military governor, and, most significantly, a section abolishing slavery and giving the new governor and legislature the power to set voter qualifications. The convention also ratified Johnson's call for new state elections as soon as possible. To prevent any conservative opposition from developing, the Radicals presented the voters with a carefully selected slate of candidates. Furthermore, the vote would be restricted to Unionists who had taken the "ironclad" or "damnesty" oath (swearing one's complete, unwavering loyalty throughout the war, and therefore disqualifying large numbers of conditional Unionists in Middle and West Tennessee). Once a new constitution was ratified, the new legislature could establish voting requirements for subsequent elections. With everything seemingly in place for Tennessee's restoration to the Union, a suddenly reinvigorated Johnson declared the "Liberty and Union Convention" a success and considered it the highlight of his administration as military governor and prepared to assume the vice presidency.[4]

The convention's haste and perceived extraconstitutional actions shattered the fragile coalition that had formed against secession in 1861. Ever since the Emancipation Proclamation had transformed the Union's war objectives, West Tennessee Unionism had been under great strain. Most West Tennessee Unionists agreed with the Radicals on the necessity of punishing the former Rebel leaders, but they remained deeply divided over the political fate of rank-and-file Confederates. Additionally, West Tennessee Unionists, who unlike East Tennesseans came from a more racially divided region, had already expressed their dissatisfaction over emancipation, the formation of United States Colored

Troops, and expanded rights for freedmen. In March 1863, an editorial letter to the *Memphis Bulletin* from an anonymous private in the West Tennessee's Sixth Tennessee Cavalry (U.S.A.) had claimed that the regiment preferred Democrats George McClellan for president and Andrew Johnson as vice president, adding, "We want no Negro regiments to serve in the Union army." At the 1864 Fort Pillow Massacre, the Unionist white troops segregated themselves from the black soldiers' quarters before the attack, a decision that contributed to the garrison's grisly demise. After the attack, the white Unionists attempted to blame the black troops for the fort's fall; however, the subsequent congressional report on the massacre ignored such charges and chose to emphasize the black garrison's fate. This decision by the congressional investigators exacerbated hard feelings among white Unionists, who felt their plight had been slighted again by federal authorities.[5]

More recently, West Tennessee Unionist Emerson Etheridge, a vocal Democratic elector in the 1864 presidential campaign and a staunch antiabolitionist, had been among the dissenting leaders at the January 1865 convention. In 1863, Etheridge's schemes to unseat Johnson's administration and his attempt to deny Northern Radical Republicans their seats in Congress while he served as Clerk of the U.S. House of Representatives got him expelled from Nashville and Washington. His campaigning on behalf of McClellan's candidacy and arguing in favor of restoring ex-Confederates' political rights in 1864 had publicly highlighted the growing rifts that had been developing among Tennessee Unionists. Etheridge's impolitic actions during the later stages of the war and his antiabolitionist stand further damaged the credibility of Southern Unionism and earned him the label of "traitor" in Radical Unionist circles. Soon after the war, Tennessee Unionists split into the Conservative faction under Etheridge, representing largely the western two-thirds of Tennessee, and the Radical faction led by William G. Brownlow, centered in East Tennessee.[6]

The West Tennessee Unionist "Executive Committee," which advised Johnson on the region's condition, engaged in bitter infighting over patronage. Personal and political animosities among the members had been kept in check by the war, but with the conflict all but over, antagonism destroyed the tenuous alliance. West Tennessean Alvin Hawkins, whose cousin Isaac commanded the Seventh Tennessee Cavalry (U.S.A.), had complained to Johnson in November 1864 about the corruption of public officials in Memphis and had denounced fellow committee member and newspaper editor James Bingham's influence over affairs in that district. "The Union men of West Te. have no confidence in Bingham of the *Bulletin*," said Hawkins, "and will never consent to follow his lead . . . without stultifying themselves and sacrificing their own self respect." On the other hand, Bingham, a Johnson sycophant who was always seeking patronage for himself or others, decried anyone who opposed abolition and despised the "imported" men brought in by federal military authorities to fill government positions in Memphis, including the recently appointed U.S. Attorney Alvin Hawkins.[7]

The Conservative Unionists' decision to boycott the constitutional referendum allowed Radicals to assume power easily, even though their victory appeared to lack legitimacy. The 26,865 to 67 vote of February 1865 in support of a revised state constitution signaled the Radicals' dominance; however, the turnout was less than half of what Radicals had predicted because of the boycott by the "strict constitutionalists" in Middle and West Tennessee, who denounced the "illegitimate" vote. Unfavorable conditions in West Tennessee further suppressed the Radical turnout there. Yet another Confederate raid into West Tennessee had prevented some polls from opening and discouraged people from voting at other polls, as did discontent over a new federal conscription order in Shelby County. Johnson had begged federal authorities to delay the draft until after the election, but the commander there argued that a draft order would not reduce voter turnout. The results indicated otherwise, as even the heavily Unionist Irish and German immigrant communities most affected by the draft (approximately 5,000 voters) largely failed to cast ballots. Regardless of these concerns, because the statewide turnout exceeded 10 percent of the state's voters in the 1860 presidential election, the state could be restored to the Union under Lincoln's December 1863 plan. In the subsequent election for governor and the General Assembly in March 1865, the "Liberty and Union" ticket received 23,222 votes. Thus, on the same day that Johnson ascended to the vice presidency in Washington, the voters elected Radical East Tennessean William G. Brownlow as Tennessee's new governor along with a Radical-dominated legislature.[8]

Unionist West Tennesseans mustering out of the federal service found conditions difficult once they arrived home. One Memphis Unionist claimed that years of suffering the federal occupation and unrestrained guerrilla warfare had altered the balance of power in the region. In areas of West Tennessee where Unionism had prevailed before the war, Rebels now seemingly outnumbered Unionists three to one. He feared that without federal protection, Unionists here were in danger from violence inflicted upon them by their former enemies, and he told newly elected Vice President Andrew Johnson that "it is as much as [Unionists] can expect to be allowed to remain in the State." The lack of security left Unionists vulnerable to attacks by guerrillas and bushwhackers, many of whom were former Rebels. Furthermore, those Unionists who remained had to be wary of their attitudes toward the former Rebels and would have to plan their future not as they would want, "but as may be *expedient*."

Unionists were already "fast leaving the state," declared a group of "greatly discouraged" West Tennessee Unionist refugees in Columbus, Kentucky. Until Unionists received protection, they deemed any attempt to restore government as "madness." They begged military officials in Nashville to reassign units, preferably ones recruited in West Tennessee, to restore order to the region. They further pleaded with Johnson to act decisively on these matters regarding restoration so that Unionists and their families could return home safely. "We have long looked for aid [from Johnson and federal authorities] until we have almost lost hope," said the refugees. Their requests were in vain; once again Johnson, preoccupied with assuming the vice presidency, did nothing to assist them.[9]

Destitute and without political and physical protection, Unionists had little choice but to watch helplessly as their defeated enemies regained economic control over their communities. Their requests for economic assistance and political patronage fell on deaf ears in Nashville and Washington, and both the state and the federal governments' desire to alleviate deteriorating Southern conditions as quickly as possible gave an advantage to the antebellum ex-Confederate elite who, unlike the usually less affluent Unionist contingent, still possessed some capital resources. Many ex-Confederates were already reopening businesses and reaping the profits of heavily inflated government contracts, effectively making up for their wartime losses. Unionists had few if any such opportunities. Fielding Hurst complained to Governor Brownlow, of this "unequal" situation and the "hardship" it was creating for Union men. Although state officials labeled the West Tennessee Unionists' situation "a great injustice," they did little to rectify the situation. At the federal level, though Johnson had recently become president after Lincoln's death and now presumably had authority to act on these complaints, he remained unresponsive.[10]

Lincoln's assassination on April 14, 1865—less than ten days after Brownlow's inauguration and less than a week after the Army of Northern Virginia's surrender—dramatically altered the course of Tennessee's Reconstruction. Tennessee Radicals took advantage of the temporarily cowed Confederates to enact further punitive measures upon their former enemies. Admonished by Brownlow "to guard the ballot box faithfully and effectually against the approach of treason," Radical state lawmakers passed restrictions on "seditious" speech and adopted a new franchise bill disfranchising former Confederates for five years and Confederate political leaders and high-ranking military officers for fifteen years. These new voting restrictions would be enforced by the state's first-ever voter registration system. The registrars in each county, chosen directly by the governor to ensure that only "unconditional" Unionists could participate in the upcoming elections, employed very strict qualifications that guaranteed Unionist East Tennesseans would qualify and vote in large numbers, thereby securing that section's hold on state power. Conservative Tennessee Unionists, primarily from Middle and West Tennessee, considered the 1865 franchise bill as part of another blatant power grab by Brownlow and the Radical East Tennesseans and worked diligently to dislodge him from office.[11]

The shifting sands of national politics that led President Johnson to pursue an increasingly conservative course opened up new opportunities for Brownlow's opponents. Many Conservative Unionists now favored a lenient course toward their former enemies, believing the support of ex-Confederates as vital to overturning "Brownlowism" and preventing the expansion of freedmen's rights. They loudly protested what they considered to be vindictive legal and franchise restrictions upon former Confederates. Ex-Confederates and Conservative Unionists therefore began forming tentative alliances to support Johnson's lenient Reconstruction program. Now claiming to have the majority of Tennesseans behind them, Conservatives decided to end their boycott of state elections and challenge Brownlow's Radical administration at the ballot box.[12]

Emerson Etheridge emerged as Brownlow's most vocal critic and became a Conservative candidate from his native seventh congressional district in northern West Tennessee. His campaign messages centered on the illegitimacy of the Brownlow government, and he argued that Tennesseans owed no loyalty to it. Etheridge wrote in late June 1865 that there could never be an Independence Day celebration in West Tennessee until law and order returned to that region. He claimed that presently there was "no law but force," and that Brownlow's government represented "no semblance of civil government, State or Federal, but usurpation enforced by the bayonets of negroes." At a public rally, he also declared that "a few desperate political and pecuniary adventurers" had assembled in Nashville earlier that year and established a fraudulent government. The "Liberty and Union" convention, in Etheridge's eyes, was "scarcely less treasonable, revolutionary and lawless than were the original authors and instigators of the rebellion." He demanded the resignation of those elected in March to the legislature. Finally, on July 3, Etheridge reportedly incited his supporters to shoot all abolitionists, black troops, and their "low and degraded" white officers stationed in the state, along with Brownlow's tax collectors and other officials.[13]

Deeming Etheridge's campaign rhetoric seditious and treasonous under the recently passed franchise acts, Brownlow, with the support of the federal military authorities, had Etheridge arrested and held in a Columbus, Kentucky, military prison for the remainder of the campaign, ensuring a Radical victory. In September 1865, after hearing only about one-third of the witnesses, a military tribunal found Etheridge guilty of "encouraging resistance to the enforcement of the law" and making "inflammatory and incendiary remarks." But the tribunal handed down no sentence, and so Etheridge ultimately went free. Etheridge's arrest and kangaroo court martial further inflamed opposition to the Radical-led government as a result of what many Tennesseans increasingly considered to be Brownlow's autocratic, repressive leadership.[14]

Realizing that Conservatives would soon take control even with the restrictions under the franchise law, Brownlow moved to solidify the Radicals' hold on state government by raising voter qualification standards. When the new legislative session opened in October 1865, he pushed Radical state legislators to overhaul the June 1865 franchise act. Conservatives filibustered and refused to show up for sessions, preventing a quorum and paralyzing the General Assembly. As the deadlock continued, twenty-one Conservative members walked out and then resigned. A furious Brownlow ordered new elections to replace these members and threatened military occupation of various districts if they did not elect Radical replacements. Voters ignored Brownlow's threats, returning nearly all the bolters to their seats. The Radical legislators, acting on Brownlow's orders, refused to admit the Conservatives, but they did allow four Radicals to take the oath of office, giving the Radicals a quorum to continue business unabated by Conservative filibusters. However, the franchise act did not apply to county elections, thus allowing ex-Confederates to participate; consequently, voters overwhelmingly elected Conservatives and former Rebels to county offices. Following race riots in Memphis and increased violence from early incarnations of vigilante groups such as the Ku Klux Klan, Radicals refashioned the franchise act in May 1866 to weaken Conservative opposition. This revised franchise bill voided all previous voter registrations, required prospective voters to register with special commissioners (to be chosen by the governor personally to ensure their loyalty) who would then decide their qualifications, and disfranchised ex-Confederates without exception for life.[15]

Conservative newspapers published the "disgusting list" of state legislators who had voted for the revised franchise act. "Each one of these persons," the May 16, 1866 *Nashville Republican Banner* stated, "forfeits the right to be considered a citizen of Tennessee or an honest man." Similar inflammatory rhetoric, accompanied by thinly veiled threats of retaliation against Radicals, filled the pages of the Conservative press for months following the controversial votes. Increasingly, too, the Conservatives' threats of violence and retaliation turned real. Frank Farris, a West Tennessee Confederate, murdered prominent Unionist and Radical West Tennessee state senator Almon Case's sixteen-year-old son, Emmitt. This crime was perhaps an errant assassination attempt intended for Emmitt's father. However, on January 11, 1867, Farris succeeded in murdering Almon Case, allegedly for his support of the revised franchise bill.

Earlier that morning, Farris had seriously wounded Obion County Deputy Sheriff Moses Kinman—a veteran of the Unionist Seventh Tennessee Cavalry—on a public street in Troy, Tennessee. The following day, Farris's rampage continued when he shot dead another Obion deputy, Roland Green. Although local officials knew Farris was responsible for these crimes, Confederate sympathizers shielded him, preventing his arrest or trial. These incidents emboldened the anti-Brownlow forces to continue their campaign of violence and served notice on West Tennessee Unionists, especially the Radicals, that the mechanisms of local justice offered them little protection.[16]

The Case assassination caught the attention of the national press and again cast the spotlight on the rapidly deteriorating situation in Tennessee. The state's Radical legislators draped Case's seat with American flags and wore mourning badges for thirty days out of respect for their fallen comrade. Letters poured into the Radical press detailing the tribulations of Unionists in the state. An anonymous West Tennessee Unionist wrote that the public "winks" at crimes committed against them by ex-Confederates and possessed a "secret satisfaction that another and another 'd—d Tennessee traitor and Yankee' has met his merited doom." Outraged by the escalating violence directed at former Unionists and freedmen across the state and determined to prove the legitimacy of their government, the Radicals decided it was time to act in an even more forceful manner against their opponents. They took desperate measures by advocating the formation of a state militia to reestablish law and order in Conservative-dominated districts. Furthermore, the Radicals suggested that to offset the swelling ranks of the state's Conservatives, Tennessee become the first Southern state to enfranchise freedmen.[17]

Conservatives, particularly those from West Tennessee, howled over the Radicals' proposals. Almost immediately after passage of the revised franchise bill, they began clamoring for a drastic solution: the overthrow of Brownlow's government through a new constitutional convention. Brownlow winced at the very suggestion of a new convention, and he declared that another civil war threatened to engulf Tennessee if the Conservatives continued to resist Radical rule. In response to intensified political and racial violence and a perceived threat of a coup, Brownlow asked the legislature for the power to form the State Guard as a military arm of the Radical administration. According to West Tennessee's Unionist military chieftain Fielding Hurst, such a force was crucial to "inspire confidence in the people." William J. Smith, who had succeeded Hurst as commander of the Unionist Sixth Tennessee Cavalry and now served as a Radical legislator, agreed. He had worked tirelessly to push a militia bill through the General Assembly for over a year. Additionally, in an effort to counter the growing Conservative forces at the polls in Middle and West Tennessee, Brownlow also urged the General Assembly to enfranchise freedmen. By February 1867, the governor and his Radical allies managed to muster the legislative majorities needed to pass both the militia and freedmen's suffrage bills.[18]

The upcoming 1867 statewide elections were an extraordinary opportunity for voters to express their opinions on Brownlow and his policies. This contest would be the first under the more stringent 1866 franchise act and the first to allow all black males to participate. The newly established State Guard, ostensibly mobilized to ensure order and fairness, would oversee the entire process. The Radicals had Brownlow at the top of the Republican ticket and tried to control the votes of the newly enfranchised freedmen. Well-organized Tennessee Union Leagues formed to mobilize black voters and to guarantee what one Radical newspaper called "a concert of action." In an audacious effort to blunt the Radicals' efforts in Middle and West Tennessee, Conservatives also decided to accept the freedmen's suffrage bill and court black voters during the campaign, even allowing select blacks to serve as Conservative delegates to their nominating convention and to speak on behalf of Conservative candidates during the campaign. Conservatives nominated West Tennessee Unionist Emerson Etheridge to oppose Brownlow for governor, betting on his presence and stump-speaking skills to counter Brownlow's political savvy.[19]

Hoping to expose the Conservatives' disingenuous efforts to gain black votes, Radicals immediately seized on Etheridge's prior statements about freedmen. The Radical press labeled Etheridge an "extravagant and unprincipled partisan, whose violent passions always carried him to offensive extremes." Illness prevented Brownlow from campaigning, but several Radicals filled in for the ailing governor on the stump. Radical speakers reminded blacks that they had been the ones who had emancipated the slaves and extended suffrage to the freedmen. To instill fear into black voters, they charged that a Conservative victory would reestablish slavery. Although confident of a success, the Radicals, believing Etheridge's speeches had threatened to siphon off the votes of moderates and freedmen, were unwilling to chance sizable Conservative gains or perhaps even victories. They had to do more than talk; they had to act forcefully to ensure total victory.[20]

Federal troops in Tennessee had refused Brownlow's request to get involved in the campaign, declaring it a civil matter because Tennessee had reestablished civil government with the state's ratification of the Fourteenth Amendment in the summer of 1866. Therefore the governor stationed the State Guard in politically hostile portions of the state, including nearly 460 militiamen to occupy half of West Tennessee's counties. Nearly two hundred West Tennesseans, many veterans from West Tennessee Unionist regiments and a sizeable number of freedmen, enlisted in and commanded several State Guard companies. Other companies were made up of East Tennesseans. West Tennessee Radicals welcomed the Guard's presence from whatever region or race they could be recruited. "The Rebills is Dispert in this County. . . . They have to be Subjugated Some how & the Sooner the Better," Weakley County's C. V. Underwood declared in his request for a State Guard commission for himself and the previously wounded Obion County deputy, Moses Kinman. According to Underwood, anyone declaring publicly for Brownlow would be killed in his county. Furthermore, he informed Brownlow that all federals still remaining in West Tennessee were Johnson supporters who were "doing more Harm than good" and allowing the Conservatives to become bolder in their attacks on Radicals.[21]

Preserving order and preventing attacks upon freedmen and Radicals were the *raison d'etre* for the State Guard, and they dogged Etheridge on his campaign tour, often spurring rather than quelling disorder. Militia commanders immediately set out to punish those who dared challenge the Radicals' authority, even if they had been sincere Unionists throughout the war. Militia officers also fostered nascent Radical organizations such as the Union Leagues. West Tennesseans charged that the State Guard exceeded its authority, using excessive force and committing numerous crimes ranging from theft to rape. Not surprisingly, the militia camps, especially in West Tennessee, came under attack during the campaign. Although the militia's presence was supposed to ensure an orderly campaign, threats of violence frequently prevented Etheridge and his supporters from speaking. On several occasions, confrontations between the two parties erupted in gunfire or fisticuffs that left two Conservatives dead and thirteen more injured, including seven black Conservatives. Nearly thirty black Radicals also lay wounded.[22]

Many Conservatives believed that Etheridge's record on race might sway enough votes to unseat Brownlow. On the stump, Etheridge criticized Brownlow's divisive politics and dictatorial management of state government. He also advocated universal manhood suffrage, even for blacks. Most accounts agree that Etheridge's campaigning skills served him extremely well in debates with Brownlow's proxies. He reminded blacks that he had always been against slavery, pointing to his stand against the Kansas-Nebraska Act of 1854, his opposition to the revival of the African slave trade, and his acceptance of the Thirteenth Amendment. He used many of Brownlow's antebellum proslavery statements, including one in which Brownlow labeled Etheridge as a "black Republican," to demonstrate the Radicals' hypocrisy. Etheridge also trotted out black supporters who claimed that Radicals had used their race as "cannon fodder to save their own lives and to end the rebellion." These conservative blacks deplored Brownlow's divisive tactics and favored ending the disfranchisement of ex-Confederates.[23]

With a state of martial law imposed upon at least thirty counties, stricter voter qualifications in place, and a climate of fear permeating the state, the results of the 1867 elections were predictable. The polling itself came off quietly, though many voters came to the ballot boxes armed. The restrictive franchise requirements significantly reduced the numbers of white voters from Middle Tennessee and the area around Memphis. The Radicals benefited from the Union League's ability to turn out the black vote, especially in the former plantation areas of Middle and West Tennessee, where apparently the freedmen remained unconvinced of Etheridge's pro-emancipation campaign conversion. Thus the Radicals soundly defeated Etheridge and the Conservatives in nearly every contest, winning every congressional seat, every state senate seat, and all but three state house seats. West Tennessean Isaac Hawkins scored the campaign's most convincing Radical victory. Only seven counties statewide recorded Conservative majorities, three of them in West Tennessee. In an ominous indication of the Conservatives' renewed strength in West Tennessee, Madison, Tipton, and Hardeman Counties voted heavily Conservative despite the presence of few qualified white voters and an overwhelming number of new black voters.[24]

Tennesseans, particularly those in West Tennessee (who had enjoyed the benefits of a highly competitive antebellum political party system), became increasingly uncomfortable with Brownlow's political tactics to impose essentially a one-party dictatorship. As a result, noticeable cracks soon began forming in the Brownlow coalition even at the moment of its greatest triumph. In West Tennessee, Radical support decreased 20 percent between the 1867 and 1868 elections, and Conservatives garnered about fifteen hundred more votes in the 1868 campaigns than they had a year earlier. As Conservatives gained political strength, peace appeared to be returning to West Tennessee. According to a Freedmen's Bureau agent in West Tennessee, no "outrages" had been reported in December 1868, and he believed that Radical newspapers had exaggerated the amount of violence. Such reports made Brownlow's mobilization of the State Guard once again for the 1869 campaigns and his declaration of martial law in three West Tennessee counties (Gibson, Haywood, and Madison) and six Middle Tennessee counties appear to be acts of desperation. Feeling the pressure of a growing Conservative opposition and realizing that the days of his administration were numbered, Brownlow used his remaining political capital within the legislature to secure one of Tennessee's U.S. Senate seats, and he resigned as governor on February 25, 1869, just five days after issuing his martial law proclamation.[25]

The militia's presence in West Tennessee actually hurt the Radicals in the 1869 elections. The militia company sent to patrol the Haywood County area soon believed itself besieged by the newly organized Ku Klux Klan and other anti-Radical elements. The State Guard embarked on an aggressive but fruitless patrol of the area, producing one militia casualty, a few firefights, and only one arrest. Frustrated by these results, the militia commander, East Tennessean Judge K. Clingan, imposed harsh punishments on civilians for trivial offenses, further angering the already annoyed populace. Exasperated with West Tennesseans' defiance and in his inability to stem the violence against the Radicals, Clingan appealed to Tennessee's interim governor, state House Speaker DeWitt Senter, for greater authority. "Our troops will never amount to anything," Clingan said, "unless those parties committing depredations have come to fear them." Although a close friend of Brownlow and an East Tennessee Radical, Senter was far less partisan than his predecessor, and he began demobilizing the militia instead of strengthening it.[26]

Without the force of Brownlow's personality or the State Guard, the Radicals collapsed quickly. Radical candidates jockeyed to replace Senter at the 1869 gubernatorial election, but he turned their own system against them. Senter knew the Conservative forces were growing too powerful to overcome, and he decided to curry their favor rather than feel their wrath. He was able to replace pro-Brownlow registrars with his own supporters and dictate more lenient voter qualifications. While campaigning for a full term as governor in 1869, Senter restored the franchise to any Tennessean disfranchised by the previous Radical administration. Of course, the measure endeared Senter to Conservative Unionists and ex-Confederates alike, and Senter achieved the most spectacular victory in Tennessee history with their support. Conservative Emerson Etheridge also gained a state senate seat on Senter's coattails, as did other Conservative candidates, who swept all but eight seats in the new General Assembly.[27]

In 1870 Tennesseans adopted a new constitution that prohibited the state from ever again infringing upon the suffrage rights of any Tennessean. Ex-Confederate Conservatives quickly pushed aside the Unionist Conservatives, despite the Unionists' role in restoring the Rebels' political rights. Even moderate Unionist Isaac Hawkins was turned out after three consecutive terms in Congress. By 1877 the state's former Confederate governor, Isham Harris, had even returned to politics and won a U.S. Senate seat. Only when Democrats were divided—as they were in 1881 over solving the state debt crisis incurred during the Brownlow era—could Republicans achieve success. Hawkins's cousin—Republican and wartime Unionist Alvin Hawkins—took the governor's chair in 1881, installed a plan to resolve the debt crisis, and then was unceremoniously turned out at the next election by the revived Tennessee Democratic Party, composed largely of ex-Confederates.[28]

The Civil War and Reconstruction had left West Tennessee Unionists to wander in a political wilderness with few friends and even fewer rewards for their loyalty to the United States. Wartime animosities lingered well into the postwar period, and former Rebels sought revenge against Unionists. Without adequate protection from the state or federal government, Unionists endured considerable persecution and torment from their supposedly defeated enemies. Observing conditions in Gibson County led Unionist and Radical W. H. Stillwell to label the federal claims of victory over Confederates in the war "the most gigantic falsehood of the age." Unionist veterans, particularly in West Tennessee, found themselves, as one North Carolina Unionist said, "ostracized and proscribed socially . . . compelled to discard the blue they have worn with honor, to protect themselves from insult and violence." As late as the 1890s, when one Unionist objected to the hiring of one of Nathan Bedford Forrest's cavalrymen as minister of his church, the congregation reminded him to follow Jesus's example and forgive those who trespass against us. "The Lord was just crucified," the Unionist veteran of the Seventh Tennessee Cavalry responded, "he never had to go to Andersonville Prison."[29]

Many Unionists held firm to their beliefs despite persecution by former secessionists. Fielding Hurst returned to his home in northern McNairy County, an area referred to as the "Hurst Nation" because of the Unionist solidarity displayed by all but a few of residents in the area. He became a circuit court judge and commander of the local Grand Army of the Republic post. Former Confederates in McNairy County still considered Hurst a traitor and an outlaw. After Hurst's death in 1882, his enemies often desecrated his gravesite. The demonization of Hurst and his Unionist regiment (derisively known by ex-Confederates as "Hurst's Wurst") became cemented in local legend. John Hallum, a former Confederate who had served under Forrest, attributed several heinous acts to Hurst and his "regiment of predatory thieves, robbers, murderers, and rapists." In one of Hallum's most vivid descriptions, Hurst's "Diggers" looted homes in 1863 and cut off the breast of a young woman, leaving her maimed for life. Continuing the cycle of "lex talionis" among the West Tennesseans, several local Confederates received news of such incidents and reportedly hunted down the men responsible. The Hurst name soon came to be affiliated with terror, evidenced by an anonymous poem that circulated throughout West Tennessee:

Despair for the children
who lie now in bed.

The widow, the aged
the soldier who bled.
For out of the "Nation"
comes a sickness and curse—
God save us all
From the demon called Hurst.

Like vandals of old
through our land they did ride
With Hunger and Death
always close by their side.
Came Terror, his herald—
but the wailing comes first . . .
We know he is coming,
That demon called Hurst.[30]

Isaac Hawkins fared much better in terms of historical memory but still found the federal government unappreciative of West Tennessee Unionists and their suffering. He served three consecutive terms in Congress and—along with his cousin, Alvin—lobbied extensively in behalf of Southern Unionists. As early as 1868, Hawkins had asked the federal government to compensate Southern Unionists for property confiscated by federal troops. Hawkins argued that the U.S. Constitution required that revenue collection must be "uniform through-out the United States" and that the Third Amendment prohibited the government from quartering troops during wartime in citizens' homes. Furthermore, as Hawkins knew from his own experiences, federal forces had violated Southern Unionists' Fifth Amendment rights by depriving them of property without due process of law or just compensation.[31]

According to Hawkins, Southern Unionists had always remained U.S. citizens, and the government was obligated to treat them as such. Yet the Union's military forces had unjustly impressed Southern Unionists' property and supplies. Hawkins noted that no law had been passed to permit this type of confiscation and that in contrast to Southern Unionists, the government had routinely compensated Northern citizens for wartime losses. He demanded that Southern Unionists be put on the "same footing of other loyal men." Congressional refusal to grant Southern Unionists compensation would set a "dangerous" precedent, inflicting a "deep wound" and leaving a "dark stain" upon the national character.[32]

Hawkins's efforts bore fruit when Congress created the Southern Claims Commission (SCC). Under this March 1871 measure, Southern Unionists could

file a claim for losses and the commissioners would make their judgment on
the basis of the claimant's loyalty during the war and proof that the claimant's
property had been taken. The skeptical and contentious commissioners
imposed strict qualifications on proving loyalty and proclaimed all Southerners
were secessionists unless they could prove otherwise. Overcoming the Northern
commissioners' prejudices toward Southerners was a task that proved especially
difficult for Unionist West Tennesseans. Wartime losses had impoverished
many Unionists, and they could not afford the legal fees and expenses involved
in filing a claim. Some prospective Unionist claimants might also have been
deterred by the public postings of their names on claimant lists compiled by
investigators seeking witnesses in their communities. A third set of Unionists,
embittered by federal treatment and Radical Reconstruction, had become discouraged and refused to file at all. Still, Tennesseans submitted nearly four
thousand claims, roughly 20 percent of the claims filed with the commission
from 1871 through 1873. The SCC took nearly ten years to adjudicate the more
than twenty-two thousand claims submitted from across the South.[33]

Although perhaps intended by Hawkins and others as a means of compen-
sating Southern Unionists for their loyalty and suffering, the SCC forced many
to relive the most terrifying experiences of their lives. More significantly, the
experience of adjudicating their claims left most of them once again believing
that federal authorities, whom they had thought of as allies, had betrayed and
abandoned them. One quarter of Tennessee's wartime claims for federal restitution originated from West Tennessee. The extant records of these claims
reveal the extraordinary circumstances West Tennessee Unionists endured,
while also demonstrating the extraordinary burden of proof required to have
claims approved. Disregarding Hawkins's assertions that Southern Unionists
had remained U.S. citizens during the war, the commissioners placed Southerners in a state of "twilight citizenship," neither U.S. nor Confederate citizens,
until their loyalty could be proven. Claimants were asked to answer more than
eighty questions about themselves, their politics, and their wartime activities.
SCC special agents would journey into the Southern communities and post a
public list of claimants. In theory, this practice was intended to solicit infor-
mants as well as to discourage fraudulent claims. In practice, it dissuaded many
Unionists from filing claims for fear of opening themselves up to reprisals by
former Confederates. Once the special agents had investigated the claimants, a
hearing was held to review the questionnaires and take testimony from additional witnesses. The investigators then forwarded recommendations to the
commissioners for a final determination. Approved claims required evidence of
unwavering loyalty throughout the war and specific losses of property. Claimants lacking adequate proof of loyalty, failing to establish their ownership of

the property taken, or unable to produce proof that federal soldiers had confiscated the property had their claims "disallowed." Claimants whose loyalty
was not in question but whose specific property losses could not be accounted
for, failed to fall under the commission's jurisdiction (such as soldiers' captured
horses), or lacked any evidence had their claims "barred."[34]

West Tennessee's wartime reputation as a den of secessionism, and the
Unionists' weakened political position after the war, dogged their efforts to gain
compensation for their wartime sacrifices. John Edwards, the SCC special
investigator for West Tennessee, Arkansas, and North Mississippi, found his
task arduous. "I am alone, against a crowd," he complained. He quickly concluded that claimants, their lawyers, and the witnesses all conspired to deceive
him and defraud the government. The only information Edwards was inclined
to trust came from freedmen. Frequently, even good white witnesses such as
Tom Dohery, a former Union scout, frustrated Edwards's investigations
because they refused to testify on record. "It might yet give him trouble with
some of his neighbors if they suspected him of being the cause of them being
'tore up' by the Yankees," Edwards explained. The hostility displayed by many
West Tennesseans and the difficulty in locating reliable, willing claimants and
witnesses (who tended to relocate frequently), combined with the hazardous
and arduous travel through some of the region's most inhospitable, rural territory to locate Unionist claimants, exhausted Edwards's health as well as his
patience. For Mary E. Allen's claim from Carroll County, he traveled nine miles
in seven hours, going through the woods "over holes and logs never pressed by
buggy wheels before" to take depositions, only to discover the claimant in a
"chronic state of lethargy" from a morphine addiction. Yet Confederates had
arrested Allen for nursing wounded Union troops, and a reluctant Edwards
reported favorably on her claim.[35]

West Tennessee claimants had a very difficult time establishing their wartime
loyalty. William Jones, a Hardeman County resident, found that unless claimants could show proof of persecution for Unionism, the commissioners were
unlikely to deem them loyal. The commissioners decided that Jones's "very
quiet life" had left him "wonderfully fortunate for a Union man in Western
Tennessee" and disallowed his claim. On other occasions, claimants who had
been persecuted, but were naively honest, such as William Dickens, fared little
better. Dickens testified that Unionists "were living under a sort of duress" in
the spring and summer of 1861. Secessionists in Madison and Gibson Counties
had promised to hang anyone who voted for the Union, and that those who
failed to vote at all "would be arrested and dragged about the country." Dickens
said he would have left the area except that he feared the breakup of his farm
and family. His wife had become ill and their eight children needed him to stay

healthy. When federal troops occupied his county, Dickens went straight to the provost marshal and asked for absolution for his failure to stand up to the secessionists. The provost told Dickens that he "had done right" and provided him with a protective guard. Despite a rare direct appeal from Edwards asking consideration for Dickens's circumstances, the commissioners rejected the claim, deeming the "fairly stated" reasons for his actions to be an unacceptable "legal excuse." Hardeman County resident William Stringfellow served with a Unionist regiment in Alabama during the war, although he confessed that his brother had hired him as a Confederate substitute in a blatant attempt to skirt military service with the Rebels. The Confederates later exempted Stringfellow from service because they discovered him to be too young to enlist. Disregarding his later service with the Unionist regiment, the commissioners could not overlook the fact that Stringfellow had once been a Confederate substitute, albeit a fraudulent and rejected one. They disallowed the claim for his failure to prove loyalty throughout the war.[36]

The disloyalty of close family members also could hurt Unionists' claims. Daniel Wright of Memphis told commissioners that he had tried to make his very vocal Unionist niece, Sarah Ann, "hold her tongue" to prevent them from being "ruined" while the Confederates had held the city, but she had refused. The politically divided family had adopted a "survival lying" strategy to avoid trouble, but she refused to go along with them. The young woman's constant arguments with family members eventually resulted in the permanent estrangement from her pro-Confederate sister. Sarah Ann even burned a Confederate flag that had been brought into the house and skipped around the stove singing "Yankee Doodle" and "Hail Columbia," much to the dismay of her uncle and the other household residents, whom she threatened to report if they attempted to silence her celebration. The commissioners ultimately rejected the family's claim because of its divided loyalties. Nathaniel Brewer had also received threats from the local Confederate home guard that urged Brewer to reassess his loyalties. Two of Brewer's sons fled north for safety, but his minor son enlisted in the Confederate army against his father's wishes. In disallowing Brewer's claim, the commissioners ruled "if the father was loyal, [then] the son would naturally sympathize with him." It was an "unusual case," they said, where the father could not control his minor son.[37]

Even those West Tennesseans able to prove their loyalty found the commissioners still unwilling to take responsibility for the actions of Northern soldiers. Commissioners frequently ruled that property taken or destroyed by Northern soldiers were just "mere depredations" or "plainly lawless and unnecessary acts of plunder and pillage." Therefore the government could not be held accountable for behavior that ran contrary to their stated policies.[38]

As during the war, federal officers often proved to be merely fair-weather friends of West Tennessee Unionists. Isaac Hawkins, whose law firm represented a large number of West Tennesseans before the SCC, found himself embroiled in a conflict with attorney Gilbert Moyers. A former commander of the Third Michigan Cavalry stationed in the region for much of the war, Moyers still questioned the loyalty of West Tennesseans. He attempted to persuade Hawkins's clients that the West Tennessee Unionist lawyers were incompetent or had given up trying to represent them. Hawkins protested Moyers's conduct to the SCC, but, as they had during the war, Washington officials did nothing.[39]

The obstacles in establishing loyalty or property claims, the bias of the investigators in the region, and the infighting between Southern and Northern attorneys made a successful claim nearly impossible for West Tennesseans. Their section had been under a more comprehensive and more extended federal occupation than other parts of the state, but they had their claims rejected at almost double the rate of East Tennessee Unionists (see Table 1). Northerners' perception that West Tennessee was the one of the most secessionist, most anti-Republican portions of the state hurt claimants' chances to win compensation for destroyed or confiscated property during the occupation. The high rate of rejections certainly caused many to question their choice of wartime allegiances, and the lack of restitution for the typically less prosperous Unionist classes of Tennessee led to further lapses into debt or bankruptcy.

The attitudes of West Tennessee Unionists during the Civil War and Reconstruction convinced many federal leaders that Southern Unionists were of little political or military value and that their wavering loyalty and military misconduct only escalated a cycle of violence that had inhibited the North's war effort. Furthermore, the nature of federal occupation in West Tennessee reinforced Northerners' perception that all Southerners were cut from the same secessionist cloth, whatever their claims to the contrary, and that Southern Unionists were unworthy partners with Northerners on the battlefield and at the ballot box.

For their part, West Tennessee Unionists repeatedly felt betrayed and deserted by federal authorities. Early in the war, the shift of Union operations to the railroad towns and counties of the region's secessionist southwest corner

Table 1. Southern Claims Commission Judgments in Tennessee, by Grand Division

	East	Middle	West
Approved	52%	28%	28%
Disallowed	31%	47%	39%
Barred	14%	21%	28%

had left Unionists in the outlying pro-Union counties relatively defenseless. The subsequent evolution of pragmatic and hard war occupation policies had further undermined West Tennessee Unionism. The Union's shift toward emancipation completed the estrangement of conservative West Tennessee Unionists who lived in a slave-based economy and culture and who desired to maintain a racially divided society.

As a result of mutual suspicions and animosities, both sides squandered the opportunity to aid one another in quelling the rebellion or establishing a solid Unionist base for Reconstruction. The less racially divided East Tennesseans further exacerbated longstanding state sectional animosities by attempting to use the black suffrage issue to regain control over state politics at the expense of conservative Unionists and ex-Confederates in Middle and West Tennessee. The Conservatives' strong reaction to the Radicals and the quick "redemption" of Tennessee by former Confederates reinforced the impression that Unionism in the western portion of the state had always been weak and ineffectual. Therefore it should come as no surprise that Radical-dominated East Tennessee has garnered the greater share of attention from students of Southern Unionism.[40]

But West Tennessee and other areas of the plantation South were far from being Confederate monoliths and contained significant Unionist pockets. West Tennessee, like many other areas of the upper South, possessed a fluid political party system that reflected, and to some degree mediated, internal demographic conflicts. Secession and war destroyed the party system and exposed the fault lines within West Tennessee communities. Community conflicts devolved into brutal cycles of retaliation and vengeance that fueled animosities for decades after the war ended. Believing steadfastly that their loyalty to "the Union as it was" would be rewarded with patronage and a greater degree of economic and social opportunities, West Tennessee Unionists failed to understand the dynamic shifts within the American political landscape during the Civil War that rendered the philosophies of the "old government" obsolete until it was too late. Many West Tennessee Unionists seeking the stability of the "old government" had their faith in it shattered by the federal occupation and the evolution of federal war aims toward emancipation. Their confidence in government had resulted in passivity during the war's early stages, making them more vulnerable to secessionist attacks and generating a great deal of skepticism in the North about Southern Unionists' commitment to the war and Reconstruction. When they finally did regroup and begin to assert themselves, West Tennessee Unionists found it impossible to regain the initiative from their opponents, North or South, and they drifted helplessly on the winds of war. They formed an uneasy alliance with their former enemies to overthrow Brownlow's Radical government, only to discover the ex-Confederates had merely used them to accomplish Tennessee's quick "redemption" and then cast the Unionists aside.

With the rapid collapse of Radicalism in Tennessee and the eventual collapse of federal Reconstruction policies, these West Tennessee Unionists believed they had been abandoned and left without protection from the very government they had fought to preserve. West Tennessee Unionists essentially became "marginal men" in the postwar era with no solid political, economic, or social standing within their own communities or their country. West Tennessee Unionists, as their moniker "homemade Yankees" implies, found themselves living between two worlds, yet were strangers in both.[41]

2

"I Wanted a Gun": Black Soldiers and White Violence in Civil War and Postwar Kentucky and Missouri

AARON ASTOR

In a grisly discovery on a cold morning in February 1865, a patrol of Unionist Missouri militiamen found "an old Negro Man" hanging from a tree just six miles from the city of Columbia, a heavily fortified Unionist stronghold. Pinned to the corpse's coat pocket was a note bearing the insignia of Jim Jackson, one of central Missouri's most notorious pro-Confederate guerrillas. With sordid irony, the note declared that the elderly African American was "Killed for knot going into the federal arma, by order of Jim Jackson."[1] H. A. Cook, captain of the Ninth Missouri Cavalry, discovered the body and explained to his lieutenant that substitute brokers regularly scoured the Columbia area for all able-bodied black men to fight in the Union Army in lieu of whites who would have otherwise been drafted into service. Though most whites had long protested the enlistment of African Americans in the Union Army, some whites condoned the presence of black soldiers in the final months of war only because they helped fill the draft quota. According to Captain Cook, Jackson pretended to be an outraged conservative Unionist and hanged an elderly black man for not relieving fellow white Unionists of their military obligations.[2] But Cook was only speculating, as nobody understood Jim Jackson's real motives for murdering an innocent old man.

In Danville, Kentucky, a town even more staunchly Unionist than Columbia, Al McRoberts met his death at the hands of a mob on Christmas Eve, 1866.[3] On the grounds of the First Presbyterian Church, once the home of an early Kentucky emancipationist minister, two hundred men and women hanged McRoberts, a black man, from an old elm tree just hours before Christmas morning.[4] Unlike the elderly man killed at Columbia nearly two years before, McRoberts carried a violent reputation. His alleged offense involved the discharge of a pistol at a white police officer who had tried to arrest him. The mob that lynched McRoberts saw in him the peril of general emancipation. In their minds only extralegal community violence could restore the honor and standing of the white population that had been undermined by emancipation, black soldier enlistment, and the potential of black equal citizenship.

These two murders—one occurring in central Missouri's "Little Dixie" region months before General Robert E. Lee's surrender and the other taking place on the outskirts of central Kentucky's fertile Bluegrass region a year and a half after the war's conclusion—bore the mark of a new kind of conflict.[5] By and large, violence targeting African Americans in late–Civil War and postwar Kentucky and Missouri was not random. Indeed, a significant portion of the black victims consisted either of soldiers in the Union Army or their family members. The prevalence of violence targeting this subset of the African American population reflected underlying tensions regarding the contours of citizenship and white supremacy within conservative border-state society during the Civil War. In the western slaveholding Union border states, large numbers of conservative whites fought for the Union precisely because they thought it would best preserve slavery.[6] The abolitionist turn of the Civil War demoralized such border conservatives who were caught between vicious and desperate guerrillas on one side and an armed African American population on the other. African Americans who took up arms and used them to target local white Confederates dramatically altered the balance of power in border state communities in the minds of white conservatives. When African Americans joined the Union Army, they not only contributed vital manpower to the Union cause but also recast the Union cause as a struggle for liberation, even though many fought on the same side as their own masters. As historian Linda Kerber points out, white Americans in the nineteenth century equated the prerogatives of citizenship with the obligations of military service: "Citizenship and civic relations in [the] republic were tightly linked to race and manhood; it was white men who offered military service, white men who sought honor, white men who dueled in its defense."[7] Black slaves who took up arms for the Union cause challenged this bedrock social principle of the American republic. For white Unionists in Kentucky and Missouri, a black soldiery mocked the conservative social basis of the Union. To outraged white conservatives, only the violent suppression of these unofficial black citizens could resuscitate longstanding social relations and restore honor to themselves and to the republic.

Scholars have long identified the post–Civil War era with the epidemic of racial violence. The rise of the Ku Klux Klan and likeminded groups in 1866 and after threatened African Americans across the South with summary violence. Explanations for this explosion of postwar violence include the political struggle of Southern whites to restore Democratic Party hegemony and the economic demands of former slaveholders to reestablish plantation discipline.[8] But the violence that engulfed the border state countryside in the years following Appomattox resembled neither of these patterns.

In the Union slaveholding border states of Kentucky and Missouri, African Americans did not attain the right to vote until passage of the Fifteenth Amendment in 1870.[9] Though Missouri fell under Radical Republican rule between 1865 and 1870, the basis for its power lay with the state's German population, whites long subject to brutal guerrilla violence in the southwest, and the more Northern-born community centered in St. Louis.[10] Instead of expanding the franchise to the African American population, Missouri Radicals disfranchised any and all Missourians who ever participated in or sympathized with the rebellion. The political alliance of former free-soil whites and Ozark Unionists coupled with the massive disfranchisement of Rebel sympathizers made formal black political participation superfluous to the Radical regime. Though African Americans actively campaigned for the franchise as early as 1865, they never achieved full political rights until the Radical government's dying days in 1870.[11] Kentucky similarly barred African Americans from the political process until 1870, offering even fewer legal and civil safeguards than in Missouri. Indeed, the Kentucky state government passed seamlessly from conservative Unionists to Democrats in the postwar era, offering Radicals and their beneficiaries no chance to gain control. If Missouri blacks offered little threat to the white political order in that state, Kentucky blacks provided even less.[12] Thus, unlike in the Deep South, black votes never threatened the white political order in the immediate postwar border states.

The traditional economic interpretation of postwar racial violence also fails to account for the persistence of racial attacks in the border states. Although slaves tilled the hemp and tobacco farms of Little Dixie and the Bluegrass through the early years of the Civil War, none of those regions relied on slave labor to the degree of plantation owners in the Deep South. Slaveholdings in the Bluegrass averaged 6.3 slaves per holding, and in Little Dixie the holdings were even smaller.[13] Many of these farms employed a combination of white family members, hired skilled laborers, hired slaves, and nonhired slaves to work the relatively small border state holdings. Though slaves performed critical work, especially the laborious task of hemp breaking, their labor was hardly indispensable to the degree it was in Mississippi or Louisiana. Moreover, the decline of the American hemp industry and the rise of white burley tobacco, which could be profitably raised by small family farms, made slave labor even more redundant.[14] Whereas Deep South planters desperately sought African American labor to grow cotton, Kentucky and Missouri farmers adjusted more easily to nonslave labor.[15] Indeed, the flexible work relations in antebellum Kentucky and Missouri—where hired slaves, free blacks, and white family members worked alongside resident slaves to till the modest-sized farms— made the transition to free labor less shocking to the white landowning class than in the Deep South. With black labor now relatively unnecessary to land-owners, border state whites had less need for violence to force former slaves back to work.

Since the traditional political or economic explanations for postwar border-state racial violence do not suffice, the origins of postwar racial terror in Missouri and Kentucky lay elsewhere. In fact, the two lynchings described above highlight a more convincing explanation for racial violence. With the rise of black enlistment into the Union Army, whites in the border states no longer viewed the war as a struggle over union or disunion, but as a struggle for white dominance in all facets of social, cultural, and political life. As African American men joined the Union Army in large numbers beginning in early 1864, they made an unprecedented bid for citizenship in a republic that long treated them as nothing but mere property. In doing so, they also asserted the masculine rights of martial self-defense that had long been restricted to white men. Indeed, whites and blacks intimately understood the gendered component of racial domination and citizenship. From the first moments of white settlement in the trans-Allegheny West, white men restricted to themselves the right to dominate the black and female members of their households and to participate as equals with other white men in the civic life of the republic.[16]

Federal emancipation edicts and abolitionist harangues may have annoyed and angered conservatives in the border states, but the arming of former slaves transformed social relations on the ground in ways that threatened the basic social and racial order. To conservatives—whether Unionist or Confederate—race relations resembled a zero-sum game; every gain for African Americans signified a loss in honor and power for whites. For decades, white Kentuckians and Missourians of all political stripes expected slaves to exercise deference to white authority both within slave households and in public spaces. Slavery was a means of labor exploitation for border slaveholders, but it also was a means of racial control; with a miniscule free black population in Kentucky and Missouri, whites found the slave system sufficient to manage the black population.[17] However, with the utter breakdown in slave-based social relations during the Civil War and the loss of trust in the newly radicalized Union, border state whites turned increasingly to mob violence to reestablish white supremacy. And because the surrender of Confederate forces in April 1865 only reified the new social order characterized by general emancipation, white violence against newly freed slaves did not diminish with the Civil War's end. The war between the Union and Confederacy had devolved into a veritable race war wherein former white foes settled old accounts and turned their guns toward the newly emancipated black populace.

Peter Bruner, a slave in central Kentucky's Bluegrass region, appeared with
"plenty of company" at the Union Army enlistment center at Camp Nelson. "I
came there to fight the rebels and . . . I wanted a gun," Bruner recalled. Joining
thousands of other slaves across central Kentucky in the summer of 1864,
Bruner fused his own liberation with the war effort against the Confederacy.
And his tool of emancipation, the gun, bore revolutionary consequences for
black liberation in the border states. This was not the first time Bruner sought
his freedom at the Kentucky River encampment. Before Camp Nelson became
a major black soldier recruitment center it was an army camp for the Union's
Department of the Ohio. In August 1863, Bruner attempted to escape his brutal
master for the safety of Camp Nelson, only to be captured and jailed by a
Unionist, pro-slavery judge in nearby Nicholasville. "Oh, how hard some of us
poor slaves labored for our freedom," Bruner wrote. In the summer of 1863,
the Union Army still rejected African American soldiers in Kentucky. "When I
had run off before and wanted to go in the army and fight they said that they
did not want any darkies, that this was a white man's war."[18] But in his successful 1864 venture Bruner found a radically altered Camp Nelson awaiting him.
Unlike the all-white unit that guarded central Kentucky for the Union in 1863,
the new army welcomed, initiated, trained, and commanded thousands of African American soldiers willing to fight the Confederates and, more immediately,
to attain their freedom.[19] Elijah Marrs, another African American soldier at
Camp Nelson, heralded the revolution at hand:

> I can stand this, said I. This is better than slavery, though I do march in line
> at the tap of a drum. I felt freedom in my bones, and when I saw the Ameri-
> can eagle with outspread wings, upon the American flag, with the motto E
> Pluribus Unum, the thought came to me, "Give me liberty or give me
> death." Then all fear banished.[20]

For African Americans at Camp Nelson like Peter Bruner and Elijah Marrs,
the transformation from slave to soldier was a potent assertion of manhood
and signified the first great step toward American citizenship.

When the first slaves enrolled in the army at Camp Nelson, they followed
tens of thousands of their brethren throughout the Confederacy who had
enlisted as early as 1862.[21] Indeed, with enrollment delayed until February 1864,
Kentucky slaves were the last to join *en masse*; the similarly late-enrolling Missouri slaves waited until December 1863. Thus the prospect of black enlistees
surprised neither black nor white in early 1864. Still, with the Lincoln administration handling the border states with great caution—exempting the states
from the Emancipation Proclamation in January 1863 and generally yielding to

conservative Unionist civilian officials in Kentucky and Missouri on all significant political matters—the reality of black enlistments in the border states
brought home to white Unionists the radical turn of the Civil War.

Throughout the South, black enlistment played an integral role in ushering
forward the social revolution of general emancipation and the transformation
of former slaves into citizens. But the effects of black enlistment were felt the
strongest in Kentucky and Missouri for four reasons: First, the number of slaves
that joined the army from Kentucky and Missouri far exceeded in proportion
and number enlistees in virtually every Confederate state. Out of 41,935 military-
age African Americans in Kentucky, 57 percent joined the Union Army; in Missouri, 39 percent joined.[22] Even these numbers downplay the total of black
recruits in the western border states, as many joined in neighboring free states.[23]
It is very likely that a significant percentage of the 2,080 African Americans
credited to Kansas actually came from Missouri.[24] Similarly, a sizable portion of
the recruits credited to Indiana (1,537) and Ohio (5,092) were black Kentuckians who crossed the Ohio River earlier in the war to enlist. And in the heavily
enslaved Little Dixie region of central Missouri and Kentucky's Bluegrass, the
proportion of slaves joining the army was even higher. In Howard County,
Missouri, for example, nearly two-thirds of all military-age male slaves entered
the army; Howard County had the largest percentage of slaves of any county in
Missouri.[25] In both Kentucky and Missouri, nearly all black enlistees were slaves
because both states possessed miniscule free black populations.[26] The sheer volume of black—and particularly slave—enlistment in Kentucky and Missouri
transformed much of the labor force into a vital weapon in the federal government's counterinsurgency campaign against rebels led, in many cases, by their
former masters.

For slaves in Missouri and Kentucky, the vast black army also signified a
critical moment in the development of a highly politicized racial consciousness.
Upon witnessing thousands of other slave enlistees in army camps from central
Kentucky to central Missouri—slaves who once toiled on isolated farms
throughout the border state countryside—African American men developed a
critical understanding of their own potential for political expression and power.
Indeed, the very act of joining the military proved the most vital political statement most of these slaves had ever made as it proved the only viable path to
emancipation; with both states exempt from the Emancipation Proclamation,
Kentucky and Missouri slaveholders were under no federal pressure to free
their slaves.

The second reason black enlistments in Kentucky and Missouri proved so
significant lay in the speed with which slaves joined the military. The slaves of
Kentucky and Missouri flooded recruitment centers; all of Kentucky's slave

recruits joined within the span of ten months, most of them in the three summer months of 1864. A local provost marshal officer wrote to commanding
General John Schofield that a "stampede of negroes" enlisting in the army had
thrown conservative white Unionists into a "state of desperation."[27] By January
15, 1864, dozens of slaves enlisted in central Missouri's slave-rich Howard
County alone. By the end of February more than 3,700 African Americans
enlisted in Missouri, with central Missouri's Little Dixie producing a significant
portion. Many slaves traveled to recruitment sites on their own, while others
joined as a group. Seven of John R. White's slaves—William, Adam, Alfred,
Sam, Andy, Preston, and Jacob—all enlisted together at the Fayette provost
marshal post in the first weeks of January.[28] White was one of Missouri's largest
slaveholders; the seven who joined represented a mere tenth of White's holdings, though it signified collective action on the part of a portion of his slaves.[29]
At the same post in Fayette, 174 African Americans joined the service in the first
two months of 1864. In Brunswick, just up the Missouri River, another 128
slaves joined in the same period. Perhaps the most impressive recruitment site
in central Missouri was Boonville, where Lieutenant C. S. Swamp presided over
the enrollment of 436 African Americans—nearly all of them slaves—into the
Union Army.[30] By the end of 1864, slaves rushing to join the Union Army
throughout central Missouri destroyed the last vestiges of the "peculiar institution," thereby making the state's constitutional abolition of slavery in January
1865 a mere acknowledgment of reality.

Slave enlistment began later in Kentucky, but once state officials removed
restrictions to recruitment in June 1864, enlistment proceeded at an even more
fevered pace than in Missouri. A February 1864 circular issued by U.S. Provost
Marshal General James B. Fry to all assistant provost marshals in Kentucky
ordered the enrollment of free blacks in accordance with the new Congressional
Enrollment Act.[31] Despite conservatives' vehement opposition to black enlistment in March 1864, General Stephen Burbridge, commander of the District of
Kentucky, began recruitment in earnest in April with the release of General
Order Number 34. Still, the new circular restricted recruitment to free blacks
and slaves "whose owners may request the enlistment."[32] The new enlistment
procedures clearly exempted the vast majority of potential black soldiers, giving
the Union Army the political grief of conservative alienation without the benefit of increased manpower. Rumors that the army would remove all remaining
barriers to enlistment reached the slaves of the Bluegrass in the next few
months. In late May 1864, a provost marshal in Boyle County, Kentucky,
reported to his superior officer, "It became known to these negroes that they
could enlist without the consent of their masters, whereupon they thronged the
office of the Dep[uty] Pro[vost] Mar[shal] clamoring to be enlisted." In

response, whites in nearby Danville "commenced abusing and threatening them," trying to prevent the slaves from enlisting at all. The provost marshal was surprised at the "stampede" of blacks to Camp Nelson and imagined, erroneously, that enlistment would continue "singly and in squads" as it had up to then.[33] But the rumors reflected reality. The army removed all remaining obstacles to enlistment two weeks after the incident.[34]

On June 13, 1864, Lorenzo Thomas, adjutant-general for the Union Army, issued General Order Number 20, accepting "any slave who may present himself for enlistment" at one of eight recruitment centers located throughout Kentucky.[35] Camp Nelson in southern Jessamine County and a recruitment center in Lebanon served the heavily enslaved Bluegrass area. With the final barrier to enlistment removed, slaves poured into Camp Nelson, most of them coming from the Bluegrass region. Nearly 2,500 black soldiers entered the Union Army by the end of August 1864 at Camp Nelson.[36] By the end of July 1864, Boyle County alone contributed 275 black enlistees to Camp Nelson.[37] The 275 enlistees represented 42 percent of Boyle County's military-age black male population.[38] The flood of enlistees continued throughout the summer of 1864, roiling the Kentucky countryside and shaking slavery to its core. The enrollment of more than half the military-age black population of Kentucky—nearly all of whom were enslaved—in less than a year suggests a revolutionary war underway in the region.[39]

The pace of enlistment shocked Union officials and white conservatives. This deluge of enlistment threatened a calamitous breakdown in social order as tens of thousands of slaves immediately abandoned decades-old relationships with their former masters. More ominously, in the white imagination, the suddenness of the black enlistment "stampede" heralded the sort of disorderly racial catastrophe befitting the onset of a slave uprising.[40] Regardless of these exaggerated fears, whites could not ignore one new reality: African Americans in their midst had become a powerful political force, and unbeknownst to the master class, the newly militarized black population drew energy and organization from decades of kin and social networks built during slavery. Henry Clay Bruce, a slave in Missouri's Chariton County, recalled in his autobiography that border state slaves were intimately aware of the politics of war and emancipation. He outlined the vast networks of communication across the scattered, small slaveholdings in the border countryside.

> The Colored people could meet and talk over what they had heard about the latest battle, and what Mr. Lincoln had said, and the chances of their freedom. . . . When the news came that a battle was fought and won by Union troops, they rejoiced, and were correspondingly depressed when they saw

their masters rejoicing. . . . Slaves who could read and could buy newspapers, thereby obtained the latest news and kept their friends posted, and from mouth to ear the news was carried from farm to farm, without the knowledge of masters.[41]

By 1864 one of the most important pieces of news to arrive was the possibility for enlistment in the Union war effort. Given this underground network through which slaves passed information, it is hardly surprising that hundreds of slaves would rise up at the first chance to enlist in Danville, Kentucky, or Fayette, Missouri. If the sheer magnitude of black enlistment in the border states heralded the emergence of a broader black political consciousness, the speed with which slaves answered the enlistment call suggests the political and organizational sophistication of a population previously underestimated and degraded by white society.

The location of blacks under arms reveals the third reason slave enlistment proved so revolutionary. After slaves entered the service, their primary duty was to guard the towns across the border from guerrilla raids and Confederate attack. Black soldiers were rarely sent to some far-off battlefield; they were stationed at home, squaring off with their own outraged former masters. Given that Kentucky remained under martial law for several months after the war's completion, many of these black soldiers continued to stand as armed guards in towns and posts across the Bluegrass. Even the staunchly Unionist Paris *Western Citizen* in Bourbon County, Kentucky, wrote with relief in June 1865 that "efforts would be made by the Administration to conciliate the people of Kentucky, and that all negro troops would accordingly be soon removed from among us." The editor remarked that "this is pleasing intelligence, and we sincerely hope it may be true."[42] Unfortunately for whites seeking the immediate removal of black troops from the state, ten thousand would remain stationed on Kentucky soil as late as October 1865.[43] In Missouri, black troops played an integral role in enforcing civil law, especially after passage of the new radical constitution in 1865. In Lafayette County, Missouri, black troops arrested two pro-Confederate judges for refusing to abdicate their offices in accordance with the new constitution.[44] For whites outraged at the presence of black troops, the continued presence of these soldiers threatened a permanent, direct, and official rejection of white supremacy. For African Americans, on the other hand, the power and obligation to keep the peace in a place where they legally served as slaves as late as December 1865 signified a dramatic reversal of the social and political order. Moreover, as new guardians of the public order, uniformed and armed blacks stationed in towns across the border states made an unprecedented bid for the equal rights and responsibilities of citizenship.

The fourth, and perhaps most important, consequence of slave enlistment was the opportunity it gave African Americans to recast the Union cause as a struggle for liberation. Since the outbreak of war in 1861, white conservative Unionists vowed to preserve the federal government precisely because it was the best way to preserve the slave-based social order. Indeed, the governors of Kentucky and Missouri encapsulated the conservative Unionist spirit throughout the war, rejecting immediate emancipation and black soldier enlistment but supporting an otherwise vigorous prosecution of the war against both external Confederate invaders and internal Confederate guerrillas.[45] Slaves joining the Union war effort threatened to overturn the conservatives' original rationale for supporting the Union. While tens of thousands of whites fought for the Union to protect slavery, tens of thousands of their own slaves fought for the Union to destroy slavery. Although slaves elsewhere in the western hemisphere—notably in Cuba during the Ten Years War between 1868 and 1878—fought alongside their masters (and ex-masters) in a war of emancipation, border state conservative Unionists were in no mood to join in spirit with a radicalized slave population.[46]

The traditional narrative of slave enlistment portrays slaves taking up arms against their own masters.[47] In Missouri and Kentucky many owners of enlistees (possibly a significant majority) supported the Rebel cause. Federal Walker, a well-known Confederate in Howard County, witnessed his three slaves—Shelby, Daniel, and St. Andrew—join the Union forces.[48] For these slaves the process of enlisting into the Union Army resembled the experience of black soldiers in the Confederate states. For other enlistees, such as those owned by conservative Unionists like Columbia's William Switzler, the social consequences of enrollment differed from those who took up arms against their own masters. Slaves understood that, despite the conservative basis of Unionism in Kentucky and Missouri, a Union victory would result in the destruction of slavery. Henry Clay Bruce recalled, "Slaves believed, deep down in their souls, that the government was fighting for their freedom, and it was useless for masters to tell them differently."[49] It is hardly surprising that a slave population scattered and isolated on small farms would offer a coherent picture of the Union war effort that so differed from that of their own masters. Border state slaves like Peter Bruner, Henry Clay Bruce, and Elijah Marrs never accepted the conservative interpretation of the Union cause offered by their own masters; regardless of their masters' loyalty, border state slaves joined the Union Army because it provided their own freedom and the opportunity to liberate their people. This recasting of the Union cause by ex-slave soldiers as a war for emancipation constituted the first great step in the social revolution of the border states.

White Kentucky and Missouri Unionists viewed the prospect of black enlistment with anger from the moment the army and the Lincoln administration first broached the subject. Like leaders in other slave states, whites in Kentucky and Missouri vigorously opposed arming their own bondsmen. The Confederate government introduced the concept of arming slaves as its prospects for independence dwindled in late 1864 and early 1865. Historians assessing the rancor within Confederate military circles over black soldier enlistment at the conclusion of the war have accurately disposed of the plan as a desperate last stand that ultimately went for naught.[50] Historians also have examined the debate over black enlistments in the free North and the effects of such a revolutionary move on long-held doctrines of white supremacy and an all-white citizenry.[51] Only in passing, however, have these historians discussed the impact of this move on the white Unionist cause in the border states, where the social effects of black soldier enlistment drew some of its most contentious criticism.

Perhaps no better exemplar exists of conservative Unionist protest against black enlistment than Colonel Frank Wolford. A longtime inhabitant of Casey County on the southern edge of the Bluegrass, Wolford was a dedicated Union commander of the First Kentucky Cavalry. As the oldest cavalry unit in the state and the most successful opponent of John Hunt Morgan's Confederate raiders, the First achieved legendary status across the Bluegrass by the middle of 1863. Its commander regularly received applause and accolades from grateful Unionists in towns like Lebanon that faced Morgan's assaults and in cities like Lexington where his presence ensured protection against guerrilla depredations. But Colonel Wolford drew the most attention to himself when he delivered a series of speeches in March 1864 denouncing the enlistment of black soldiers into the Union Army.

With Governor Bramlette standing by his side, Colonel Wolford declared in a Lexington speech that President Lincoln was a "traitor, tyrant and usurper" for daring to enlist African Americans into the army from Kentucky.[52] He insisted that it is the "duty of the people of Kentucky to resist it as a violation of their guaranteed rights."[53] Wolford's grievances extended beyond black soldier enlistment to the entire abolitionist course of the war. A Lexington newspaper's paraphrased Wolford's comments:

> The purposes of the war were the same today that they were when Mr. Lincoln in his inaugural and Congress by resolution declared that they were not for conquest or subjugation, nor for interference with the domestic institutions of the States, but simply to preserve the honor and maintain the supremacy of the Constitution—The effort to pervert the war from this legitimate purpose, and to make it a war upon slavery, was an issue which

the dominant party had no right to make—it was a startling usurpation of power.[54]

Soon after Wolford's incendiary speech he was arrested and sent to Nashville to meet with General Ulysses S. Grant. Bramlette immediately sought to defuse the crisis by insisting that the highest priority at the time was to employ Kentucky's "gallant soldiers" to defeat the rebellion, after which Kentuckians could redress their grievances over the enlistment of slaves through constitutional means at the ballot box and in the courts.[55]

Bramlette's attempt to quell the anger did little to prevent an outbreak of violence.[56] Just days after Wolford's speech, one hundred Kentucky Union troops fired on members of the Eleventh Michigan Cavalry, declaring that they would "clean out the town of Michiganders and Yankees."[57] The reason for the disturbance was the presence of a mulatto soldier standing guard near the Michigan regiment. A Kentucky colonel warned the Michigan regimental commander, "If [the mulatto guard] was not immediately removed there would be trouble, as his men would not suffer a nigger soldier to be on duty in their presence." A Union officer stationed in Lexington wrote to the War Department, "The excitement about the enrollment of negroes is intense, and many professed friends of the Govt say that it shall be resisted and they rely upon their own (Kentucky) officers and troops to do it."[58]

Open attacks against fellow Union troops initially threatened to destroy the entire Union war effort in Kentucky. Consequently, from Bramlette on down, conservative Union officials preached restraint and acquiescence to the law. While outbreaks of violence between units disappeared after the Eleventh Michigan incident, white Kentuckians—and Missourians—merely redirected their anger at the slaves who sought entry into the Union Army. Although many of these attacks came from Rebel guerrillas, not all can be traced to supporters of the Confederacy. Even when conservative white Unionists did not openly attack African Americans, they expressed virtually no disapproval of these increasingly common acts of racial violence. Their acceptance encouraged further depredations and made Union military prosecution of assailants difficult.

In some cases military authorities had to alter recruitment procedures for fear of violent interference. James Fidler, provost marshal in Lebanon, Kentucky, began sending black recruits by train to Louisville to protect them from guerrilla attacks. "There is no possible chance," he wrote, "to disguise the fact that there is great opposition, amounting almost to an outbreak, to these enlistments, all through the centre of the state." Fidler, like other Union Army officials, implied that vehement opposition came from all quarters of the white population, Unionist and Confederate. Opposition grew so intense that the he worried that transporting the recruits to Louisville would not sufficiently protect them. "Information came to me yesterday that a band of guerrillas were on the RR ten miles from Lebanon, there living to burn the train."[59] Fidler also witnessed local citizens catching and whipping potential slave recruits. As the whip represented the crudest tool of control over the slave, employment of it to prevent slaves' enlistment in the army served as a visible reassertion of the traditional prerogatives of slaveholders' power.

In other cases whites mutilated African Americans attempting to enlist. Near Lebanon, two "boys" named James and Jasper Edwards encountered an Irish immigrant named Michael McMann on the road to the enlistment center in town.[60] McMann accosted the two boys and cut off their ears. An officer at the Lebanon post immediately arrested McMann and an accomplice named William Burns, though the victims only positively identified McMann as the assailant. Recruit mutilation undoubtedly served to intimidate other blacks, who considered joining the military; mutilation, including cutting off ears, was an occasional punishment of slave runaways by slave patrols.[61] With the slave code in full effect in Kentucky until passage of the Thirteenth Amendment in December 1865, slaves seeking the safety of enlistment camps were considered runaways under Kentucky law, regardless of the presence of Union troops or the state's official standing within the Union. McMann, who likely served on a slave patrol in the community around Lebanon, maintained full civil authority to inflict whatever punishment upon slave runaways he deemed appropriate, including bodily mutilation.[62]

Whites angry at black enlistment also directed their violence at the families of recruits. The wife of a black recruit appeared before the office of Hiram Cornell, an assistant provost marshal in Fulton, Missouri, and reported that she and her child were severely beaten and driven from her home by her master. She asked to follow her husband into the army, offering to work at the camp if necessary.[63] The black recruit, unable to protect his wife and children from the master's assault either at home or in the army camp, faced a dilemma that would survive the war. Violence against the families of recruits continued as long as blacks served in the army, in many cases until late 1866. Masters also attacked slave families because the labor value of the remaining women and children did not warrant continuing to support them. In the Fulton case, the slave owner was an "aged man" and had already complained to the army that he could not afford to feed and clothe the remaining slaves. These attacks represented, in some ways, an expulsionist campaign designed to intimidate slaves into leaving the border states outright. Ironically, earlier in the war, masters despised the Union Army for luring their slaves away. Yet once they decided to rid themselves of their remaining slave property, the army proved an inviting destination.

Whites in central Missouri and Kentucky regularly harassed, intimidated, and attacked black recruits en route to enlistment camps to prevent them from entering the army. They also attacked black soldiers already in uniform carrying out their duties, especially when guarding or traveling through the border countryside. In Woodford County, Kentucky, which held the largest percentage of slaves of any Kentucky county in 1860, a black soldier transporting official army dispatches was stopped by a man who stole his bridles, led him for two miles into the woods, and shot him.[64] The murderer, identified by witnesses as Maddox, told the tollkeeper guarding the road that he intended to kill the black soldier.[65] According to the tollkeeper, the only reason Maddox killed the soldier was that he was black and he was wearing a federal uniform. Blacks in uniform, like the Woodford County soldier, represented an affront to prevailing white conceptions of citizenship; for many whites, racial violence against blacks was required to enforce this restrictive understanding of citizenship.

As the war entered its final months, the state of Missouri formally abolished slavery.[66] Bushwhackers and other Rebel sympathizers transformed their existing practice of threatening African Americans who joined the military into a generalized terror campaign, in some cases aimed at the expulsion of blacks from the border states. Near Columbia, just days after Captain Cook found the elderly black man hanged by Jim Jackson's gang, Union officer F. Russell discovered another black man murdered by Jackson. According to Russell, Jackson's men had promised "that all blacks were to leave in 10 days or be killed by them." The officer noted that most black men from the vicinity were already serving in the army, leaving behind the "unarmed and helpless," in a state of "terrible alarm."[67] With the abolition of slavery in Missouri, bushwhackers who once threatened violence against slaves escaping their masters now used terror and violence to remove all remaining African Americans from the region. Though Kentucky did not formally abolish slavery—only ratification of the Thirteenth Amendment in December 1865 brought the institution to an end— slaveholders in the Bluegrass also recognized the demise of the peculiar institution. Like their Missouri compatriots, they viewed freed slaves with complete disdain. Not only had their former slaves forcibly severed their bonds of slavery, but they had the audacity to claim the prerogatives of equal citizenship commensurate with a Union soldier. As the Civil War came to a conclusion and the Union destroyed the last redoubts of Confederatism in April 1865, the battle over the place of African Americans in Kentucky and Missouri society merely entered a new phase. Patterns of violence committed by white Rebels against black soldiers, and especially by white conservatives of both loyalties against all African Americans, would change after Appomattox, but they would not diminish.

The Danville Fair held in Boyle County, Kentucky, in the fall of 1865 provided one of the first public recreational spaces for central Kentuckians, regardless of race or previous loyalty, to congregate openly and peacefully after the close of the war. At county fairs in nineteenth-century America, farmers and townsfolk gathered to discuss business matters such as crop prices and new market conditions, show off livestock, and participate in a rare moment of social revelry. The county fair also offered an arena for rural men and women to discuss current political matters, hear politicians speak, and resolve local disputes. Boyle County's first fair after the war brought to the surface simmering tensions over emancipation, guerrilla war, and the use of black soldiers— tensions that continued to roil the community months after Lee's surrender. The racial makeup of the Danville Fair added a novel dimension to social relations in the region. Never before had African Americans legally assembled in public in Boyle County without direct white supervision. Whites long feared that an all-black meeting would lead to general insurrection, regardless of whether or not the congregants were enslaved. At the same time, whites insisted that blacks refrain from interaction across the color line for fear of miscegenation. As a result, the fair's organizers divided the crowd by establishing a separate zone for black fairgoers to mingle, and vowed to enforce the segregation rule with force. The volatile mix of black soldiers, returning Rebels, and conservative whites at the fairgrounds exploded into violence when newly freed African Americans challenged the segregated boundaries.[68]

According to U.S. Army Major A. H. Bowen, charged with investigating the incident, several blacks had attempted to "pass out of the ring" allotted to them. Two white men, one a conservative Unionist parade marshal named Thomas Moore and the other a "returned rebel soldier" named Thomas Tadlock, tried to force the blacks back into their specified section. Bowen reported that Moore "fancied" that he saw a black soldier pull out a gun, and Moore promptly shot the would-be assailant. Immediately afterwards, other black soldiers fired back at Moore and Tadlock, causing a general riot. Thirty white "citizens" with pistols and bowie knives chased the entire population of African Americans out of the fairgrounds, firing at them along the way. Moore caught a black sergeant and began kicking him, threatening to "blow his brains out" if he did not give up his pistol. As black soldiers and civilians regrouped outside the fairgrounds, many demanded that they return to the fairgrounds with reinforcements and guns, but by then the affair was over.[69]

The Lexington *Observer and Reporter*, the largest conservative Unionist newspaper in central Kentucky, described the incident differently than Major Bowen. According to the newspaper,

Four negro soldiers were promenading in a careless manner among the gentlemen and ladies when the Marshal, named Moore, told them to go around
and occupy a place amongst other negroes. Three of the four started willingly but the fourth grew somewhat stubborn and was being pushed along
by Moore and another gentleman, when he drew his pistol and fired, shooting Mr. Thomas Tadlock of Perryville.[70]

After shooting Tadlock, the "negroes ran into Danville and being re-inforced
by their entire company declared their intention to go to the Fair Ground and
shoot every white person they saw." Inexplicably, according to the newspaper,
the blacks did not attack the fairgrounds, instead shooting "promiscuously"
at people coming from the fair and shooting a black woman in the streets of
Danville.

The two explanations of the Danville Shooting Affray, as it came to be
known, reveal competing narratives of racial violence in postwar Kentucky.
They also uncover, in their contradictions, the tensions within a border state
society undergoing a revolutionary challenge to the existing social order. Major
Bowen presented the fair marshal and his rebel compatriot as primarily culpa-
ble for the incident. The officer made sure to describe Tadlock as a Rebel, thus
identifying his Civil War loyalty with his propensity to commit violence against
African Americans and black soldiers in particular. While conservative Unionists shared local Confederate disdain for black soldiers, most Union officers,
particularly those from the North, had long accepted African Americans as courageous and effective soldiers.[71] Though conservative white Unionists often participated in, and even led, episodes of violence against African Americans, white
Rebels clearly took the lead in inciting attacks.[72] Thus, by describing Tadlock as
a "Rebel soldier," the officer placed blame for the incident on the whites. Moreover, the officer's account claims that Moore "fancied" he saw a black soldier
pull out a gun, raising doubt as to whether Moore was telling the truth. This
statement is especially significant because Kentucky forbade the right of African
Americans to testify in court on the basis of old prejudices regarding the inability of blacks to speak truthfully and the belief that blacks had no claim to the
same civil rights accorded whites. By doubting the word of a white man in a
case involving violence between blacks and whites, the officer revealed the difference between the values of white Kentuckians and himself, at least in this
instance.[73] Most importantly, the officer concluded after taking evidence from
numerous witnesses at the fair, "I can see nothing in the conduct of the negroes
that is deserving of censure." And while the officer mildly chastised the black
soldiers for returning to the fair with guns and reinforcements, "this is little

more than could be expected even from men supposed to possess cooler judgment than the colored soldier." As respectable soldiers, they held the right to
use violence for self-protection. To him, the black soldiers behaved honorably,
especially when they sought revenge against those who attacked them. Perhaps
more significantly, a white man believed that African Americans *had* honor to
defend.

The contrasting account offered by the Lexington *Observer and Reporter* dramatically highlights the different attitude concerning race and the right to commit violence held by conservatives. In the newspaper account, primary
responsibility for the violence lay with the black soldiers, not with Moore. In
addition, the newspaper represents the black soldiers' conduct as both dishonorable and dangerous. First, the newspaper claimed that of the four black soldiers "promenading in a careless manner," only one chose to fight back against
the marshal when told to return to the black section of the fairground. Like the
prototypical "bad slave" who negatively influences or "demoralizes" his fellow
slaves, the instigator, out of "stubbornness," set the bad example and the
remaining blacks followed along. Second, without any reference to the white
attacks against African Americans at the fairgrounds, the article plays up the
decision of blacks to return with arms and reinforcements. It claims that the
black soldiers and their compatriots planned to "shoot every white person they
saw." However, the utter incompetence and timidity of the blacks convinced
them to halt their offensive and shoot "promiscuously" at random targets, killing only a black woman. The newspaper account thus portrayed the black soldiers as cowards who illegitimately claimed access to the right of organized
violence. To conservatives, blacks were not respectable soldiers capable of keeping order—they were a degraded mob hell-bent on race war and anarchy.

Not all white violence against newly freed African Americans in central Missouri and Kentucky targeted black soldiers or their families. As the Union Army
mustered black troops out of the service by late 1865, the immediate threat to
white sensibilities of a black military died down. However, the level of violence
against blacks continued apace, and it rose in some parts of the Bluegrass and
Little Dixie. New white paramilitary organizations—known commonly as the
"Regulators"—emerged in late 1865 and committed hundreds of acts of violence from arson to lynching. The stated purpose of the Regulator campaign
was to restore order where ex-slaves had resorted to acts of theft and murder.
The superintendent of the Lexington Sub-District of the Bureau of Refugees,
Freedmen, and Abandoned Lands (Freedmen's Bureau) reported a "regular
organized mob known as Negro Regulators who go about through these counties at night in disguises, beating and abusing these people in a most shocking
manner."[74] In Lebanon, site of the earlier mutilation of the black recruits, a

gang of thirty Regulators, under the leadership of Captain Skaggs, in 1866 attacked a black grocer named Edward Tucker and a black restaurant owner named Allen Drake. They also ransacked the homes of Tucker, Drake, and seven other black families in the area, where they "broke down doors, tore down chimneys, unroofed houses, shot at men and women, and scattered in every direction the papers and books of the Rev. Wm. Miles, a Methodist colored minister, who was absent from home."[75] A Radical newspaper in central Kentucky noted that Skaggs's men had targeted Drake and Tucker before this incident as well, and that all of the victims were "the most quiet and industrious colored men in our county."[76] The Regulators likely targeted men like Drake and Tucker precisely because they were relatively successful, and they served as inspiration for African Americans seeking autonomy and the right to own land.

Some violence targeted blacks who refused to acknowledge the demands of racial segregation and restriction from white public spaces. In Versailles, Kentucky, Captain Campbell of the Shelton House violently ejected a black man who had "cooly sat at the table and ordered supper."[77] For this, the conservative newspaper reported, "Cuffee receive[d] a pretty severe drubbing, and afterward [was] lodged in the jail for disorderly conduct." Before 1865, white Kentuckians long restricted free blacks' access to public spaces. In the years after the war, white businessmen maintained the right to exclude any patron whom they deemed "offensive"; violation of segregationist custom met swift violence in response.

Foreshadowing the major lynching epidemic in the late nineteenth century, many whites justified racial violence by appealing to the protection of white womanhood.[78] In Paris, Kentucky, a mob lynched a black man named Burt for raping and murdering an Irish woman named Millie Dolan.[79] The staunchly conservative True Kentuckian mocked a visiting abolitionist who dared to question the propriety of lynching in an argument with an Irish waitress named Maggie Short. After the visitor claimed Short should be tarred and feathered for defending lynching, Short rounded up a collection of "ladies and gentlemen" and threatened the man with a stick. Short accused the visitor of being "no better than the negro" and chased him out of the town.[80] Here, an Irish woman rose in defense of the honor of a fellow countrywoman allegedly "outraged" by a black man. Indeed, community violence in defense of white womanhood was not restricted to men.

In some cases, whites killed blacks for no explicit reason. After consuming several bottles of liquor, three brothers named Elson entered Miami, Missouri, and announced to all present that they planned to "kill a nigger."[81] Shortly afterward, they shot a randomly chosen black man. After the black man ran into a hotel for protection, the brothers shot at the white hotelkeeper. Perhaps because of the second transgression—attempting to murder a prominent white businessman—a white mob retaliated and shot the Elson brothers. Though drunk, the Elsons apparently felt they could murder with impunity any African American they chose. The random nature of the attacks undoubtedly contributed to a generalized fear among the black community in central Missouri. But neither of the two published accounts of the incident suggests any community outrage at the attempted murder of the black man.[82]

Indeed, the conservative press that emerged after the war, including the Lexington *Gazette*, offered a lens into the rising racial violence. These newspapers characterized the great political struggle of postwar Kentucky and Missouri as a struggle for the survival of white supremacy in an age of emancipation. Editors from longtime Unionist papers such as the Fulton *Missouri Telegraph*, Paris *Western Citizen*, and the Lexington *Observer and Reporter* made common cause with ex-Rebel sympathizers (and ex-Rebel soldiers, in some cases) who produced such popular Democratic Party tracts as the Danville *Advocate*, Paris *True Kentuckian*, and, perhaps the most virulently white supremacist newspaper of all, the *Caucasian* of Lexington, Missouri. Ex-Whigs and supporters of John Bell's Constitutional Union Party joined forces with stalwart Democrats to defend Andrew Johnson's rejection of the Civil Rights Bill, the Freedmen's Bureau Bill, and the congressional Reconstruction bills advanced by Radical Republicans. All of these newspaper editors vehemently opposed black soldier enlistment during the war and continued their rejection of the Radical course of the Union cause long after the war's conclusion.[83]

Establishing itself as the pre-eminent white supremacist newspaper in the West, the Lexington (Mo.) *Caucasian* unified political protest against radical claims of racial equality. Billing itself as the largest newspaper west of St. Louis, the *Caucasian* affirmed, "We are Caucasian in blood, in birth, and in prejudice, and do not expect to labor to place above us in the scale of civilization, in morality, in usefulness, in religion, in the arts and sciences, in mechanics either the Mongolian, the Indian or the Negro."[84] The *Caucasian* consistently argued for the rights of ex-Rebels within Missouri who were disfranchised by the new Radical regime. But as the *Caucasian* duly noted, the more pressing concern for conservatives of all prior loyalties was the status of African Americans in border state society. "Today the question is whether these liberated slaves shall be enfranchised—made the equals of the Caucasian. Radicals say they shall. Conservative Union men say they shall not."[85] For ex-Rebels like the editor of the *Caucasian*, the threat of racial or "social" equality united all white conservatives, regardless of past loyalties. Though the *Caucasian* never explicitly advocated violence against African Americans, its harsh editorials in opposition to the rights of ex-slaves gave voice to conservatives who, up to that point, had expressed their opinions under the cover of night, in disguise, and with arms.[86]

The *Caucasian* did, however, describe black soldiers as dishonorable whenever possible. Citing a story in Hermann, Missouri, where an anti-Radical school board voted to eject all black students from the town's schools, the *Caucasian* titled the article "And the Colored Troops Fought Nobly."[87] Hermann, in the heart of central Missouri's burgeoning German immigrant population, proved to be one of Missouri's most steadfast Unionist strongholds, and it continued to support the Radical programs in the Republican Party for the first few years after the war. Citing, approvingly, the conservative drift in Radical Hermann, the *Caucasian* mocked the "myth" of noble black soldiers often employed by Radicals to justify black education and other civil rights for ex-slaves.[88] The *Caucasian*'s disparagement of black troops' honor was especially important because, as elsewhere in the South, Missourians associated honor with the right to self-defense and the ability to wield that right to protect one's social standing. Under the slave system, white men "defended" their honor in myriad ways, including duels, militia participation, and the public demonstration of authority over slaves.[89] Black men entering military service during the Civil War also associated military prowess and fearlessness with public honor. For most border state whites, only those willing to defend their honor with violence deserved the rights of citizenship. By mocking black military service, the *Caucasian* directly attacked African Americans' claims to equal citizenship in a biracial republic.

In many ways, the Regulator campaigns of the late 1860s that afflicted black men and women across central Kentucky and Missouri resembled the lynch mobs that terrorized communities across the South in the 1890s and early 1900s. But the social and political context for Regulator violence differed from the lynching wave of the turn of the twentieth century. Whereas latter-day lynching apologists like South Carolina's Ben Tillman or Mississippi's James Vardaman cited the generation growing up after slavery as insufficiently respectful of white authority, white border state supporters of racial violence in the 1860s viewed the revolutionary changes *within* the last generation of slaves as particularly threatening. In particular, white conservatives identified the disturbing potential of armed ex-slaves for upending social relations. Even as ex-slaves mustered out of the army, whites feared that freedpeople would summarily reject the longstanding social mores and customs that held central Kentucky and Missouri together. The threat of political "Negro domination" was a chimerical fear in the border states; however, the critical role that African Americans played in emancipating themselves revealed uncomfortable possibilities for whites accustomed to unchallenged rule.[90] The use of extralegal violence, committed with "solemnity" by organized white mobs, helped fend off the revolutionary challenge of an armed, assertive black citizenry.[91]

The epidemic of racial violence afflicted the central Kentucky countryside more than in central Missouri for a number of reasons. First, the Radical Republican state government in Jefferson City effectively deployed militia throughout the Little Dixie region, preventing the growth of large, organized white supremacist groups like the Regulators. Second, what violent response existed targeted the officers of the Radical government and the symbols of the new Radical-driven economy; the infamous James-Younger gang of ex-Rebels that prowled the towns of central and western Missouri attacked white employees of the armored express companies and the Radical county government officials much more often than they did freed African Americans. Third, the violence against African Americans *during* Missouri's guerrilla war forced a significant portion of the black population to flee to St. Louis or Kansas even before the war's completion. And fourth, because of the existence of a large white Unionist militia in Missouri, black soldiers established a much greater presence in Kentucky than in Missouri; white refusal to serve in either side of the Civil War in Kentucky yielded a disproportionately high percentage of black soldiers.[92] Correspondingly, the fears and subsequent violence associated with a black soldiery ran higher in Kentucky than in its western neighbor.

A cumulative effect of this ongoing racial violence was the permanent emigration of African Americans from the border countryside.[93] The black population in Little Dixie and the Bluegrass dropped considerably between 1860 and 1870. Kentucky and Missouri were the only Confederate or Union states to witness a decline in their black populations during this ten-year period.[94] By 1870 the black population of Kentucky dropped by 6 percent from its 1860 total, while Missouri's black population dropped by a smaller margin. Within the Bluegrass and Little Dixie, the black population dropped even further. In eight Bluegrass counties, the black population dropped from 42,033 to 40,190, or 7 percent.[95] However, if Fayette County, home of the burgeoning city of Lexington, is removed, the black population dropped by 10 percent. Thus many African Americans in the surrounding Bluegrass countryside emigrated either to the relative urban safety of Lexington or to a different region altogether. In Missouri, the story is even more dramatic. Of seven Little Dixie counties along the Missouri River, the black population dropped 19 percent. Lafayette County, home of the *Weekly Caucasian*, witnessed the greatest drop: 37 percent. Like Kentucky, however, not all African Americans left the state. The two largest cities in the Missouri, St. Louis and the newly developing Kansas City, experienced a growth of 325 percent and 30 percent, respectively, in black population between 1860 and 1870.[96] Black populations in states and counties immediately outside Kentucky and Missouri grew exponentially as well, with Kansas growing from 625 African Americans in 1860 to 17,108 in 1870. Ohio River counties, from Cincinnati's Hamilton County to sparsely populated Switzerland County, Indiana, likewise experienced major increases in black population between 1860 and 1870.[97]

It is impossible to implicate racial violence for all black migration from the border countryside. Indeed, a significant portion of black migrants escaped bondage during the war to enlist in Union Army regiments in Indiana, Ohio, and Kansas. Still, it is significant that so few of these migrants moved back to their homes in the border countryside after the war while African Americans across the North returned to states in the former Confederacy to reconnect families and communities torn apart by slavery, especially as the immediate prospects of Radical Reconstruction portended a better life.[98] Life in postwar central Kentucky and Missouri proved uninviting for African Americans. The epidemic of racial violence played a central part in keeping blacks away, with Radical Reconstruction either nonexistent or irrelevant to the fate of African Americans.[99] At the vanguard of antiblack violence were gangs led by the likes of Jim Jackson, who had threatened to expel all African Americans from rural Boone County in 1865. In the postwar years, violence by gangs of Jackson's sort and the lack of economic opportunity in the white-dominated countryside created the first of many Great Migrations from the rural border states to cities and to states to the north and west.

African Americans suffered arbitrary acts of racial violence from the moment slavery arrived in Kentucky and Missouri. Even as border state propagandists insisted that the "peculiar institution" in Kentucky and Missouri represented the "mildest" forms of slavery, personal violence played an integral role in maintaining social and labor control. As the decades-long sectional struggle over slavery led to a civil war that pitted Kentuckians against Kentuckians and Missourians against Missourians, violence against border state blacks continued. Indeed, the nature of violence against many border state blacks during and after the Civil War, including the mutilation of potential army recruits and the whipping of family members of black soldiers, closely mimicked the sort of violence that had characterized slavery. But the context of racial violence shifted dramatically during the Civil War as African Americans made an unprecedented bid to free themselves from the thrall of both Unionist and Confederate whites. For slaves, the Civil War brought a chance at self-liberation, the assertion of human dignity, and the martial rights, responsibilities, and honor of citizenship. The Civil War heralded a revolution that overturned social customs, slave labor relations, and rituals of racial deference. Few blacks or whites could have imagined the final outcome.

For border state whites, the revolution brought on by emancipation and, especially, the enlistment of former slaves in the Union Army signaled a coming reign of terror. If not the great race war of Saint Domingue, the newly armed black citizenry would at least usher in the rule of what the *Caucasian* termed "The Jacobin Party."[100] In a war hijacked by radicals bent on social revolution, the use of violence could help conservatives restore the long-held prerogatives of white supremacy. Whether bushwhackers in the late-war central Missouri countryside vowing to return slave runaways to their "rightful" owners, or Regulators prowling the black districts of Lexington, Lebanon, and Danville in postwar central Kentucky, extralegal mobs asserted the right to maintain a racial order based on black deference and subservience to whites in all facets of social, cultural, and economic life.[101] Regulators even established a mock court of "Judge Lynch" wherein they published their "official proceedings" in the Kentucky newspapers.[102] Regulators believed that white control of the civil law had weakened under the yoke of the Freedmen's Bureau, and they thus assumed the "legitimate" right to exact community vengeance upon social, and especially racial, transgressors.[103]

Though white radicals, both within and outside Kentucky and Missouri, played a critical role in reshaping the Union cause into a war for emancipation, it was the slaves themselves who most dramatically altered the conflict within the border states. From the beginning of hostilities in 1861, the Lincoln administration yielded to the social and political demands of conservative whites in Kentucky and Missouri. The Emancipation Proclamation never applied to the border states, and the enrollment of African Americans into the Union Army was postponed there until manpower requirements rendered further delay impossible. After the army lifted the final restrictions against black enlistments, the rush of slaves from the farms of Little Dixie and the Bluegrass stunned white conservatives and Union military officials alike. Sporadic violence against enlistees hardly stemmed the tide of African Americans who "stampeded" into the army of liberation. Liberated slaves with guns now manned posts in communities where slavery still legally existed. The new social order patrolled by armed African Americans rested upon a revolutionary biracial conception of the body politic. Blacks declared themselves equal citizens of the biracial republic, having served with honor on the battlefield.

The Union cause that many border state whites long espoused had now fulfilled Confederate prophecy; whites across Kentucky and Missouri who once rallied to the Union side in 1861 precisely because it promised to respect slavery now found their cause usurped by their own slaves. The rumblings of discontent threatened to sever the Union coalition in the latter years of the Civil War, as popular officers like Colonel Wolford demanded the right of Kentuckians to resist black enlistment by any means necessary. After April 1865, many conservative Unionists joined forces with their former Confederate foes to stem the radical tide. Primarily targeting families of black soldiers, border state whites attacked the most salient symbols of the Civil War's social revolution. With the refusal or inability of civil authorities to stop the violence, African Americans fled the border countryside for towns and cities like Lexington, Danville, and Columbia, and then for the Northern states like Kansas, Indiana, and Ohio. After years of violence between white Unionists and Confederates, white conservatives in central Kentucky and Missouri laid to rest their old quarrels and directed their guns at the nascent black citizenry.

By 1870, the mass of former conservative Unionists and erstwhile Rebels in Kentucky and Missouri helped undermine the Radical project in the border states and even in the former Confederacy. Border state whites served as the vanguard in a white conservative "redemption" campaign by publicizing stories of white suffering gathered by sympathetic border men and women traveling throughout the South. Alas, not only did former conservative Unionists and Confederates threaten the lives of radicalized former slaves and their white allies, they also constructed a nationally resonant narrative of Radical "corruption" and "abuse" that convinced many Northerners to abandon Reconstruction altogether. The racial violence at the heart of the border states and the heart of the country as a whole symbolized the fervent opposition to radical egalitarianism in the American heartland and directly inspired the resurgence of a new racial conservatism at the national level.

3

"The Rebel Spirit in Kentucky": The Politics of Readjustment in a Border State, 1865–1868

ANNE E. MARSHALL

On his postwar journey through the South in 1865–66, journalist Whitelaw Reid noted during his stop in Louisville, Kentucky, that it was the only place on his trip where slaves waited on him. "They were the last any of us were ever to see on American soil," he claimed. Not coincidentally, Reid found the city to be a "rebel community" whose residents displayed about as much loyalty to the federal government as those of Charleston, South Carolina, and even less than those of Nashville, Tennessee. These claims may have struck his readers as curious given that Kentucky had, at the outset of the Civil War, first declared neutrality, then loyalty to the Union. But as Reid suggested, by 1866 white Kentuckians' stance toward the federal government had undergone a marked shift.[1]

Reid's observations regarding the state of slavery and disloyalty in the "Southern" but Unionist slave state of Kentucky were, of course, intimately intertwined. The "peculiar institution" had disintegrated in most of the South, and much of the nation was readjusting to peace, but by the war's end slavery was in limbo in Kentucky—neither dead nor alive. Exempt from the Emancipation Proclamation, Kentucky's slaves had not yet been officially freed by the federal government. While nearly 70 percent of them ended their bondage by serving in the Union Army or marrying someone who did, an estimated seventy thousand Kentucky slaves existed in a frail form of slavery through the spring and summer of 1865. This meant, ironically, that a place where slavery once existed in its most tenuous form became one of the institution's last outposts. Indeed, with the exception of Delaware, white Kentuckians clung to the dying institution longer than people in any other "Southern" state. Many did so in a desperate attempt to control African Americans, while others still harbored hope that they might receive some sort of compensation for their property. As white Kentuckians stubbornly refused to let go of slavery, the state's African Americans fought in myriad ways for their freedom.[2]

Whitelaw Reid's estimation of antifederal sentiment in Kentucky pointed to another wartime development that continued into the postwar period. While white Kentuckians were famously divided during the war—"brother against brother"—most residents of the Bluegrass State had been loyal to the Union at the outset. During the war, however, emancipation and federal military policy caused many Kentucky whites to change their minds, and by 1865 the questions raised by black freedom led to another civil war within the state, this one largely between white males. No longer fighting as Rebels or Yankees, Kentuckians were in an all-out political battle to shape the state's postwar social order. As residents of an unreconstructed state, former Unionists and Confederates alike enjoyed unfettered access to the polls, where they cast their ballots for conservative Democratic candidates in overwhelming numbers. These postwar political battles bore all of the vitriolic rhetoric and violent imagery of bloody Civil War engagements, and more often than not—despite significant efforts made by both black and white Republicans—conservative, pro-slavery, pro-Confederate forces emerged victorious.[3]

Democratic politics enveloped in a Lost Cause narrative quickly came to define the state in the years following the war, and it ultimately redrew the lines of Kentucky's Civil War historical memory. The voting tendencies of white Kentuckians gained national attention, and in Northern eyes, especially those of Republican newspaper editors, the ballot box became the first grounds on which Kentucky rebelled *ex post facto*, appearing to, as E. Merton Coulter would famously write, "[wait] until after the war was over to secede from the Union." As one disgruntled Kentucky Republican lamented, it soon became clear that "a majority of her voters believe the war for the Union was wrong and that their hearts as well as their voices, are in sympathy with the 'lost cause.'" An examination of political rhetoric about Kentucky, from both inside and outside of the state, reveals how battles over wartime issues continued after 1865 and not only forged a new postwar image of the state, but also remade its wartime identity.[4]

To both those Kentuckians who owned slaves and those who did not, the uncertain status of slavery in their state and the incumbent ever-shifting racial relations proved to be the biggest source of anxiety in the aftermath of the war. While black Kentuckians began to test the boundaries of their status, whites wondered how long they might count on their labor and subservience. Even as whites clung tenaciously to slavery, they realized the inevitability of its demise. "We would not however be surprised to see the whole flock take flight someday," Harrodsburg resident Lizzie Hardin said of her family's servants in July 1865, knowing it was only a matter of time before they would "blossom into freedom."[5]

Indeed, the very next week Hardin reported that "liberty fever" had "broken out" among the family's servants. One of them, whom the family referred to as Uncle Charles, left his work at the Hardin household and walked to the nearest army encampment to obtain his "Palmer pass," the eponymous document Kentucky's federal military commander John Palmer began granting to African Americans in the spring of 1865, enabling them to travel freely in and out of the state. Emboldened and determined to take advantage of this freedom, Uncle Charles told Hardin's grandfather that his pass "allowed him to hire himself to whom he pleased." Hardin denounced it as "only a permission to go to Cincinnati, or in other words, to run off." Hardin's grandfather, trying in vain like many Kentucky slaveholders to wield any coercive power he had left, threatened to sue anyone who would hire the black man. For Uncle Charles, however, the documentation was assurance that he could act upon this liberty if he wished, and for a time Hardin noted that he seemed "perfectly satisfied with the consciousness of having the pass in his pocket, and came back and went to hauling wood without any mention of his freedom."[6]

Doubtless hundreds of such encounters between "slaves" and "masters" took place in the summer and fall of 1865. Across the state there existed a three-way struggle between the occupying Union forces that tried to extend and protect the rights of freed blacks, freed blacks who were seizing those rights, and whites who attempted to limit them. As thousands of African Americans moved away from rural areas and congregated in the urban centers of Kentucky, white fears about their concentrated numbers escalated. In October 1865, Lexington mayor Josiah Wingate, in denial that slavery was dead, demanded that slave owners retrieve the African Americans and "take care of them" or face legal charges. Palmer countered the mayor, threatening use of military force should any people calling themselves "owners and claimants" try to seize former slaves. Furthermore, he asserted, "All the people of the state are presumed to be *free and protected as free until orders are received to the contrary.*" In November, one Kentucky judge, seeking economic remuneration while he could, tried to sell the child of one of his slaves. In an attempt to save her child, the mother feigned marriage to a federal soldier, and the judge narrowly escaped the embarrassment of being arrested by a group of black soldiers. Everywhere there were reminders that the prewar order was irrevocably gone. During the August 1865 elections, armed black troops stood at Mercer County polls to deny access to expatriated Confederates. When a white sheriff seized two black men accused of a crime, a group of black soldiers on a train passing through Bowling Green seized the prisoners and threatened the sheriff and anyone who attempted to interfere.[7]

As African Americans seemed to abrogate the racial order in numerous ways, Kentucky whites voiced a multitude of fears in newspapers and other public forums. They worried about the lack of control over where former slaves lived and traveled, and they feared the concentration of bitter, and possibly retaliatory, blacks. Landowners and those who rented slaves for seasonal labor worried about the labor supply and whether African Americans could be compelled to work without the coercive power of slavery. One former slaveholder described the feelings of many Kentucky whites when he stated candidly, "The negroes have been among us for centuries. They are among us now. The mere fact of the negroes being a part of our society, is not offensive. It is only when the negroes are free that it is assumed they will be a bad element of the population." To the problem of control and the matter of "reconstruct[ing] a system of efficient labor out of the ruins of slavery," Kentucky whites passed the same sort of stringent vagrancy laws as existed in other Southern states and provisions for every county with a large number of freedmen to manage a farm "under a competent overseer," upon which "vagrants" would be forced to work for the county. Trading one vision of coercion for another, the former slaveholder argued that "wise, judicious, and humane laws can be readily devised, enacted, and enforced as the new exigencies of the new system may require."[8]

Other Kentuckians shared with their fellow Southerners the fear that freedom would lead to sexual equality and miscegenation. "The great staple argument of the Kentucky Conservatives who oppose the [Thirteenth] amendment," scoffed the *Cincinnati Gazette*, "is that if slavery is abolished, negro equality will result, and their daughters will walk with and marry colored men." The paper cynically added, "They have a very poor opinion of their daughters."[9] Other slaveholders simply mourned their loss of authority. As one man told a reporter regarding slavery, "It wasn't the pecuniary loss that hurt me. The truth is, I had all my life, been accustomed to having someone call me master, and I can't get along without it now." These worries often took on an apocalyptic tenor, as when the *Lexington Observer and Reporter* stated, "The African at home is the lowest of savages, and although enlightenment of two centuries of contact with whites has wonderfully improved this savage of four thousand years, his domination means ruin and decay."[10]

Though they shared many of the fears of their fellow Southerners, Kentuckians soon faced them without federal aid or federal interference. In October 1865, President Andrew Johnson finally heeded Kentucky's request to end martial law. Crucially, its "loyal" border state status exempted Kentucky from federal Reconstruction, leaving whites free of its implications and African Americans void of its protective measures. As a result, white Kentuckians charted a political path unique among the border states. While Maryland, Delaware, and Missouri each had strong pro-slavery, antifederal factions, they all for various reasons came under Republican control by the end of the war. Even when the Democratic Party later revitalized in these states, Republicans had strong enough footholds to be an effective minority party.[11] The story was different in Kentucky, where the political landscape had been a mass of shifting alliances that had gone by ever-changing monikers since the demise of the Whig Party in the 1850s. Despite voting for Constitutional Union Party candidate John Bell for president in 1860, the majority of Kentucky voters considered themselves Democrats at the war's outbreak. After the war, white Kentuckians began carving out new political identities for themselves on the basis of their wartime experiences, the outcome of the war, and their visions of the future. Voters formed political coalitions around their economic interests, their level of support or disapproval of presidential and congressional Reconstruction policies, and the role they felt African Americans should play in postwar life.

This fluidity resulted in a political landscape that scrambled the lines of wartime loyalties. As Kentucky voters searched for the party that shared their best interests, some Unionists pledged allegiance to the Republican Party, which also went by the titles Unconditional Union, or Union Party. Self-styled to be more moderate than the congressional Radical Republicans, the state party nevertheless wished to see Kentuckians embrace, or at least accept, a new economic and racial order. Between 1865 and 1867, another party faded in and out of influence. The Conservative Union Party (also incarnate as the Union Democrats) steered a middle course between the "radical" Republicans and the "reactionary" Democrats. It became the party of choice for Unionists dismayed by the federal government's altered war aims but unwilling to ally themselves with former secessionists. Most Unionists, however, feeling betrayed by the Lincoln government's emancipation and Reconstruction policies—and fearful of its successors—called themselves Conservatives or Democrats.[12]

Indeed, politics became one of the first meeting grounds for former foes as they soon realized that their wartime sympathies were less important than their postwar problems. The phenomenal level of Unionist Democratic voting was for many whites not simply an attempt to redress past grievances but rather an attempt to seize control of the present. Together they faced personal loss, physical and economic devastation, the legacy of ruptured families and communities, and most of all, a world in which African Americans lived outside of bondage. With this issue in mind, many former Confederates and former Unionists came together at the polls, making the politics of race common ground for white Kentuckians following the Civil War and leaving the state dominated by what would be termed the "rebel Democracy."

Historian C. Vann Woodward wrote that, "despite Kentucky's failure to secede and join the Confederacy, no state below the Ohio River presented a more solidly Confederate-Democratic front in the decade after Appomattox."

But not all Kentuckians "seceded" after the war. A significant number of African Americans and white Republicans imbued their politics with a different vision of Kentucky's wartime experience, one that recalled the state's loyalty to the Union. For these whites, the end of slavery had been a long time coming and meant Kentucky might finally become fertile ground for industry and white labor. Black Kentuckians, meanwhile, called on their service and sacrifice for the Union in their efforts to seize their freedom, negotiate new labor arrangements with whites, and extend their claims of citizenship to the courtroom and the ballot box.[13]

In August 1865, in the first postwar elections in the state, eligible Unionist voters—ex-Confederates still could not vote under the terms of expatriation— filled five of Kentucky's nine congressional seats and the majority of the state legislature with Conservatives and Democrats. Although anti-Republican sentiment accounted for some of the vote, it also was an expression of the racial conservatism of white Kentuckians. As the *Cincinnati Gazette* observed, the Democratic Party had "one single rallying point and that is the negro. On that narrow neck of ground they find common ground. Every other principle which has governed these different factions in days that are past is laid aside, and the negro is made the one grand cornerstone of their building."[14]

In November, the Conservative-dominated legislature proved this point when they rejected the Thirteenth Amendment as well as the Republican initiative to admit black testimony in state courts. When Congress ratified the amendment the following month, the state General Assembly repealed the Act of Expatriation to mark its protest, thereby restoring full constitutional rights to ex-Confederates. The reward for such insubordination came when General Oliver O. Howard extended the Bureau of Refugees, Freedmen, and Abandoned Lands (Freedmen's Bureau) to Kentucky in December 1865. For the next four years, blacks would look to the agency for help and protection while whites would add the agency's presence—which they considered a "naked usurpation"—to their list of grievances. In February 1866, the state General Assembly adopted resolutions requesting the removal of federal troops from the state, condemning the Freedmen's Bureau, requesting restoration of the writ of *habeas corpus*, and, yet again, rejecting the Thirteenth Amendment.[15]

Some Kentuckians looked on with anger, frustration, and embarrassment at the Conservatives' intransigence. Louisville native James Speed, who had served as Lincoln's attorney general, was particularly pained by the attitude of his home state. "Kentucky seems to know less than a blind puppy that has not the sense to find the mother's teat and not to wound it," he wrote to his mother from Washington in December 1865. In striking at the agenda of the federal government, he continued, Kentucky was "making ugly sores upon her own body, and future history will not let the scar disappear. I blush for her record in history . . . Kentucky is more unbelieving than Thomas. She has had her hand in the death wound of the monster slavery, the last desperate struggles of the hideous creature have been upon her soil, and yet she is unbelieving. Poor Kentucky!"[16]

The loudest voices of protest appeared in Northern newspapers, whose reporters watched the intransigence of Kentuckians with keen eyes and critical pens. While the ever-proximate Cincinnati dailies—the *Gazette* and the *Commercial*—had reported wavering white loyalty in the state throughout the war, they responded to the state's postwar actions with invigorated resentment, rhetorically linking Democratic voting to Confederate sentiments and what they called "the rebel spirit." The *New York Times*, the *New York Tribune*, and the *Pittsburgh Gazette* soon joined them on a regular basis. "He is hardly a responsible being," said the *Cincinnati Gazette* of the Kentucky slaveholder in 1865, "[the] poor, silly creatures are standing with their short-handled brooms attempting to sweep back the ocean tide of this mighty revolution." The *Gazette* returned to the subject later in the year:

> Oh, wise Democracy of Kentucky, hugging the relic of slavery to your bosoms, bowing before this your idol, and worshipping—calling everybody fanatical that opposes your foolishness, holding on to slavery because it used to pay, forgetting that the times have changed . . . the people of this country are not going to take a single step backward on this slavery question.[17]

In 1866, with their voting rights restored, Confederates quickly reentered political life. They soon joined ranks with conservative Unionists and, despite the fact that much of the Conservative/Democratic constituency consisted of former Unionists, the Confederates began quickly to lead and define the party. In 1866 Alvin Duvall, a Southern sympathizer, ran for clerk of the Kentucky Court of Appeals against Unionist Edward Hobson. Though the contested office was a relatively minor one, the sectional credentials of the candidates and their racial politics resulted in an election that played out in terms of wartime loyalties. Duvall, running as a Democrat, had gained his rebellious reputation when Military District Commander Stephen Burbridge forced him to leave the state in 1864 because of his well-known Confederate proclivities. Meanwhile, Hobson, whom both the Conservative Union and Republican Parties backed, had forged his valiant reputation by capturing the elusive and hard-riding John Hunt Morgan on one of his Kentucky raids. Furthermore, he was a racial moderate who supported the passage of the Thirteenth and Fourteenth Amendments.

In the public debate surrounding the contest, commentators completely wrapped the contemporaneous politics of race in the sectional rhetoric of war. J. Stoddard Johnson, the ex-Confederate editor of the *Frankfort Yeoman*, admonished the people of Kentucky to "remember that they have been robbed of more than one hundred millions of slave property" by Hobson's party. On the other side, George Prentice, editor of the *Louisville Daily Journal*, attacked both Duvall and his party for their wartime connections, charging that "every man in Kentucky" knew the Democrats to be "pro-rebel and rebel-sympathizing." He later cautioned, "If you vote for Duvall to-day Kentuckians, you vote BLACK AND BLOODY SECESSION." Criticism of Duvall and those planning to vote for him rained down from across the Ohio River, including this from the *Cincinnati Gazette*: "Democracy in Kentucky means secession is right, the rebellion was a patriotic duty, the rebels patriots and heroes, and all Union men murderers and tyrants . . . if a man is a Union man he is not a Democrat. If he is a Democrat now, he is not a Union Man." On another occasion, the *Gazette* wrote that conservative Democrats "hate the Union, hate the flag, hate its defenders."[18]

Despite the preoccupation with wartime loyalties, the election also turned on practical fiscal concerns for white Kentuckians, some of whom were still hoping to be repaid for their freed slaves. Along with sectional rhetoric, state newspaper editors enlisted economic issues to make their case. By voting for Southern sympathizer Duvall, Walter Haldeman reminded *Louisville Courier* readers, they could curry favor with the Southern states and help secure trade for Kentucky merchants. Meanwhile, George Prentice's *Louisville Daily Journal* argued that Kentuckians should vote for Hobson if they wanted any congressional compensation for their lost slave property.[19]

Tensions came to a head on election day as violence broke out and at least twenty people were killed in conflicts around the state. White Kentuckians, it seemed, were refighting the war at the polls. Some Republican observers had optimistically estimated Hobson would win by twenty thousand votes, but when the ballots were counted, Duvall emerged victorious, winning by thirty-seven thousand votes. Recognizing that Duvall's success had as much to do with racial fears as his Confederate status, the *Frankfort Commonwealth* reported that the Unionists had been, "out-numbered, or out-generaled, the great engine used against them having been, as usual, the negro."[20]

For Northern onlookers, Duvall's election appeared to be "a straight out rebel victory." Once and for all, Kentucky had exchanged war loyalties. "It is a sad record for Kentucky, claimed to be the most thorough Union state in the Union. That she is rebel and thoroughly rebel is proven beyond doubt by the election," wrote the *Cincinnati Gazette*. "The rebel gray has whipped the Union blue at the polls and as humiliating as it may be, it is nevertheless true. The same rebel spirit that rules in Memphis and New Orleans against all who sustained the Union there, voted . . . in Kentucky against all that respected the Union here." Furthermore, recognizing that Kentucky's loyalty to the Union had been based in part on the preservation of slavery and lost with the institution's demise, the *Gazette* asserted that the state had "been rebel" since the fall of 1862, when Lincoln issued the preliminary Emancipation Proclamation.[21]

In the end, the Court of Appeals race in 1866 exhibited not only the extent of conservative sentiment in Kentucky, but also the power and pervasiveness of sectional rhetoric in postwar politics. In an atmosphere where whites feared the loss of their place in the racial hierarchy above all else, having been a Union hero carried little weight, and when coupled with the rhetoric of race, it could be spun into a liability. The contentious political atmosphere continued in 1867. The *Frankfort Commonwealth* heralded the new political year with a warning about the "the designs of the conspirators in our midst, who are plotting and scheming to place this State under the rule of those who favored the rebellion." Sending up a political battle cry, they declared that loyal Kentuckians must continue to suppress the rebellion as they had during the war.[22]

Despite the Republican call to arms, 1867 proved to be another successful year for the Democrats. They defeated the proposed Fourteenth Amendment in the state legislature by a wide margin and swept all nine seats in a special congressional election held in May. Their victory prompted one angry Republican to claim, "Kentucky is today as effectually in the hands of rebels as if they had every town and city garrisoned by their troops. With a rebel Governor, rebel Congressmen, rebel Statehouse and Senate, rebel Judges, rebel Mayors, rebel municipal officers, rebel policemen and constables, what is to become of the poor blacks and loyal white men God only knows." The election results so angered Republicans in Congress that they initially refused to seat four of the newly elected congressmen from Kentucky.[23]

The most important victory of the year for the Democrats came when John L. Helm won the governor's seat. The race featured three parties: the Republicans, the Democrats, and the Conservative Union Party, which was led by several prominent conservative Unionists who could not tolerate the Confederate-dominated Democratic ticket. Significantly, the Conservative Union Party garnered just 13,167 votes, with the Republicans netting 33,939 and the Democrats 90,225. The lopsided Democratic victory caused the Republican editor of the *Kentucky Statesman* to lament, "What Bragg failed to do in 1862, with his army and banners, the people of Kentucky, five years later have done; they have given the State over into the hands of those who have been enemies of the Union."[24]

Newspapers in Chicago, Cincinnati, and Washington, D.C., responded to the election results by calling for the state to undergo federal Reconstruction. "Kentucky needs reconstruction, and must have it," unsuccessful Republican congressional candidate Sam McKee proclaimed.

> She is to-day the most disloyal of all the states. To-day she is more hostile to the national authority than any other State. . . . Today we witness in Kentucky a State avoiding and defying the acts of the nation's Congress. Here the theory of State rights, as contended for by Davis and his collaborators, is a success.[25]

McKee's call for reconstruction drew a clear connection between politics and postwar rebellion. He asked, "why should congress treat Kentucky different from any rebel State?" and concluded that "the mistake of the administration was treating her thus during the war . . . Now that [Kentuckians] have been conciliated to such an extent as to join the rebel ranks and vote the rebel ticket . . . there is no excuse for Federal government not to intervene."[26]

Northerners continued to look at the political behavior of Kentucky with a mixture of anger and bewilderment. In the aftermath of the election, the *New York Times* printed a list of all of newly elected "rebel" state officers. The list included Helm, whom federal authorities arrested twice during the war for disloyalty, and Lieutenant Governor John Stevenson, a "Calhoun school politician" who was once arrested while trying to raise a regiment of Confederate fighters. Readers also learned of the scores of "rebel" officials elected to various positions, including the state's attorney general, auditor, treasurer, and superintendent of public instruction. Lastly, there was James Dawson, the register of the State Land Office, who had during the war climbed to the rank of lieutenant in the Union Army, but had since "expressed regret that he ever wore the blue." Dawson, the *Times* claimed, "would have preferred seeing the South succeed, to witnessing the incidental overthrow of slavery, in the triumph of the Nation." When John Helm died after only five days in office, Stevenson succeeded him. Stevenson won the seat in his own right in an 1868 special election, becoming second in a line of six former Confederates or Southern sympathizers to serve as governor between 1867 and 1894.[27]

Indeed, though the rank and file of the Democratic Party had been Unionist during the war, former Confederates quickly assumed leadership of the party. Ex-Confederate William Preston put it diplomatically: "Without a doubt after the close of the war, the Southern element was the most energetic power in reviving the exanimate Democracy of the State." In most areas of the state, with

the exception of some eastern mountain counties where antebellum slaveholding had been less common, Confederate credentials soon became almost a pre-
condition for election. One Confederate veteran stated that a majority of the
Democrats in his area refused to vote for anyone who had not "seen service in
the Confederate army." According to historian Lowell Harrison, "If you
wanted to be elected, it was by far best to be an ex-Confederate. If you had lost
one or two limbs, for public display, you were almost a shoo-in." Unionists, in
many cases, could only get ahead in the party by denouncing their wartime
cause. A "rebel" county committee purportedly gave a former Unionist the
position of county sheriff after he remarked that he had become ashamed of
the Union uniform after "the negro had worn it."[28]

The lopsided prominence of Confederates in postwar politics obscured the
significant participation of conservative Unionists. Democratic U.S. Senator
Garrett Davis, who had been a staunch Unionist before the emancipation, won
reelection in 1867. Similarly, Kentuckians elected Lovell Rousseau, a (successful)
Union general who had commanded the Fifth Kentucky Volunteers, to the U.S.
House of Representatives as an Unconditional Unionist. Mirroring his constituency, however, Rousseau strongly opposed federal Reconstruction policies,
and these views came to a head in 1866 when he debated Radical Iowa Congressman Josiah Grinnell over extending the power of the Freedmen's Bureau.
The discussion turned ugly as Rousseau opposed the Bureau and its purposes,
and Grinnell insulted Rousseau and slighted the entire state of Kentucky for its
racial conservatism. In a subsequent confrontation reminiscent of the Preston
Brooks–Charles Sumner incident almost ten years prior, Rousseau struck Grinnell with a rattan cane until it broke. Because of the incident, Rousseau resigned
from Congress in July 1866, but promptly returned to fill his old seat several
months later, this time elected as a Democrat. As Davis and Rousseau illustrate,
Unionist politicians were usually only successful when they embraced conservative politics and turned their backs on Radical Republican federal racial policies.

Whites who chose to align their politics with the "old Union element," on
the other hand, found themselves held political hostage by Conservatives. The
situation in Kentucky was unusual: Republican men who were on the winning
side of the war had become pariahs after the war, persecuted by those whom
they defeated on the battlefield. They faced social ostracism, lawsuits, threats to
their property, and violent mobs. One Radical lamented, "Combinations
formed to ruin you in business, to exclude you from society, to turn you out
of your houses of worship, to compel you to send your children to school to
[be taught by] rebels." In Mason County a landowner informed one of his tenants that if he voted the Radical ticket, he would have to leave the farm. The
man followed through on his political convictions and left. Other tales emerged

of former Confederates refusing to buy goods at stores whose owners did not vote Conservative. The *Cincinnati Gazette* claimed that after the 1866 political contests, many men who had voted Republican were "discharged from work" and replaced by Conservatives. One Union veteran feared for his fellow Unionists who were unable to "earn a living, owing to the wounds received battling for this Government. Place the Government in the hands of rebels, and God help all such."[29]

Whites were not the sole agents of Republican politics. The fact that African Americans so willingly engaged in the political life of the state from the earliest days of their freedom was both a help and a hindrance to white Republicans. Despite the mighty effort whites put forth to limit the scope of black citizenship, black Kentuckians wasted little time after emancipation organizing political action. As they gathered at Emancipation Day and Fourth of July celebrations and at church assemblies and conventions around the state, they not only celebrated their freedom, but also demanded full rights of American citizenship.[30]

In January 1866, four thousand blacks gathered in Louisville, where military commander John Palmer told them to seek the aid of the Freedmen's Bureau and declared that legally they were on "equal footing," with whites. In March of that year, at a convention in Lexington, African Americans launched their fight for suffrage. In the following years, thousands pursued both the right to vote and to testify in state courts, working within fraternal societies such as the Union of Benevolent Societies and the United Brothers of Friendship to gain civil rights. One Cincinnati correspondent asserted, "Any one who supposes that the negroes are indifferent spectators of what is going on in Kentucky is greatly mistaken. They observe closely all that transpires and reason with a logical clearness which is perfectly surprising. White men tell them that they shall never have the right to vote in Kentucky, but the negroes laugh and say, 'It's a comin', massa.'"[31]

With the promise of black suffrage hanging in the air, white Republicans quickly realized that black memorial celebrations provided excellent opportunities to capture votes. Prominent Kentucky Unionists and Republicans made themselves a fixture of black public celebrations from the beginning. James Speed addressed Louisville celebrants in 1867, offering them "some very good advice," and as the *Cincinnati Commercial* reported, urging them to "continue in their exertions for promoting their race." At another political gathering, General John Palmer underscored the difference between white Confederates and black Unionists, and the potential of black citizenship: "All of those intelligent white men were *rebels*—therefore *foolish*; and all of this senseless, ignorant

niggers were loyal—therefore wise; and I am in favor of giving the right of suffrage to wise men."[32]

White Republicans also tied postwar black political rights to their wartime
military contribution. At an 1867 convention sponsored by the Benevolent Society of Winchester, J. S. Brisbin sent the following advice: "You black people
have a great mission to perform in Kentucky—no less, indeed, than regenerat-
ing your native State, disenthralling it from rebel rule and making it what it
ought to be, a loyal member of the Union. . . . You helped to cut the head off
the rebel rattle snake down South, and now with ballots you must trample the
life of the tail in Kentucky." One white Republican spoke at a 1868 picnic in
Winchester, offering twenty commandments that, if followed, would lead to
African American prosperity. The first was to read the Bible and trust God, the
second was never to vote for a Rebel or a Democrat for office.[33]

Black Kentuckians understood that the Union victory and their role in that
triumph formed the basis of the rights they sought. When the Negro Republican Party held its first convention in Lexington in November 1867, Louisvillian
William Butler proclaimed, "First we ha[d] the cartridge box, now we want the
ballot box, and soon we will get the jury box." He tied black armed service in
the Union Army to the rights of citizenship: "We went out and fought the battles of our country, and gained our liberties, but we were left without means of
protecting ourselves in the employment of that liberty. We need and must have
the ballot box for that purpose." Butler also stated what African Americans
knew well, namely that Confederates stood against their freedom after the war,
just as they had during it. But if armed with the vote, they could fight back. "I
stand here for universal suffrage for rebels as well as black men," he claimed.
"I'm not afraid of rebels voting if you give us the same weapon of dissent." But
such assertiveness made the latent African American electorate a curse as well
as a blessing for white Republicans. The more African Americans staked their
claims of citizenship on the scaffolding of Union victory, the more dissonance
conservative Unionists, with their fear of "Negro domination," saw between
their own interests and the rhetoric of Union victory.[34]

Outsiders continued to notice this opposition, and its racial roots. One sign
of the political times in the Kentucky appeared when fictional Ohio Copper-
head Petroleum V. Nasby relocated to the state following the war. The literary
creation of Republican Toledo *Blade* editor David Ross Locke, Nasby had been
one of the most popular characters of American political satire since 1862.
When the coarse, semiliterate scoundrel decides he needs a more hospitable
political climate after the war, he moves to the Bluegrass town "Confederit X
Roads" in Locke's 1868 book *Ekkoes from Kentucky: A Perfect Record Uv the Ups,*

Downs, Experiences uv the Dimocrisy, Doorin the Eventful year 1867, Ez Seen By a Natrualized Kentuckian.[35]

Soon after moving to town, Nasby obtains the position of postmaster of Confedrit X Roads by petitioning Andrew Johnson in person. "I am the only Democrat in ten miles who kin write," he informs the president, "and [you] dare not deprive Kentucky, wich never seceded, uv mail facilities." Locke's Confedrit X Roads represents the "typical village in the unreconstructed South," stocked with a few admirable, but mostly unlikable, characters that are illiterate, racist, former slave owners. As eager to talk politics as they are to imbibe local firewater, Nasby and his friends frequently discuss their fears of "Nigger Equality" and miscegenation. They applaud the burning of a Freedmen's Bureau school and the occasion upon which Louisville lit up "in a blaze uv glory" in celebration of Johnson's policy of "yooniversal amnesty" for Confederates.[36]

If the nation's readers missed Kentucky's political misdeeds in the newspapers, they could find them in exaggerated form in Locke's satire. Under Locke's pen, Nasby and his indolent associates Kernal Hugh McPelter, Squire Gavitt, and Elkanah Pogram became objects of disparaging critique of the postwar political circumstances in Kentucky. The only thing they seem to work hard at is maintaining the town's prewar social, racial, and political order. One of their more ambitious endeavors to this end comes when they decide to tackle the problem of sectional bias in education. Rather than send their children to colleges in "Ablishn" states, they found "the Southern Classikle, Theologikle, and Military Institoot," where "Southern yooth," can be educated without being "tainted with heresy." Professors are, of course, ex-Confederates, and Nasby and friends even propose to help the down-and-out Jefferson Davis by offering him a teaching position. Nasby and his compatriots thrived in this unreconstructed environment as "the waves uv Ablishinism rolled over all the other States, but aginst Kentucky they struck harmless." For Nasby, "Kentucky [was] a brite oasis in the desert" where Democratic supremacy means white supremacy: "Here we kin flog our niggers,—here we shall hev the Institooshen [of slavery] in sperit, ef not in name," claims Nasby, "Here Dimocrisy kin flourish, ef nowhere else." Nasby states with satisfaction, "So long ez we're left to ourselves, so long will Kentucky be troo to Dimocrisy."[37]

Locke's character sealed Kentucky's postwar political character in American literature for all time. The Democratic voice of Kentucky politics became only somewhat less incendiary when Henry Watterson arrived in the state in 1868 to take over the editorship of the *Louisville Journal*. Once he merged that paper with the *Louisville Courier*, his editorial voice began to channel the Democratic politics of the state away from the unreconstructed platform of white supremacy and agricultural economy to the New South racially moderate, pro-industrial politics of modernization. But the die was cast: Republicans and Unionists remained politically marginalized for decades.[38]

Conservative Kentuckians' political wrangling in the years following the war was merely the beginning of a larger process by which they began to rewrite the memory of their participation in the conflict. With white Democratic dominance secured, they turned their labor to other memorial endeavors over the next five decades: building many more Confederate than Union monuments, observing Confederate holidays, publishing Confederate periodicals and literature, and hosting Confederate veterans reunions, all while leaving the victory of the Union largely uncelebrated. Though these cultural efforts took place far from the ballot box, they were nonetheless saturated with political and racial meaning. Like conservative postwar politics, these cultural manifestations served to reinforce white supremacy and to suppress Union memory. The Lost Cause would be found again and again in Kentucky for decades to come.[39]

4

The Crucible of Reconstruction: Unionists and the Struggle for Alabama's Postwar Home Front

MARGARET M. STOREY

During the Civil War, few areas in northern Alabama were as rife with local violence as Cherokee County, situated on the state's northeast border with Georgia.[1] Emblematic of Cherokee's general state of instability was an ongoing feud between Unionists and Rebels living near the little town of Ringgold. Though the origins of the conflict remain unclear, by 1862 Joseph Baker, Joseph Maples, James Davis, and Ebenezer Leath had become so renowned for their Unionism that a mob of "bitter rebels" had decided to run the men out of the county or, it was rumored, to kill them outright. When this news reached the Unionists, one of them—Ebenezer Leath—took it upon himself to confront the leader of the pro-Confederate gang, R. W. Wilkes, whom the Unionists believed had fraudulently obtained an exemption from military service by pretending to be Presbyterian preacher. "I went after him," Leath later explained to the Southern Claims Commission (SCC), "and . . . at first he denied [threatening us and] got his pistol and made some. threats." Undeterred, Leath persisted. "I then went at him with a double barreled shotgun and made him lay down his pistol and I kicked him about till he begged like a dog and acknowledged what he had done, but said he did it under excitement and passion." Leath concluded derisively, "He would not fight."[2] Though Ebenezer Leath bested Wilkes on this occasion, his friends acknowledged that Leath's victory was exceptional.[3] Most Unionists in Cherokee County, as elsewhere in Alabama, were intimidated and driven underground by such Confederate harassment.

Hostility between Cherokee County's Unionists and Rebels continued to fester after the war. In the late 1860s, Leath, who "took the liberty to join the Methodist Episcopal Church" and "voted for the Republican ticket," found himself again targeted with violence, this time from anti-Reconstruction vigilantes, including Wilkes, who was now garbed in the guise of the Ku Klux Klan.[4] As he had during the war, Leath gave as good as he got. A member of his wartime gang, Joseph Baker, explained to the SCC,

His reputation was that of a union man and every man in his neighborhood knew of his loyalty. And the rebels still know it and he has had trouble since the war from the Kuklux. But he had stood up to them and they have never dared try to abuse him for he was not the man to be abused with out killing somebody. . . . I knew him and Sam Elliott to guard my house one whole night when they expected the Kuklux to attack me.[5]

Likewise, one of Cherokee County's most renowned conscript officers, Bratch Porter (whom Leath referred to as "a villain"), continued his abuse of loyalists during Reconstruction, causing Baker to rechristen Bratch "KuKlux Porter."[6] For another Cherokee Unionist, John Smith, Bratch Porter was the embodiment of Confederate continuity—Smith referred to Porter as "a rebel and a Kuklux." Porter perceived this continuity of identity as well; when he attacked Smith, swearing to have his "hearts blood," he also cursed the Unionist as " a D—d Blue Coat."[7] Once Smith had "stood it as long as I could," he attacked Porter, shooting and wounding him.[8] Though "KuKlux Porter" survived his run-in with Smith, his was a short reprieve. As Leath noted, Porter was later "killed with a Kuklux disguise on, breaking into a house."[9]

These stories from Cherokee County are representative of the larger reality shaping political life in postwar Alabama: for Unionists and Confederates alike, Reconstruction was a local event that was frequently experienced by Southerners as an extension of the war itself. In the words of John Ramsey, a native Unionist of the county and assistant commissioner for the SCC, "In parts of Cherokee Co Alabama it has taken almost as much nerve to be a Republican in the midst of KuKlux bands as it did during the war in the time of vigilance committees and bands of cutthroats and scouts."[10] Reconstruction for wartime Unionists was thus not simply a major period of political readjustment and realignment; it was characterized by the concentration of the formal war into the "informal" or home-front war that had always played a major part in the battle between the Union and the Confederacy.[11]

Just as Civil War historiography has benefited from incorporating the complexities of violence on the home front into the larger narrative of the war, our understanding of Reconstruction can be likewise expanded by attending more carefully to the ways that postwar conflict was bound up in the experience of war itself. Alabama's Unionists are a case in point: they conceived of the purpose and significance of Reconstruction in local terms because many of them had fought the war primarily on the home front. For them, the Union's vindication meant a safe return to home and hearth, the end of personal and familial suffering, a lasting peace for friends and kin, prompt and decisive punishment of traitors, and the elevation of the "truly loyal" Unionists to positions of community and state power as a reward for wartime contributions. Thus they believed that victory should be as visible in their neighborhoods as it should be in the halls of Congress, and that this would be ensured by the power of the federal government, just as the Union Army had provided security during the war in those areas it occupied.

Before discussing the postwar world further, a brief summary of Unionists' wartime experiences is necessary. During the war, most of Alabama's loyalists clustered in the state's northern tier of counties, located along the state line with Tennessee and continuing south through the Tennessee River valley and into the hill country.[12] Of those who self-identified as loyal to the Union in postwar petitions to the SCC, and for whom there are socioeconomic records, the vast majority were nonslaveholding yeomen farmers; this population also included a diverse range of individuals, including planters, manufacturers, professionals, artisans, and propertyless farm laborers.[13] They all had vigorously opposed secession during the winter of 1860–61, though their reasons for doing so were as varied as their livelihoods and economic circumstances. A few remained loyal to the Union either because they opposed slavery itself or slaveholders' dominance of Southern politics; many more opposed secession as a politically radical, dangerous, and unconstitutional doctrine. Creed Taylor, a tanner by trade, was typical in believing "[W]e had no right to that privilege— . . . the makers of our constitution never intended to give that [right] to any state."[14] Some chose the Union out of deference to leading members of their families or communities who stood against secession, while others felt the obligation to honor the patriotism of ancestors who had fought in the Revolution or the War of 1812. Archibald Steele understood his loyalty to the Union in this light: "I was raised in South Carolina by my old father," he explained, "and taught first, to reverence my God; second, the Bible; third, the Constitution; and fourth, the Union—to regard all these things as sacred."[15] Others simply held to the idea that the Union could not be improved upon. Repeatedly, loyalists expressed a desire to preserve what they had, not to overthrow it for a new venture whose prospects were murky at best. "I loved my government," explained Jasper Harper, "and I was not in favor of no other one."[16]

Among those who clung to the Union were slaveholders. In addition to harboring concerns about political legitimacy and family honor, slaveholding Unionists also feared that slavery would be more readily destroyed in the armed conflict they were sure would follow secession.[17] Most frequently, the men who endorsed such politics had long been identified as Whigs or "old fashioned" conservative Democrats in the late antebellum period, and had long endorsed conservative political approaches to solving the sectional conflict over slavery.[18] SCC claimant Thomas Nation certainly counted these anxieties among his reasons for opposing separation. "I had worked a long time and had got a little property," he explained, "and I felt that it would all go up if there was a rebel-lion." His "little property" included fourteen slaves in 1860.[19] John Morgan Brown, who owned thirty-six slaves and ran a sawmill and plantation just out-side Mobile, likewise insisted that the better course of action for slaveholders was to "fight for their rights in the union" rather than to secede and fight a war that would likely destroy the thing they claimed to want to protect. "I do not mean fighting with arms," Brown explained, "I mean to fight for them in Congress."[20]

Many of the sentiments advanced by Unionists were not all that uncommon among moderate Southerners before the outcome of the November 1860 presi-dential election.[21] However, Lincoln's victory prompted secession conventions throughout the Deep South and sharply reduced the number of citizens willing to publicly endorse an unconditional Unionist course. As was the case else-where, Alabama's loyalists became increasingly convinced that maintaining fidelity to the Union would require considerable fortitude in the face of at best social ostracism and at worst actual violence. Their decision to maintain their loyalty despite Lincoln's election, Alabama's secession, and increasing hostility from fellow Alabamians made their loyalism "unconditional." Unlike reluctant secessionists who ultimately went with the state, unconditional Unionists refused to accept the legitimacy of separation under any circumstances. Herein lies the great irony of Unionists' experience: The impulse that drove them to first identify with the Union cause was a conservative one rooted in a deeply held desire for stability and security. The consequences of that identification, however, ultimately undermined that security as their steadfast loyalty relegated them to the fringes of their communities. Their Unionism became a brand—it was as telling about them as who their parents were or what church they attended. Viewing themselves as defenders of the status quo, Unionists none-theless seemed radical to their opponents. They were thus made extreme—or "true blue" Union men—by the shifting sentiments of the majority around them.[22]

Once the war began, Alabama's Unionists were subjected to ever-intensify-ing persecution and threats from the Confederate majority with an animosity that only intensified and hardened after April 1862, when the Confederate Con-gress passed the Act to Provide for the Public Defense, the fledgling nation's first draft. As one loyalist put it, "Things got . . . hot about the time the con-script law passed."[23] Conscription transfigured the implications of Unionists' dissent and raised the stakes for resistance because it flattened out the distinc-tion between "sedition" (disloyal speech) and the more serious "treason" (dis-loyal acts). The draft made criminals of those who refused the Confederacy not only their hearts and minds, but ultimately their bodies. Unionists who resisted the state's call were now legally subject to arrest, imprisonment, and forced service in the Confederate Army. Moreover, because conscription was a national matter, efforts to suppress draft resistance were not only a question of state and local governance, but a problem to be solved in part by military authorities.[24] Consequently, all Unionists now became the target of both state law enforcement and Confederate conscript cavalries. After 1862 it thus became a regular occurrence, in the words of one man, "for union men to be arrested, put in the county jail, others sent to military prisons, some hung and others shot, families of some . . . abused, their property taken, others . . . forced to go within the union lines for safety."[25]

By the end of the war, many loyalists in the state had suffered retribution and violence at the hands of their Confederate neighbors and the Confederate Army. Many of them had also found ways to aid and abet the Union Army, which commenced its tenuous occupation of northern Alabama in February 1862. This assistance took many forms, from providing casual intelligence to participating in organized espionage to enlisting in the Union Army or pro-Union irregular partisan units. Union Army commanders benefited from the strong relationships they developed with these loyalists—particularly in the Tennessee Valley, where Unionists were an important counterinsurgency weapon. Such alliances accomplished something far more personal for loyalists on Alabama's home front: vindication and revenge. As historian Noel C. Fisher has argued, individuals embroiled in Civil War guerrilla warfare rarely drew neat lines between "violence motivated by political ends and violence originating in personal grievances."[26] For Unionists, the distinction between the political and personal was simply impossible, for it required a disaggregation of concerns about family, home, and property from concerns about the war's purpose and conduct.[27] For them, the war had long been coterminous with a defense of kin and community; as kin and community suffered humiliation and brutality, desire for personal justice only intensified. As one federal soldier from southern Alabama pointed out, "There was a strong thirst for revenge among men whose housetops had been burned over the heads of their defenceless [sic] wives and children."[28] For Unionists, being a spy or soldier for the United States was thus not just about helping a cause in which they believed but also about gaining power over specific enemies.

Unionists gained leverage in their fight against local Confederates only because they had the Union Army behind them, a fact that boded ill for loyalists once the war ended. Of the approximately thirty-five thousand federal soldiers stationed in Alabama in May 1865, all but a tiny proportion had returned home by the end of that summer. For these Northern soldiers and their families, the war was over. Though their communities had lost numerous young men, most

Northern towns remained physically untouched by the devastation that marked much of the South, including northern Alabama, which had been traversed heavily by armies and guerrillas. Even more importantly, Northern towns were substantially free of embittered neighbors and enemies. Southern Unionists, by contrast, found themselves indelibly marked in a ruined land, alone and left to fend for themselves surrounded by defeated and disillusioned Rebels. What would become clear over the course of Reconstruction was that, when and where Union troops had a substantial presence during Reconstruction, they were often effective in minimizing the worst excesses of Southern resistance. However, as historians have demonstrated, the federal government did not countenance, and many of its citizens would not support, a truly widespread military occupation of the South. It was not only an unpopular idea among people who had suffered through four years of warfare, but it was also a notion incompatible with dominant ideas about peacetime republican government.[29]

In light of these realities, confrontations between Unionists and their old enemies were commonplace well after hostilities formally ended.[30] In July 1865, "parties of marauders" were reported running rampant in northwestern Alabama, "burning houses [and] murdering Union men."[31] Three months later, Union scout George W. Ridge (whose father and brother had been murdered by Confederate guerrillas in 1863) and a number of "loyal men and discharged U.S. Soldiers Resident of Jackson County" were so harassed by Rebels in their neighborhood that they petitioned for permission to form a loyalist militia. Without it, they argued, "union men can not live here any longer."[32] More than a year after the armistice, First Alabama U.S.A. cavalryman Joseph H. Davis and his son watched in shock as ex-Rebels strode into the polling area at a local Randolph County election, gathered "about the ballot box," and began "over aweing [sic] union men, intimidating them to such an extent as to prevent their votes." When Confederate veteran Robert Richards stepped to the front of the crowd to shout curses like " 'God damn the Government, hurah for secession & the Rebel army & God damn them that don't believe it," Davis and son gave vent to their own frustration. A fistfight ensued, with the Davises tearing into Richards and "his party of late rebels."[33] In a letter to Alabama's Bureau of Refugees, Freedmen, and Abandoned Lands (Freedmen's Bureau), Davis made a dire prediction: "Unless the Union men in my part of the country can get the protection of the Government of the US, they are in danger of losing their lives."[34]

For Unionists, the great calamity of the postwar period was that the federal government was rarely forthcoming with its support and protection. From the start, as historian Michael Perman has argued, President Andrew Johnson reflected widespread thinking on postwar policy in his "assumption that a real reunion demanded reconciliation at the expense of reconstruction." Believing that only "time and sympathetic circumstances . . . could sow feeling of cooperation among Southerners," Johnson endorsed lenient measures to restore many former Confederates to the full rights of citizenship.[35] He thus remained unwilling to do what Unionists wanted most: punish in severe and lasting ways the men who had attempted to take the South out of the Union. Though this Southern-born president had vigorously opposed the Confederacy, he nonetheless set in motion a program for Reconstruction that sacrificed the most treasured ideals Unionists held about political legitimacy. The evidence that Johnson was pardoning an ever-expanding number of former Confederates only exacerbated loyalists' feelings of anger and frustration and heightened their forebodings about the future.[36] As loyalist William Miller complained to a friend, "I thot [the president] declared Emphatically that he will put the government in the hands of its friends make treason odious & that the leaders in the Rebellion must take back seats. [But] he then commences pardoning all of the worst & most bitter enemies of the Government."[37]

Johnson was not alone in endorsing a postwar policy devoted to amnesty and conciliation. Most Republicans also remained deeply ambivalent about the feasibility or legality of establishing loyalist-controlled governments in the South, especially in the Deep South, where consistently loyal white men represented a tiny proportion of the population. During the war, the Union's overwhelming mandate to pursue victory, like Unionists' all-consuming desire for vengeance, justified acting with little concern for democratic processes and—as the policies of emancipation and confiscation ultimately demonstrated—even less respect for property rights. The political contestations of the postwar era, however, represented quite a different matter, largely because the federal government no longer sought to crush the enemy. Instead, most Northerners in Congress wanted speedy reconciliation with the South and a relatively painless return to peace and prosperity.[38] The Republican Party was thus fundamentally unwilling, during both Presidential and Congressional Reconstruction, to sacrifice the goal of pacification for the sake of severely punishing former Confederates or for the sake of establishing a long-standing military occupation of the South to assert and defend the political authority of Unionists over their wartime enemies.[39] Elevating true-blue Unionists to positions of control would mean broadly disfranchising Southern citizens, a step that many feared would upset the peace by fostering renewed opposition. To prop up such an obvious and vilified minority in charge of Southern state governments would also have been politically dangerous for other reasons. The Republican Party had been firmly associated with violations of civil liberties during the war, particularly Abraham Lincoln's suspension of the writ of *habeas corpus* to suppress antiwar dissent. After the war, Northern Democrats remained eager to exploit for political gain any Republican policies that might be deemed equally unconstitutional or antidemocratic.[40] Moreover, the alternative of building Southern majorities was equally risky, for the only way to do it was to enfranchise freedmen. Before 1867, most Republicans were sure that any attempt to establish black political equality (and possible domination of Southern politics) would enrage many of their border state and Northern constituents.[41] Through such calculus the Republican Party pushed aside the political aspirations of loyal Southerners.

Unionists, by contrast, gave almost overwhelming allegiance to the Republican Party from the first. For most loyalists, the Democratic Party remained the party of secession and copperheadism. They believed that Republican activism offered them a chance to advance a postwar Reconstruction policy devoted to punishing the betrayal of *known* traitors and honoring and rewarding *known* loyalists. This belief represented a profoundly local understanding of political legitimacy and the aims of Reconstruction; it rested not on a desire to pacify Confederate enemies but to have also significant power over them. Consequently, when federal policy during the first two years following the war allowed former Rebels to take positions of local judicial, political, and economic authority, Unionists were stunned and bitterly disappointed. Hugh McVay of Limestone County, a veteran surgeon of the federal army, reported to the Freedmen's Bureau in March 1866, "The Rebels hold almost all the offices in our state . . . the most rampant secesh are now to hear them speak the most loyal."[42] Others complained that even unpardoned Rebels had stood for and won election. In June 1866, a number of "late Officers in the U.S.A. and loyal citizens of Morgan Co." protested to federal officials that the fall elections had placed a man named George P. Charlton in the office of probate judge. His victory came despite having held "at different times two offices of trust under the so called Confederate Govt." (They included a copy of his oath of office to prove it.) Moreover, according to the veterans, Charlton had never received a pardon as required by Johnson's amnesty plan and thus had taken his office illegally. "We hold it our duty as Union men to have the facts known that the matter may be investigated, and we protected in our rights." They tersely concluded, "As the U.S. Govet says, Union men must rule and not rebels who bid defiance to the U.S. laws."[43] Unionists not only objected to former Confederates holding office as a matter of justice, but as a matter of self-preservation. Many believed that leniency to their enemies only encouraged continued recalcitrance among former Confederates, a recalcitrance that meant nothing but trouble for loyal Alabamians. As George White and ninety other petitioners from Blount County explained to Congress in 1866, "We say to you that Rebellion is [now] more strong more Resolute more Hell Bent [and] that the Rebels wold Be more savage than at any time during the war if tha[y] had the opitunity."[44]

The opportunity for increased violence came with what should have been Unionists' greatest reprieve: the intervention of Congress into postwar politics and society with the passage of the Military Reconstruction Acts in 1867, which placed all former Confederate states except Tennessee under martial law and divided the region into five military districts. Each district was to be overseen by a military governor, who would quickly register voters and hold elections for delegates to new state constitutional conventions.[45] Proscribed from the franchise was any man who had taken an oath to the United States before 1860 and subsequently taken an oath to the Confederacy. By virtue of these limits, many former Confederate officials, including men who had gained political positions during Presidential Reconstruction, were now barred both from voting and from holding local, state, and national offices.[46] Finally, Congress made the granting of suffrage rights to black men an unavoidable price for Southern states' readmission to the Union. Lawmakers mandated that in the election for delegates to the state constitutional conventions (and all subsequent electoral contests), African American men could both vote and run for office.

The political empowerment of African Americans had been long advocated by Northern radicals, and by 1866 many white Unionists had added their voices to the chorus. In September of that year, southern loyalists gathered at an anti-Johnson conference in Philadelphia. At this meeting, representatives from Alabama and the other unreconstructed former Confederate states approved a resolution supporting the enfranchisement of blacks.[47] Pragmatism, of course, rather than egalitarianism, prompted most Unionists to move so far ahead of all but the most extreme members of the Northern Republican Party. Just as many had aligned themselves with slaves during the war out of a practical need for allies rather than an ideological opposition to slavery, many now saw the wisdom of supporting African American voting rights.[48] This, they believed, would solve the problem of minority rule, bolster Republican Party membership in the South, and thereby help defeat Rebels in elections. Regardless of the means employed, only the creation of loyal Southern governments, they argued, would provide security to loyal people. In the words of the Union League's state council, the question was simply, "Shall we have [the freedman] for our ally or the rebel for our master?"[49] With the proscription of leading Confederates and the enfranchisement of blacks, many loyalists hoped that Reconstruction was finally on the course they had advocated since the war's end.

Initially, Unionists' hopes for a new political order seemed well founded; they soon acceded to positions of greater political power, particularly in north Alabama. In particular, many were called upon to fill federal appointive offices operating at the county or local level because those jobs now required the "iron clad oath," in which the oath-taker swore to having never supported the Confederacy. Because Unionists could pass this bar, they were now asked to serve as Freedmen's Bureau officials, election registrars, postmasters, and tax assessors. Unionists also filled state and local positions, replacing office holders that were now barred by virtue of having taken oaths to the Confederacy.[50] Another capacity in which Unionists flexed political muscle was as delegates to Alabama's constitutional convention mandated by the Military Reconstruction Acts. Wartime Unionists, many of them Union League activists, represented about 25 percent of the delegates, a far larger proportion than the 10 percent they had constituted in the 1865 convention. At least twelve of these delegates had either fled or been driven from their homes during the war; six of these had served in the Union Army as soldiers or independent scouts.[51]

During the convention, Unionists advocated some of the most radical proposals put forward for debate, particularly as regards two issues. The first was land redistribution, an idea that many wartime Unionists and white Union Leaguers embraced.[52] Representing loyal men who came out of the war poorer than they had been in 1860—and who placed the blame for this fact squarely at the feet of the Confederacy—these delegates understood postwar poverty as inseparable from Confederate power and abuse. They believed Rebels were not only responsible for the war and its devastation but had caused and compounded Unionists' privation by targeting them for punitive foraging and vandalism throughout the war. In this view, economic suffering after the war was yet another manifestation of the political and military injustices inflicted upon them both by the Confederate government of Alabama and by Rebel neighbors. The confiscation and redistribution of the land of leading Confederates promised economic relief, but just as important, it offered a way for the state to make restitution to loyalists by punishing those who had caused injury in the first place. Despite broad support among north Alabama whites, Unionists at the convention could not deliver on this agenda. No proposal for land confiscation or redistribution ever reached the floor for debate, much less for a vote. With the exception of a few Radicals, the national Republican Party was never willing to pursue land confiscation as anything more than a threat to impress the South with the seriousness of the Reconstruction Acts.[53] In the end, proposals to undermine the land rights of anyone, even men seen as traitors to the Union, were too revolutionary and threatening to individual property rights throughout the nation.[54] Moreover, the national Union League, and even the black leadership of Alabama's Union League, abandoned their earlier pro-confiscation sympathies once the opposition of moderate Republicans became clear.[55]

In addition to land confiscation, loyalists at the convention aggressively pursued broad-ranging Rebel disfranchisement. Their hope was to permanently alter the political landscape of Alabama by denying the rights of U.S. citizenship to those they viewed as unredeemable traitors. For many, this was "the great object which ought to govern the convention."[56] Shortly before the constitutional convention met, in fact, the Grand Council of Alabama's Union League publicly advocated that delegates should award the franchise only to wartime Unionists, a resolution heartily endorsed by a number local Leagues, particularly in north Alabama.[57] Accordingly, loyalists at the convention attempted to extend disfranchisement well beyond the provisions established by the Military Reconstruction Acts (and by the as-yet-unratified Fourteenth Amendment), which nullified the voting rights of individuals who had taken an oath to the United States and subsequently aided the Confederate state.

Most of the wartime Unionists' franchise proposals embodied judgments about and exacted punishment for a particular Confederate "crime" and were likely appealing because their provisions would fall heavily on particular, known Confederate "criminals." For instance, William C. Garrison, a Unionist refugee during the war and Union League organizer, proposed to disfranchise "those men who were members of the State Convention of 1861, and voted or signed the ordinance of secession," or "who were members of the Confederate Congress, and voted for the conscript law."[58] Garrison argued that the betrayals of 1861, as well as any act that resulted in the persecution of Union men, should not only be remembered but also penalized. Likewise, Thomas Haughey, Union war veteran from Morgan County and Union League organizer, lobbied to disfranchise anyone who had held an officership in the Confederate Army above the rank of captain, had "ever held a seat in any pretended Legislature, or held any executive, judicial, or ministerial office under any government, or pretended government, in hostility to the government of the United States," or had "killed, or otherwise abused citizens of Alabama because such citizens were known to be friends of the government of the United States."[59] Haughey explained his proposal to the *Montgomery State Sentinel* by noting that "'his constituents demanded the disfranchisement of nearly all who participated in the rebellion.'"[60]

As went plans for land redistribution, so went radical plans for franchise restrictions. When leading Republican politicians in Washington got wind of the proposed new disfranchisements, they began lobbying General John Pope, commander of the Third Military District, and General Wager Swayne, head of the Freedmen's Bureau in Alabama, to restrain the Unionist delegates. Any

restriction of voting rights that went further than the Military Reconstruction
Acts, not to mention the strictness of wartime Unionists' proposed amendments, conflicted sharply with the agenda of the national Republican Party.
Aware that such punitive measures would provoke resentment among former
Confederates (thereby delaying the process of Reconstruction), and fearful of
a backlash from Northern voters opposed to unseating moderate white politicians in favor of a majority composed of blacks and white Unionists (both of
whom they held in doubtful esteem) the national party balked at supporting
Unionists' bid to punish ex-Confederates at the polls.[61] Matters became so
delicate at one point as to require an emissary be sent from Alabama to Washington in search of guidance "on the wording of the disfranchisement clause"
in the new constitution.[62] The Washington worriers were buttressed in their
concern by an anti-disfranchisement faction within the convention itself—
fifteen conservative native whites threatened to walk out. As a result, all but
one of the radical efforts to restrict the franchise were either tabled or
defeated. Thus, with the exception of the proscription of those who were
guilty of war crimes, the new constitution limited the vote only as far as did
the Fourteenth Amendment.[63]

Despite the new constitution's limited disfranchisement measures, Unionists
soon were confirmed in their hope that the presence of black voters made
Republican Party ascendancy possible in the state, ushering wartime Unionist
William H. Smith into the governor's office and the Republican Party into control of the state legislature during the election of 1868. Local and statewide political power, however, came at a steep price. Terrorism and intimidation aimed
at white and black Republicans by a range of vigilante groups, including the Ku
Klux Klan, soon created the most repressive and violent environment loyalists
had encountered since 1865, largely as a consequence of their continued alliance
with the Republican Party and its advocacy of black voting. The failure of
Reconstruction policies to deliver security to Unionists who had finally won
some measure of local control was devastating. Unionists began to see that
though the Union had been victorious in the war, they would not be victorious
at home.

From the summer of 1868 through 1870, increasing numbers of disguised
vigilantes took to demonstrating in the public areas of Southern towns and
night riding through rural neighborhoods, intimidating, abusing, and murdering freedpeople and Unionists.[64] The goals of this violence were simple: scare
whites and blacks away from the Union League, pro-Republican political gath-
erings, and, during elections, the polls themselves. Although most vigilantism
during Congressional Reconstruction was associated with the Klan, it would be
a mistake to understand these groups as part of a tightly organized, centralized

movement.[65] Instead, many small groups of citizens banded together as vigilantes in sympathy with the Klan's mission to restore racial and political "order"
in their neighborhoods. Victims of violence usually referred to their persecutors
as "KuKlux" less because they knew them to be part of any organization in
particular than because news of "the Klan" was ubiquitous in their newspapers
and communities. As Unionist C. S. Cherry explained in testifying before the
congressional committee investigating the Klan in 1871, the name was generic
rather than specific. "The term Ku-Klux . . . is sort of understood to cover all
political outrages, all these political disorders," he explained. "People are sort
of called Ku-Klux whether men are in disguise or not." William Shapard concurred, noting that few loyal people were "particular about the name."[66]

For Unionists, the name was less important than the identity of the men
persecuting them. Hooded or not, Klansmen or not, their enemies were the
same men whom they had been fighting for the last seven years: Rebels. Many
Unionists protested to the state government and the Freedmen's Bureau that
their old enemies were on the warpath again and that they felt they had been
abandoned. William Powell of Calhoun County demanded to have "something
dun or the Union Men will have to leave their homes and farms, for their is
men that has to ly out every night to keep the KK from whipping them."[67]
Without help, Union Leaguer S. S. Plowman explained, loyal men would "be
crushed under foot again by the hatred [sic] rebs." Dr. T. C. Brannon of Lawrence County concurred. Characterizing Klan violence as "another Bloody
war," Brannon pleaded with the governor for protection. "If this thing is suffered to go on," he predicted, "it will not be long till everybody who will say a
word for Law & order & union will be intimidated one by one & the secesh will
rule the country with a rod of Iron." Brannon felt confident that the Klan
would kill him and demanded help "quick," adding tersely, "I shall not need it
when my wife has become a widow & my children orphans." C. P. Simmons,
an 1867 constitutional convention delegate, feared for his life. "In the name of
God," he pleaded to Governor William H. Smith in 1868, "what ar [sic] we to
do, when will we ever get Protection in this State?" Four months later, Simmons had given up entirely and was preparing to flee his home in Tuscumbia
"to hunt for Peace." Thrown off his landlord's farm—"he rote me a note the
other day that he was advised by the old citizens not to hav any thing to do
with me if he des[ire?] to live Peacible in this county"—Simmons was plainly
beaten. "I hav lived in hopes of a change for the better as longe as there was
any shadow of cause for hope. I now se and am Perfectly Satisfide that I cannot
live hear in any Peace or Safety. They the Rebs hollow [hosanna?] for Jeff Davis
on the Strets & Bidds defyance to the U.S."[68]

Vigilante attacks sometimes seemed like full-blown military maneuvers. In 1870, St. Clair County Union Army veteran and constitutional convention delegate Henry J. Springfield was besieged by some two hundred men "armed with Rifles, Shot guns, and revolvers" as well as members of the "county sheriff's posse." Denouncing Springfield "as a dangerous man and a 'Scalawag'" and for his "long service in the Union Army, the attackers opened fire on his house at eight a. m. and continued firing until the morning of the next day." Springfield finally surrendered, but not before narrowly cheating death. An army investigator later examined the house and "found on the side windows of his bedroom Twelve distinct bullet holes—in the front window of same room Ten—in the side wall of same room Thirty Five, in the front Fifty, all of which passed clear through the room and partitions and cut many of his wife's dresses which were hanging on the partition." The rest of the house and its outhouses, too, were "riddled with bullet holes" to such an extent that the officer could not count them. The officer interviewed the attackers, and discovered that "the universal sentiment among [them] was that the Springfields must be killed or leave the County." The attackers were

> young men varying from 17 to 26 years who had seen some little service in the rebel army and when armed with a navy revolver and supported by a half dozen sympathizing friends, similarly equipped, felt all their native chivalry in arms against men like Springfield who had been true and loyal to his Country, and this hatred to him and friends, was increased by the fact that he was to the "manor born" as were most all his friends. As an encouraging Vendetta in this background I found some old lawyers and politicians who prevented from political disabilities from monopolizing all the offices of the county as in the olden time, stormed and railed against this loyal element, who robbed them of their accustomed influence and spoils.[69]

The former Rebels of Springfield's neighborhood clearly viewed local Unionists as legitimate targets in a continuing war for local control of the South.

Violent contestation over social power and influence was not confined to the political sphere. Among the hardest-hit of "nonpolitical" arenas were churches, particularly congregations associated with the Methodist Episcopal Church. Alabamians variously referred to this denomination as the "loyal Methodist Church," the "Northern Methodist Church," or the "Republican Methodist Church" to distinguish it from the Methodist Episcopal Church, South, which in 1844 had split from the national church over the question of slavery. These nicknames also served to dissociate the church from secession and the Confederacy, and they continued to be used long after Reconstruction. As historian

William W. Sweet noted in 1915, "Every 'Northern' Methodist was a Republican, and even today in some sections of Alabama, the members of the Methodist Episcopal Church are know[n] as 'Republican' Methodists as distinguished from the southern Methodists or 'Democrat' Methodists."[70]

An early critic of President Johnson's reconstruction policies, the Methodist Episcopal Church had not hesitated to take up the cause of both freedpeople and Southern Unionists.[71] A church newspaper, the *Western Christian Advocate*, frequently highlighted Unionists' tribulations in its editorials. One such piece, published in November 1865, drew a direct connection between Southerners' faith in the Union and their faith in God:

> For the sake of the Union of these States men have renounced father, mother, wife, children, home, friends, and every thing which could seduce men into disloyalty, and, unhallowed and unknown to fame, have died in the mountain fastnesses, whither they had been hunted by dogs and men more brutal and ferocious than dogs, thanking God that they were honest men, and not rebels and traitors. Could the religious of Jesus be divine if it required any thing less than martyrdom for truth and holiness? A religion for which men would not die, could not meet the necessities of the human soul.[72]

The *Christian Advocate and Journal*, another prominent Methodist periodical, promised in February 1865 that Northern missionaries would minister to the "genuine Union men of the South whose abhorrence of the rebellion will lead them to reject the religious services of a set of men by whom they have been so fearfully misled."[73] Indeed, according to Sweet, "Loyalty to the government of the United States had become practically a part of the Methodist creed, and disloyalty was discredited as much as the worst types of heresy."[74]

For its outspoken endorsement of loyalty, the Methodist Episcopal Church appealed as a haven for Unionists. During the war, loyalist women and men had frequently worshipped separately from the secessionist-dominated congregations of the Methodist Episcopal Church, South. Its firm associations with the Confederacy prevented many Unionists from returning to the fold after 1865. Instead they yearned for the opportunity to build congregations associated with the regular M. E. Church. In October 1867, Bishop David W. Clark and Reverend Arad S. Lakin established a Methodist Episcopal Church mission conference.[75] North Alabama men attending the organizational conference at Talladega were "from the rural districts," who had "suffered much, as Union men, during the war, and now, since their connection with the Old Church, . . . suffered almost as much from the persecutions of the ministry and membership of Churches which were rebels through the war, and remain so still."[76] More than eight thousand northern Alabamians joined the new conference. One-third of them were African-American members who soon separated, both by their own choice and in response to white pressure for segregation, into separate congregations within the denomination.[77]

Unionists' membership in the Methodist Episcopal Church represented a public statement about continuing fidelity to the Union, to Reconstruction, and to a South dominated by loyal men, not former rebels.[78] Opponents of these ideas understood perfectly well what the church and its congregants stood for. As a consequence, the church buildings, ministers, and congregants all became the targets of vigilante groups. In 1871, Unionist Isaac Berry testified before the congressional joint committee investigating the Klan that "two or three" such churches were burned in Blount County, but by whom was never proven. Nonetheless, "it was generally supposed it was these Klans that did it . . . because [the churches] were composed of loyal characters to the Government."[79] Missionary preacher Arad S. Lakin reported on November 4, 1870, to the national Methodist Episcopal Church of similar trials in Scottsboro, where he was busy helping establish a small congregation of thirteen members. "Under the most violent opposition from . . . the Ku Kluk Klan, we have organized a small society. What we have done is permanent, and the prospect is flattering for building up a fine congregation and membership, though we are now passing through the fires of persecution."[80] Presumably, the "fires" to which he referred involved an October 1870, attack on Lakin and other citizens by men who were later indicted in the U.S. District Court for violating the Enforcement Acts. Lakin and his congregants were interrupted during religious worship as their attackers "did then and there with force and arms, blow whistles, shoot pistols and Guns, threaten and intimidate [and] and did threaten assault and unlawfully seize arrest and imprison them."[81] A twentieth-century biography reflected on the state of siege that pastors like Lakin and his fellow Methodists experienced during Reconstruction:

> [Lakin's] churches were burned, his ministers beaten, driven off and some killed, the roads to his meetings were frequently picketed, and a guide sent by faithful friends would meet and lead him around some by-path to a place of safety. Men attended church service armed, as in colonial days, for the defence of their families.[82]

It should be remembered, however, that Unionists did not have to look back to "colonial days" to find models of how to survive guerilla warfare; their own war had provided plenty of training.

Reverend Levin Clifton of Cherokee County, who was "bitterly opposed to Ku Kluxism and [a] firm Republican," had also been "much persecuted" for being one of the founding members of the 1867 conference and a traveling minister in its circuit.[83] The intensity of his devotion to the Union and the church seemed only to be heightened by his experience of persecution during and after the war. As an obituary written upon his death in 1924 noted, "His loyalty to country was next in his religion to his loyalty to the church and God. Indeed they seemed to intertwine and became inseparable."[84] Likewise, Ebenezer Leath of Cherokee County attributed his hard treatment at the hands of the Klan in part to his religious affiliations, which grew directly out of his wartime Unionism. "After the war was over . . . [I] took the liberty to join the Methodist Episcopal Church and voted for the Republican ticket and the Kuklux come after me to my house and threatened to break down my door if I did not open it."[85] Although Leath escaped unharmed, the Reverend M. B. Sullivan was not so lucky. On May 11, 1869, Sullivan—the presiding elder of Big Cove Circuit of the Alabama Conference of the M. E. Church—was awakened to see "a band of armed men" surrounding his bed, with their "pistols . . . cocked and presented at my breast."[86] The vigilantes forced Sullivan out of bed, ransacked his possessions, stole his pistols, and carried him about two hundred yards away from the house. Telling Sullivan that he had preached his "last sermon," and swearing that no other Methodist institution should "exist South of Mason and Dixon's line but the Church South," the men began to beat Sullivan "horribly." Throughout the attack, they threatened him with even worse treatment unless he abandoned the "northern" church. "If I did not join the Church South, work for my family through the week, and preach for the Church South on Sabbaths, they would kill me."[87]

Unionists looking for protection from Klan violence found that there was little military power to deploy in their behalf. Alabama's readmission to the Union after the ratification of the new constitution had lifted martial law, as it did elsewhere in the South. Though the numbers of federal soldiers stationed in the former Confederacy had increased marginally during Congressional Reconstruction, fewer than twenty thousand remained in the entire South in the fall of 1868; of those, only just over six hundred were stationed Alabama, most assigned to a few remaining federal garrisons or to the Freedmen's Bureau.[88] In the absence of federal forces, Alabama's governor could have mobilized the state militia. And, indeed, Unionists pleaded with Governor Smith to allow them to organize branches of the state militia for their own defense. DeKalb Countians recommended that Captain T. J. Nicholson, a Union veteran, be put in charge of a military force to put down Klan activity in their county.[89] Likewise, J. Pinkney Whitehead and Union veteran J. F. Morton, a delegate to the 1867 Constitutional Convention, also nominated a number of Union men, including a First Alabama Cavalry veteran, for officerships in the state militia. Without a reliable militia, Morton and his fellow petitioners believed that "Fayette County is ruined." Indicative of the dangers these men felt, Morton hastened to add this postscript: "Do not make our names Known as it would cost us our lives."[90] Despite pleas like these, Smith failed to call Alabamians to arms. He likely faced the difficulties plaguing many Southern governors: The Military Reconstruction Acts prohibited the formation of militias in the former Confederacy in an attempt to prevent uprisings against the establishment of military rule. As a result, the entire militia system was in disarray across the South. Even if militias could be organized, impoverished Southern legislatures were unable to pay for necessary materiel. Though sympathetic congressmen had in July 1868 proposed a bill to federally subsidize the arming of Southern militias in reconstructed states, the legislation was ignored by the Republican majority, which allowed Congress to recess before taking up the proposed legislation.[91]

With little, if any, assistance from the federal military or state militias, white Unionists had to turn to local authorities for help. Many such officials, however, were unwilling to act. One loyalist complained that Blount County's sheriff and justice of the peace were too intimidated to help him: "I have asked them frequently why they don't enforce the law, and they have told me they were afraid; even afraid to issue warrants."[92] Whatever the prerogatives of holding a judicial or political office, it offered little protection against vigilante groups and the community that supported them. In DeKalb County, officers who had successfully arrested Klansmen complained that they could not keep the lawbreakers in jail for very long before fellow riders broke into the jail and liberated their comrades.[93] Cursing the Klan for its seeming immunity to authority, they exclaimed, "It rides with high handed impunity over all who do not bow to its miserable behests."[94]

For many Unionists, there seemed to be only one real solution: taking matters into their own hands, just as they had during the war. As William Powell of Calhoun County explained to the governor, "If I can find out whar the K K will pass, I will get my Radical croud and I will find . . . if Powder and le[a]d will do any execution . . . I am willing to do any thing to Stop the K. K."[95] W. T. Beard of Marshall County likewise killed "one of the ring-leaders of a K. K. Klan" who had contrived one of the most "hellish murderous plots" against him.[96] Although Beard had reported the plan to local officials, they had refused to issue warrants for the arrest of the men implicated. Frustrated to the point of recklessness, Beard acted where the law would not and killed the Klansman himself. "I had been abused as long as it was human to bear."[97] Similarly, Union veteran Henry Smith of DeKalb County resorted to using violence of his own.[98] After being continually harassed by the Klan for his Unionism and steadfast association with the Republican Party, Smith killed at least two Klansmen in the spring of 1869.[99]

As stories like these make clear, Unionists were still battling their wartime persecutors and Confederate neighbors well into Reconstruction. Indeed, Reconstruction would be the last front of their war, a front they ultimately lost for a number of reasons, including the unwillingness and inability of the federal government to protect Republicans (black and white) from violence and terrorism. Perhaps most crippling to the Unionists' cause, however, was the fact that the war they fought during Reconstruction was different than the war they were fighting in 1861, or even in 1865, despite appearances to the contrary. During the secession winter of 1860–61 and throughout the war, Unionists embedded their political choices within neighborhood and kinship; loyalty to the Union grew out of a conservative impulse to protect the world they knew. Reconstruction, by contrast, demanded that Unionists commit to defending a new and alien order, one that was not deeply embedded in long-standing social and cultural traditions, especially those governing race relations. That the price of power would mean such insecurity—and even a sense of isolation from one's allies—was simply intolerable to most white loyalists in the state. In 1869, Alabama's Union League collapsed under the pressure from vigilantism and neglect from national leadership, soon followed by the state's Republican Party. Though there remained Unionists who never abandoned their dissident stance, and who continued to run as and vote for Republican candidates in local elections, by the mid-1870s loyalists' battle for political control of the home front had been well and truly lost.[100]

5

"A New Field of Labor":
Antislavery Women,
Freedmen's Aid, and
Political Power

CAROL FAULKNER

The humanitarian crisis following emancipation provided many Northern women, white and black, with a new opportunity to advise government officials and implement federal policy.[1] Responding to the
demand for missionaries and teachers in Union-controlled areas of the South,
women explained their participation in the freedmen's aid movement by citing
their gender's presumed role as caretakers of the young, sick, and poor. As the
war developed, female activists, most of them seasoned abolitionists and wom-
en's rights advocates, argued that their work in behalf of former slaves justified
access to real political power. Like many Radical Republican politicians, they
envisioned a federal government with power to protect the rights of citizens.
But female reformers saw their own benevolent presence in the halls of government—as employees, lobbyists, teachers, entrepreneurs, and potentially voters—as central to their vision of a reconstructed nation. Women's physical and
ideological movement into the world of national policy did not go unchallenged. Beginning during the war and intensifying after 1865, military officials
and male reformers set limits upon both activist women and their gendered
vision for Reconstruction.

Historians frequently describe the Civil War as a watershed in the public
lives of Northern women, but few trace the continuation of women's wartime
activities after Appomattox. Historians of Civil War women usually end their
analysis at the Confederate Army's surrender and demobilization. Between
1861 and 1865, women's role as nurses, writers, freedmen's teachers, and organizers of the U.S. Sanitary Commission gave them a new, if fleeting, visibility.
As Lyde Cullen Sizer concludes, "The rule remained: women in the mid-nineteenth century had few options for employment or for public or political
power."[2] Studies of women's reform during Reconstruction focus on freedmen's teachers or suffragists, disguising the true extent of women's postwar
activities.[3] In fact, women's participation accelerated when government and
Northern voluntary associations took on the burdens of aiding former slaves.
The Bureau of Refugees, Freedmen, and Abandoned Lands (Freedmen's
Bureau), a temporary division of the War Department established in 1865, and

freedmen's aid societies cooperated to reorganize labor, establish schools, distribute aid, and protect the basic rights of former slaves in the South. Abolitionist women viewed the Freedmen's Bureau as their own, an official arena for freedmen's relief and a vehicle for the political and economic rights of women and African Americans.

Despite women's hopes for the Freedmen's Bureau, the end of the war heightened anxieties about both freedmen's aid and women's public labors. An expanding federal government, which placed women in positions of authority and created a newly entitled citizenry composed of African Americans, threatened commonly held assumptions about male privilege, white supremacy, and limited federal power.[4] During the war, the military only half-heartedly endorsed the efforts of female reformers, viewing them as an unfortunate necessity in helping impoverished slave refugees. The officers who staffed the Freedmen's Bureau voiced a similar disapproval of women's assumed authority over the distribution of clothes and food to former slaves.[5] Though gender did not divide freedmen's aid associations during the war, the new alliance between male abolitionists and the Republican Party isolated female coworkers after 1865. Only by extending the boundaries of the war into Reconstruction can we understand the gendered battles over emancipation, charity, and women's work.

Women's interest in freedmen's aid grew not only from their antislavery convictions but also from their self-proclaimed empathy for former slaves. In 1863, for example, the Rochester Ladies' Anti-Slavery Society (RLASS) noted that "a new field of labor has opened to us" in "comforting, cheering, advising, educating the *freed* men, women and children."[6] The society hired its own freedmen's agent, former member Julia A. Wilbur, to go to Washington, D.C., and Alexandria, Virginia, to investigate and respond to the needs of former slaves. Welcomed by the male leaders of the National Freedmen's Relief Association of Washington, in October 1862 she headed to Alexandria, where large numbers of refugees from slavery had gathered. When she arrived, she informed the RLASS that "there are none but white men to care for [freedwomen] & minister to their most delicate necessities. I was sick. I was disgusted." She believed that former slaves desperately needed female agents, writing, "There are women here that need woman's care & counsel & kind words." Though the nation's middle-class and elite women had long devoted themselves to benevolent enterprises, Wilbur and the RLASS nonetheless described their plan to work with former slaves as a "new field of labor." Abolitionist women assumed the guardianship and care of recently freed women and children, hoping for a broader social and political transformation.[7]

The Ladies' Contraband Relief Society of St. Louis, Missouri, also viewed the care of freedwomen and children as their special province. Located at an urban crossroads between North and South, the Contraband Relief Society served a large number of former slaves displaced by the war. They reported, "There were at least 100,000 on the river between St. Louis and Vicksburg who were in suffering condition. These sufferers were mostly women and children whose husbands and fathers had in many cases entered the Union Army."[8] As freedwomen and children lacked the protection of male relatives, the women of St. Louis concluded that someone must care for them. As in the antislavery movement, women lamented the effects of slavery and war on African American families. Their language was often paternalistic, imagining former slaves as a population of needy women and children. Still, female reformers called the nation's attention to the problems of former slaves, highlighting their own initiatives to assist the government.[9]

In 1864, Ohio abolitionist and women's rights activist Josephine Griffing petitioned Congress to commission women to visit camps, raise funds for freedmen's relief, hire teachers, and "in short, to look after, and secure the general welfare of these women and children." She explained that women "fully understood" the "wants and necessities" of freedwomen and their children, establishing an interracial connection on the basis of motherhood. Though her argument relied on a traditional gendered division of labor, she asked for something far more radical. At the 1850 women's rights convention held in Salem, Griffing and other participants had urged the women of Ohio "to assert their rights as independent human beings; to demand their true position as equally responsible co-workers with their brethren." Now Griffing asked Congress to appoint women as official representatives of the Union government, with full legal authority to distribute aid to former slaves.[10]

As Griffing and other women worked with former slaves, they realized they needed more power to remedy the careless treatment of freedpeople by the military and even other missionaries. Emily Howland, a New Yorker who worked in freedmen's camps around Washington, resisted pressure to affiliate with the New York National Freedmen's Relief Association, noting that she could use any donations she received more effectively than if they "were put into the treasury of a society." Her comments expressed skepticism of the society's allocation of funds, particularly in the high salaries of its male leaders.[11] Julia Wilbur wrote to Secretary of War Edwin Stanton to protest the injustices she witnessed in Alexandria. She informed Stanton that the Provost Marshal, Lieutenant Colonel H. H. Wells, was a person of "little experience." Wilbur had conducted an intense lobbying campaign for the government to build barracks in Alexandria to house African American families while they looked for work and permanent homes. Instead, Wells instituted a policy to rent rooms to freedpeople, a policy Wilbur adamantly rejected. She wrote Stanton that she had "not thought for a moment that either yourself or the President intended to extort from the Contrabands in Alex $17 00 a year as rent for these rude barracks." She also opposed the appointment of her fellow reformer, the Rev. Albert Gladwin, as Superintendent of Freedmen, calling him "altogether unfit" for the position. Although she did not presume that she could become the superintendent, she wrote, "I did think of asking for the position of *Assistant Superintendent*." She went on to describe the importance of women's efforts in Alexandria, concluding that women also deserved to get paid for their work: "I could do still more were I invested with a little more authority. Although a *woman* I would like an appointment with a fair salary attached to it, & I would expect to deserve a salary."[12] Wilbur wanted official recognition of her contributions by the government. Already paid for her work by the RLASS, she knew a government salary would carry more weight as she negotiated with Wells and other officials in Alexandria.

Wilbur faced strong resistance from military officials and male reformers in Alexandria. Even with broad social acceptance of women's benevolent activities, their incursion into military areas violated the boundaries between private and public, home front and war zone. The Rev. Gladwin, the future Superintendent of Freedmen, expressed his outrage at Wilbur's presence, informing her that she was out of her sphere and he did "not like to see a woman wear men's clothes."[13] Wells complained that Wilbur wanted "the control, the management of the contrabands." He dismissed her goals for the barracks, saying the plan to rent them was "calculated to benefit the colored people, and not render them more dependent and indolent than they now are." Further, he informed his superior officer that he did not intend to be directed by a woman.[14] Both the Rev. Gladwin and Wells had a visceral reaction to a female freedmen's agent in the male world of occupied Alexandria, but they also characterized her proposals as misguided charity. Instead, they wanted refugee women and children to become self-sufficient—and thus leave the army's care—as soon as possible. Such views reflected the army's frustration at their unexpected responsibility for freed families as well as a political aversion to dependency in any form. In their minds, the dependency of slave refugees was linked to the presence of benevolent women.[15]

Yet government officials also recognized the value of women's contributions to the relief effort. After her 1864 petition to Congress, Josephine Griffing moved to Washington to work with the National Freedmen's Relief Association. Like other women, she saw the need for an independent government agency to oversee freedmen's relief. In a letter to abolitionist William Lloyd

Garrison, Griffing articulated her ideas for the future Freedmen's Bureau. In Griffing's view, the agency would be the basis for a "new & purer system of Politics," which would include the participation of women. She acknowledged that a man would head the bureau, but believed he should be "fully committed to give us *women* what we do so much need in the *Gov.*—in *Commissions* to carry forward the work of Relief to the Freedmen which he sees to be *our* work *legitimately*." Griffing saw freedmen's relief as women's work and "of great importance to the Freedmen, Women, and the country."[16] From the care of freedwomen and children, Griffing extended women's sphere of influence to all former slaves and suggested that women's labors were essential to Reconstruction. She lobbied politicians in Washington vigorously for the Freedmen's Bureau. Suffragists later described her as the originator of the Freedmen's Bureau: "Few cared to listen to the details of the necessity, and it was only through Mrs. Griffing's brave and unwearied efforts that the plan was accepted."[17] In appreciation, General Oliver Otis Howard, commissioner of the Freedmen's Bureau, appointed Griffing assistant to the assistant commissioner for Washington in 1865. Her appointment was a victory for women in the freedmen's aid movement as it acknowledged their important role in aiding former slaves.

Abolitionist women hoped the establishment of the Freedmen's Bureau would inaugurate a new era of equal rights in American politics. The Freedmen's Bureau did indeed expand the female presence in the federal government, especially in the nation's capital, as women took jobs as visitors, matrons, and teachers. Despite her negative experience with the army in Alexandria, Wilbur had enormous faith in the military officers who staffed the Freedmen's Bureau. "I hope and believe Gen. Howard is equal to the task he has assumed," she wrote the Rochester Ladies' Anti-Slavery Society. "Since the Freedmen's Bureau went into operation, many wrongs have been remedied."[18] On a visit to Richmond shortly after the end of the war, Wilbur found forty soldiers guarding the almshouse who "were rough, ignorant, and prejudiced; they took to negro driving naturally. Such men should never be out where they can wield any power over others, especially the weak and helpless." Wilbur saw the soldiers stand over freedwomen with a whip, "and in several instances women were beaten and otherwise abused."[19] In addition, small children were hired out, or apprenticed, under the army's watch. Wilbur saw women's presence as the only remedy to these injustices. But after Colonel Orlando Brown, the Freedmen's Bureau superintendent, informed Wilbur he would return the apprenticed children to their mothers, she expressed her confidence in him: "I felt that he could be trusted with the interests of the Freed-people, and then, and not till then, did I feel at liberty to leave Richmond."[20] In Wilbur's view, this male Freedmen's Bureau agent and military officer was an effective substitute for a female reformer. She and other antislavery women viewed the Freedmen's Bureau as both an extension of women's charitable activities and an official endorsement of their efforts. Emma Brown, a native of Washington, D.C., and one of the first teachers in its segregated "colored" public school system, wrote, "I don't think women have ever before had so glorious an opportunity to do something—They have always been such insignificant creatures—so dependent." She noted that she and a female colleague had "a little Freedmen's Bureau of our own."[21] As Brown and her friend distributed clothes and other goods from their schoolroom, they associated the bureau with their own version of Reconstruction, combining female benevolence with a national program to ease former slaves' transition to freedom.

Though now agents of the federal government, and thus representatives of the general public, female reformers continued to advocate for freedwomen and children. In 1865, Josephine Griffing published an appeal in Garrison's antislavery newspaper the *Liberator* that described the impoverished condition of "twenty thousand" freedpeople in Washington. She claimed these former slaves, "miserable women, with large families of children, besides old, crippled, blind and sick persons" were the "mothers and sons, and wives and children, of soldiers still in Government service as Regular U.S. Troops." According to Griffing, they needed housing, fuel, beds, blankets, food, and clothing.[22] She earnestly solicited donations from friends and sympathizers, emphasizing the nation's debt to black soldiers and their families.

Despite her emphasis on these deserving groups of former slaves, Griffing's appeal was unusual and controversial for its emphasis on direct relief to destitute freedpeople. Since the beginnings of the freedmen's aid movement, women had stressed the need for donations of money, clothing, and other items to ameliorate the poverty of former slaves. By the end of the war, the tone of the freedmen's aid movement, spurred by the demands of Republican politicians, the military, and the public, had evolved to focus on education and free labor rather than charity. Such pleas for donations of necessities embarrassed officials because they highlighted the failures rather than the successes of emancipation. But women still viewed their principal duty to be benevolent in nature. They did not see the poverty of former slaves as a racial characteristic, but a result of the specific circumstances of war and the abolition of slavery. Female activists believed that neither women nor slaves could gain independence without short-term assistance.

Griffing's appeal for the "twenty thousand" also redirected the attention of Northerners to the capital, an antebellum symbol of slavery's corrupting influence on the republic. After the abolition of the peculiar institution in the District of Columbia in 1862, female abolitionists, nurses, and visitors noticed the city's growing population of freedpeople, many of whom migrated to the city seeking shelter from slavery and the ravages of war. Though Griffing may have exaggerated the number of destitute, she accurately assessed the change in the city's black population, which grew by more than twenty thousand between 1860 and 1870. Griffing and other antislavery women, such as Rachel Moore of the Philadelphia Female Anti-Slavery Society, flocked to the district to aid impoverished former slaves, creating a population of politically active female reformers. They alerted Northerners to the continued suffering of district freedpeople and the inability or unwillingness of government officials to cope with the problem. But many Freedmen's Bureau officers, uncomfortable with direct charity or the national focus on their headquarters, preferred education, employment, migration, and other solutions to those advocated by the benevolent women at their doorstep.[23]

As politicians began demanding freedpeople's adaptation to a free labor system, women's activism began to focus on work. Aid rolls swelled in Washington, D.C., between 1866 and 1868, and the Freedmen's Bureau strongly encouraged underemployed freedpeople to leave the overcrowded district for work on Southern plantations or Northern farms. Though Griffing continued to urge the government and private individuals to donate generously to freedmen's relief, she and Sojourner Truth also worked as employment agents for the Bureau, ultimately aiding the Northern migration of almost seven thousand former slaves.[24]

To find occupations for former slaves, Truth and Griffing used their antislavery connections throughout the Northeast and Midwest. Truth asked Rochester, New York, abolitionist Amy Post if she could find "some good places for women that have children."[25] After advertising in the Rochester *Democrat* and the Rochester *Express*, Truth received approximately three thousand requests. As one advertisement for their services read, "We exhort everyone in want of farm hands or household service to write to Mrs. Griffing, No. 394 No. Capitol St., Washington City, enclosing two postage stamps. It would be better still to inclose $5 at once, and ask her to send such help as you need. Our women are overworked, our farms not half tilled for want of help."[26]

While well intentioned, their efforts ultimately pitted against one another the interests of white and freed women as well as abolitionists and former slaves. Former slaves came to the North only to find themselves working as domestic servants and farmhands, which, as the advertisement suggested, eased the labors of white farm families.[27] Though the Freedmen's Bureau paid to transport freedpeople to the North, Truth and Griffing sought additional compensation for their efforts, a practice some attacked as slave trading. Since neither woman was independently wealthy, each depended on the money they could raise for their survival. Sojourner Truth justified her fee: "The people come and are willing to pay what I ask 5 cts. or 1 dollar for the sake of having help and they think it is no more than right for me to have it."[28] Both women struggled for economic security even as they assisted former slaves to achieve a measure of financial independence.

Although northern migration fulfilled the hopes of Truth and Griffing by offering former slaves new employment opportunities, the program was often paternalistic and sometimes exploitative. For example, Anna Lowell of the Howard Industrial School for Colored Women and Girls in Cambridge, Massachusetts, helped freedwomen and children resettle in the North. Her school was a branch of the Freedmen's Bureau's migration network, and she regularly received freedwomen from Washington, D.C., trained them, and found them employment in Massachusetts. The goal of her home, she explained to C. H. Howard, the assistant commissioner of the Freedmen's Bureau for the district, was "to take girls and women and teach them and then get them good places."[29] She believed that the women in her school were thus saved from "evils which can only be realized and appreciated by those who have been familiar with it," presumably referring to enslaved women's sexual vulnerability in Southern homes. "Instead of living in poverty and dependence they are all supporting themselves by honest labor," she claimed, "and their children will be more benefited than they." But Lowell's perspective on the employment of freedwomen presumed their inferiority to whites and the wholesomeness of the North; she trained African American women for jobs as domestic servants only. Though she found her pupils "good places" removed from the sexualized atmosphere of the Southern household, she offered them positions that were often isolating, demeaning, and abusive—one reason why elite white women like Lowell faced servant shortages throughout the nineteenth century. Lowell's school gave freedwomen the chance to exchange one white mistress for another.[30]

Migration limited the newfound freedoms of former slave women in even more important ways. To protect "the moral good of the next generation," Lowell created a self-consciously female environment and requested that the Freedmen's Bureau send her young girls, preferably orphans, though she also accepted women with small children because "it is not difficult to get a place for a woman with a child over 18 months—when younger than that they will meet with much that is disappointing." Lowell told C. H. Howard that she did not want men or boys, however, "as it interferes with all our arrangements."[31] Such strictures broke up married couples, including one preacher and his wife, and probably separated mothers and sons.[32] In the zeal of the Freedmen's Bureau and its agents to transfer thousands of freedpeople from Washington, these problems were inevitable, but from the perspective of some abolitionists this practice displayed eerie similarities to the slave market. In 1867, Worcester abolitionist Anna Earle complained to the Freedmen's Bureau that Griffing and her colleague Sarah Tilmon, an employment agent with the nationalist African Civilization Society, had taken a girl named Kitty Brooks to New York City without the permission or knowledge of her mother. Since then, Griffing, Tilmon, and the Freedmen's Bureau had been unable to locate Kitty. Earle wrote, "I refrain from expressing my feeling in regard to Mrs. Griffing, who it seems to me as clearly kidnapped little Kitty as if she had been a slave trader."[33]

Frederick Douglass expressed a more general skepticism of the freedmen's aid movement. Concerned that charity encouraged white Americans to view blacks as dependents, he urged abolitionists instead to work for equality: "My mission for the present is to ask equal citizenship in the state and equal fellowship for the Negro in the church. Equal rights in the street cars and equal admission in the state schools . . . this is what we count and must not lose sight of in all our schemes of benevolence with special reference to the Negro." Douglass noticed the similarities of such "schemes of benevolence" to the paternalistic ideal of plantation slavery, but his reluctance to wholeheartedly endorse freedmen's aid also represented practical politics.[34] Few Americans supported a national system of charity for former slaves, especially one that relied on the labors of politically active women. Women in the freedmen's aid movement found their vision for Reconstruction severely circumscribed. Many former slaves undoubtedly agreed with Douglass that they would rather be left alone, but other impoverished freedpeople temporarily needed the assistance of the government and freedmen's aid associations.

The story of Diana Williams shows how one former slave used the assistance of female reformers and the Freedmen's Bureau to forge a new life in freedom. In 1868, Williams visited Griffing's employment office, hoping to secure a job and transportation to Hartford, Connecticut, where she had relatives. Other bureau agents frequently challenged Griffing's judgment, but she justified the use of government transportation by noting that Williams was "a constant applicant for help and employment" and that her husband approved of the move. Nevertheless, Williams's husband hid their children, forcing a change of plans. Clearly intent on leaving, Williams departed for Philadelphia several days later. The Freedmen's Bureau fielded complaints from the husband about the disappearance of his wife, demanding action from Griffing. She responded that Mr. Williams "was a worthless overbearing man" and counseled him to find work.[35] Griffing believed that she had helped Diana Williams flee an unhappy marriage while also giving her a chance at economic independence. She urged the Freedmen's Bureau to recognize Williams as an individual, independent of her husband. Juggling the demands of free labor with interrelated concerns about appropriate gender roles, Freedmen's Bureau officials sought to restore the traditional relationship between Diana Williams and her husband.

What had changed since Griffing, Wilbur, and other women expressed their hope for a new "system of Politics" embodied by the Freedmen's Bureau? The end of the war transformed the relationship of the freedmen's aid movement to former slaves. Responding to the concerns of citizens, soldiers, and politicians, the staff of the Freedmen's Bureau began to distance themselves from direct relief of freedpeople almost immediately. General Oliver Otis Howard assured the public he would not support former slaves "in idleness." As a result, the agency cut back on its charitable operations, preferring to spend its budget on transportation rather than fuel and food whenever possible. In the case of Diana Williams, Howard's subordinates linked African American self-sufficiency with the nuclear family structure, reinforcing women's status as dependents rather than economic actors in their own right.[36] As with Julia Wilbur's experience in Alexandria, fear of African American dependency coexisted with anxieties about women's new public presence. Griffing fell victim to this political reality. During and after the war, she toured the North raising funds and awareness of freedpeople's condition. But Griffing's speeches, published appeals, and her official appointment as assistant to the assistant commissioner raised questions about the Freedmen's Bureau. Was the agency funded by taxpayer money or private contributions? Was the Bureau a government charity for former slaves? What was the nature of Griffing's position in the Bureau? As a result, Griffing lost her position in the fall of 1865, less than six months after her initial appointment. Fielding inquiries from the public, Lieutenant S. N. Clark, a staff member in the district office, informed one E. Carpenter of Colchester, Connecticut, of Griffing's dismissal: "That connection has ceased. She has no authority to solicit funds for the Freedmen's Bureau and no official information to sustain her statements of the suffering among the Freedmen."[37] Explaining that Griffing had no authority or official information, the Freedmen's Bureau thus reassured the American people that the social upheaval and economic exigencies of the war were not permanent.

Male abolitionists also undermined Griffing's status at the Freedmen's Bureau. After emancipation, antislavery men like J. Miller McKim, Jacob Shipherd, and others celebrated their victory by joining the Republican Party and forming organizations with close ties to political power. McKim, former agent of the Pennsylvania Anti-Slavery Society and publisher of its paper the *Pennsylvania Freeman*, left the American Anti-Slavery Society in 1865 to found the American Freedmen's Union Commission (AFUC), an umbrella organization for freedmen's aid societies that assisted and supplemented the Freedmen's Bureau's efforts. Many Garrisonian abolitionists found such a close connection to the government disturbing, but abolitionist women found the lack of women in the commission hierarchy even more problematic. As Lucretia Mott wrote, "I told him [McKim] it was objected, that Woman was ignored in their organizn., & if really a reconstructn. for the Nation she ought not so to be—and it wd. be rather 'a come down' for our Anti Slavery women & Quaker women to consent to be thus overlooked."[38] Though McKim denied any deliberate exclusion of women, the commission helped undermine Griffing's position at the Bureau, ostensibly because she presented a threat to its political existence. Jacob R. Shipherd, the commission's secretary, wrote to General Howard that "Mrs. Griffing is simply irrepressible: & yet she must be repressed, so far as you and I have to do with her, or else we must bear the odium of her folly. She still represents the '20,000 utterly destitute' as needing *outright support* from northern charity."[39] Shipherd believed that Griffing's appeals for impoverished former slaves hurt the ability of the American Freedmen's Union Commission and the Freedmen's Bureau to sustain their educational and legal work with freedpeople. Shipherd viewed charity to former slaves as harmful because it undermined free labor values and encouraged "copperheads" in their belief that African Americans were better off under slavery. Throughout his letter, Shipherd stressed Griffing's incompetence, implying that her sex disqualified her from a job meant for "sensible men."[40] By the end of 1865, the male officers and reformers in the Freedmen's Bureau and the AFUC controlled freedmen's aid, limiting the place of both women and direct relief in the movement.

Despite this transformation, abolitionist women continued to view the Freedmen's Bureau as the only government agency that embraced the political needs of women and former slaves. Griffing remained a regular at the offices of the Freedmen's Bureau because of her employment agency and industrial school. She continued to press the Bureau for greater authority, though it generally pushed back. The Freedmen's Bureau itself was fighting for its own survival throughout the 1860s, increasingly limiting operations to education starting in 1868 before finally closing in 1872. Though she acknowledged its flaws, Wilbur speculated that "if the whites behave so badly with the Freedmen's Bureau in operation, we can easily imagine what the situation of the freedpeople would be were the protection of the Bureau withdrawn."[41] In Virginia, teacher Caroline Putnam echoed this sentiment. After Putnam informed freedman Steptoe Ball of the demise of the Freedmen's Bureau, she reported "the look of being forsaken suddenly came on him, that was pitiful to see. '*Who then is going to see justice done us now?*'"[42] In 1869 Griffing wrote a desperate last appeal to General Howard for money to distribute aid to former slaves and to support herself and her daughters, writing "I feel that I am called to work in this District—and shall be greatly strengthened by your encouragement in this matter."[43] But women's plans for a true reconstruction of the nation foundered on the image of women distributing aid to thousands of destitute freedpeople in the nation's capital, an image that threatened the uneasy consensus over emancipation with sexual and racial disorder.

If the Freedmen's Bureau disappointed them in the end, many female activists hoped that the government might repay their contributions to the relief effort with political rights. Julia Wilbur witnessed the first election in Washington in which African American men voted. She wrote that she "rejoiced that I had lived to see so much progress" but admitted that she felt "a little jealous—the least bit humiliated" when she realized the male voters did not know how to read. But she concluded, "No earthquake followed these proceedings, and I presume no convulsion of nature would have occurred, had white *women* and black *women* increased that line of voters." Women in the freedmen's aid movement agitated for universal suffrage, and Wilbur attempted to register to vote with other white and black women in the district.[44] But in this, too, they were disappointed. Though African American men gained the vote during Reconstruction, women did not. In frustration, suffragist Elizabeth Cady Stanton used the example of the freedmen's aid movement to argue that women's aid to former slaves demanded equal treatment with their charges:

Did the Negro's rough services in camp and battle outweigh the humanitarian labors of woman in all departments of government? Did his loyalty in the army count for more than her educational work in teaching the people sound principles of government? Can it be that statesmen in the nineteenth century believe that they who sacrifice human lives in bloody wars do more for the sum of human happiness and development than they who try to save the multitude and teach them how to live?[45]

Stanton's remarks also indicate the historic break between women's rights and abolition prompted by Reconstruction and the Fifteenth Amendment. Many in the women's rights movement adopted racist rhetoric to argue that white women (no longer white *and* black women) deserved the suffrage before black men.

Stanton's view was hardly universal among women's rights advocates. Many suffragists viewed the issue of freedmen's aid as a link between the rights of women and African Americans. Griffing, for example, understood the misguided policies of the federal government and the Freedmen's Bureau as a direct result of sexual inequality. She wrote Stanton, "I see the want of regulation in national affairs, that can never be accomplished, while Govmt. is administered on the *male* basis of representation."[46] Rather than seeing the sexual

inequality inscribed in the Fifteenth Amendment as a reason to deride freedmen, women like Griffing saw the former slaves' cause as justifying and even
necessitating women's suffrage. For such advocates, equal rights were means to
an end rather than an objective in its own right.

The political opponents of women's rights and freedmen's relief also associated the two causes and discredited both. It was because military officials linked
women's charity with African American dependency that they condemned the
new public presence of women and free blacks. Such anxieties only increased
after the war, when it seemed that women had made inroads into politics, joining with African Americans to demand full citizenship rights and economic
opportunity. Reformers and government officials placed harsh limits on both
populations. While former slaves learned that freedom too often meant working for their former owners with pay, women learned that in the Freedmen's
Bureau and other government offices they would remain subordinate to men.
In the freedmen's aid movement, women extended their sphere of influence,
only to meet fierce resistance from reformers and government officials attempting to reassert sexual and racial hierarchies upset by the Civil War.

If the nation resisted women's political equality, the freedmen's aid movement nonetheless offered women significant opportunities. Women forged new
connections to the government during the Civil War and Reconstruction. They
forced the government to be concerned not only with the labor of former slaves
but also with their education and welfare. Their testimony contributed to the
establishment of the Freedmen's Bureau and ensured that its mission incorporated some provisions for the neediest populations of former slaves. Women
petitioned politicians, negotiated with military officials, and frequented the
halls of government as employees and concerned citizens. These changes were
permanent. After Reconstruction, women continued to lobby for suffrage, tem-
perance, and other issues. This new relationship between women and the federal government shaped women's reform into the Progressive era.

6

"Objects of Humanity": The White Poor in Civil War and Reconstruction Georgia

Denise E. Wright

On October 31, 1865, Nancy Estes, a white woman from Cobb County, Georgia, just northwest of Atlanta, wrote to President Andrew Johnson requesting food and money. Describing her family's desperate conditions, she claimed to be a long-time Unionist who "drank a cup of Uncle Abraham's coffee" with the Union soldiers who had come to her home. Estes claimed that the "secesh" people would not help her—the president was her only hope. On November 30, a local agent of the Bureau of Refugees, Freedmen, and Abandoned Lands (Freedmen's Bureau) investigated Estes's claim. He determined that Estes and her family, who still resided in the family home, were not "objects of humanity," and forwarded a copy of his findings to Georgia's assistant commissioner. The Estes family received no aid from the Freedmen's Bureau. The letter raises compelling questions about the white poor in the Confederacy and the evolution of charitable aid programs during the Civil War and Reconstruction. The Estes family was not alone in its desperation or appeal for assistance.[1]

Despite numerous historical and sociological studies of the South's white poor during the Civil War and Reconstruction, the lives of the Estes family and thousands of other Georgians who survived those desperate times remain somewhat mysterious. But there is a common thread that can shed some light on this population: access to aid in varied forms. During the war, Georgia implemented massive aid programs that provided cash, food (primarily in the form of corn), salt, and the materials necessary for the home production of cotton cloth. Immediately after the war, the newly established Freedmen's Bureau provided rations, clothing, and transportation. That aid was supplemented by donations from Northern charitable associations, many of them organized specifically to assist starving Southerners. Even the U.S. Department of Agriculture provided seeds for crops. One can hardly expect this population, largely illiterate and living in the midst of a catastrophic war and ongoing drought, to have left behind the diaries and letters that have contributed so greatly to illustrating the story of the Southern white aristocracy. But the histories of these aid programs, and the rare surviving evidence of white Georgians' interactions with them, provide a better understanding of the privations and challenges poor white Southerners faced during this turbulent period. By examining the relationships between the aid organizations, and the influences they had upon one another, we can establish connections between Civil War and Reconstruction in Georgia and throughout the South.[2]

The historiography of Southern welfare in this era often focuses almost exclusively on the Freedmen's Bureau, the most well-known Reconstruction welfare agency, and its aid to former slaves. That focus is understandable. But in 1970 John Hope Franklin published an article in *The Social Service Review* that offered a compelling way to understand the Bureau's history through an examination of the origins of Southern welfare policy. Franklin clearly established the connections between wartime and Reconstruction aid, especially aid provided by the Freedmen's Bureau. He found that wartime relief was the first welfare policy for most Southern states. He determined that state legislatures had realized the need to provide some aid to soldiers' widows and families. They moved quickly to do so, partially motivated by the necessity of avoiding the threat to social order that might occur if the "rich man's war, poor man's fight" cliché came too close to describing reality for the white poor. Poor relief, available to whites only, would maintain the race-based social order. Highlighting the significant percentage of Freedmen's Bureau rations that were issued to whites, Franklin concluded that the initial phase of Reconstruction—the period of so-called Radical Reconstruction—was not so radical after all. Confederate state and local welfare policy had established a precedent; when it came to providing material aid to the poor, the Freedmen's Bureau continued a practice already in place. Franklin placed the Bureau within the context of wartime welfare programs.[3]

Elna C. Green's 2003 study of welfare in Richmond, Virginia, *This Business of Relief: Confronting Poverty in a Southern City, 1740–1940*, provided an example of new directions in American welfare history. In chapters 4–6, she details the changing focus of poor relief in the Civil War, Reconstruction, and the early New South period. State aid, the Freedmen's Bureau, and Northern charitable associations all play significant roles in the story, and the white and black poor receive equal attention. Though Green is careful to point out that her study of a Southern city has limited applications to the rural South, her focus on relief as the central thread of the story brings all the aspects of welfare, and its evolution in Richmond, to center stage. The goal of the current study is to combine Franklin's and Green's approaches and place the Freedmen's Bureau in Georgia within the larger context of state and federal welfare both during and after the Civil War. By doing so, Georgia's white poor necessarily become a larger part of the story, offering a new vantage point from which to examine the evolution of welfare in Georgia. The story begins during the war.[4]

Before the war, Georgia had "virtually no role in education, welfare, health, or police and regulatory functions." But as the war progressed, the state's role in providing aid to its white citizens changed radically. Several factors contributed to a growing number of white Georgians who desperately needed assistance. The April 1862 Confederate conscription law took farmers from their fields, and food shortages became a growing concern throughout the South. As Emory Thomas stated in *The Confederacy as a Revolutionary Experience*, "The fact was that Southern agriculture failed the Confederacy. Not only did the great staple crops decline in value and production, but the wartime South proved unable to feed herself." Georgia was no exception; by late 1863 the state faced the additional problems of an ongoing drought, an early frost, and numerous skirmishes within its borders. In 1863 and 1864, the Georgia legislature approved corn appropriation acts, totaling $1,890,000, to provide food for destitute white Georgians.[5]

These were not the state's only appropriations for aid. The legislature also set aside more than $1 million to procure and distribute salt, which was necessary for preserving food, tanning leather, dyeing fabric, and for horses and livestock. It was provided without charge to the indigent, at reduced rates to soldiers' families, and at controlled prices to those who could afford it. Though not exclusively a welfare measure, the system of salt distribution was put in place primarily because of the suffering of Georgia's soldiers' families. Home production of cloth also was important in Georgia, as it was throughout the Confederacy, for making clothing and blankets, both for soldiers and those at home. Georgia had cotton in abundance, but to process it into useable thread, people needed cotton cards—wire brushes with wooden backings and handles. As existing supplies dwindled and cards in use wore out, shortages developed. In three separate appropriations beginning in 1862, the legislature approved a total expenditure of $1.3 million to produce or purchase cotton cards.[6]

But by far the largest welfare expenditure in Georgia during the war was for the state's "support of indigent soldier's families," referred to as the Indigent Soldiers' Families Fund. The earliest precedents for this program are found in late 1861. Georgia's governor, Joseph E. Brown, believed it necessary for those who could most afford it to assist people in need. In November 1861, in his annual message to the legislature, this idea took shape in a suggestion that planters and others in possession of cotton (which could not be easily sold because of the blockade) who would warehouse the cotton and insure it, would be eligible to receive from the state an advance, in treasury notes, of two-thirds of its market value. Those with a crop to sell could thereby access much-needed funds, especially to pay state and Confederate taxes. Though the legislature took this suggestion in a different direction, this first step toward "relief for the people" is startlingly conservative compared with later efforts.[7]

By the opening of the 1862 legislative session, Brown's proposed relief measures were more specifically aimed at relieving soldiers' families. Some counties had adequate resources to assist their indigent, but others did not. Brown argued that the state should offer its resources in the form of an appropriation for "a bounty of one hundred dollars" to soldiers' families whose property values were less than one thousand dollars. The "bounty" would be funded by the "whole net proceeds of the Western & Atlantic Railroad for the ensuing year." He also suggested that every soldier be exempt from the poll tax and from paying any taxes on their first one thousand dollars of taxable property.[8] The legislature implemented these measures on December 13, 1862, and also appropriated $2.5 million to be distributed by each county's inferior court justices to indigent soldiers' families. The act was amended the following April because of reports that some justices were not issuing funds unless those eligible were "utterly penniless and beggared." The amendment directed them to use their discretion to "assist all indigent and needy families."[9] By November 5, 1863, Brown called for an appropriation of $5 million to aid soldiers' families, and was careful to point out that he was not suggesting "supporting them in idleness." On December 12, the legislature passed a bill requiring the counties' ordinaries to turn over any surplus educational funds to the inferior courts to be added to the funds for indigent soldiers' families.[10]

By the end of the 1863 session, the legislature responded to Brown's urging and appropriated $6 million for indigent soldiers and their families, including widows, orphans, and families with soldiers in active service as well as disabled soldiers and their families. The governor was authorized to borrow money or issue state bonds if necessary to fund the appropriation.[11] The language of the appropriation bill is exact, and is an indication of the increasingly detailed and sophisticated legislative approach to public welfare in the state. For the first time, "indigent" was defined to include "Wives, Mothers, Grandmothers, and all those who have to leave their ordinary business in the house, and to labor in the field to support themselves and children, and who are not able to make a sufficient support for themselves and families." Soldiers who were "detailed for the purpose of working in workshops, and transacting other business, for which they are drawing [m]echanics wages" were specifically excluded from the appropriation. Additionally, inferior court judges or their representatives could offer partial relief to those who were not "actually indigent," provided they did not take supplies from those who required them. Families of "substitutes" in the army were to be considered the same as other soldiers' families.[12]

The distribution process was also more complex than in earlier appropriations. Funds for the appropriation would come from the "'income tax act,'
assented to April 18th, 1863." The original tax law directed that the funds would
be distributed among Georgia's counties on the basis of "representative population." This new act superseded it and required the inferior courts in each
county to "make out a schedule of persons within their respective counties,
who may be entitled to . . . benefits." The list of those "entitled" was specific
and extensive. Beneficiaries included widows whose husbands had been killed
in service or who had died as a result of wounds or illness resulting from their
service; disabled or ill soldiers, as well as their wives, who resided within the
county; the wives or dependent mothers or other relatives of soldiers in service;
and children under twelve who were dependent on soldiers, including orphans.
Inferior court officers were allowed discretion in distribution as long as the
method was "efficient." There was no mention of dependent slaves. Harking
back to Brown's assurances that no one who could support themselves would
benefit, the county representatives were instructed to "make diligent enquiries"
into each potential beneficiary's status. To ensure diligence, any agent who was
found guilty of misappropriating funds would be sentenced to two to seven
years in the state penitentiary. County grand juries were instructed to "make
diligent enquiry" into the actions of the county's representatives. Only Georgia's "deserving" poor were eligible for aid.[13]

The quarterly distributions could take the form of cash, or "articles of prime
necessity" in lieu of cash. Considering rising inflation and scarcity, goods were
probably more valuable than cash. But distribution to counties that were occupied by Union forces would, of course, be difficult. Recognizing that the citizens
in those counties often were the most desperate, the legislature directed Brown
to retain an "appropriate" percentage of the fund for distribution in those
counties as soon as practicable. The law also anticipated the potential problems
posed by "refugeeing" as citizens of one county moved to another. In such
cases, those leaving could collect their allotted amount at their current address
and apply for a certificate from the court representative. That certificate could
then be taken to the court representative in their next county of residence. One
can only imagine the difficulty of this procedure in the midst of war, but the
fact that there was such a procedure indicates how common "refugeeing" had
become.[14]

The difficulties of fulfilling this plan are noted in Georgia Comptroller General Peterson Thweatt's October 1864 report. The deadline for submitting
county estimates of the number of recipients was February 1, 1864; however, by
that date "not one-third of the counties" had done so. It was not until late

March that "a sufficient number had made returns to authorize an apportion-
ment" from Thweatt's office. Three counties in far northwestern Georgia had
made no returns by October because of the Union Army occupation. Total state
expenditures for the fiscal year 1863–64 were $13,288,435. Of that, despite the
challenges of receiving reports and collecting income taxes, Thweatt's offices
disbursed $4,481,305 from the Indigent Soldiers' Families Fund in fiscal year
1863–64, one-third of the state's expenditures. Combined with expenditures for
salt, cotton cards, and corn, which totaled $6,730,533, the state spent a stagger-
ing 50.6 percent of its appropriated funds on direct welfare measures. Other
welfare-related expenditures included Educational Fund payments of $135,844,
which were turned over to the counties to use at their discretion; Small Pox
Fund payments of $64,580, which paid physicians and purchased supplies to
stem outbreaks of the disease; payments in the amount of $15,000 to support
the state academy for the blind; payments of $111,990 to support the state luna-
tic asylum; a $15,000 payment from the Military Fund for "Location and Sub-
sistence of Atlanta Exiles" who were living in the Fosterville settlement in
Terrell County; and the annual payment of $500,000 to the Georgia Relief and
Hospital Association, which helped fund hospitals in and out of the state to
meet the needs of Georgia's soldiers. Altogether, direct and indirect welfare
support totaled $7,587,947, or 57.1 percent of the state's total expenditures that
year.[15]

Georgia's welfare spending was slated to continue at a similar level for the
fiscal year 1864–65. In fact, the legislature increased the appropriation for the
Indigent Soldiers' Families Fund to $8 million. But Lee's surrender in April 1865
ended most disbursements in late April or early May.[16]

It is important to note that though these wartime aid programs were never
specifically identified as for whites only, the implication throughout the
debates and the language of the bills that established Georgia's programs is
clear: They were established to assist white soldiers' families. When Comptroller General Thweatt made his report to the provisional governor only
months after the end of the war, he argued that much of the state's debt was
incurred to feed and clothe Georgia's soldiers and to take care of their families, who had been left "dependent upon the maternal care of the state."
There was no mention of any slaves those families might own. The soldiers'
families could look to the state for "care," but the slaves had to continue to
look to their masters. There is no doubt that Georgia's black population benefited from the state's wartime programs, but they are significantly absent
from welfare debates and legislation.[17]

Throughout the war, county inferior court judges administered the state's
relief programs. After the war, this system continued as Georgia faced wartime

destruction and the ongoing drought. On March 13, 1866, the Georgia General Assembly appropriated $200,000 to purchase corn for soldiers' widows and orphans, as well as "wounded or disabled soldiers" and "such aged or infirm white persons as must suffer without aid, on account of their destitution and inability to work for a living." The justices of the inferior courts were ordered, within a month of notification, to report the number of such persons in their counties. The governor would then appoint a purchasing agent, and the justices would appoint county agents, to procure and distribute the aid. In December 1866, the General Assembly appropriated an additional $100,000 with the same restrictions, but with the added proviso "that no part of the same shall be expended until the Governor shall become satisfied that a sufficiency of corn will not be contributed from voluntary sources."[18]

But there also were two significant changes in welfare programs serving Georgia. The first was the arrival of the Freedmen's Bureau, whose mission was to aid both black and white Georgians. The second was the formation of numerous private charitable organizations in the North, those "voluntary sources" noted in the December 1866 Georgia legislation, whose sole aim was to provide material aid, most without regard to race, to the devastated South.

The Freedmen's Bureau had been established in March 1865, and subsequent legislation in February 1866 clarified the Bureau's mandate and expanded its administration. But from the beginning, the Freedmen's Bureau did not exist only to support former slaves. The white poor also benefited from the Bureau's programs, and this aspect of its operations is important. The Bureau's responsibilities regarding poor whites was made clear in a statement by Congressman Thomas Dawes Eliot, Republican from Massachusetts, during debate over the 1866 Freedmen's Bureau bill. Eliot had shepherded the original bill through the House, and when confronted with the question of exactly who would have access to Bureau aid, he simply stated that "the refugees have all the rights under this bill that the freedmen have and have been cared for from the beginning by the Commissioner and the assistant commissioners under him, wherever that care has been called for." In defining "refugee," Eliot stated that he interpreted it to mean "white" in a situation where one was discussing "freedmen" and "refugees." The individual states of the former Confederacy had established welfare policies and programs during the war; by providing assistance to the South's white poor, the Freedmen's Bureau continued an established practice. But the Bureau simultaneously established radical new policy when it offered aid to former slaves and continued established practice when it assisted the white poor whose lives had been disrupted by war. The connections between state wartime aid programs and the Bureau are often-overlooked aspects of Bureau history.[19]

In the early months of Reconstruction, one of the Freedmen's Bureau's most basic methods of addressing Southern destitution was issuing rations. From June 1865 until November 1868, the Bureau issued approximately 20.3 million rations in thirteen states and the District of Columbia—26 percent of those rations were distributed to white refugees. But this simple statistic does not explain the diversity of ration programs within each assistant commissioner's jurisdiction. There was great variation in the number of rations issued in each state, as well as in the percentage of rations distributed to freedpeople and white refugees. Virginia distributed the greatest number of rations of any state (4,257,178). But less than 5 percent of those rations (203,478) were distributed to white refugees. In stark contrast, Alabama, which distributed the second greatest number of rations (4,219,579.5), issued 65 percent of its rations (2,727,406) to whites.[20] An attempt to explain the variations between states is beyond the scope of this work, but an examination of the details of Georgia's ration program reveals how one state implemented a policy that was, at best, fluid.

The Georgia Freedmen's Bureau distributed 1,476,579.5 rations from August 1865 to October 1868, fifth most of all the states. Only Alabama, Arkansas, and South Carolina distributed a greater number of rations to whites than Georgia. White refugees received 285,933.5 of Georgia's rations (or 19 percent, which also ranks fifth). However, the full implication of Georgia's ration program is not found in its rankings but in the detailed monthly reports the assistant commissioners forwarded to Bureau headquarters. Unfortunately, the extant reports do not span the entire period from June 1865 to November 1868. There are, however, consecutive reports from December 1865 until December 1867, which provide a large enough sample to identify areas in which white refugees received rations.[21]

During the war, the forty-five counties composing the upcountry and mountain regions, and the home counties of the population centers of Savannah, Augusta, Columbus, and Macon, received 52 percent of the aid distributed in fiscal years 1863–64 to 1864–65. Though Cherokee County, Governor Brown's home county, received the largest portion of any county, it was followed by Savannah's Chatham County, Columbus's Muscogee County, Macon's Bibb County, and Augusta's Richmond County. After the war, Freedmen's Bureau ration distribution followed much the same pattern, with one notable exception: Fulton County, home of Atlanta, replaced Cherokee County as the top recipient. This would support the conclusion that the county's large wartime welfare program had been at least partially attributable to Brown's influence. Atlanta's ascendance on the list of postwar aid recipients is likely explained by an influx of refugees, especially after Sherman's army moved through northwestern Georgia. As a growing transportation hub and the city nearest those areas devastated by Sherman's March, Atlanta was a logical destination for destitute people of all races. After Fulton, the counties that received the next largest numbers of rations were, in order, Macon's Bibb County, Augusta's Richmond County, Savannah's Chatham County, and Columbus' Muscogee County. Georgia's major cities continued to function as primary aid distribution centers.[22]

But did early Reconstruction ration distribution follow other patterns established during the war? Yes, as proven by a regional comparison of wartime aid and postwar ration distribution. During the war, a significant portion of Georgia's wartime welfare was distributed to the northern portion of the state—the seventeen counties designated "mountains" and the twenty-four "upcountry" counties—areas that, according to the 1860 census, were majority white. This was not surprising during the war, as whites were the sole intended recipients of wartime aid. What is surprising is that the Freedmen's Bureau's ration distribution followed the same pattern. Though only nine of the seventeen mountain counties and nineteen of the twenty-four upcountry counties were listed as ration distribution stations from 1865 to 1867, the Bureau distributed 574,597.5 rations in those areas—56 percent of Georgia's total rations. This area includes, of course, Atlanta's Fulton County, the top distribution station, but that does not alter the fact that more than half of the Bureau's rations were distributed in 28 of Georgia's 130 counties, and that those counties, without exception, had black populations of less than 42 percent according to the 1860 Census.[23]

Though the 1860 Census provides an understanding of the location of Georgia's slave population, its obvious limitation is its static nature. It cannot provide information on the movement of populations during the war or in the first years of Reconstruction. It cannot tell us if the percentages of black and white populations remained the same in Georgia's counties. But the Freedmen's Bureau's monthly ration reports can shed some light. Since these reports designate the numbers of rations distributed to "freedmen" and "refugees" at every station in the state, the percentages issued to each group identify the areas in which whites, or "refugees," received the most rations.

Not surprisingly, the mountains, the area with the largest 1860 white population, led the way in refugee ration distribution. Of 152,940 rations issued in nine mountain counties, 101,254 (66 percent) went to whites. In the nineteen upcountry counties that had ration distribution centers, 33 percent of the 421,657.5 rations issued went to whites. The percentage of rations distributed to whites dropped precipitously in the ten eastern Black Belt counties, where only 7 percent of the 287,016.5 rations went to whites. The pattern continued in the three (of six) counties in the coastal region that included ration distribution stations, where only 2.5 percent of the 103,630 rations went to whites. Only four of the nineteen counties that composed the western Black Belt had ration distribution centers, but less than 1 percent of the 54,154 rations went to whites. The nineteen counties of the Pine Barrens-Wiregrass region had no ration distribution stations. Though Georgia's population was undoubtedly shifting during the war and after, the racial composition of the different geographical regions of the state did not change significantly. As evidenced by the Bureau's ration reports, in the early years of Reconstruction large white populations were still found in the mountains and upcountry counties while large black populations continued in the eastern and western Black Belts and the coastal region.[24]

The statistics found in the ration reports also confirm that Georgia's Freedmen's Bureau agents, on average, appear to have implemented the Bureau's mandate to assist both blacks and whites. In areas with large white populations, a large percentage of rations were distributed to whites; in areas with large black populations, a large percentage of rations were distributed to blacks. The inclusion of whites in the Bureau's mandate to assist the South's poor was not peripheral; it was clearly part of its mission as described by the second Freedmen's Bureau bill. But the Bureau also was coordinating the distribution of private assistance, often through the very offices of the inferior court judges who had overseen wartime relief. That aspect of its operations was not so clearly defined in any legislation. It evolved from necessity as the demands of the South's poor overwhelmed the Bureau's resources.[25]

The Freedmen's Bureau worked closely with private charitable organizations, primarily based in the North, who solicited funds and donations to aid the South. It was through these organizations that the white poor and freedpeople found access to even greater amounts of aid. Private charitable aid was distributed by a variety of people, including Freedmen's Bureau agents, the ubiquitous county inferior court judges, and local ministers. The Freedmen's Bureau commissioner, General Oliver Otis Howard, played a role in facilitating the fundraising and distribution activities of private charities. An examination of one such agency further clarifies the role of the Bureau in assisting poor whites and freedpeople at a time when the question of assisting white Southerners who had not been loyal to the Union was being debated in Congress and in the nation's newspapers.

One of the earliest public charities founded to assist the South was the New York Ladies' Southern Relief Association (NYLSRA), created in December 1866. A pamphlet by Anne Middleton Holmes, published in 1926 by the Mary Mildred Sullivan Chapter of the United Daughters of the Confederacy (UDC), provides detailed information from the association's founding until its final report in November 1867. The information found in the pamphlet is invaluable to understanding the workings of the association, the needs of Southerners who wrote requesting relief, and the motivations of the women and men who served the association.[26]

The NYLSRA's founder, Mary Mildred Hammond Sullivan, and her husband, Algernon Sydney Sullivan, were prominent in New York society and had numerous ties to the South. He was born in Indiana, moved to New York, and became a celebrated attorney and philanthropist with political connections. She was a Virginia native who, in addition to founding the NYLSRA, also founded the UDC chapter in New York. During the war, Mrs. Sullivan had, with government permission, traveled to Virginia and gained first-hand knowledge of Southern devastation after the war. Her Southern sympathies were well known. Mr. Sullivan was the first president of the New York Southern Society, an organization he founded to meet the needs of New York's expatriate Southerners. With such ties to the South and the Confederacy, and a reputation for philanthropy, the Sullivans' interest in postwar Southern charity is not surprising. According to Holmes's pamphlet, Mrs. Sullivan was "familiar to hundreds of southerners . . . because of her work with the Confederate prisoners during the war." This reputation led to an influx of mail having "the proportions of an avalanche." Her response to these calls for assistance was to found the NYLSRA, and she served as secretary throughout its yearlong existence.[27]

The association's entire slate of officers, executive committee, and managers were women, with one exception: Arthur Leary, who served as treasurer. There were many notable names on the roster, including Mrs. J. I. Roosevelt, president, and executive committee members Mrs. J. C. Frémont, Mrs. Cyrus McCormick, Mrs. G. Ticknor Curtis, Mrs. Egbert Viele, and Mrs. E. W. Stoughton. The list of managers includes such surnames as Van Buren and Vanderbilt. In roughly eleven months, these women raised more than $71,000 in cash, and the association's Brooklyn auxiliary raised more than $12,000 in cash. Additionally, they collected donated goods and "fifty boxes of new and second-hand clothing." All were sent South via a carefully orchestrated disbursement system.[28]

The NYLSRA chose to distribute its aid via "well-known clergymen in the destitute districts at the South." Arthur Leary's importance as treasurer is apparent in the association's system of cash distribution. The procedure was "for the Treasurer of the Association to draw his checks on his bank in New York for an amount designated by the Disbursing Committee, payable in the name of, and only to the order of, the clergyman who was to distribute the funds, and these checks were sent by mail to the persons named therein." The first checks were issued on January 31, 1867, and regular disbursements continued until November 1. A total of $60,634.52 reached the Southern clergy in cash, while roughly $7,000 was used to purchase provisions for distribution and another $3,500 went to miscellaneous expenses.[29]

The association's "Statement of money distributed, with the names and residences of the Clergymen through whom the distribution was made" is as detailed as the name implies and provides an excellent basis for analysis. A chronological list, it includes the name, location, and monetary amount sent to every clergyman. The total sent to Georgia clergy was $11,633.91, or 19 percent of the total cash contribution. The largest single payment was $866.66 to Reverend C. H. Coley of Savannah on April 5, 1867. The smallest payments were $25 each. More than fifty percent of the money sent to Georgia went to clergymen in the major population centers of Savannah, Atlanta, and Augusta. Savannah's portion was by far the largest at $4,126.66, while Atlanta received $1,400 and Augusta received $1,320.00. This is not surprising, as major cities were established aid disbursement locations and were located along transportation routes.[30]

When examined by region, the coast received the largest amount of cash ($4,226.66), but the majority of this went to Savannah. The eastern Black Belt received the second largest ($4,065.00), which included the cities of Augusta and Macon. The upcountry counties, which included the city of Atlanta, received $1,042.25. The western Black Belt and the mountain regions both received $450.00 each, which is a surprisingly small amount considering that the city of Columbus is in the western Black Belt and the destitution of the mountain counties had been publicized even before the war was over. The cash distributions of the NYLSRA deviated from wartime state and Reconstruction Freedmen's Bureau aid patterns. It did not focus its relief efforts on the mountain and upcountry counties, though it did continue to distribute aid through most of the state's major population centers, with the exception of Columbus.[31]

It appears, however, that despite some variation in distribution patterns, the NYLSRA interacted with the Freedmen's Bureau to some degree. On December 8, 1866, General A. McL. Crawford, subassistant commissioner for the Bureau in Charleston, wrote to Mr. E. W. Ayers, who had apparently requested information about the state of affairs there. Crawford's reply was that there were "large numbers of Ladies and children in an utterly destitute condition . . . [who] belong[ed] to the upper classes of society." Their social position led them to feel "great repugnance to making their wants known." Therefore, the general took it upon himself to ask for aid. He requested "supplies of any kind," but specifically requested "dresses, underskirts, stockings, flannels, shawls, in fact any and all articles the ladies can spare, and children's clothing, shoes too, even if partially worn." He asked that the boxes be shipped directly to him. This request for private charity on behalf of formerly wealthy—and at least some presumably Confederate—white women and children provides evidence that some Bureau officers did not restrict themselves to assisting "loyal" refugees and freedpeople.[32]

Most of the forty-eight letters (eight from Georgia) contained in Holmes's pamphlet, however, are from individuals who wrote either to request assistance or thank the association for their aid, and they provide more clues to understanding aid distribution in Georgia in 1867. Two of the Georgia letters came from Mrs. Bachman, a self-described "poor farmer's wife" in Tilton, Whitfield County, in April 1867. The first, dated April 18, is a request for aid for destitute people in Whitfield and Gordon Counties, both in the northwest mountain region on the Tennessee border. She stated that she had "been requested by several persons to apply to your society for aid for the suffering." In describing conditions in the counties, she explained that

> where shall we get bread, is the constant cry. All are willing to work but there is no money. Provisions are not in the county, & if it had not been for the Bureau, "and that in our section did not give any bread," and a little corn from charitable persons in Kentucky, many would have died from starvation ere this. Some poor women have to walk 30 or 40 miles with their infants, some barefoot, to try to get rations, when alas! They have to return faint and weary as they were too late!—all was issued . . . North Georgia is a scene of much suffering, it having been occupied so long by both armies, and the crops proving a failure the past two seasons.

She also offered the names of two men who would be willing to distribute any aid, and three others who would vouch for her statements. Only four days later, on April 22, Mrs. Bachman sent an additional letter because

> since that time others have called on me and begged me to state to your society that this was a class that had not received any aid from any source and without help, many would be obliged to abandon their crops for the want of corn to feed the stock necessary to carry on the work. Many have to depend entirely on grazing, and that the spontaneous growth of the earth, as but few here have yet paid any attention to grasses etc.

She also noted that yet a third county, Murray, was "in as deplorable a condition as the ones [previously] mentioned." She closed the letter by stating that she was "not a person of much notoriety—a plain farmer's wife—but you probably have noticed the reports of Gov. Jenkins and Gen'l Howard, & therefore will not doubt the truth of what I have written." Her final words were a simple plea: "Please answer." According to the distribution records in Holmes's pamphlet, her requests were ineffective. No cash was sent to a representative in any of the three counties Bachman described in her letters, though it is possible that a more distant representative may have answered her pleas.[33]

A very different letter described the plight of Mrs. Joseph Huger, originally of Savannah, who had relocated to Athens during the war. No farmer's wife, Mrs. Huger is described as coming from "one of the oldest families of South Carolina." A description of her family's circumstances was included from M. G. Harison, who made a plea for aid to the association on Mrs. Huger's behalf. Her description of destitution was much different than Mrs. Bachman's. The Huger's property had been worth $200,000 before the war, but she explained that attempting to farm with hired labor had only "created debts, which, increasing at interest, we can perhaps never pay." Her husband was "re-studying the profession of medicine," while two of her four grown sons were employed but "receive only small salaries." One son had given them money, but illness had taken much of it. She noted that "at this moment I do not own $5.00" and that "several times [they had] not had a cent in the house, nor a week's provisions." Her health and four small children prevented her from finding work. One daughter gave dancing lessons and "took in work," and friends had assisted them in times of great need. Additionally, two of her daughters had "been furnished education by the Society of Baltimore." It is not known if the association agreed with Mr. Harison that this family was deserving of aid, but a $100 donation was sent care of Reverend W. H. Henderson in Athens on October 15, though the recipient is not noted.[34]

The other letters from Georgia were not written to request aid, but to acknowledge receipt of donations. M. D. Woode, the minister of a Presbyterian church in Decatur, Dekalb County, wrote to thank the association for a $100 disbursement he received in April 1867. Though the list of recipients is not included, Woode stated that all were "respectable ladies, formerly in independent circumstances & themselves generous to the poor and suffering." He also described conditions in the area. "Our people are suffering for even *bread* in numerous instances. I know of cases,—aged men and women, most respectable people, who know not today where their trembling hands will find tomorrow what they may eat; widows and orphans who are needy, indeed, living off the line of the railroad & unable to come to town for supplies from the hand of charity." Assuring the association that the "benefaction and succour" of the association was "most gratefully received," he closed by stating that "the blessing of those ready to perish is coming upon you."[35]

In a similar letter, J. H. George of La Grange wrote on May 23 offering two examples of the people he had assisted with the association's $100 donation. He "made a contribution to a widow with six children, of $10. who said she never thought to eating meat, that being too great a luxury: she was thankful to get bread once a day. She is trying to support her family by making baskets." Although he did not divulge the amount he gave another widow, he described her family of nine as "all depending upon the exertions of herself and married daughter." And, in the only disclosure of its kind in any of the letters, he noted that "I am among the sufferers, having lost everything, being obliged to take my furniture to buy bread for my family, consisting of eleven children only one of which is old enough to provide for herself. I must avail myself of your kind offer and retain fifty for the use of my family." It is worth noting that no additional funds were sent to Mr. George.[36]

Letters from Augusta and Macon provide even more distribution detail. J. H. Cuthbert wrote on May 27 that he had received $100 on April 9 and distributed it as follows:

A single woman (cripple): $5.00
Poor widow, husband killed in war: 2.50
Family from N. Carolina for bread: 5.00
Old widow lady: 2.50
To woman whose only son crushed to death by car: 10.00
Family half starved: 5.00
Widow whose sons were killed in war: 2.50
Poor old colored man: 1.00
Colored woman with large family: 5.00
Family of women and children, son helpless by illness: 7.00
Women and children (9) very poor: 5.00
Ministers of different denominations in the neighborhood, among the poor: 15.00
Left with minister in Columbus who said that within sound of his bell were a thousand at least, who did not know where their bread was to come from tomorrow: 20.00
Poor woman, single, confined to her room: 5.00
Invalid destitute woman: 2.50
Old woman, very poor: 2.50

E. W. Warren reported a similarly detailed distribution of $100 in Macon on July 20, and noted that "the pressing necessity for contributions from abroad for the poor is rapidly passing away. A gracious Providence has blest us with most fruitful seasons, and the present prospect now gives earnest of a very good provision crop." His distribution actually listed most recipients by name. All were women, and they received between $.50 and $13.50 each. He also noted that he gave 30 cents to "poor child in bread," and $3.80 was expended for "provisions for poor children." Additionally, he sent $5.00 to "poor widows and orphans" in Rome and $15.00 to "poor widows and orphans" in Marietta.[37]

Despite the clues they offer, the letters sent to the NYLSRA also complicate our understanding of aid distribution in Georgia. The letter from Augusta notes that funds sent there were actually distributed in Columbus, on the opposite side of the state. The letter from Macon, in central Georgia, discloses that some of the funds there went to Rome and Marietta, both in the northern part of the state. And apparently some requests for aid were unanswered for unknown reasons, though there is the suggestion that the NYLSRA preferred assisting "ladies" of "good families." Of course the NYLSRA was not the only organiza-tion of its type. Though organized slightly later, the Southern Famine Relief Commission, founded by prominent men in New York, provided even more aid than the ladies' organization, and there are scattered references in both organizations' records to similar organizations based in California, Kentucky, Massachusetts, and Ohio.

A letter published in the March 12, 1867 edition of the Brooklyn *Daily Union* likely spurred what would become a very public debate over the role of such organizations, and especially the gender of their members. Signed by "Inkgall of Andersonville," the author rejects all charitable aid to the South and refers to any attempt to do so as "an idle folly originating in the brains of a few impractical women who have no knowledge, or care for, the world about them." He continues, and asks, "Upon what line in God's revealed will or what principle in morals must these women, who are dying for something to do, take to relieving the other and remote end of the line of miserable consequences of the war?" His words for Southern women were no kinder. "A she clay-eater of the Carolinas, or a sand-hiller of Alabama, with but one garment to her body, and that a cotton frock, would elevate her nasal protuberance to its utmost aspiring flexibility at her sister of Brooklyn Heights, although the hand that holds the proffered loaf were covered with [j]ewels. The loaf might be taken but the hand would not be grasped." A response, signed "E. B.," followed on March 14. "I know very little of the Ladies' Association to which he refers; but I do know that the Southern Famine Relief Commission, of which Mr. James M. Brown, 61 Wall Street, is the Treasurer, and which was organized at the Cooper Institute meeting of January 25, *did not* originate with the ladies, whether practical or 'impractical.'" "Inkgall" was unusually vehement in his thrashing of charity for the South, but his letter indicates the very public debate that surrounded the issue.[38]

The question of how best to relieve the suffering there was not only being posed in the nation's newspapers; it was also being posed in Congress. The issue of loyalty was central to the congressional debate. By 1867, General Howard's role as commissioner of the Freedmen's Bureau made him an expert on the condition of the South. On March 9, Howard testified before the Senate Judiciary Committee, offering statistical evidence of the potential starvation in the South. His testimony concerned a joint resolution then in the Senate (HR 16), which proposed to appropriate an additional $1 million "for the relief of the destitute in the southern and south-western states." It directed the Secretary of War to "issue supplies of food sufficient to prevent starvation and extreme want among all classes of the people . . . where a failure of the crops and other causes have occasioned wide-spread destitution." The disbursement would be supervised by Howard and carried out through the officers and agents of the Freedmen's Bureau. Howard had written a letter the day before his testimony that offered estimates of what was needed in the South to relieve "thirty-two thousand six hundred and sixty-two whites, and twenty-four thousand two hundred and thirty-eight colored people, making in all fifty-six thousand nine hundred who will need food from some source before the next crop can relieve them." Rations for these people would total 1,707,000 per month and, as the famine was expected to continue for five months, the aggregate number would reach 8,535,000 rations. At a cost of $.25 per ration, his estimated cost was $2,183,750. After subtracting $625,000 that was already appropriated, Howard would need an additional $1,508,750. Again, he was careful to distinguish between those persons who fell under the Bureau's jurisdiction in its original mandate and those who would be relieved by this new appropriation: "The present appropriation is ample, provided the issues be confined to the classes named in the Freedmen's Bureau act; but the additional sum named will be required should the issue be extended as contemplated in the foregoing estimate." Included in the letter was a "tabular statement" of numbers of destitute people in all eleven former Confederate states.[39]

In the end, there would be no $1 million appropriation. The joint resolution met fierce debate in both the Senate and the House, and portions of those debates were reprinted in newspapers and were the subject of editorials and letters from citizens. In the House debates, Benjamin F. Butler, Republican of Massachusetts, offered an argument that would be echoed by others in newspapers. He offered a substitute for the bill that would use the funds "in relieving the widows and children of Union soldiers starved to death in the Rebel prisons at Andersonville, Salisbury, Libby, Millen, and Bell Isle." Similarly, William Williams, Republican of Indiana, argued that he could not tax the "one-armed and limbless soldiers of the Republic" to support the "women and children who with malignant hatred spat upon our soldiers wounded and weary in their march to the sea." He lodged his "protest . . . in behalf of the widows and orphans of the men who were starved to death at Andersonville."[40] This debate was reprinted in the New York *Tribune* on March 14, and discussion of the bill itself is found in the pages of the Albany *Express, Commercial Advertiser,* the *Evangelist,* the *Express,* the Brooklyn *Daily Union,* the New York *Sunday Mercury,* the New York *Herald,* and the *New York Times.*[41]

Supporters of the appropriation met these charges, in Congress and in the public debate, with varied responses. Congressman Benjamin Boyer, Democrat of Pennsylvania, based his argument upon a British example: "Twenty years ago, the Parliament of Great Britain voted $50,000,000 for the relief of the starving population of Ireland. . . . And shall it be said that the great Republic of America is less merciful to her perishing children than was that nation we have been accustomed to denounce as the tyrant of the Indies and the oppressor of Ireland?" Another reference to Ireland was found in a New York *Express* editorial "Famine at Home," printed February 20:

> We have been sending money to Crete and elsewhere, and years ago sent ships laden with bread to feed the poor of Ireland. It was said in Congress at that time, by an old Southern Senator, that he could not comprehend such a thing as a famine abroad, as he had never seen anything but its very opposite at home. The scene now changes. Famine stares us in the face, and among a people who are our brothers and sisters, or if this is not admitted, then at least our life-long countrymen.

The editorial closed with an appeal commonly found in arguments supporting the appropriation: "Christian charity and common humanity demands that, as far as in us lies, there shall be an end of this deplorable suffering and sorrow." An editorial in the same paper offered a more matter-of-fact argument on March 14: "We have appropriated millions to killing the people of the South in lawful battle. Can't we conscientiously and consistently do something to feed them?"

On March 22, 1867, the House passed a greatly altered joint resolution that allowed the Freedmen's Bureau to use its "unexpended" funds to assist "destitute or helpless persons." Bureau funds were officially available to anyone Bureau officers deemed "deserving." As described on March 21 by William Lawrence, Republican Representative of Ohio, the bill would

> direct the officers of the Freedmen's Bureau to expend the $2,100,000 appropriated for the refugees and freedmen for the benefit of all people of all

classes, loyal and disloyal, in the rebel States who may be in a destitute condition, thus diverting in part this money from the purpose for which it was
appropriated, and taking it in part from the suffering classes for whom it
was designed.

Before the initial Bureau legislation was passed, loyal whites were included in
the "Freedmen's" Bureau. Two years later, loyalty was no longer an issue. The
Bureau of Refugees, Freedmen, and Abandoned Lands could, with congressional sanction, assist anyone deemed "destitute or helpless."[42]

The defeat of the $1 million appropriation bill provided private charitable
organizations added incentive to press forward with their campaigns; their
efforts would be needed because there would be no forthcoming additional federal aid. They continued to advertise the plight of destitute Southerners in
Northern papers. In the March 25 edition of the *New York Times*, a plea for aid
noted that

> the sickening revelations of our correspondents concerning the difficulties,
> embarrassments, privations and sufferings of the women and children who
> are reduced from wealth or ease to want and poverty are fully corroborated
> by private letters in the City by reports of O. O. Howard and the Freedmen's
> Bureau agents. These of themselves constitute a claim, as absolute as the
> right of a child, upon the generosity of the more prosperous sections of the
> country.

On March 25, the New York *Herald* noted that

> the condition of the Southerners is such that Congress found it necessary to
> make some provision for them, though appropriations are rarely made and
> scarcely within the legitimate legislation of that body. But this is a case that
> could not be overlooked. Consequently an act has been passed to afford
> relief from the Freedmen's Bureau fund. Major General Howard . . . says
> "suffering is great and on the increase" in the South, and that his means for
> relieving it, with this fresh draft upon his resources, will not last beyond next
> December. He urges that additional aid be given by voluntary contribution.

Without the additional appropriation, and faced with assisting all "destitute
or helpless" Southerners, Howard needed the associations' assistance, and they
needed his name to give credence to their descriptions of destitution. The
arrangement proved fruitful for starving Southerners.[43]

Georgia Governor Charles Jones Jenkins was concerned with another class of Georgians, and he, too, made a public appeal concerning the destitution that found its way into Northern papers. As described above, the state government made appropriations for the purchase of corn totaling $300,000 in 1866. It also appropriated an additional $20,000 to pay for freight on the supplies coming from the "benevolent societies." There was a restriction, however, that "all supplies on which the State shall pay the freight, shall be distributed under the same provisions as are contained in the resolution of last session." Presumably, this meant that supplies could only be issued to people whom county agents could confirm were unable to work. Even in the midst of such a crisis, the state legislature still emphasized only offering aid to the most destitute. No matter the amount, Jenkins anticipated further suffering and deemed it necessary to issue "an address" to the people of Georgia in May. The *New York Times* printed both an interpretation of the address and a verbatim transcript; both further our understanding of how several sources of aid worked together in Georgia.[44]

Jenkins sought to explain the distribution restrictions on all sources of aid for destitute Georgians. Aid from the state as well as "noble charitable associations of the more fortunate States" were restricted to the poor without property as "it would be a violation of the trust to distribute them among property holders, in aid of agriculture." Those propertied individuals were Jenkins's primary concern. They, too, were starving in some areas. He described the situation this way. "All that the State Government and the United States Government and the ever memorable charities of benevolent individuals have done will fall short of full relief." The solution he offered was simple: Those with land should plant "cereals and other articles of food." Jenkins "fear[ed] there [was] too much land devoted to cotton, cotton, cotton." As had happened during the war, some Georgia farmers were opting for cash crops, much to the detriment of the state. Jenkins urged them to change tactics as "a dictate of patriotism." If state, federal, or private charity was unavailable to the landed poor, this was the only way for true recovery.[45]

No thorough examination of private charitable relief during Reconstruction exists. However, Alice B. Keith of Meredith College in Raleigh, North Carolina, writing for the sociology journal *Social Forces* in 1939, shed some light on the complexity of the aid process. Keith described how "the story of the sympathy and the assistance given to the white people of the South by the people of the North during [Reconstruction] is not often heard." Focusing her work exclusively on North Carolina, she found newspapers and magazines the best sources of information. Those sources continue to hold great potential to further our understanding of the evolution of Southern welfare from the Civil War through Reconstruction and beyond.[46]

The story of welfare aid in the South during the Civil War and Reconstruction cannot be fully understood by studying organizations in isolation. Georgia and other Confederate states established welfare programs during the war. After the war, the federal government as well as private organizations provided additional aid as Georgia continued to provide its own relief. When we study the relationships between these organizations—when we recognize the continuities between wartime and postwar programs—we begin to approach a more thorough understanding of America's nineteenth-century welfare history. The reasons this aspect of American history has remained obscure are puzzling; it is, after all, a compelling story. But in 1937 Keith provided what is perhaps the most eloquent answer to that question: "Man is not given to advertising his indigencies nor to eulogizing his creditors."[47]

7

Racial Identity and Reconstruction: New Orleans's Free People of Color and the Dilemma of Emancipation

JUSTIN A. NYSTROM

In his famous 1911 memoir of New Orleans' Creoles of color, Rodolphe Desdunes commented acidly on those members of the Afro-Creole community who had "disowned and rejected not only their fellow blacks but even their own kin" by crossing the color line after the Civil War. In "passing" for white, charged Desdunes, these individuals lived "in a moral depression that seems to represent the last degree of impotence." A generation later, historian and fellow Creole of color Charles Barthelemy Roussève observed with only slightly less disdain that during Reconstruction some fair-skinned free people of color had crossed the color line to avoid losing status.

> To accomplish this purpose they resorted to various subterfuges. Pages are missing, it is said, in the notarial acts in the office of the recorder of conveyances at New Orleans. . . . Yet it is definitely reported that in certain cases these records were destroyed to obliterate all legal evidence of Negro blood in persons (in some cases of high rank in the city) who were then transferring into the white group.

Racial passing clearly distressed Roussève and Desdunes as well as countless other Creoles of color, and it is easy to understand why. Writing in the early decades of the twentieth century, these men could reflect back with regret on the battles for racial equality fought and lost during the era of Reconstruction and Redemption.[1]

As the historian David Rankin has noted, it is indeed "difficult" to quantify how many of the city's free people of color who were capable of doing so actually elected to cross the color line. Roussève suggested optimistically that "most free people of color chose more nobly to remain with the underprivileged Negro population and to work loyally toward the improvement of its status." The evidence presented in this essay, however, suggests that racial passing in its many forms was not at all unusual among those who had once belonged to New Orleans's free colored community. While many individuals who crossed the color line undoubtedly harbored misgivings, cross it they did.[2]

If those who crossed the color line had hoped to form a new (presumably white) identity, it is important to define first what that identity entailed. The recent outpouring of scholarship on the subject of whiteness has made it possible to define what the term *white* meant to those engaged in racial passing. Since the early 1990s, historians and sociologists have put forward thought-provoking arguments about the formation of white identity, particularly among ethnically or economically marginalized segments of the American people whose forbearers hailed from continental Europe. In short, many ethnic groups sought not just visual identification with whiteness but a broader cultural embrace of what Toni Morrison has called the "master narrative." Viewing racial passing in both regional and historical contexts—the South in the late nineteenth and early twentieth centuries—the main focus of this study must lie with the denial of African ancestry. While the literature on whiteness and white identity formation has illuminated the plight of various marginalized groups who occupied a racial borderland in the era of American apartheid, to Desdunes—and certainly other turn-of-the-century New Orleanians of both African and European ancestry—passing was less about becoming "white" as defined by modern identity studies and much more about severing one's ties to their African past.[3]

For the Francophone culture of Afro-Creole New Orleans, passing involved important cultural dimensions. It entailed not only the rejection of African heritage, but a full embrace of Gallic, and at times elements of Spanish or Germanic ancestry along with retention of Roman Catholicism and often the French language. Indeed, in passing, Afro-Creoles rejected only a *portion* of their past. Even Desdunes's *Nos Hommes* is testimony to the fierce pride Afro-Creoles took in cultural accomplishments that were decidedly Gallic in origin. This strategy also made perfect sense when one considers it in the context of whiteness studies, for the white ancestors that many Afro-Creoles could claim did indeed belong to the "master narrative." If one agrees with the widely accepted notion that race is more social construction than biological fact, it is possible that elite Afro-Creoles had already formed a partially white identity, a fact that would have made the self-denial of African blood less philosophically problematic.

Invariably, the question of racial passing has led to a debate over the political actions and moral rectitude of New Orleans's free people of color during the antebellum, Civil War, and Reconstruction eras. Desdunes and Roussève portrayed elite, fair-skinned Creoles of color who had crossed the color line as either self-serving or at the very least weak in their devotion to the cause of racial equality. In a similar vein, and marshalling a large amount of statistical evidence to support his point, Rankin detected the presence of a "pigmentoc-racy," or racially conscious caste-system, within New Orleans's Afro-Creole community. According to Rankin, the most elite Creoles of color found greater identification with white New Orleanians than they did with their darker-skinned associates. Other historians downplay such divisions, depicting instead the solidarity and racial activism of the city's Afro-Creoles. The influential work of Joseph Logsdon and Caryn Cossé Bell posits that economics and not skin shade was what most frequently divided the city's free blacks. Writing on the topic of racial passing among Louisiana Creoles of color, Shirley Thompson probably most accurately defined the issue as being "at the nexus of an official history of celebratory achievements and an unofficial but collective memory of painful and problematic episodes."[4]

Instead of engaging in a debate over the morality of passing, however, this essay focuses on the motivations of Afro-Creoles who crossed the color line in the decades that followed emancipation. The moral component of racial pass-ing is neither here nor there, for as the evidence presented suggests, within the same person could lay both the desire to champion racial equality *and* to pass for white. Those who sought to cross the color line often lived public lives that stood at odds with their private aims. For this reason, this essay dwells on the utterly human dilemma faced by fair-skinned free people of color who, beset by familial and societal pressures, redefined their self-identity to combat the perils of an uncertain future.

There were many different paths taken by Creoles of color who passed for white. A few crossed the color line so dramatically that it could have come straight out of a Charles Chesnutt novel. Discarding their black identity at New Orleans's city limits, these people began life anew in a distant town where they might prosper from the opportunities that white America could bestow upon one of its own. Far more common, however, were those who stayed in place or made incremental moves, dancing around the margins of the color line, employing subtlety and long-term tactics in their precarious balancing act between New Orleans's black and white worlds. For most of these individuals, passing was incremental in action and multigenerational in outlook. It was an insurance policy against an unknown and unknowable future—one in which the acknowledgment of African ancestry might forever foreclose on their (and, more important, their children's) aspirations for full citizenship. Sometimes this approach worked; other times it did not.

While the evidence presented here supplies a relatively concrete picture of the methods used by mixed-race people to cross the color line, the same evi-dence delivers far less certainty about the motivations behind such actions. For those who lived in the immediate post-emancipation period, the preservation of status—both social and economic—must have played a significant role in the decision to pass. More difficult to quantify, and without doubt more controversial, is the question of whether free, fair-skinned, mixed-race people ever fully conceptualized themselves as black in the same fashion freedpeople had in the post-emancipation environment. Yet, much as the work of David Rankin suggested twenty-five years ago, some of the cases presented here reveal that some members of this caste identified strongly with the white, Francophone aspect of their heritage.

In antebellum New Orleans, free people of color occupied the middle stratum of the city's three-tiered racial caste system. While they did not fully enjoy the benefits of white society, neither did they suffer the degradation of slavery. Although this dynamic had taken root in other parts of the American South, it was in New Orleans, with its large and prosperous segment of free people of color, that the middle caste came to play such a crucial role in the larger social pyramid. About half of the city's people who possessed some amount African blood were free, and their presence made a vital contribution to the overall dialogue of race in New Orleans. Despite the value they brought to the community, free people of color were second-class citizens with circumscribed legal rights and absolutely no political voice. The arrival of the Americans to New Orleans in 1803 signaled the beginning of a gradual tightening of manumission laws aimed at stemming the growth of this community. The free colored population not only represented a dangerous contradiction to the philosophical underpinnings of race-based slavery, but by mingling and at times cohabitating with slaves, they blurred the boundary separating the free people and slaves. As in many other slave states, Nat Turner's 1831 slave rebellion in Southampton County, Virginia, spurred Louisiana's legislature to adopt increasingly restrictive laws governing the movement of the free people of color. Along with New Orleans's reconsolidation in 1852 (the city had been separated in three municipalities) came repressive laws that required free blacks constantly to prove publicly their free status. Some Afro-Creoles with sufficient financial means chose to leave such indignity behind forever, fleeing to France, Haiti, Mexico, or other countries where their status as free men went unchallenged. In 1857 Louisiana outlawed manumission entirely. [5]

The fall of New Orleans to Union forces on April 26, 1862, contained an element of double-edged irony for the city's free people of color. On one hand, the invasion rendered null and void the increasingly oppressive race-based laws passed by the slaveholding regime over the previous decade, and it renewed hopes for full citizenship. On the other hand, the upheaval and the tangible prospect of Confederate defeat also brought with it significant disadvantages, not the least of which was the ultimate liberation of slaves held in bondage by free people of color. Of more pressing consequence for a larger portion of free blacks, however, were the dramatic demographic changes taking place. During the war, the arrival of freedmen from the plantation regions around New Orleans began a trend that resulted in a fast increase in the city's black population. According to John Blassingame, during the 1860s African Americans jumped from roughly 12 to 25 percent of the Crescent City's population. Not surprisingly, many whites in New Orleans were not happy to see this change— but they were not alone. Some of the city's free Afro-Creoles also expressed displeasure with these newcomers, noting that most came with no prospects and lived by the largesse of charitable operations. Furthermore, unlike the Afro-Creoles, they were Anglo, Protestant, and largely uneducated.[6]

Many elite Afro-Creoles did not immediately react to emancipation by trying to pass for white. Instead, from the start of the Union occupation through the Radical ascendancy in 1868, this caste played an active and conspicuous role in fighting the war and in shaping the racial politics of Reconstruction. Although a substantial number of the city's prominent free blacks had organized under the banner of the Confederacy's Louisiana Native Guards, this gesture yielded little tangible support to the slaveholders' cause. While a few wealthy free blacks may have felt some loyalty to Louisiana and its slaveholding regime, many others who joined the Native Guards did not share this view, joining only out of a sense of community pride, obligation, and perhaps even fear. The arrival of Union forces in 1862 led to a rapid reorientation of loyalties and priorities. As a result, many of these same men, along with other free blacks, quickly pledged their loyalty to the Union and served in the federal army despite suffering great prejudice. The French-speaking Afro-Creole elite viewed itself as the natural social and political leadership of all blacks in Louisiana, and this attitude drew criticism from non-Creole blacks. At the same time, this same caste worked diligently to achieve racial equality for all blacks. Even at Reconstruction's bitter end, and indeed well beyond it, elite Creoles of color and their descendants continued their activist politics.[7]

Despite their notable activism, however, the more imperiling dimensions of emancipation clearly affected the racial self-identification of those mixed-race New Orleanians who had always been free. The elimination of laws that governed the movement and behavior of the city's free blacks also removed key obstacles to crossing the color line. While the removal of such restrictions did not immediately grant the free black population anything approaching citizenship, combined with the upheaval of war and occupation and the suspension of normal civil government, conditions were far more conducive to the forging of new identities than they had been in the antebellum era.

While the case studies presented in this essay do not form a statistically complete picture of racial passing in New Orleans between the fall of the city to the Union in 1862 and the turn of the twentieth century, they do illustrate the different mindsets of mixed-race individuals who struggled with their own self-identity in the wake of emancipation. One common factor shared by all of them, however, was a sense of vulnerability. Whether they bravely faced such adversity or succumbed quietly to its influence, those who had once belonged to the city's free colored population recognized that they had much to lose in the post-emancipation ebb toward a strictly bichromatic racial paradigm.

Documenting the lives of such individuals would have been much more difficult only ten years ago. Census records, so crucial in tracing an individual's trajectory over a broad expanse of time, have been made far more accessible by online genealogical tools. More important, such electronic search engines linked to federal census data have allowed for a fairly accurate reconstruction of an individual's chronology, telling us where and when those who sought to secure a white identity may have first taken action. The ability to digitally cross-reference the indexes of multiple states has also allowed, for the first time, tracing of the diaspora of those who in crossing state lines seem to have also crossed the color line. Likewise, the compilation of birth, marriage, and death records into electronic databases by both private enterprises and state agencies has facilitated such research. When used in conjunction with more traditional sources, such as court testimony and government documents, one can successfully uncover the paper trail of passing. Unlike the statistical analysis of Rankin, this article does not examine a broad range of individuals across a brief time span. Rather, it considers the multigenerational legacy of emancipation and Reconstruction on free people of color by tracing family units over a span of forty to eighty years, beginning in the antebellum period and lasting until the era of Jim Crow. The family case studies presented here underscore the importance that heritage, blood ties, time, and geography had on the decision to pass.[8]

The uppermost echelon of New Orleans's elite, free colored population belonged to an even more finite subset of individuals who had always lived their lives on the margin of both free black and white societies. Their light skin tone, Francophone cultural outlook, and wealth defined their social station and informed their worldview. Family ties and family interests were of paramount importance.

The dealings of the extended Esnard and Raynal families between 1850 and 1920 illustrate the presence of a multigenerational vision for preserving privilege. This vision included not only the drive for financial success but also a flexible attitude toward racial self-identification. Joseph Raynal and John Benjamin Esnard may have become publicly involved with the racially charged arena of Reconstruction-era politics, but behind the scenes both the Esnards and the Raynals placed an insurance policy on their families' futures by moving the next generation into the orbit of white society.

Joseph Raynal moved within the most elite circles of antebellum New Orleans's Afro-Creole society, and as such had much to lose in the upheaval of war and Reconstruction. Unlike the wealthy Saint-Domingue black planters who had fled the island to Louisiana during the American period, the mixed-race branch of the Raynal clan could trace its ancestry back to the Spanish colonial period, and perhaps even earlier. Although the records that speak to the matter are incomplete, Auguste Raynal, and later his son Joseph, described themselves as "planters" and as such might have been slaveholders. Without question, the family was one of means. By the time a census official came to their home in the Fifth Ward in 1860, Joseph Raynal's mother Suzane had amassed a personal estate that she valued at $15,000. It is therefore not surprising that like many other free men of color of his class, Joseph's sixty-five-year-old father volunteered to serve as a sergeant in the First Native Guards once the state seceded.[9]

As with millions of Americans of his generation, the Civil War profoundly altered the course of Joseph Raynal's life. After New Orleans fell to the Union in the spring of 1862, he received and briefly held a commission as a captain in the Sixth Louisiana Colored Infantry. After the war, he doubly identified himself with the Republican regime of Governor Henry Clay Warmoth, serving as both a colonel in the state militia and as a commissioner for the metropolitan police board. The "Metropolitans" served as the police force in New Orleans and in surrounding parishes. This heavily armed force also functioned as the Republican Party's paramilitary wing and served as probably the single most conspicuous reminder to all of the new political order. In accepting these prominent positions, Joseph Raynal had seemingly set out on a bold course as both a Republican and as a man of color.[10]

The 1860s had also proven eventful in Joseph Raynal's private life. Sometime during or immediately following the war, he married Marie Rose Olympe Esnard, a young woman from a large and prosperous free black family. In December 1867, they welcomed their first and only child into the world. Their daughter, Marie Ella Raynal, had neither a white parent nor a white grandparent, but that did not stop them from procuring a birth certificate that identified their child as white. In February 1870, Olympe Raynal died at just twenty-seven years of age, making Joseph Raynal a widower and leaving behind a young daughter who would one day seek passage into white society.[11]

Joseph Raynal's brother-in-law, John Benjamin Esnard, was of the same generation and as such faced many of the same heady decisions as war engulfed his homeland. Like Raynal, both of Esnard's parents were people of color. His father, Siméon Esnard, was born in Cuba in 1805 and was likely part of the large migration of free blacks whose odyssey had begun with the revolution in Saint-Domingue. By the late antebellum period, Siméon Esnard was the head of a large family and operated his own shoe store in New Orleans's First Ward. As with Raynal, John Benjamin Esnard joined the Union Army after the occupation. After the war he came home and became a representative from St. Mary Parish, a sugar planting region in Louisiana's Acadiana region. There he remained until 1868, when violent elements inimical to his career as a Republican forced Esnard's retreat to New Orleans. The ensuing investigation by the House of Representatives into that year's violent election, however, revealed that Esnard was quick to differentiate himself from the freedmen. Under oath, Esnard declared that he was "of French descent" and that he could not tell whether he were "a white man or a colored man."[12]

On June 6, 1874, Esnard married Josephine Florentine Krach, an unremarkable detail in of itself except for the fact that his bride was a white woman. Esnard's marrying across the color line seems to answer the question of his self-identity, but the reality was far more complex. The details of this union offer a rare glimpse into the sort of fluid racial identities that occupied the margins of Southern urban life in the mid-nineteenth century. Indeed, although white, Josephine Krach was no stranger to interracial marriage—her stepfather was a Creole of color. She was most likely born in the Alsatian region of France to a Louisiana man and a French woman. Josephine's father died a few years after her birth, however, and her mother sailed to Louisiana, presumably leaving Josephine and another daughter in the care of relatives in France. There she grew into womanhood, learning French as her only tongue. Meanwhile in New Orleans, Josephine's mother met and in 1858 married an Afro-Creole man by the name of Pierre Dejean. Although antimiscegenation laws forbade such unions, the couple had their marriage solemnized in a ceremony at the city's Holy Trinity Catholic Church, an institution that served primarily the German community in the Bywater area of town. Mme Dejean probably first became acquainted with Esnard during Reconstruction. A keen businesswoman, she had amassed a considerable amount of capital that she sought to invest in both real estate and commerce. Impressed with Esnard's financial skills, Dejean placed a large portion of her fortune under his management. Like the servant in the parable of the talents to whom much was given, Esnard had proven himself worthy of greater rewards. When Dejean's daughters came to New Orleans from France in 1871, Esnard began to court his future wife.[13]

Even before the Republican Party lost control of Louisiana, the Esnards and Raynals had already begun their journey across the color line. With the Compromise of 1877, these efforts intensified, but with mixed results. Marie Ella

Raynal, the daughter that Joseph and Olympe Raynal had registered as white in 1867, married in New Orleans a presumably white man from Michigan named August Summers. Unlike her parents, however, Olympe Raynal Summers encountered difficulty in registering her firstborn as white. Instead, Louis Aristide Summers received a "C" denoting race on his January 1895 birth certificate. Perhaps unsure himself, the recorder a year later merely left blank the space denoting race on younger brother Charles Henry's birth certificate. Possibly because of this setback, the Summers family changed Louis Aristide's name to August Jr.—the name that he would successfully carry not only into adulthood but also across the color line.[14]

Despite his brief but conspicuous stance as a Louisiana "black" Republican, John Benjamin Esnard and his descendants seem to have passed into white society more easily than his older sister's grandchildren. Undoubtedly his marrying a white woman facilitated such a transition. At the same time, crossing the racial line created a division of color within the Esnard clan. By the turn of the twentieth century not only did Esnard and his six children live as white, so did the family of his business partner and younger brother Siméon Jr. Yet, unlike John Benjamin, Siméon had not married a white woman, nor had he ever registered his children as white at their birth. In 1910 Siméon found his family recorded as "mulatto" on the census. His claim that his parents had been born in France—a false claim—went recorded by the census official but did not change the clerk's verdict on racial classification. The white classification of John Benjamin and his family went unchallenged that year, but his brother's experience might have served as a cautionary tale. Perhaps such close geographic proximity with next of kin who were clearly too dark-skinned to pass for white posed too great a risk to his children's futures. Whatever the inspiration may have been, by 1920 John Benjamin Esnard and his family had moved to Los Angeles, where they would remain forever white. To underscore the point, just as his brother Siméon had done in New Orleans a decade earlier, John Benjamin Esnard informed census officials in 1920 that both of his parents had been born in France.[15]

One might easily dismiss the experiences of the Esnards and Raynals by suggesting that they were mere bit players in the grander scheme of Reconstruction-era politics, but even far more politically prominent men faced a similar dilemma of self-identity when confronted with the hard facts of a rapidly changing racial environment. The son of a wealthy white Frenchman and a free woman of color, Charles St. Albin Sauvinet came from a similar background as Joseph Raynal and John Benjamin Esnard. Thirty years old on the eve of the Civil War, he was a man of considerable substance and cultural refinement, and by all accounts so fair-skinned that anyone who did not know otherwise would have described him as white.[16]

Like many other men of his generation and caste, Sauvinet recognized the possibilities that accompanied the regime change in 1862. Although he had served as an officer in the Confederate Native Guards, he quickly tendered his services as interpreter to General Benjamin Butler after the fall of New Orleans to the Union. From that moment, Sauvinet's political star was on the rise. When Butler formed the first black regiments from Louisiana, Sauvinet received a captaincy. What was unusual about his service in the war was that, unlike most of his fellow elite Afro-Creole officers who nearly to a man resigned their commissions in protest against ill-treatment, Sauvinet managed not only to serve out the entire war as an officer but even received a promotion to regimental quartermaster. When the war was over, he returned to New Orleans and served as the head cashier for the Freedman's Bank, won a seat as a city alderman, and in the election of 1870 attained the office of Orleans Parish Civil Sheriff.[17]

An event took place in January 1871, however, that would publicly challenge all of Sauvinet's assumptions about his own racial identity. He and two white men had gone to the Bank Coffeehouse on Royal Street in the French Quarter to discuss business over a midday drink. It was a place that Sauvinet knew well. Only a few weeks earlier he had gone to the Bank in his official capacity as Civil Sheriff of Orleans Parish to discuss rent payments with the bar's proprietor, Joseph Walker. As the two sipped cognac and wrapped up business in Walker's upstairs office, the barman paused and asked if Sauvinet might be able to do a favor for him. Walker had been told that Sauvinet was a colored man and that he would appreciate his no longer coming to drink in the bar because it would hurt his business. Sauvinet responded that he "had always drank in all houses and that it was too late now to go back." Now, as he sat at the table with his two drinking companions, it became clear to Sauvinet that the Bank Coffeehouse meant to deny him service. He refused to "cause a fuss" at the time, but a few days later he filed suit against Joseph Walker for being in violation of Louisiana's civil rights law of 1870.[18]

The trial that ensued revealed the confusion and contradictions that resided in a man like Sauvinet. One might interpret his actions in court as those of a man crusading for racial justice, but one could also just as easily see the deep personal outrage felt by a man who sensed the imperiled nature of his own privileged status. By his own admission, Sauvinet had "been in the habit of going to all the bar-rooms [in New Orleans] for the last twenty-five years" and had visited the Bank "times and times over," even drinking "on special invitation of the proprietor at his own bar, once if not more." Ironically, new laws intended to protect the rights of black people now threatened Sauvinet's ability to move freely within white society. When the defense's counsel asked point-blank if he were a colored man, Sauvinet responded, "whether I am or not I do not know myself—but I am, and was legally for this reason; that prior to the war and before the Congress of the United States had passed laws granting and giving citizenship to men born on the soil whether colored or not, you had always refused me." Others had defined him as black, according to Sauvinet. Such a temporizing reply only encouraged further cross-examination. When asked, "Have you not stated that you are as much a white man and of white blood as any man in the community?" Sauvinet retorted, "I have stated so.—Ain't I?"[19]

While one might not be able to completely define Sauvinet's own sense of self-identity from his court testimony, other evidence suggests that he wished his children to be considered white. When registering his three children with the recorder of births in Union-occupied New Orleans, Sauvinet made sure to secure a white racial categorization for each of them. These three children would not see their parents grow into old age. Sauvinet's wife, Angela Chesse, died in 1868. A decade later, distraught over his youngest son's terminal case of yellow fever, Charles Sauvinet committed suicide in the front bedroom of his family's home. When seventeen-year-old Charles Silas Sauvinet died two weeks later, the medical examiner produced a death certificate that bears a "C" denoting race. Eldest son James Nelson Sauvinet, however, had by 1890 passed into white society—first as a traveling musician in Texas and later as a music instructor in Memphis. A daughter born in New Orleans in 1867 later married one of the thousands of Italian immigrants who came to the city in the latter part of the nineteenth century. Whatever struggles Italians may have encountered in being accepted into white society in turn-of-the century New Orleans, their children all passed successfully into white society, perhaps never knowing the entirety of their own heritage.[20]

The decision to become involved in politics made by some free men of color could also jeopardize the aspirations of family members who sought to cross the color line. One particularly unusual case involves the siblings of a prominent black Republican politician named William H. Vigers. The offspring of a wealthy slaveholding white commission merchant who had emigrated from Denmark and a mixed-race mother, the Vigers children clearly enjoyed the privileges granted to free blacks of high birth in antebellum New Orleans. While such evidence might not fully indicate the community's perception of them, like many other members of their racial caste and economic status, antebellum city directories failed to add the denotation "f.m.c." or "f.w.c." behind their names. Coming into their majority before the start of the Civil War, both

William and older sister Caroline had begun work as school teachers while the remaining younger siblings—ranging in age from eighteen to four—lived at home with their recently widowed mother. Positioned as they were, it is not difficult to imagine the family quietly passing into white society amid the upheaval of war, occupation, and Reconstruction. When the war was over, however, eldest son William saw an opportunity to become something more than merely the privileged mixed-race offspring of a white man.[21]

William Vigers had made himself every bit as conspicuous during Reconstruction as Charles Sauvinet, and this fact foreclosed on his siblings' efforts to quietly cross the color line. As early as 1865, Vigers had become involved in Louisiana's universal suffrage movement, and he eventually served as the chief clerk of the Louisiana House of Representatives under the Republican regime and as the recording secretary of his party long after the Compromise of 1877. Vigers's post-Reconstruction employment in the Custom House on Canal Street also identified him squarely with Republican politics. Yet his public life contrasted sharply with the actions of his siblings, who came of age during the turbulent years of Reconstruction. Immediately after the war, city directories failed to identify Caroline or William Vigers as colored, but as William became more readily associated with the Republican regime, his racial classification as a colored man appeared in print beside his name. Caroline and her other younger stayed out of politics, and as a consequence, temporarily avoided a public designation as black. Although Caroline had taught at a segregated school for colored children, she and her other siblings continued to engage in the precarious exercise of straddling the color line. In 1890 William and Caroline, along with younger siblings Charles and John, all lived under the same roof at 206 Conti Street, where all but William incongruously passed. Twenty years later, and a decade after William's death, Caroline, now retired; John, a city policeman; and a niece were all recorded in the census as white. How successfully they had crossed the color line remains unclear, however, as each received a "colored" classification on their death certificate.[22]

For mixed-race people who had earnestly championed the cause of racial equality after the war, probably one of the most frustrating legacies of the period was the brutal lesson of failure that seemed to inform the decisions of the next generation. While the Esnards, Raynals, and Sauvinets quietly laid the groundwork for their children's racial passing—and perhaps themselves questioned the extent of their own common cause with the freedpeople—others fully embraced the goals of equality only to find their aspirations crushed by an inherently racist society. It must have been doubly bitter when even the most steadfast supporters of civil rights found that their children rejected the burdens associated with being an agent of social change.

Peter Joseph had given over the better part of his adult life to Republican causes. After serving as a private in the United States Colored Troops during the Civil War, Joseph returned to his native New Orleans, where he became an officer in the state militia as well as a captain in the Republican administration's Metropolitan Police. In March 1874, he successfully brought suit against the owner of a popular theater known as the Academy of Music for violation of state civil rights statues after the establishment's doorman had refused his admittance to a show. In September of that same year, he quite literally laid his life on the line for his party when the "Metropolitans" engaged in a bloody battle with the White League in the streets of New Orleans. Undeterred by increasing violence against authority figures, Joseph continued in the service of the police until spring 1877, when the "Redeemers" (conservative Democrats, also known as "Bourbon Democrats") put this force and most other remaining state-run apparatuses devised by the Republicans out of business.[23]

Not long after the Democratic Party regained control of Louisiana in 1877, Peter Joseph managed to parlay his connections within the Metropolitan Police and Republican Party into a federal patronage job at the U.S. Custom House. By 1880 he had been promoted to captain of night inspectors and worked alongside other prominent Afro-Creole political activists like William Vigers, Paul Trevigne, and Arnold Bertonneau, some of whom later engineered the landmark segregation case *Plessy v. Ferguson*. Yet by the 1890s, even a dedicated individual like Joseph had seen enough. In the three decades since the end of the Civil War, he had witnessed the slow erosion of the rights he had fought so tirelessly to secure. Perhaps for this reason he moved his family to Denver, Colorado, and returned to his prewar trade of bricklayer. Although the Joseph family did not cross the color line in the West, the lesson of postbellum defeat was not lost on his eldest surviving son, the ironically named Sumner Geddes Joseph. When he walked into the Kenosha County, Wisconsin, courthouse to register for the draft in 1918, Sumner Joseph declared himself a white man.[24]

Emancipation and its attendant social change presented yet another set of challenges to free women of color. While freedom represented a giant step forward for thousands of enslaved black women, it also posed an enormous threat to the caste-conscious distinction held by black women who had always been free. No matter whether one belonged to the elite or more middling classes of New Orleans's free women of color, one's status as a lady, and not merely a woman, was something to be guarded jealously. For poorer free women of color in particular, emancipation swept away the one characteristic that had elevated their status under the antebellum regime. For this group to preserve their social status, marrying a man of means or somehow attaching one's self to white society proved to be attractive options. Only through the acquisition of wealth or a white identity could a woman of color hope to preserve, let alone improve, her position in society. Conversely, life as a single black female with few private resources in post-emancipation New Orleans could lead directly to a life of drudgery in a low-status, low-wage job.

The social upheaval that accompanied emancipation must have been particularly upsetting for financially marginal single young women of color, such as Louise Drouet and her older half-sister Sylvanie Morgan. Eighteen and twenty-one years of age, respectively, at the end of the war, they were not old enough to have established themselves in society during the antebellum regime. Now they had to do so in a social terrain that was much different than the one in which they had been born. Their mother, herself a fair-skinned, mixed-race free woman of color, had been a *placée*—a professional mistress—to their respective fathers, who had both been white men. Their mother's abrupt death in 1858 had left the girls under the care of extended family in the city's free colored community.

Louise Drouet had one advantage that her half-sister did not. Unlike Samuel Morgan, who had disappeared from New Orleans not long after the birth of his daughter Sylvanie, Louis Flourange Drouet had taken a particularly active interest in the life of Louise. By 1861 Louis Drouet had instructed his daughter's mixed-race relatives to enroll Louise at the St. Augustine Convent, a boarding school operated for young women of color on St. Claude Avenue in the historically Afro-Creole neighborhood of Tréme. As societal norms collapsed all around the convent's walls, Louise Drouet remained within, acquiring both education and moral instruction befitting a young lady.[25]

A chance event in the fall of 1865 opened the door to a kind of social mobility that Louise Drouet might have only dreamed about. Her wealthy, bachelor father collapsed in his garden one afternoon and had to be carried inside by a very concerned tenant, a German immigrant named Schwartz. When he awoke later that evening, Drouet openly acknowledged the poorly kept secret of his daughter's existence to Schwartz. "Why do you not take her with you?" quizzed Schwartz, to which Drouet replied, "Perhaps it would be better for her to remain in the convent." The tenant was incredulous and urged Drouet to bring his daughter to live at the house. After all, he pointed out, Drouet was terribly ill and needed someone to take care of him. "I'm afraid people will talk about that," fretted the sickly old Creole. "Let people talk," Schwartz fired back. Two weeks later, eighteen-year-old Louise came to live with her father.[26]

Over the next seven years, Louise grew into womanhood under the roof of her father and lived the life of a young, *white* lady. With a few notable exceptions, Louis kept little counsel with the rest of his vast extended family, and Louise became the central focus of his attention. If those around him did not suspect the fair-skinned Louise to be the illegitimate issue of his union with a free woman of color, her father did nothing to disabuse such notions. Indeed, this aging white Creole seemed to be complicit in his daughter's subtle bid to cross the color line. When a census official came to their home in 1870, he undoubtedly believed that a young woman with such a father and an Irish domestic servant was white.[27]

Sylvanie Morgan also seemed to enjoy her half-sister's proximity to white society. She became a frequent visitor to the Drouet house while Louise lived there, even after Morgan's marriage to an Afro-Creole man named Eugene Duvernay. Indeed, she also seems to have had aspirations of crossing the color line—if not for herself, certainly for her children. Like other mixed-race people of fair complexion, Sylvanie Duvernay acquired birth certificates declaring her children as white, starting with her firstborn in 1868. Her half-sister's public association with white society was but one additional step toward her own family's incremental change in racial identity.[28]

Louise Drouet's plans of living the life of a white lady came to an abrupt end with her father's death in the fall of 1872. The few white relatives who had met Louise suddenly became far less cordial to their first cousin and moved swiftly to cut her out of any possible inheritance from her father. When Louise sued the estate for alimony, one of her primary claims outside of paternity was that she had been brought up as a lady and was of "too delicate a constitution" to perform the sort of menial work that her cousins now suggested she undertake to support herself. Although she had won her case at the lower court, an appeal to the state supreme court reversed the decision, and Louise was left penniless. In 1878 she married a politically active Afro-Creole man named E. P. Ducloslange, but none of their children ever passed into white society. Her children worked as seamstresses once they reached their late teens. It was an occupation that Louise's white relatives had suggested she take up to support herself instead of praying for support from her father's estate.[29]

In contrast, at least one of Sylvanie Duvernay's children managed to cross over into white society, though with great travail. Eugene Duvernay, born in 1869, moved in 1900 to Mobile, Alabama, where he married a mixed-race woman. Both successfully passed for white on the 1910 census, but by 1920 their racial classification had reverted back to mulatto. It required a move to Cleveland, Ohio, sometime before 1930 to finally make the transition permanent. As an illustration of how multigenerational in outlook racial passing could be, according to a living ancestor who had always defined herself as white, her grandfather, the son of Eugene Duvernay, had told his children that he had been adopted.[30]

The presence of complicit relatives, both black and white, could make a great deal of difference as to whether a mixed-race individual successfully passed for white. Such was the case with the ironically named Blanche Penn. She was born in January 1859 to Josephine Keating, a seventeen-year-old free woman of color, and Davidson Bradfute Penn, the son of one of the city's wealthiest white men. By the time of the 1860 census, Blanche and her mother had gone to live with the extended mixed-race Keating family. The coming decade, however, brought great change to all parties. Shortly after Blanche's birth, Penn married a white woman, then served for the duration of the Civil War as an officer in the Confederate Army. After the war he became involved in Reconstruction-era fusion politics and eventually became the favored candidate for governor under the banner of Liberal Republicanism. Things did not turn out so well for Josephine Keating, who died in 1868 at the age of twenty-five. Blanche went to live at her Aunt Olivia's mixed-race boarding house. Perhaps confused by the unusual array of white and mulatto boarders—not to mention that Blanche carried her father's family name—the census worker recorded the eleven-year-old as white. Indeed, on the actual census record, she had been grouped with white boarders with whom she had no blood relationship. The entire household—black as well as white—must have known about her mixed-race background. As Virginia Domínguez points out, "Many colored Creoles protect others who are trying to pass, to the point of feigning ignorance of certain branches of their families." Eight years later, Blanche Penn gave birth to a son, Alfred, the issue of her marriage to a white man named George Wright. A young widow by the time of the 1880 census, Blanche and her son had successfully passed into white society.[31]

Taken collectively, these case studies help to form some preliminary assumptions about members of New Orleans' free black community who crossed the color line in the decades following emancipation. Antebellum blood ties with white New Orleanians undoubtedly influenced not only their decision to pass, but also informed their self-perception as being something other than strictly white or black. Indeed, for much of the free colored population of New Orleans, the construction of their unique racial identity had been generations in the making by the time emancipation threw the entire racial order into disarray. Ill at ease with the uncertainty of the postbellum racial dynamic, some members of the free black community sought to preserve their family's status by redefining themselves as exclusively white.

Perhaps the most revealing aspect of these case studies, however, is that racial passing appears to have been less often an individual enterprise than it was a collection of incremental deeds that spanned multiple generations. While some did not cross the color line, this did not prevent them from enabling the eventual passing of their children. Indeed, with many of these cases, the journey across the color line began with a birth certificate declaring a mixed-race child as white. Those who crossed the color line also seem to have uniformly done so with the complicity of either white or black relations. The act of passing, at least until a new identity had been secured, was simply too complicated for most individuals to accomplish alone. Conversely, uncooperative black or white relatives could, and did, prevent a mixed-race person from passing.

Until a more systematic analysis that encompasses a broader cross-section of the free black population of New Orleans is conducted, many questions about identity and racial passing within this culture will remain unanswered. Nevertheless, as this essay has shown, the journey across the color line was far more complex and time-consuming—though no less dramatic—than the fictitious tales of passing written by turn-of-the-century novelists. Moreover, these tales of individuals struggling with their own identity testify to the long-lasting effects of war, emancipation, and Reconstruction on America's racial consciousness.

8

"My Children on the Field": Wade Hampton, Biography, and the Roots of the Lost Cause

Rod Andrew Jr.

My son, my son!"[1] It was October 27, 1864, along the Boydton Plank Road near Petersburg, Virginia. Confederate cavalry commander Wade Hampton III was leading a successful counterattack against a federal cavalry probe of the far right of the Confederate lines. Choked with emotion and crying out in despair, Hampton cradled the body of his twenty-year-old son, Preston, in his arms. As Hampton's troopers charged ahead and away from him, Hampton sat weeping with his son's head in his lap. Preston had been shot in the groin a moment before, while shouting encouragement to the men around him. Now he was barely conscious. Hampton whispered something in his son's ear. A look of recognition crossed the young man's face; then his eyes rolled back into his head, and he died. Meanwhile, Hampton's oldest son, Wade Hampton IV, had been shot in the back while dismounting to tend to Preston. As young Wade was helped away, Hampton rode beside the makeshift ambulance that carried Preston's body to the rear. Hampton stayed abreast of the cart for a short time before suddenly announcing, "Too late, doctor!" and riding away to continue directing the battle. Outwardly stoic, Hampton's heart was broken. He carried the memory of that devastating day, and of many others, to his deathbed.[2]

Biographical details such as these are essential to a complete understanding of the nature and roots of Lost Cause mythology in the post–Civil War South. Hampton is well known, of course, as the aristocratic and talented cavalry officer who became commander of Robert E. Lee's cavalry corps after the death of "Jeb" Stuart. He is even better recognized as the South Carolina Democrat who led the ouster of the Republican state government during the 1876 campaign as many of his followers initiated the infamous 1876 "Red Shirt" campaign of intimidation against "carpetbaggers" and black voters, ultimately unseating the Republican state government. Later, as a "Redeemer" or "Bourbon Democrat" he served two terms in the U.S. Senate until ousted in 1890 by the forces of racial extremist and self-proclaimed agrarian reformer Benjamin R. Tillman. He is far less recognized as the doting family man who lost a brother and a son on the battlefield, as the proud South Carolinian who unsuccessfully defended his hometown of Columbia against William T. Sherman, or as the man who lost his home and ancestral mansion to Union "arsonists," only to be blamed for the fire in Sherman's official reports. Historians gloss over the implications of the fact that Hampton, a wealthy planter who cherished his reputation as a man of his word, faced the humiliation of bankruptcy in 1868 followed by charges in Republican newspapers that he was a "moral bankrupt" and swindler as well.[3]

This essay cannot be a complete biography of Wade Hampton's life, nor even of his postwar political career. It aims to show, however, that the biographical perspective is essential to a complete understanding of the nature and roots of Lost Cause mythology in the postwar South. It also argues that the roots of the Lost Cause can be found in the experiences of the war years. The Lost Cause legend was not simply a postbellum reaction to racial and social change, a deliberately dishonest means to reestablish white supremacy. For Wade Hampton, one of the major spokesmen of Lost Cause mythology in the late-nineteenth century, the Lost Cause represented a persistent, deeply felt need to find validation and meaning in all that he had suffered and in all that his beloved had given for the Confederate cause. The experience of war and tragedy was so deeply engrained in Hampton's mind that it influenced his understanding of postwar political and social issues. It was not always the other way around. Historians remember Hampton as a soldier and politician, but rarely as a distraught father holding his dying son. Unless we remember that part of his life as well, we may never truly understand his postwar political assumptions or his motivations in espousing the Lost Cause.[4]

The Hampton family was one of the wealthiest in the South in the early to mid-nineteenth century. Hampton, his father, and his brothers owned thousands of slaves and hundreds of thousands of acres around Columbia, South Carolina, and in the rich cotton lands along the banks of the Mississippi River in Mississippi. In 1838, at the age of twenty, Hampton married Margaret Preston and began expanding the holdings given to him by his father. Over a period of ten years, Margaret bore him five children: Wade, Preston, Sally, John, and Harriett. For fourteen years, Hampton mostly avoided public affairs and apparently enjoyed the life of an aristocratic planter, sportsman, and family man. In 1852, however, tragedy struck. Margaret died at the age of thirty-four, and eighteen months later little Harriett died. Hampton was devastated, though he seems initially to have tried to delay facing the tragedy squarely or grieving fully. More than three years later, as if just confronting a recent disaster, he finally poured out his heart to his younger sister, Mary Fisher Hampton: "Again I hear the voice & see the smile that once were dearer to me than all else on earth. . . . Every scene, every emotion, every memory wrings my heart & I can scarce realize that the weak & broken down man, who mourns here over blasted hopes, & lost happiness, is the same, who years ago, had every dream of joy fulfilled."[5]

Perhaps to take his mind away from his sorrow, Hampton began to play a serious role in state politics. He served several terms in the South Carolina General Assembly, where he was an advocate of public schools and a state lunatic asylum and an opponent of the efforts of many South Carolina politicians who advocated secession. One pet project of South Carolina secessionists designed to widen the rift between North and South was asserting South Carolina's right to reopen the Atlantic slave trade, banned by federal law since 1808. Hampton forcefully opposed such a move as inhumane to Africans and as a violation of the compact made between the founding fathers in the Constitution.[6]

Hampton, who would become one of the loudest voices after the war asserting that the South had fought nobly for the principle of self-government, always believed that a state had the constitutional right to secede from the Union, though he did not think it wise or necessary. Nor was he a proslavery ideologue. As South Carolina moved steadily toward secession during the 1850s, Hampton cooperated with the state's dwindling number of conditional Unionists. After the election of Abraham Lincoln, however, as "Fire-Eater" sentiment engulfed the state, Hampton quietly announced that he would support the state's bid for independence, though he clearly hoped there would be no war. After the shelling of Fort Sumter and Lincoln's announcement that he would raise troops to suppress the "rebellion" of Southern states, Hampton no longer hesitated. He raised his own troops, the Hampton Legion, paid for much of its equipment himself, and was appointed a colonel in the Confederate Army.

Hampton fought as an infantry officer in the first year of the war. He was wounded while playing an important role at the battle of Manassas in July 1861 and wounded again while leading a charge at Seven Pines in 1862. Shortly after returning to duty, he took over a brigade in Jeb Stuart's cavalry division. Though his personality clashed with Stuart, he rapidly built his reputation as an officer of quiet competence, hard fighting, and grim determination.

Hampton was wounded twice at Gettysburg. When he had fully recuperated, he returned to the army as a division commander. After Stuart's death in May 1864, Hampton became the senior cavalry officer in Lee's army, and Lee formally made him the cavalry corps commander in August. As Lee and Ulysses S. Grant sparred in eastern Virginia and conducted siege warfare around Richmond and Petersburg during the rest of 1864, Hampton's cavalry performed well and Hampton earned Lee's full confidence. At the end of 1864, however, William T. Sherman's Union army was in Savannah, Georgia, and poised to strike South Carolina. Hampton asked to be reassigned so that he could help defend his home state.

These bare outlines of Hampton's military career through January 1865, while familiar enough to Civil War military historians, do not include several incidents that were vitally important to his postwar assumptions, beliefs, and outlook. During the war, Hampton saw countless friends, relatives, and comrades killed or maimed. Every death made him increasingly bitter toward what he saw as the "Yankees'" perverse determination to fight and kill to deny Southern men the right to run their own affairs. As early as May 1862, Hampton confessed to his sister, "When I think how much our people are suffering my heart burns with indignation & I have the most vindictive feelings towards the whole Yankee race." Hampton longed and prayed for peace, confessing that it was

> a grievous thing to see our best young men falling daily before these vile wretches who are desolating our country. . . . We gain successes, but after every fight comes to me an ominous paper, marked *"Casualties"* & in this I often find long lists of "killed" and "wounded." Sad, sad words which carry anguish to so many hearts. And we have scarcely time to bury the dead, ere we press on in the same deadly strife.[7]

Yet Hampton was fiercely proud of his men, including his two sons, Wade and Preston, who served on his staff. He was apt to write of them in the lofty, romantic prose commonly associated with Lost Cause rhetoric after the war. After the battle of Seven Pines, in which eighteen-year-old Preston dismounted, seized the guidon of the Hampton Legion, and led a charge, Hampton wrote, "They both behave nobly & I may well be proud of them. . . . Two braver & nobler boys never lived & I pray God to spare them to me." He also praised his troops. After Seven Pines, in which the Legion suffered grievous casualties, he wrote, "Well does the Legion deserve its praise, for it fought as only the best troops can fight. Poor fellows! They are down to a handful now. Soon there will be, I fear, none of them left."[8]

Hampton eulogized or praised all his dead soldiers. Rather than let the losses discourage him from continuing the fight, however, the opposite occurred. Each death required a statement of the dead man's gallantry, courage, and patriotism. Those words, in turn, made it impossible to give up fighting; to quit would render their sacrifices useless and make a mockery of their virtues, as if those virtues were not important after all. That was a possibility that Hampton refused to accept. Thus a grim equation helped determine why Hampton and so many Confederates continued to fight into the spring of 1865: the more that good men died, the more quitting became a moral impossibility.

It was an even greater moral impossibility when the dead were beloved family members. One of those dear ones was Hampton's younger brother Frank. Frank served the first part of the war in South Carolina so he could be near his terminally ill wife, Sally. When she died in September 1862, Hampton arranged for Frank to be transferred to Virginia, where he served as the lieutenant colonel in one of Hampton's cavalry regiments, the Second South Carolina. Hampton grieved for Frank, but thought that service on the Virginia front would "distract his mind from his sorrow."[9] But Frank was mortally wounded on June 9, 1863, while leading a countercharge of thirty-six cavalrymen against a federal attack at Brandy Station, Virginia. He was taken to a nearby house, where he asked repeatedly that couriers be sent to summon Hampton. Hampton did not come immediately. The Confederates had been surprised at Brandy Station, and now that the battle was over Hampton wanted to make sure that all his pickets were posted properly. Around dusk he finally arrived at the house where his brother lay. "Am I in time?" he asked Captain William Bachman. "No, General," replied Bachman, "You are too late." Frank had died moments before. Hampton's voice "twitched with emotion," and he eventually spoke in a choked voice. "Bachman, you know that nothing but the sternest duty could have detained me." With tears streaming down his cheeks, Hampton strode into the room where his dead brother had waited for him.[10]

The death of Hampton's son a year and a half later was even more devastating. For nearly three weeks after Preston's death, Hampton could not bear to write home about it. On November 14, he finally confessed to his sister that "God only knows how much I need comfort, for my heart is sorely bruised. It cries out for my beautiful boy, all the time, & I cannot become resigned to his loss."[11]

The death of the handsome, popular Preston (as well as Hampton's reaction on the battlefield) left a profound impression on Hampton's contemporaries. Every one of the many eyewitnesses to this poignant scene commented on Hampton's act of turning away from his son and back to the battle. Each one also commented on Hampton's profound grief. One veteran wrote that he learned "here my first great lesson of life from General Hampton, which is self-control." Hampton, he remembered, "dismounted and kissed his brave boy, wiped a tear from his eye, remounted and went on giving orders as though nothing had happened. How can we control others if we do not control ourselves?"[12] Captain Zimmerman Davis reported that Hampton spent the next few hours until dark directing the fire of one of his horse artillery batteries. The battery was dueling against a federal battery, and Hampton gave specific orders on fuse length and tube elevation with each round. After dark, the broken-hearted Hampton relinquished command to a subordinate so that he could spend the night beside the body of his dead son.[13]

Back home in Columbia, the Hamptons' friend Mary Boykin Chesnut marveled, "The agony of that day—and the anxiety and the duties of the battle-field—it is all more than a mere man can bear. . . . Until night he did not know young Wade's fate. He might be dead, too."[14] Varina Davis, wife of the Confederate president, wrote, "I know nothing in history more touching than Wade Hampton's situation at the supremest moment of his misery—when he sent one son to save the other and saw them both fall."[15] Meanwhile, Hampton's friends and relatives did all they could to comfort him. His daughter Sally and his second wife, Mary, Preston's stepmother, journeyed to Virginia to be with him. Hampton's sisters wrote to console him, as did Confederate President Jefferson Davis and Generals Braxton Bragg and Robert E. Lee. He sent his son's body home to Columbia with his slave and body servant Kit Goodwyn, instructing that Preston be buried in Trinity Episcopal churchyard next to his mother Margaret, Hampton's first wife. Here others gave what support they could. Dr. Robert Wilson Gibbes of Columbia pronounced that there was not enough space to bury Preston next to his mother, so another grave was dug nearby. Jacob Motte Alston, a wealthy planter and neighbor, intervened at the last moment, asserting that there was enough room after all. As Preston's coffin was lowered next to that of his mother, the other grave several yards away yawned open, haunting those attending the burial.[16] Mary Boykin Chesnut wrote her diary that "[I]t was sad enough, God knows, without that evil augury—or omen."[17] Hampton told his sister Mary Fisher to thank Jacob Alston "for his great and thoughtful kindness. I will not forget any kind acts performed for my boy."[18]

The eulogization of the handsome and popular Preston Hampton began almost immediately. One critical element of Lost Cause mythology that was so influential in the postwar South was the glorification of the valor of Confederate soldiers. Modern historians have been increasingly aware of how the mythology of the Lost Cause could serve to justify the restoration of white supremacy in the postwar South. There has been a growing tendency, in fact, to assume that Southerners promulgated the Lost Cause in a conscious, deliberate effort to rewrite the history of the war in order to reestablish white supremacy during and after Reconstruction. David Blight, for example, has correctly emphasized how important the memorialization of valor became in postwar collective memory, but has called the Lost Cause a "quest for thought control," and Catherine Clinton has described it as conscious "reconfiguring facts to conform to political agendas." By remembering the war as a heroic struggle, the argument goes, white Americans, especially Southerners, succeeded in rede-fining its meaning as a test of virtue and valor rather than one for racial justice and the meaning of citizenship.[19]

For Wade Hampton, the eulogization of the Confederate dead was initially, at least, a grieving father attempting to come to grips with his son's death. Hampton's first epitaph for Preston was properly restrained and suitable for an official military report. In his official report to Robert E. Lee on November 21, 1864, he wrote only, "In this charge, whilst leading the men & cheering them by his words & example, Lieut. Thomas Preston Hampton A.D.C. fell mortally wounded, & Lt. Wade Hampton who was acting on my staff received a severe wound."[20] In 1867, however, Hampton wrote far more, privately, to Lee. Lee was attempting to write a history of the Army of Northern Virginia and had sent out a circular to his former officers asking for their reminiscences and records. Appearing immediately after Hampton's copy of his 1864 report of the Boydton Road fight was a passage in which Hampton elaborated at length on his son's death. One cannot help suspecting that race and postwar politics were the last things on Hampton's mind when he wrote Lee that Preston deserved more than "the mere mention of his death" in an official military record. "But even after the lapse of three years," he wrote, "I fear to trust myself to speak of that brave boy, who had stood [by] my side in more than seventy fights . . . lest my words of praise should be attributed more to the fond partiality of the parent, than to the just commendation of the commander."[21] After several more sentences of praise, Hampton got to the point: Preston's military record provided "not only his noblest eulogy, but my only consolation for his loss."[22] This one phrase by Hampton explains much of the postwar rhetoric that aimed to immortalize Confederate valor. Hundreds of thousands of Southerners were still deeply grieving the loss of loved ones. Reflecting on such themes as wasted sacrifices and misguided causes could bring no comfort. To most, denying that the cause had been noble, or stating that their sacrifice had no moral value would be akin to spitting in their loved ones' graves. Only praise for the virtues of the dead and their cause could bring "consolation."[23]

Hampton described his son in the language of nineteenth-century chivalry. Preston, he remembered, was gentle and kind with others, except when he was fiercely courageous in combat. He had "an almost womanly tenderness . . . with his friends," but his courage on the battlefield was conspicuous even among an army of men in which courage was "the rule." "[H]e fell at last," Hampton concluded, "as he was leading his way to Victory, dying as he had lived—brave, true, and thank God, free."[24]

Another reason for the South's glorification of its dead was the romantic bent of the age itself. Nineteenth-century Americans looked for heroes, particu-larly tragic ones who blended the virtues of duty, courage, and tenderness. They

tended to honor those heroes with poetry and flowery prose.[25] As a Carolina
newspaper wrote of Preston Hampton, his short life was "crowned with deeds
of chivalry," and he "died as a hero would wish to die—on the field of glory,
with the Christian's God for his friend and the last sound in his ear the triumphant sound of victory." The article continued:

> And how can man die better
> Than facing fearful odds
> For the ashes of his fathers
> [A]nd the temples of his God?[26]

These sentimental lines appeared not at the height of the Reconstruction or
Redeemer periods, but in an 1864 obituary, within weeks of Preston's demise.

The deaths of Preston, Frank, and countless others, along with acts of valor
on the battlefield, were just a few of the events that influenced Wade Hampton's
version of the Lost Cause. Hampton's understanding of the Confederate experience was important, in part, because he was such an influential spokesman for
the Lost Cause after the war. In 1869 he became president of the Survivors'
Association of the State of South Carolina, a group dedicated to helping Confederate widows, orphans, disabled veterans, and "the vindication of the cause
and the memory of . . . former comrades."[27] In the 1870s he also played a prominent role in the Southern Historical Society, an organization that published
Southern Magazine and was dedicated to telling the Confederate side of the war.
When the Hampton Legion Survivors held a reunion in 1875, Hampton was
unanimously elected chair of the meeting. In all of these organizations, and on
many other public occasions, Southerners called on Hampton to speak on the
legacy of the Confederate dead. As a state governor from 1877 to 1879 and U.S.
Senator from 1879 to 1891, Hampton had many other opportunities to lecture
his audience on the valor and virtues of Confederate soldiers. During the 1890s,
as he became politically irrelevant both within and beyond the borders of South
Carolina, he ironically became more of a cultural icon of the Lost Cause. He
was the star attraction and a keynote speaker at a reunion of the United Confederate Veterans (UCV) in Charleston in 1899, at a convention of the South
Carolina chapter of the UCV in Columbia in 1901, and numerous other veterans' reunions. He was elected a departmental commander of the UCV in 1900
at the age of eighty-two, long after he could achieve any political gain from his
heartfelt eulogies of Confederate veterans. The grim, stoic Hampton shed tears
on more than one of these occasions when South Carolina veterans filed by to
shake the hand of their old commander.[28]

A close reading of Hampton's speeches reveals that there were four essential elements to his understanding of the Confederate past. To a great extent, Hampton's experiences in a brutal, heartbreaking war influenced all of them. The first was the emphatic insistence that the Southern cause had not been wrong, but right. Hampton was well aware that slavery was the catalyst for most of the sectional tension preceding the war. To him, though, the central issue was whether states had the right to secede and form their own governments. Hampton had not wanted his state to secede, but was adamant that it had the right to do so. Still, one must emphasize that Hampton's conviction that the South was right came mostly from wartime experiences, not abstract constitutional thought. From his point of view, plenty had happened in the war to prove that the Yankees were the bad guys—Southern soldiers were desperately and nobly defending their homes against barbaric invaders. Hampton had played a key role in stopping Dahlgren's Raid in the winter of 1864, which most Southerners believed had the express purpose of assassinating President Davis and his cabinet, freeing prisoners of war from Libby Prison, and burning the city of Richmond. Even before that, Hampton was deeply distressed over the suffering that the North's invasion had brought to Southern civilians and soldiers. As he participated in the defense of Richmond in 1862, Hampton hoped that a sound whipping of the federals would bring an end to the war. As much as he desired peace, however, he did not want it to come "until we have carried the war into Yankeedom. *They* should be made to feel the horrors of war & then perhaps peace would be lasting."[29]

In late 1864, Southerners' worst fears came true when Sherman's federal army blazed a wide path of destruction and plunder from Atlanta to Savannah, and then turned north to wreak devastation on South Carolina. Hampton and many other Southerners considered Sherman a war criminal. Hampton was placed in charge of a disorganized and outnumbered collection of Confederate units in February 1865, just in time to make an unsuccessful defense of his hometown of Columbia. When the city suffered a disastrous fire on the day of the Confederate evacuation and the federal occupation, Hampton and most other Columbians were sure that Sherman had either ordered the city's destruction or was guilty of criminal neglect in making no effort to stop it. The unquestioned fact that Sherman's men had burned more than a dozen other South Carolina towns made his assertions that he was not to blame for Columbia's fire farcical to most Carolinians. As Sherman's men continued to plunder civilians and burn houses, Hampton warned Sherman that he had ordered his troopers "to shoot down all of your men who are caught burning houses."[30] The issue was personal to Hampton; he knew that Sherman's men had deliberately fired his own house and another in which his sisters, nephews, and nieces lived. The crowning insult was when Sherman claimed that Hampton was responsible for Columbia's fire by ordering that cotton be burned in the streets before the Confederate evacuation. (Hampton actually countermanded an earlier order from his superior, General P. G. T. Beauregard, to burn the cotton, but the latest order may not have reached some of his troops in time.) Many pamphlets and books have been written on this controversy, but what is undeniable is that Hampton was outraged by Sherman's charge and believed it to be a deliberate slander. Sherman's accusation enraged Hampton more than any other event in his life. As late as the 1880s he wrote articles trying to prove that Sherman was a liar. As far as Hampton was concerned, the war proved that Yankees stole, Yankees burned, and Yankees lied.[31]

In contrast, Hampton witnessed countless heroic deeds by his own men, from Manassas to Bentonville. What was even more common was intense suffering from hunger, disease, and the elements. Hampton had to be aware of the problem of desertion and occasional cowardice in the Confederate ranks, but even during the war he tended to be far more impressed by the courage, sacrifice, and endurance of his men. If Hampton was guilty after the war of ignoring Confederate desertion and cowardice and praising heroism and perseverance, it was a habit that he formed as early as the day after Manassas. For men like Hampton, who had seen the mud and the blood, the desperate charges and mangled corpses, the hardy few who refused to desert even when they could, valor and sacrifice would always be at the heart of their Civil War experience. They had experienced enough of Southern valor and Yankee cruelty to assert the existence of both without engaging in deliberate "thought control." And even if they ignored other verses in America's Civil War saga, it was the images of burning homes, pillaging foragers, and dying loved ones that would remain seared in their memories and define the entire conflict for them.

A second fundamental element of Hampton's Lost Cause was that white Southerners must accept the verdict of arms and abide by their paroles, but must never renounce the cause of their dead heroes. In 1870, for example, Hampton spoke at a monument dedication to the dead of the Charleston Light Infantry, a volunteer company from Charleston that had been part of the Hampton Legion. Like much Lost Cause rhetoric, his speech combined Christian motifs, political advice, and personal and collective mourning. The cause that is right, he asserted, does not always triumph. "The religion of the Savior does not promise that virtue will always triumph on this earth, but does promise trials and afflictions for His followers." In this case, Hampton asserted, the bad guys had won; sometimes God delivered the righteous into the hands of oppressors. Hampton also had political advice: his audience must carefully observe the terms dictated by the sword and accepted by the South, but never must they fail to honor the sacrifice of those who had died to defend "those inalienable rights established by our fathers."[32] Hampton then looked out over his audience of veterans, widows, and bereaved parents—and got to the heart of the matter. The speaker and his audience knew they shared a common bond, their personal grief.

> I know that many a parent in our mourning land, as he looks through eyes blinded by tears . . . at some loved name, perhaps on that tomb, or on some stone that covers all that was mortal of one who was his pride, his hope, his darling, cries out in the pathetic language wring from a bereaved father's heart: "O my son Absalom! My son, my son Absalom! Would God I had died for thee! O Absalom, my son, my son!" I understand, I can feel—I have felt all this. But still . . . knowing how and for what our sons died, cannot . . . the father . . . say proudly, as he stands by the grave of his son:
>
> "Why then God's soldier be he!
> Had I as many sons as I have hairs,
> I would not wish for them a fairer death."[33]

For Hampton and many others, the Lost Cause message transcended politics and even race—it was personal.

Lest one suspect that Hampton's real message was a hidden political one understood only in the context of Reconstruction, he was still saying the same things twenty-five years later. In 1895, he lectured the Sons of Confederate Veterans and Daughters of the Confederacy in Charleston, imploring Southerners to recognize the "integrity of the Union, and all the obligations we assumed when we laid down our arms." But would the survivors "who followed the Starry Cross on hundred[s] of battle-fields ever consent to denounce their dead comrades as traitors?" Would the sons of veterans or women of the South ever accept the notion that their fathers were "rebels" in an unjust cause? "These things can never be," Hampton thundered, "as long as patriotism, honor, virtue, and . . . courage, are respected."[34] Hampton uttered these words long after there was any serious challenge to the supremacy of white Democrats in South Carolina.

Sometimes Hampton's Lost Cause did serve his politics, and those are the times that indicate the third theme of his Lost Cause message: Just as the Civil War defined and revealed the true character of men, war records served as a reliable guide to who could and could not be trusted with leadership after the war. Hampton made this argument in an open letter to President Andrew Johnson in 1866. Why could the North not understand, he demanded, the

South entrusting leadership to men who had proven their virtues on the battle-field? Hampton, of course, was a conservative who wished to see elite whites such as he in charge. He was less enthusiastic about black men serving in office, but recognized by 1866 that educated and property-holding blacks would have to be given a role in the Democratic Party and in government. As governor, he appointed approximately 120 black men to office.[35] Black participation in government may have been a necessary evil to Hampton, but black judges and legislators were preferable in his mind to former Union officers and to South Carolinians who had proven disloyal to their state during the war or immedi-ately afterward. Could Carolinians really trust Southern white men who took the "loyalty oath," swearing that they had never supported the Confederacy? Such men, he thought, were either cowards in wartime or traitors willing to renounce their former comrades and the South's noble dead for personal gain. Explaining to a fellow veteran and political associate, James Conner, in 1867 why he favored suffrage for educated or property-holding blacks, Hampton asserted, "I am willing to send negroes to Congress. . . . and I should rather trust them than renegades [Southern traitors] or Yankees."[36]

Often, especially after Reconstruction, Hampton's rhetoric included the theme of reconciliation with the North. In a 1879 speech in the U.S. Senate, Hampton defended the presence of ex-Confederate officers in Congress. He argued that sectional reconciliation would be far more advanced if the North-ern states had sent more of their own veterans to Congress, for "the men who served in the opposing armies. . . . learned in a common school how to respect our enemies; we learned that personal courage and honor and truth were better guarantees of patriotism than constitutional learning or eloquent speech."[37] Former Union officers who had fought honorably (in Hampton's eyes, this did not include Sherman) would have been more likely to treat a defeated foe with honor. Hampton's expression of confidence in Union veterans sounds like a contradiction of his earlier attitude, but in two ways it was not. First, white South Carolinians were firmly in charge within South Carolina by 1879; Hamp-ton was speaking of reconciliation on the national stage, not with "carpetbag-gers" and "scalawags" within South Carolina. Hampton found it far easier to seek reconciliation with the North once some measure of "redemption" had occurred—particularly the expulsion of Northern influence in South Carolina's state government with Hampton's capture of the governor's seat in 1877. Sec-ond, the basic message was the same as before—a man's war record was a reli-able indicator of his patriotism, virtue, and suitability for leadership.

Hampton believed, of course, that the history of the war also validated his own right to lead in peacetime. It helped him that most white South Carolini-ans agreed. Hampton was the senior Confederate general from South Carolina and widely recognized as the state's most prominent hero from the war. He frequently reminded Confederate veterans of their service together when asking for their political support or urging them to keep the peace during the violent state campaigns of 1868 and 1876. While praising the steadfastness of the former soldiers in his audience, he made it clear that he felt he had a right to ask for their continued loyalty.[38]

A fourth point that must be made about Hampton's Lost Cause was that for Hampton, the issue of race was far less important than his own public vindication. That point requires elaboration because of the common assumption among modern historians that the Lost Cause usually served as a cover for the reestablishment of white supremacy in the postwar South. For many South Carolina conservatives, that was undoubtedly true. It was especially true among the next generation of South Carolina Democrats led by Ben Tillman, most of whom had been too young to fight in Hampton's ranks in the 1860s. Even many of Hampton's contemporaries convinced themselves that the tragedy and humiliation they had suffered excused or even justified the violence inflicted on black Republicans during Reconstruction. Possibly much of Hampton's rhetoric had the unintended effect of condoning such violence.

Hampton, though, rarely spoke of African Americans in the same speeches in which he glorified Confederate valor. When he did, he argued that it had been a mistake for the North to enforce immediate, universal emancipation and to confer universal suffrage immediately on illiterate blacks.[39] Now that slavery had disappeared, however, no white people in the South desired or should desire its return. He also told veterans and other white audiences that it was their duty to deal with ex-slaves "frankly," "justly," "kindly," and "generously."[40]

Race was obviously a central issue of Reconstruction and the Gilded Age, as it is today. Hampton, though rightly considered a moderate for his time, shared the racist assumptions of his day that blacks were inferior. The point here is not to excuse Hampton's racial views or his politics after 1865. Nor can one ignore the fact that although Hampton publicly eschewed violence, he was elected governor in 1876 and 1878 by men who were willing to use violence and fraud to reinstate white supremacy. Like other elements of Hampton's worldview, however, it was antebellum and wartime events that formed his attitude toward African Americans at least as much as events occurring during Reconstruction. As the previously cited letter to James Conner reveals, he rarely saw blacks as a threat unless misled by unscrupulous Northerners. Events from his antebellum and wartime years created that view. In their antebellum correspondence, the Hamptons had written to each other about their slaves fondly, but condescendingly. Hampton was raised by "Mauma Nelly," a slave woman

who also cared for his younger siblings and who stayed with the Hamptons
after the war. When Mauma Nelly died in 1866, her last words were "a long
farewell to Marse Wade."[41] The last person to see Hampton's father alive was
"Daddy Carolina," a body servant who was washing his ailing master's feet
when he died. When trying to emphasize the close ties that "should" exist
between masters and ex-slaves, Hampton once indirectly referred to the devotion of Kit Goodwyn, his own body servant whom he praised for staying with
him throughout the war. Hampton was guilty, of course, of glossing over the
inhumanity of slavery and over-romanticizing master-slave ties. But there were
good reasons for doing so besides postwar political goals—reasons that are
apparent from biographical details of Hampton life. One was that it was Kit
Goodwyn to whom Hampton entrusted "his beautiful boy" when he sent Preston's body back to Columbia. In all likelihood, Goodwyn performed his task
faithfully and returned to Hampton in Virginia. He continued to live with
Hampton for the rest of Hampton's life. When Hampton died in 1902, Kit
Goodwyn drove the horse-drawn hearse in the funeral procession.[42]

However, most of these references to African Americans by Hampton,
including the praise of Goodwyn, did not appear in speeches in which Hampton discussed the legacy of the war. Race was not always Hampton's primary
concern after 1865, but personal vindication almost always was, especially when
it came to discussing the war. He longed for vindication and redemption for all
that he had lost—his brother, his son, his house, his grandfather and father's
house, his fortune, and, in Northern eyes, his good name.

The intent here is not to argue that Hampton's particular Lost Cause message was always the dominant one. Each ex-Confederate and Lost Cause adher-
ent came to his or her understanding of the war in the immediate postwar years
via their own personal journeys. Jefferson Davis's Lost Cause message, for
example, dwelt on constitutional issues; Jubal Early focused on the fighting
superiority of Confederate officers and troops. Hampton would have wholeheartedly agreed with most of their assertions, though his Lost Cause had a
different thrust. But nearly every white Southerner of Hampton's generation
who glorified the Confederate experience in the postwar years had suffered
crushing disappointment, deep humiliation, and psychic pain; all were attempting to cope with regional and personal tragedy on a scale unlike anything nineteenth-century white Americans had ever experienced.[43]

Historians are right to recognize that white Southerners could manipulate
the glorification of Southern valor and the Confederate cause to serve postwar
political and social goals. Sometimes the rhetoric and thrust of the Lost Cause,
including Hampton's version, flowed from postwar concerns as well as wartime

events. Biography, however, allows us to pay closer attention to personal experience and to recognize that the roots of the Lost Cause lay in wartime suffering and even antebellum assumptions and world views. When Southerners spoke to each other in the language of mourning and commemoration, they were trying to find meaning and redemption for all they had lost. Even when they demanded that outsiders acknowledge Southern valor, they were often seeking vindication of their reputations and that of their loved ones, and not necessarily manipulating the facts of history for cynical purposes.

On the night of April 10–11, 1902, Wade Hampton lay on his deathbed in a state of semiconsciousness. He seemed finally to accept that his ultimate vindication was not within his own grasp, for in his last words he called out for his "Redeemer, . . . my Jesus." Only a few hours before, though, his mind had returned to the memory that had haunted him since that gloomy October day on a damp battlefield in Virginia. It was the memory that best defined his own Civil War experience, that best explained why white Southerners immediately after the war were too preoccupied with their own loss to recognize the just claims of their ex-slaves, to condemn their failed bid for independence, or to accept the Northern argument that their cause had been wrong. It was memories like this one that demanded that before all else, before reconciliation could take place, the North must accept Southern claims to valor and virtue. As Hampton's mind drifted back, he saw his two beloved sons on the ground, prostrate and bleeding. That old feeling of helpless misery and gut-wrenching despair returned. "All is black," he exclaimed in a hoarse whisper. "My children on the field—heroes forever! Forever!"[44]

9   Rebels in War and Peace: Their Ethos and Its Impact

Jason Phillips

A conversation with a captured Rebel officer still fascinated Union General John Schofield thirty-two years later. At Nashville on December 16, 1864, Schofield helped annihilate General John Bell Hood's Army of Tennessee. The federals inflicted six thousand casualties and captured fifty-three artillery pieces, the highest number claimed in a battle by either side during the war. As waves of blue overwhelmed the Confederates, Schofield asked the captured officer when his men realized they were conquered. "Not till you routed us just now," he replied. At first Schofield doubted the answer. Surely the Rebels knew they were finished weeks earlier at Franklin, where seven thousand Confederates fell, including twelve generals and fifty-four regimental commanders—half the army's total. But when he reflected on the prisoner's response, Schofield thought, "He probably told me the exact truth. I doubt if any soldiers in the world ever needed so much cumulative evidence to convince them that they were beaten."[1]

Schofield's story raises two questions. First, why did some Confederates need "so much cumulative evidence" before they admitted defeat? In other words, how did diehards sustain optimism and justify persistence in the last years of the war? Second, why does the perseverance of these Rebels matter? What can diehards reveal about the South; what mark did they leave on the region and its war legacy? The solid divide between Civil War and Reconstruction scholarship tends to separate these intimately linked questions, labeling one Confederate history and the other New South history, relating the former to the military and the latter to political science. This essay combines such issues within a larger study of invincibility and defeat, faith and disbelief, and war and peace. The answers offered here are necessarily brief, but they illuminate a misunderstood group and encourage scholars to transcend the prevailing war and postwar typology. If historians are to understand white Southern culture during the "middle period," they must tackle the same challenge that haunted their subjects—namely, how did Southerners try to overcome the chasm of defeat. Only then can history appreciate which elements of the Old South informed the New and which perished in the crucible of war.

The roots of Confederate persistence can be found in the private chronicles and uncensored letters of men in gray. In these sources, even after Gettysburg, Vicksburg, Atlanta, and Lincoln's reelection decreased Confederate chances for independence, Rebels still expected to win the war. In July 1864, for example, after retreating for months during the Atlanta campaign, an Alabama soldier declared, "I dont remember a time within the last year that I felt more confident of our final success." When Atlanta fell, Georgian J. Frederick Waring considered it "a trifling success" for the enemy because "we shall as certainly win our independence as the sun shines in heaven." In February 1865, South Carolinian John McLure expected "a renewed zeal . . . throughout the country." According to McLure, "a victory or two on our part would change the phase [face] of things very much, and perhaps open the eyes of the Yankees a little."[2] Apparently, McLure did not consider how *his* perspective might have been cloudy in 1865.

After reading such language, many historians have shared General Schofield's disbelief. Hindsight separates scholars from the Confederates' war. Like Schofield, we expect Union victory in 1865. This anticipation colors our reception of diehard sentiments. Confederate hope, particularly late in the war, often seems a charade or self delusion.[3] Nonetheless, calling diehards irrational, bombastic, or dense hampers our efforts to understand these people and their place in American history. By accepting diehard views as honest expressions of their beliefs and perspectives, this essay uncovers cultural elements and wartime experiences that bolstered Rebels' abiding faith in their superiority. Throughout the war, stalwart Confederates knew they were not conquered, but more than this, they thought they were unconquerable. This powerful belief in themselves and their people created an ethos of invincibility that echoed through generations of Southern life.[4]

Clunky terms like "ethos of invincibility" require explanation, even justification. Confederates combined a host of ideas, assumptions, and fears into a system of beliefs that affirmed the indomitable nature of the South. The elements of this ethos were older than the Confederacy, but the war forged them into a cohesive culture that diehards espoused. Slave owners and junior officers—the educated, young elites of Southern society—were the most vocal diehards, but common soldiers from the yeoman class and poorer whites shared this culture. Moreover, men of every rank expressed profound confidence late into the war.[5]

Not all Southerners shared this faith. Thousands of soldiers deserted the armies; thousands of civilians abandoned the cause. This essay does not challenge scholarship on Southern disaffection, nor does it quantify notions of

invincibility; it explains the significance of the steadfast hundreds whose persistence seems so illogical and extreme. For decades historians have stressed how
the Confederate war regressed into a "rich man's war, poor man's fight."[6] Conscription, the tax-in-kind, and the "twenty-negro law" increased class tensions,
but military life also transformed diverse groups into brothers in arms. As W. J.
Cash explained,

> The armies had brought men together from the four quarters, molding them
> to a common purpose for four years, teaching them more and more to say
> and think the same things, giving them common memories—memories
> transcending all that had gone before and sealed with the great seal of pain
> and hunger and sweat—binding man more closely to man and class more
> closely to class.[7]

It is equally important to consider what this ethos was *not*, because impreci-
sion has exacerbated debates over Confederate persistence and its legacy. Faith
in Rebel invincibility strengthened military morale, but ethos is not *esprit de
corps*. Diehards experienced gloom and elation like everyone else, but beyond
the rise and fall of emotion they were certain they could not lose the war. In
short, faith in final success ran deeper than morale; for many Rebels, it was an
undercurrent that retained its pull despite war's ebb and flow. Likewise, the
ethos boosted Confederate nationalism, but they were not one and the same.
On this point, the author disagrees with Gary Gallagher, Anne Sarah Rubin,
and others who insist that Southern persistence confirms the power of Confederate nationalism. Diehard assumptions of their innate courage, noble lineage,
and divine blessing *adorned* the Confederacy for four years, but thoughts of
Southern dominance predated and outlasted the rebellion.[8] This distinction is
critical. Confederate nationalism, a unifying ideology meant to attach Southerners to the Confederacy, failed. The ethos of invincibility, a fierce faith in
Southern superiority, prevailed. In war, diehard Confederates remained faithful
nationalists against external resistance and internal collapse. In peace, these
unreconstructed veterans sustained their sense of self-importance, even great-
ness, against the realities of defeat and military occupation. Throughout these
trials, diehards drew strength from the notion that white Southerners were not
merely a separate group (as Rubin insists), but a superior people. With or without the Confederate nation, this abiding faith in the *supremacy* of white Southerners remained the diehards' distinguishing characteristic; it shaped their
identity, influenced their view of the war, and guided their actions after
surrender.[9]

Rebels founded their notions of invincibility on two Manichean elements: faith in Southern righteousness and hatred of Northern barbarity. Most stalwart Rebels tied Confederate invincibility to Southern religion. Antebellum evangelicalism, Confederate propaganda, and revivals in the ranks convinced Rebels that God favored their cause and would deliver them independence. Many soldiers witnessed God's hand on every level of the war effort. The Almighty shielded soldiers' in combat, led their armies to victories, chastened them with defeats, and oversaw their bid for self-government. Throughout the war thousands of soldiers found Christianity because it helped them make sense of the war, and it guided them past the temptations of camp and the perils of combat. For diehards, religion offered another gift: an all-powerful ally to defeat the Yankees. When Confederates suffered major defeats in 1864 and 1865, no other element—not foreign powers, Copperheads, General Robert E. Lee, or even devotion to the cause—could guarantee victory like God's protection. Christianity, more so than causes or comrades, sustained Rebel hopes of victory.[10]

Certainty of God's favor shaped Confederate behavior late in the war. In July 1864, as Sherman's columns marched toward her home, Martha McCorkle shared her anxiety with her husband, John, a private in the Army of Tennessee. John told Martha not to worry because "if we are in the right we will triumph in spite of mr Shermond whitch I trust we are. . . . Put your trust in him who reules the universe and do not murmer and I think he will do all things right."[11] Martha was sending her husband distress letters, a type of correspondence that convinced other troops to desert. Instead of heading home, John told his wife to start praying and stop grumbling. McCorkle's Christianity kept him in the ranks until he was captured at the battle of Nashville. He died of pneumonia in February 1865.

Major setbacks failed to rattle the faith of devout Rebels. After the fall of Atlanta, a North Carolinian was convinced that "all will be well," because "I cannot believe that Providence intends the Confederate States for a subjugated nation." When Lincoln was reelected, an Alabama trooper reminded his wife, "If God is on our side, we will triumph nevertheless."[12] Like McCorkle, the Alabamian was confident; however, both men used language that noted the conditional nature of God's favor. *If* Rebels trusted the Almighty and earned divine aid, Confederate victory was certain. As the war worsened, many diehard soldiers seemed more assured that God would help them. After the Hampton Roads peace conference failed in February 1865, Texan Thomas Hampton saw no reason to despair because "in God we may look for redemption." Even after the loss of Richmond, another Texas diehard expected divine intervention:

"Through His Omnipotent power we will yet triumph."[13] For these men, faith in victory was not bravado or ignorance—it was their religion.

Within the Rebel worldview, setbacks did not signify divine anger; God loved those who believed in Him. Major reverses resulted from God chastening His people for their sinfulness. Stalwart Confederates made sense of destruction on the home front, military catastrophes, and international isolation with Scripture, like Hebrews 12:5–6:

My son, despise not thou the chastening of the Lord, nor faint when thou art rebuked of him: For whom the Lord loveth he chaseneth, and scourgeth every son whom he receiveth. If ye endure chastening, God dealeth with you as with sons; for what son is he whom the father chasteneth not?

Adversity, hardship, and bloodshed galvanized peoples' faith in themselves and their deliverer. Some Confederates drew parallels to the American Revolution: The Continentals endured Valley Forge before they reached Yorktown.[14] As Louisiana Rebel Reuben Pierson told his father

God will never suffer a determined and united people to be enslaved and though many of us may never live to see the day I feel assured that our separation from and freedom of the yanks is sure. . . . Our fore fathers endured the revolution for 7 years. . . . Why may we not with their examples before us go on & take courage at our past successes?[15]

Hundreds of Confederate letters and diaries confirm religion's power to cope with major defeats. In July 1863 troops looked to God after Gettysburg and Vicksburg. In Tennessee, Joshua Callaway was "not out of heart" because "our trust is in God and our cause is just." He expressed his view of the war's course in verse: "Judge not the Lord by feeble sense,/But trust him for his grace./Behind a frowning Providence/He hides a smiling face." However dire the present seemed to mortals, God would smile on the Confederacy in the end. Pierson had "little fear of the final result of the war" because the Bible predicted Confederate victory in Scripture like Ecclesiastes 9:11. He told his father, "Our hopes must rest on the God of battles who hath assured us that the race is not to the swift nor the battle to the strong." He expected "adverse fortune" to "darken our prospects but in the end we will come out conquerors." After Vicksburg, South Carolinian Tally Simpson prepared for the surrender of Savannah, Charleston, and Richmond. "These cities will be a loss to the Confederacy," he reasoned, "but their fall is no reason why we should despair." Simpson wrote his wife, "If we place implicit confidence in Him and go to work in good earnest, never for a moment losing sight of Heaven's goodness and protection, it is my firm belief that we shall be victorious in the end." The corporal satisfied himself that "God's hand," not Lincoln's or Grant's, caused defeats, "and He is working for the accomplishment of some grand result."[16]

This steadfast faith accompanied Confederates through the horrors of 1864–65. After a month of the grinding Overland campaign, William Casey admitted that he was "very nearly broken down from fighting and working." Even worse, he learned all his family's slaves left with enemy forces that ravaged his home. Casey wrote his mother, "I know that you are not in good spirits[.] But you must try and put your trust in the Lord, and every thing will turn out for the best." When Atlanta fell, John McLure thought the news was "decidedly discouraging . . . yet I comfort myself with the belief that such a seeming great calamity had not been sent to us without a design by the great Ruler of Nations." Henry Chambers shared McLure's perspective: The loss of Atlanta "lengthens the duration of this cruel war" because "God for some good purpose has seen fit to bring this upon us. Let us submit to His will." When facing major defeats, devout Rebels like Casey, McLure, and Chambers did not dwell on real-world consequences because religion clarified the conflict. God intended these calamities for a higher purpose. Catastrophes like the fall of Atlanta were proof that white Southerners were God's children. Piety meant accepting the dire course of events without question.[17]

When Confederates speculated as to which Southern sin provoked divine wrath, they seldom considered slavery. Clergy occasionally pointed to the Southern *treatment* of slaves as God's provocation, but soldiers preferred other explanations. James Drayton Nance thought God sent defeats "to chasten that boastful and self-confident spirit with which we entered . . . this contest." Nance deemed Southern bravado a national sin that God was beating out of the Rebels. In his view, Rebel élan fostered heroism, but the Almighty was forging "fortitude . . . a virtue much rarer than heroism." John Shaffner disagreed. For him the concept of a national sin was a comfortable way for Christians to ignore their individual shortcomings. He thought "the prevailing idea of 'National Sin' as the cause of our present chastisement" was an "error." For Shaffner, "A nation's Guilt is but the aggregate sum of *Individual* sins," and God would punish Confederates until they personally repented. John McLure focused on the national sin of extortion. He wrote his wife that extortion was a "crime . . . [that] has submerged our whole land, & until we rid ourselves of this we can not expect Heaven to reward us with blessings." Arrogance, impenitence, and greed: Countless Confederates pointed to these sins, not slavery. The "peculiar institution" was so deeply imbedded in their culture that few diehard

Rebels considered the possibility that human bondage was immoral. The correspondence of James Blackman Ligon, a member of Hampton's Legion, illustrates this mentality. Ligon's mother complained that her ungrateful slaves were abandoning her. "Now Mother," Ligon responded, "I hope if every negro and every dollar's worth of property you possess was to be destroyed in an instant, that you would feel like it was caused by a higher power and to greave after any thing is a besetting sin." From Ligon's perspective owning slaves was not a sin, but grieving over the loss of property was, because God willed it to be. Ligon tried to convince his mother that her slaves "have been a perfect neusance and distraction." Their absence would be a blessing in disguise; an inscrutable deity planned this event, like the fall of Vicksburg, for some greater good. The mystery of God's ways helped diehards maintain their faith in victory. Defeats were unexpected bumps along the road to independence.[18]

In short, devout Confederates thought chastening was temporary; God brought setbacks to discipline Rebels, not to bless Yankees as conquerors. Many soldiers expressed this point, but none more clearly than J. Frederick Waring in 1865: "I know that God will bless this land. We have sinned and he is now chastening us, but he will *never, never* deliver us over to our enemies."[19] This belief braced troops for the war's interminable length. Baking under a July sun in the trenches of Petersburg, Henry Conner surveyed the stalemated front and admitted that the present campaign may not be the last. Though Conner desperately wanted to win the war and return to his wife, he explained, "We must trust the issue to God alone and he will in his own good time bring it about when he thinks we are prepared for it." In December, peace with independence seemed even more remote, but Conner stuck to his beliefs. With Sherman heading for Savannah, Conner stoically remarked, "It seems as tho we are destined to lose more of our country yet but we have no cause for despondence." God, not General Sherman, was directing these calamities. "Surely it is for our sins as a nation and people that we are suffering this dredful scorge of war and if we will forsake our sins and turn to god he will remove his rod of chastisement from us and give us peace and prosperity when he sees we are prepared for it." For religious Confederates, the surest route to independence was national penitence, not conquering the peace. Within their faith, many harbored an implicit assumption that it would be easier to earn God's forgiveness than to conquer the North. As one minister expressed on a fast day, "More effective than disciplined brigades, armed with the deadliest implements that science has invented—more effective than heaviest ordnance most skillfully served—is the favor of the Lord; and that favor can be gained."[20] Confederate armies could lose battles and abandon territory without changing the war's outcome because God loved them.

Other diehards stressed Northern inferiority rather than Southern righteousness as the central reason for Rebel invincibility. Poetry, music, cartoons, political speeches, sermons, and newspaper editorials reinforced a simplified image of the enemy as barbaric hordes. Yankees were immigrant scum, urban recreants, and sinister secularists hell-bent on defiling the South. At first glance, these perceptions were mere abstractions reinforced by propaganda. But emancipation, Union destruction, and black federal troops breathed life into stale stereotypes during the second half of the war. Just as defeats strengthened Confederates' religious faith in victory, the war's increasing destruction hardened Rebel prejudices and determination. Both developments reinforced diehard convictions that Southerners were God's chosen people fighting against satanic legions. Rebel self-righteousness denied the enemy's claims on morality and seemed to uncover the evil behind federal war aims: Restoring the Union was an excuse to pillage and subjugate the South, and freeing the slaves was a cover-up for racial warfare and the rape of Southern ladies by freedmen and Negroes in blue uniforms. Atrocity stories transmitted these jarring images, elevating Rebels to the status of innocent victims and martyrs and raising Confederate fears that Northern fiends challenged the foundations of Southern society and manhood. Even individual enemy soldiers reinforced these base images in unintended ways.

Rebels' impressions of individual Union soldiers exhibit how close proximity to one's enemy often reinforced base abstractions. Most of the federals that Rebels observed closely were captured, wounded, or dead, but besides an occasional expression of pity for such opponents, these encounters reinforced Confederates' low opinion of the other side and confirmed stereotypes. Under the veil of postwar reconciliation, veterans recalled a brothers' war in which enemies fraternized and helped each other. This unusual behavior did exist, but most interaction across the lines was anything but cordial. Wartime writings include broken cease fires, insults, trickery, and retaliation. One Mississippi private admitted that his comrades called Yankees over to trade goods and captured the unsuspecting men. Such episodes remind us that the war could be a base business of prejudice and deceit.[21]

For many Rebels, enemy corpses represented the folly of federal invasions. In June 1864, Virginian Robert Stiles found himself near Malvern Hill, "the old hill of fire & terror," and Frazier's Farm, "which gave me my first real view of a field after the battle fought & the victory won." Investigating the old ground, Stiles discovered "piles of human bones—sculls bare & ghastly crunching under the horses feet & wagon wheels, & many other memorials of the former invasion & defeat." Surveying the scene, the Virginian remarked, "Grant has ever to the last followed the track of McClellan, only he does not do quite so well."

Dead Yankees marked the site of Confederate triumphs because Union troops left too hastily to care for their own. Over time, Rebels described enemy corpses with indifference; carnage stripped adversaries of their individuality. After artillery had repulsed the foe, William Casey "had the pleasure of seeing some of their dead lying in the ditch." Likewise, Tennessean surgeon Urban Owen surveyed the enemy dead after an unsuccessful charge during the Atlanta campaign. He counted forty-seven bullet holes in one of the Yankees and joked "he was too dead to Skin." Such language bares the hardening of war. Samuel Foster noted, "We cook and eat, talk and laugh with the enemy dead lying all about us as though they were so many logs." The common sight of dead Yankees dehumanized survivors who wore the same uniform.[22]

Confederates who looted the dead found items that confirmed their opinions of Yankee depravity. Owen searched dead Union soldiers who died in his care. While rifling through the knapsack of a dead Iowan, Owen found "a certificate belonging to a lady in Georgia, certifying that her husband had died in the Southern army & that there was money due to him for his services in the army." Owen surmised that the barbarian "had robbed some widow's house" and stolen the certificate as a souvenir. The doctor also enjoyed reading dead men's letters. Confederates stressed the immorality and lewdness of enemy correspondence. Sergeant Edwin Fay concluded, "One would certainly form a very exalted opinion of the Yankee nation to judge from the letters captured both from their soldiers, home & from their wives to the army." Fay claimed, "I have never yet seen a decent Yankee letter and I have read many since I have been in the Army."[23]

Prisoners offered Confederates a unique opportunity to interrogate the enemy, and Rebels had no difficulty categorizing real Yankees within narrow stereotypes. The despondency and fear that affected prisoners' demeanor seemed to confirm Yankee inferiority and barbarity. Captives appeared weak, divided, shifty, critical of federal leadership, and ethnically diverse. In March 1865, Richard Maury declared a group of 476 captives from Sherman's army "the most villainous looking set of scoundrels that I ever saw anywhere. . . . And these fellows we are assured are a fair *specimen* of Sherman's forces." What word better than "specimen" expresses that Rebels observed captives as representative samples of the enemy? Mississippian Edmund Eggleston noted when "three or four hundred Yankee prisoners with hang dog countenances and ragged dirty clothes passed our camp," the captives looked drained of will and defeated. Likewise, Alabamian Sam Pickens watched "a lot of Yankee prisoners" being transported to Savannah, Georgia. "They were by far the most filthy, miserable, wretched set of human beings I've ever seen," Pickens remarked.

When North Carolinian Richard Webb interrogated some captives in November 1864, they confirmed his suspicion that the enemy was deeply divided over the course of the war and the presidential election. The Yankees claim "they were put into the fight, because they were for McClelland." In May 1864, captives told South Carolinian David Crawford that Grant deceived them with "orders that Richmond had fallen." The news supported Crawford's opinion that "their army is pretty demoralized" and "fighting themselves." Prisoners told Lieutenant Leonidas Polk that Grant's ranks were terribly sick. Polk wrote home, the "Prisoners say, whom we capture daily, that they are almost perished, & that his army is very much demoralized. They all look the worst I ever saw & say the rank & file of their army have despaired of taking Richmond." Other captives begged for food and water and swore they fought to feed their families. When a Georgia captain heard this, he concluded that "men who fight for money are easy whiped . . . [and] we who fight for our wives and children our homes and Property cannot be whiped." He saw no correlation between the enemies' professed motives and his own. Instead, prisoners' words were music to Rebel ears; they validated Confederate perceptions that the war was going well for the cause.[24]

Deserters also reinforced Rebel images of the foe. By stressing Confederate desertion as a cause of defeat, historians have unintentionally shifted our gaze away from thousands of disgruntled federals who deserted the winning side. In many respects, Sherman and Grant's troops suffered hardships in the final campaigns that rivaled the plight of their opponents: Grant's ranks sustained unprecedented casualties, and Sherman's foot-sore columns trekked hundreds of miles. Troops who abandoned the Union cause presented a disaffected demeanor and often shared Confederates' opinions of federal commanders, emancipation, and the war's progress. In May 1864, Creed Davis reported, "Now and then some of them may be seen coming into our lines—deserting. A squad of 20 has just come in. The Yankee army is said to be very much demoralized." After the battles of the Wilderness and Spotsylvania Court House, Union deserters who met Reuben Pierson's unit "report their loss as being the heaviest of any battle of the war—between 50 & 75 thousand in all & over ten Gens. in all." In June 1864, deserters from Sherman's ranks informed John Cotton and his comrades that the federal army was critically short of rations, so much so that mules and horses were starving to death. After Kennesaw Mountain, Captain George Knox Miller claimed that deserters from Sherman's army "come to us every night." In October 1864, eight deserters surrendered to North Carolinian Abe Jones while he was on picket duty in Virginia. They favored McClellan in the upcoming election and promised that Little Mac "will get a Majority in [the] Yankee Army." Though Union soldiers probably talked this way to ingratiate themselves with their captors, Rebels treated Yankee deserters as accurate representatives of the enemy. The Northerners were jaded, cowardly, unprincipled, and conquered. Some Yankees claimed thousands of federals would desert if given the opportunity. Others did more than reinforce Rebel stereotypes; they informed Confederates of federal plans and aided in the capture of unsuspecting comrades.[25]

The federals' hard war policy also contributed to enemy stereotypes by convincing thousands of diehards to avoid "subjugation" at all costs.[26] By January 1865, the destructiveness of Union forces convinced a Georgia officer that "anything is better for us than to submit to Yankee rule."[27] Some soldiers received letters from parents and spouses who suffered occupation and devastation. Traditionally, historians have stressed how such correspondence convinced men to desert, favoring family over nation. Some soldiers received a very different message from loved ones. Fred Fleet's mother wrote him that "death is far preferable to subjugation to the vile Yankees—I know something about it now."[28] When Tennessean James Brannock imagined defeat, he thought it "better that every man, woman & child in the South should be buried together in one wide, common grave." A Confederate camp song, "Call All! Call All!" echoed this idea of a sacrificial effort for independence: "Shoulder to shoulder, son and sire!/All, call all! To the feast of fire!/Mother and maiden, and child and slave,/ A common triumph or a single grave." For diehards, the message in such songs and in Sherman's destruction was the same: Catastrophe had to be avoided at all costs, kill or be killed, defend your loved ones or watch them perish. In 1864 and 1865 submission seemed worse than war. Charles Fenton James thought surrendering meant having "our property confiscated, our slaves emancipated, our leaders hung, and we become serfs in the land of our fathers." The "alternative of submission or war" was theirs, and men like James preferred resistance to subjugation. Visions of vile defeat induced thousands of Confederates to prolong the war.[29]

Southern Christianity and Northern barbarism were the positive and negative forces behind Rebel persistence. While religion sustained hopes of victory, enemy stereotypes amplified fears of defeat. In other words, while cause and comrades mattered, the extremes of God and enemy clarified the war. For diehards, such polarities encapsulated their struggle and pointed to one outcome: victory. In the hearts of religious rebels, divine providence made defeat impossible in a world ordered by God. Furthermore, even in the minds of secular Confederates, Northern cruelty and perversion made surrender unacceptable. Because diehards staked everything—their lives, livelihood, and worldview—on victory, the possibility of defeat weighed heavily on them. Throughout the conflict they searched for signs of divine favor and Union doom. Plenty of evidence sustained their faith: enormous enemy casualties, Northern peace movements, wish rumors in camp and the press, pessimistic enemy prisoners and deserters, zealous Confederate prayer meetings, and the possibility of foreign intervention. By focusing on these sources of hope, diehards downplayed the "cumulative evidence" that Schofield and historians see as portents of defeat. Stalwart Confederates received bad news and felt discouraged, but they focused on information that upheld their worldview.[30]

The significance of the culture of invincibility is most evident during and after surrender. The ethos and its adherents could not stave off conquest. At Appomattox and Durham Station, the diehards' view of the war increased the shock of surrender. The realization that they had lost was too much for some to bear. When Alabamian Robert E. Park heard of Lee's surrender, he wrote in his diary, "The news crushed our fondest hopes." "Such a shocking disappointment," he continued, "is bitter, cruel, and crushing." When David McIntosh received the news, he admitted, "A thunderbolt from heaven could hardly have shocked me more." McIntosh and his comrades "could not brook the thought of witnessing the spectacle of surrender." They tore off their military insignia and escaped through the swamp. One of them wrote home, "We refused to take part in the funeral at Appomattox." He assured his family, "I am by no means conquered." When diehards like McIntosh's group stopped running from the reality of defeat, they faced a momentous decision: Should they reject an ethos that led them and their people to disaster or maintain it despite the enemy's force and the logic of events?[31]

Diehards chose the second, fateful option: They used the culture of invincibility to overcome defeat, avoid humiliation, and uphold the status quo in the face of radical change. As Robert Park explained, "We feel deep, unutterable regret at our failure, but no humiliation. We have done nothing wrong. Our rights were trampled upon, our property stolen, and our liberties attacked, and we did but our sacred duty to defend them as well as we could." In defeat Park saw himself and his comrades as victims, not losers. This self-perception and an abiding faith in Southern superiority helped diehards remain rebellious. Many of them performed surrenders and oaths of allegiance but stayed defiant to the core. On the day he surrendered, North Carolina captain Henry Chambers prayed that God would yet strike "some terrible retribution" against "this motley crew who have waged upon us so unjust so barbarous a warfare." A leg wound received just days before Appomattox kept North Carolinian Reuben Wilson from going home. Stuck in a Union hospital, with "the fire of revenge flying from my eyes like sparks from a furnace," Wilson determined to take the oath of allegiance so that he could help to send "good men" to state conventions and Washington. Wilson reasoned that "if every southern state will send two good senators we will . . . be able to check the republican party in their wild schemes." Letters like Wilson's caution us against overstating the trauma of defeat. By May 1865 Wilson was already shifting from wartime to postwar defiance, from fighting Yankees on battle-fields to resisting them on election day.[32]

Many soldiers countered defeat by holding on to military customs and com-rades. Amid anxiety they coveted order, unity, and normalcy. This collective behavior, born in the camaraderie of war, marked their final acts as soldiers. In late May, Junius Bragg watched his division disband as units rather than dis-solve as individuals and mobs. One day, 186 troops "formed in an old field" near their camp in Marshall, Texas, "and marched away in order with loaded guns." The next night, "about eight hundred men from the Division left. . . . They went in a body and well armed." Marching off together with loaded rifles served many purposes. It separated these men from deserters who sneaked away singly and in smaller groups, and it provided safety in numbers against Confed-erate authorities willing to stop them and lawless bands waiting to pounce on them throughout the journey home. At the end, Bragg counted 132 men and officers left in his regiment; he remarked, "They will, of course, go in small squads," as if there were no alternatives to military organization. For veterans, military conventions mattered most during chaos. Though shocked by defeat, soldiers used martial rituals to see them through the ordeal. Thousands of them perpetuated this culture of campfire, rank, and bugle call in veterans' organiza-tions to the end of their days.[33]

Whether they traveled home by boat, train, horse, or foot, diehard Rebels encountered signs of defeat along the way. Many of them saw war's culminating acts of destruction: Sheridan's work in the Shenandoah, Sherman's path through the Carolinas, and Richmond's burnt district. When Henry Robinson Berkeley reached Richmond, he walked to Main Street "to take a look at the burnt district." Though a four-year veteran of artillery, Berkeley was shocked by the spectacle. "One could hardly tell where Main Street had been. It was one big pile of ruins from the Custom House to the wharf." At dockside, "the Yanks had collected all kinds of debris of war: cannon, muskets, bayonets, cartridge boxes, swords, broken gun-carriages, broken wagons, etc." Standing before the wreckage of the Confederacy, Berkeley thought of "our noble dead" and asked himself "is it better with them or with us?" He decided the dead were better off. "We almost know it is well with them," Berkeley reflected, "but who knows what the future holds for us; only God." When Kena King Chapman saw Rich-mond, his reaction was less philosophical. King noted in his diary, "Old Rich-mond is sadly changed—all the business portion of the city being a heap of ruins—thanks to the Dutch Irish, and the everlasting 'nigger.'" Fleeing Confederates had burned Richmond, but Chapman blamed the immigrants from the North and freed slaves.[34] This habit of re-writing history would continue in Lost Cause legends.

Veterans stressed the superficial, forced nature of reunion. In their view, federal troops and black henchmen bullied Rebels into swearing an oath to the Union. As Henry Berkeley put it, they "thrust their vile oath of allegiance down our throats with bayonets." When Samuel Pickens took the oath at Point Lookout Prison, he mocked the process as a "machine where U.S. citizens are made out of rebel soldiers." Such expressions confirm Anne Rubin's point that "oathtakers often claimed that they owed their enemies nothing more than lip service." For diehards, oath-swearing did not dishonor Rebels; it deprecated the government that foisted such nonsense. George Mercer thought "the arbitrary power of the United States Government seems to increase daily." He noted incidents when former Confederates were harassed, imprisoned, and fined for speaking against the federal government or challenging a Union officer. In August 1865, Henry Calvin Conner thought "the United States Government is and has been tottering on its base for many years and the last four years it has been more corrupt than ever." Wartime stereotypes continued to influence Conner's opinions. He had "seen so much of them and know the nature of a yankee so well that I expect nothing good from them." Another diehard who saw "no prospect of improvement" for the nation deemed emancipation arbitrary and foolish. In his opinion, the slaves "are free according to Yankee say so but they are the greatest sufferers in the end."[35]

Unwavering devotion to the South and their stature as veterans made diehards the natural leaders of the Lost Cause and staunch defenders of Southern orthodoxy. Unreconstructed Confederates wrote the first histories of the conflict. David Blight has described their efforts as "one of the most highly orchestrated grassroots partisan histories ever conceived." General Jubal Early published his take on the war's final years in 1866. In an introduction to a reprint of Early's work, historian Gary Gallagher notes, "Anyone susceptible to the deeply flawed, though admittedly comforting, notion that national scars healed rapidly after Grant and Lee set a conciliatory public example at Appomattox should read Early's book as an example of widely held opinions in the postwar white South." Throughout his account, Early injected the base stereotype of barbaric Yankees. Addressing his former enemies, Early wrote, "There is a wide and impassable gulf between us, in which I see the blood of slaughtered friends, comrades, and countrymen." Early filled footnotes with atrocity stories and other evidence that the enemy was undeserving of victory. He

described "delicate ladies, who had been plundered, insulted, and rendered des-
olate by the acts of our most atrocious enemies." Like so many diehards during
and after the war, Early attributed defeat to overwhelming numbers, "an
immense horde of foreign mercenaries, incited by high bounties and the hope
of plunder . . . flocked to the Federal army," and "southern negroes were forced
into its service." Countless diehards like Early continued hostilities in lectures,
articles, and books. This movement in speech and print elevated Confederates
to epic stature and degraded Yankees as artless hordes. As authors, diehards
maintained ideas that had sustained them as soldiers; they minimized slavery's
role in the contest and linked their cause with Christian virtues and the legacy
of the American Revolution. The Daughters of the Confederacy sustained the
veterans' worldview and culture for generations. As William Faulkner
explained, Southern mistresses like Rosa Coldfield lionized diehard Rebels and
their fallen comrades with "poems, ode, eulogy, and epitaph, out of some bitter
and implacable reserve of undefeat."[36]

This relentless ethos of "undefeat" persisted long after Appomattox. As with
thoughts of Southern invincibility and superiority, the vagueness of "undefeat"
increased its popularity and resilience to change. During the war, Confederates
maintained a faith in their invincibility despite numerous defeats. At capitula-
tion, Southerners insisted they were superior regardless of the fact that the
enemy had beaten them. For generations, Southerners insisted that their people
were undefeated despite signs to the contrary, such as Reconstruction, military
occupation, and black male suffrage. The irony of these positions was lost on
hundreds of diehards; somehow being both bitter and undefeated was not a
contradiction for them.

This peculiar culture of unconquered losers grew under the leadership of
stalwart veterans who became politicians, professors, editors, ministers, lawyers, and, above all, icons of Southern defiance. By assuming these important
positions, hundreds of diehards achieved in peace what they could not accomplish in war. As civic leaders and living relics, diehards lectured and set the
record straight. Some added a contemporary veneer to their rhetoric, but their
central points remained constant from the war forward. To the end of the
century and beyond, diehards continually insisted their cause was righteous,
their soldiers were incomparable, and their leaders were demigods. Edmund
Jones, a veteran of the Confederate cavalry, became an attorney and served in
the North Carolina legislature. This career brought him in frequent contact
with the state constitution, a document written during Radical Reconstruction that infuriated Jones. He particularly hated the preamble, which
expressed North Carolinians' gratitude to God for preserving the Union. That
section, Jones explained, "was placed in the constitution by a horde of foreign

carpet baggers, assisted by an army of emancipated slaves and a few native scalawags, while the real citizenship of the State were shackled and helpless." The "real citizenship of the State" included diehards like himself. Jones complained that one of the "woes of the followers of a lost cause" was "the distortion that History makes of their motives and aims." Speaking to a memorial association in 1896, Jones sought to educate the coming generations: "Child of a hero sire!" Jones proclaimed, "Little do you know of the pure flame of patriotism that burnt in the bosom of [your father . . . and] of the matchless courage that for four long, terrible, bloody years, maintained the rights of his State, and the integrity of her laws against a world of arms." He urged Southerners to pass on the heroic legacy of the diehards: "Let the living do justice to the dead. It is a poor boon to ask. You can do no less without being an . . . ingrate." Thirty years after the war, Jones's words still betrayed passion for the cause and hatred for Yankees. [37]

Diehards funneled their passion and ethos into the Lost Cause. The central elements of their wartime culture—Southern righteousness and Northern barbarity—shaped postwar legends. Instead of doubting that God was on their side, white Southerners saw defeat as providential; they viewed their trials in biblical terms and looked forward to resurrection and redemption. Confederate exiles fashioned themselves as the surviving vestiges of God's plan, the stalwart few who would build a shining civilization elsewhere and return to the South at the appointed hour. Religious leaders, including William Bennett and J. William Jones, depicted Rebel legions as God's army on earth. Reflecting on the final months of the war, Bennett recalled, "The anchor of hope held more securely as the storm increased. The serene courage and perfect trust of the Christian soldiers were the richest legacies of those gloomy days." Jones argued that those legacies continued to bless the South after defeat, because he "always found our returned soldiers the most tender and impressible part of the congregations."[38] Like the defeats at Vicksburg, Atlanta, and Nashville, the death of the Confederacy somehow confirmed God's love of the South and fit within His higher plan for it. Moreover, Reconstruction provided more evidence of Northern barbarism. Corrupt carpetbaggers, black armies of occupation, and meddlesome federal agents seemed to confirm Northern immorality and justify Southern defiance. When unreconstructed Rebels cried against their "enslavement," they did so not only as former masters familiar with racial bondage but also as Christians familiar with Old Testament scripture. Withstanding "subjugation" affirmed the righteousness of their cause. David Goldfield has argued that white Southerners performed a "mental alchemy . . . on the war itself. They spun the straw

of defeat into a golden mantle of victory."[39] To us, white Southerners' treatment of defeat seems magical and transformative; to them, it was a continuation of old ways, a response deeply rooted in their culture.

Postwar speeches illustrate how the Lost Cause offered diehards an acceptable channel to express their continued defiance. Virginian Charles Fenton
James became a minister and president of Roanoke Female College. In 1901
James insisted that the origin of the war was not slavery or even states' rights.
These, he claimed, were mere "pretext." The real cause was "the irreconcilable
antagonism between . . . the two representative classes of English people who
settled these United States." Faithful to the Cavalier myth that had justified
secession and fostered enemy stereotypes, James delineated how ancient, ethnic
differences between the "Cavalier" and "Puritan" erupted in civil war forty
years earlier. Doctor John Shaffner had served as a Confederate surgeon, and in
1902 he recalled the profound suffering of diehard Rebels. Weeks earlier Shaffner had listened to Booker T. Washington speak and was struck by a comment
Washington made about slavery. Washington had remarked how much he
looked forward to Sunday's breakfast because it included a touch of molasses
to sweeten the simple meal. "It occurred to me then," Shaffner recalled, "that
very probably at the time this negro boy was happy in absorbing the small
allowance of black sweetening; his young master, possibly in camp, marching,
or fighting, would have been more happy to have shared in this, at that time,
impossible luxury." The point of comparison was clear: Blacks complained
about how they suffered during slavery, but white Southerners endured worse
during the war without grumbling. Speaking to veterans at a Memorial Day
service, Shaffner stressed "the propriety of teaching to your children and drum-
ming it into their heads, the many heroic deeds, you and your comrades
accomplished during the four years of civil strife!" The soldiers' accomplishments mattered, not the outcome of the war. Echoing wartime exaggerations of
the odds, Shaffner insisted, "It should be indelibly impressed on your descend-
ents, that, with blockaded ports;—shut off from communication with the world
at large, it required more than 3,000,000 men to overcome, by starvation and
exhaustion, less than 600,000 Southerners, and that four long, bitter years were
required to accomplish the result." Shaffner concluded, "The heritage left coming generations is one of the grandest in history."[40] Many scholars stress how
the Lost Cause responded to defeat or postwar socioeconomic changes, but the
cult also sustained wartime mentalities. Edmund Jones, Charles Fenton James,
and John Shaffner used the Lost Cause as a medium through which they could
safely express their Confederate ethos.[41]

When bridging the divide between Civil War and Reconstruction scholarship, the permanence of white Southern culture is striking. Historians often

stress how these periods changed the South. C. Vann Woodward counted "slavery and secession, independence and defeat, emancipation and military occupation, reconstruction and redemption" as the major disruptions Southerners
faced. According to Woodward, "Southerners, unlike other Americans, repeatedly felt the solid ground of continuity give way under their feet."[42] The ground
may have shifted, but white Southern minds hardly budged. On this point,
W. J. Cash was correct. "If this war had smashed the Southern world," Cash
argued, "it had left the essential Southern mind and will . . . entirely
unshaken."[43] Rebels responded to anomie as most people do, by clinging to
their innermost convictions. The federal government could alter Southern politics and economics, but it could not change white Southern culture, which
remained diverse, diffuse, and unconquered.

This continuity confronts the assumption that defeat deeply traumatized
Confederates. Scholars expect—perhaps want—to find Rebels crushed by capit-
ulation. But if diehards, the Southerners most certain of victory, overcame
defeat and sustained their wartime ethos, how traumatic was Appomattox? To
be sure, linking Confederate notions of invincibility to Lost Cause legends does
not address other pieces of Rebel lives that may have been broken or lost in the
war. This essay does not measure postwar incidences of divorce, abandonment,
alcoholism, suicide, or other self-destructive behavior that might tell a different
story of Confederate failure. Some writers marvel at the calm reunion of 1865
and attribute it to swift reconciliation.[44] Given the failures of Reconstruction
and white Southern intransigence, it seems more likely that the quiet of April
1865 marked Confederates' silent conviction to continue their war by other
means. Defeat and its attendant changes provoked diehards who still believed
they could not be conquered by Yankees and blacks. Robert Penn Warren once
wrote, "In the moment of death the Confederacy entered upon its immortality."[45] It is an elegant idea, but glorifying the Confederacy was a long process
stretching back to the war years; it was not a transformative event contingent
on defeat. Armed with God's love and an undying hatred of the North, diehard
Rebels immortalized themselves and their nation *before* defeat. The Lost Cause
merely continued wartime reverence.

The story of diehard Rebels also challenges the legacy of the Civil War. The
most popular studies of the conflict depict an inevitable struggle that strengthened the nation and expanded equality. Novelists Shelby Foote and Michael
Shaara, historian James McPherson, and filmmaker Ken Burns are most
responsible for this story of America reborn in the fires of fratricide.[46] They
stress common courage, growing freedom, and reconciliation after a "brothers'
war." Unfortunately, their sanitized war can corroborate buff history and
Southern "heritage" claims that glorify the past. Inspiring narratives often

deemphasize the dark legacy of the Civil War: Lasting hatred and pettiness, broken promises of emancipation, and white Southerners' "implacable reserve of undefeat," are a few of its murkier elements.[47] Since McPherson's *Battle Cry of Freedom* topped bestsellers' lists in 1989, historians have been rediscovering the war's darkness. Most notably, Charles Royster studied America's penchant for destruction and its lasting effects, and David Blight recovered the abandoned emancipationist legacy of the war.[48] Certainly a more complex account of the Civil War would be more accurate if we, as Edward Ayers put it, have "the faith to approach these threatening years without a comforting story already in hand."[49] In war and peace, the diehards point to a more complicated narrative. They show us how this bloody war spilled into Reconstruction and stained generations of Southern life.

10

Reconstructing Loyalty: Love, Fear, and Power in the Postwar South

CAROLE EMBERTON

W riting in the fall of 1865, a gloomy Charles Eliot Norton predicted a rough road toward Reconstruction even though all indications from the Johnson administration suggested a quick and relatively quiet reconciliation. "Though the South has sullenly laid down its arms," Norton cautioned, "it has not laid down its hate . . . we have not yet secured a moral Union, a civil unity; we have the harder part of our task before us." Like his fellow *Nation* founders, Norton not only questioned Johnson's amnesty plans but also the larger assumption that the war itself was over. Although the president and his generals officially declared peace, the question of the South's acquiescence to defeat and the problem of rebuilding Southern loyalty to a Union it had given so much blood to dissolve worried many. Radicals in Congress, such Ohio Representative Hezekiah S. Bundy, convulsed with patriotic fervor, declaring "Loyal Men Must Rule." To ensure this policy, they supported the creation of an "iron clad oath" for Southerners who wished to assume a role in public life and the government. Unlike previous test oaths, the iron-clad oath required its takers to swear to their faithfulness both present *and* past—a decidedly more difficult burden of proof than Johnson's oath to future loyalty only. The oath's opponents, including the president, found the presumption that loyalty could be tested—much less guaranteed—absurd. Democrat Garrett Davis from Kentucky joked that Congress should offer "a reward for the discovery of an invention which would provide a proper way of determining loyalty."[1]

Most scholars of loyalty testing share Davis's skepticism, if not outright ridicule. As Harold Hyman points out, no consensus existed among politicians or the public about what actions constituted loyalty or if a person's devotion to the nation could be measured or objectively judged. Even among military leaders, who had witnessed first-hand the bloody effects of the Southern commitment to the Confederacy, inconsistency defined the application of the iron-clad oath. Hyman notes that the stringency of test oaths varied by time, location, and "the predilections of the officials" charged with administering the oaths. While General John Pope demanded extensive swearing as commander of the

Third Military District in Georgia, General Don Carlos Buell saw it as little more than a formality and haphazardly dispensed with it in Louisiana.[2]

To Hyman, these inconsistencies symbolized a deeper problem with Civil War test oaths. Enraged by Senator Joseph McCarthy's redbaiting in the 1950s and the proliferation of laws demanding Americans pledge their allegiance with loyalty oaths most Congressional investigations into "un-American" activities ignited, Hyman did not mask his disdain for such contrivances. Hyman, whose work remains the standard narrative of loyalty oaths during the Civil War and Reconstruction, argues that not only did loyalty oaths fail because of the impossibility of measuring loyalty, but also that they "crippled the courts" in the South and made it impossible to staff Southern governments and federal posts with reliable men. He cites complaints from Treasury Department officials who were unable to collect revenue because there were so few Southerners whose pasts were not tainted by Confederate service. But more important, Hyman believes the quest for loyalty in the South was "patently useless" because the oaths were nothing more than "partisan weapons" that measured not national devotion but the lengths to which politicians would go to ensure patronage and political power. Like McCarthyism and allegiance-swearing in the 1950s, loyalty oaths in the Civil War era, Hyman declares, "debased the notion of patriotism and the very concept of loyalty."[3]

However, Hyman's belief that loyalty lies somewhere outside the boundaries of politics and should remain untainted by the workings of partisanship misrepresents the true purpose of political allegiance. Rather than seeing loyalty as an "abstract and mystical quality" that emanates from some undefined place (but often having a religious origin or quality), this essay understands both loyalty and patriotism as important tools for imagining communities (to borrow Benedict Anderson's phrase) and for building the institutions necessary for the modern nation-state.[4] As such, loyalty becomes essentially political, imbued with the language of partisanship and competition. As a function of state-building, the loyalty oaths that Hyman so despises reflected Republicans' attempts to legitimize their state through patronage and the promise of political participation that oath-taking held for white Southerners. These activities were not antithetical to the American political tradition, nor did they diminish the victors' calls for patriotism and national unity. On the contrary, the political exchange that Hyman despises is the essence of loyalty.

Hyman's skepticism of loyalty-swearing disregards two important insights into Reconstruction politics. First, expressions of loyalty, including oath-taking, were tools of Republican statecraft intended to foster a new biracial nationalism. As a vehicle for African American citizenship, patriotism, love for the Union, and fealty to the federal government offered freedpeople a means to secure their place within the body politic by distinguishing themselves from Southern whites. By using patriotism as a point of comparison between themselves and their former masters, freedpeople advanced their claims to political inclusion and participation. African Americans in both regions pointed proudly to the military service of approximately 180,000 black Union troops and seized upon the language of sacrifice and duty to propel black men into the political arena alongside whites. For African Americans, swearing an oath of allegiance was not a perfunctory performance.[5]

However motivating the idea of national loyalty was for freedpeople, it was not enough to secure their place within American society for very long. The problem with the postwar quest for Southern loyalty was not oath-taking *per se* but rather the inability of government officials to enforce allegiance. What Norton realized when he cautioned against Confederate amnesty was that sometimes loyalty must be compelled. Some politicians worried about the authenticity of Confederate declarations of allegiance, but the true test of the loyalty oath's reconstructive potential lay not in the hearts of the swearers but rather in the power of the federal government to use military force and other coercive means to ensure obedience. This essay explores the unspoken relationship between loyalty and power in the Reconstruction South as a way to re-imagine the nature of Reconstruction politics as more warlike than not, thus blurring the boundary between war and peace that historians typically rely on when thinking about the 1860s. It is of no small importance that the Southern states that existed in a protracted state of war throughout the 1870s—such as South Carolina, where black militias enforced Republican policies—were the last to be "redeemed" by conservative Democrats.[6]

The idea of loyalty motivated African Americans, who seized upon it to advance their claims for political and civil rights and to demand that the federal government protect them from disloyal attacks and white violence. However, their claim to a place of special importance in the pantheon of American patriotism was not new to the Civil War era. Revolutionary-era blacks who had cast their lot with Patriot cause in the War for Independence made the first case for the incorruptibility of black loyalty. Black participation in the war effort against the British had given them "high notions of liberty," to quote one white Charlestonian who feared Lord Dunmore's Proclamation had made it impossible for the colonists not to draw on slaves' sense of duty to both their masters *and* their country. By acknowledging that slaves could possess a commitment to an ideal above and beyond mere servitude, the American Revolution offered blacks their first opportunity to try on the patriot's clothes—and they fit. Although more slaves escaped to British lines than joined the American cause, the renown that some black patriots achieved served future generations of African Americans with leverage in their fight to end slavery.[7]

In the nineteenth century, black abolitionists resurrected the image of the black patriot to highlight the nation's broken promise of liberty and citizenship to those who had aided in its birth. The most daring writers and speakers used the legacy of black patriotism to call for a renewed armed struggle for freedom. David Walker, Henry Highland Garnet, and William C. Nell each devoted considerable effort to reclaim the history of black Revolutionary soldiers to establish a tradition of black loyalty to the nation in its most idealistic form. In his historical treatise, *Colored Patriots of the American Revolution*, Nell pointed out the irony of Anthony Burns's 1854 trial and conviction in Boston taking place only steps from where African American Crispus Attucks—"the first to defy and the first to die"—fell in the Boston Massacre in 1770. Nell decried the 1850 Fugitive Slave Act, which allowed Southern slaveholders "to put our fellow-citizens under practical martial law; to beat the drum in our streets; to clothe our temples of justice in chains, and to creep along, by the light of the morning star, over the ground wet with the blood of CRISPUS ATTUCKS, the noble colored man, who fell in King street before the muskets of tyranny, away in the dawn of our Revolution." After decades of silence, the name of the first black American patriot once again rang through the streets of Boston to invoke the indignation of the antislavery movement and the Northern black communities that watched in horror as slave power crept up to their doors.[8]

By the time the federal government began recruiting black men as Union soldiers, the declarations of black loyalty reached a crescendo. Frederick Douglass and Martin Delany drummed up support for black troops and urged black men to prove their loyalty again through military service and thereby make it impossible for the state to deny them their rights as citizens. Douglass's famous call to arms revealed the beguiling simplicity of his faith in the power of loyalty in the Civil War era: "Let him get an eagle on his button, and a musket on his shoulder, and bullets in his pocket, and there is no power on the earth or under the earth which can deny that he has earned the right of citizenship in the United States."[9] The sacrifices of black regiments at Fort Wagner, Milliken's Bend, and Fort Pillow, among other bloody encounters with the enemy, seemed to confirm the veracity of Douglass's political calculus as a once-skeptical Northern public began to sing the praises of black valor and patriotism. Supporters of black citizenship repeated stories like the one of Sergeant William H. Carney of the 54th Massachusetts, a former slave from Norfolk, Virginia, who upon seeing the regiment's color bearer fall dead rushed to retrieve the flag and rally his comrades to continue their assault against Fort Wagner. Seriously wounded, Carney managed to hoist the flag atop the Confederate parapet and uttered these final words to the soldiers who carried his riddled body away: "The old girl never touched the ground, boys."[10]

Just as he carried the Stars and Stripes atop Fort Wagner, Carney's comrades carried his image—the image of black men giving their lives for freedom and a new nation—into the postwar fight for civil rights. At conventions across the nation, black veterans and their supporters demanded that the government recognize the loyalty they had demonstrated on the battlefield. In Pennsylvania, black men recalled the history of black patriotism that began with the Revolution and reminded government officials that "the negro everywhere, without the incentive of large bounties, full pay, or promotion, interposed his body between his country and its enemies, bared his breast to the storm, and contributed his full share towards saving the flag and the Union." According to the convention, this proved that despite "all the trickery and deceit of the politicians" who refused to acknowledge their service, "there is not a disloyal negro." A convention of black men in Illinois echoed this sense of irony. Praising black soldiers as "defenders of our Republic," the convention pointed to them "as proof of our devotion to a country that had enslaved us and is still unkind." The black abolitionist William Forten expressed a more bitter denunciation of the nation's failure to extend voting rights to blacks and end racial segregation in the North, calling such inaction "base treachery." "We have been deserted by those whom we faithfully supported," Forten proclaimed, deserted by a country "that none love so well as we."[11]

Black veterans demanded the vote as well as protective legislation to aid freedpeople in the South who were caught in political limbo between slavery and freedom. No longer bound to serve white men, freedpeople nonetheless found themselves at the "tender mercies" of their former masters. New England blacks called attention to the "whipping, scouring and murdering" of freedmen as well as the institution of Black Codes that effectively negated the Emancipation Proclamation. "We plainly see either a design to forcibly drive the Negroes from the country, or to provoke such resistance on their part as would excuse a general massacre of them," the conventioneers surmised. They called on Congress and the Bureau of Refugees, Freedmen, and Abandoned Lands (the Freedmen's Bureau) to "throw around the loyal blacks such protection as shall secure them from the hatred of their former masters—a hatred caused by the assistance which the blacks have given the loyal cause." In addition to calling for the government to reward black veterans for their loyalty on the battlefield, these petitioners also pointed out how freedpeople continued to suffer for their loyalty. Loyalty became an important locus of political ideology for African Americans and the Republican Party as they embarked on the road to Reconstruction, a path strewn with dangerous obstacles, not least of which was hatred and violence.[12]

While their Northern counterparts had to prove their loyalty to the nation through battlefield sacrifice, freedpeople rarely had their loyalty questioned by government agents. In an ironic twist of logic, their status as slaves acted as a guarantee of their opposition to the Confederacy and their devotion to the Union. Although the condition of slavery ostensibly precluded the possibility that a slave could possess any independent political identity, the presumption of a slave's loyalty to the Union offered freedpeople a means through which they could establish a favorable relationship to the state. By recognizing a slave's inherent political character, white officials, like the agents for the Southern Claims Commission (SCC), made it possible for freedpeople to assert their own political subjectivity.[13]

However, the records of the SCC reveal that freedpeople who petitioned for compensation from the federal government for property confiscated during the war by Union troops usually faced a heavier burden of proof of ownership than whites. Such evidence shows that the presumption of loyalty did not extend smoothly to all Southern blacks.[14] Black petitioners who had been free before the war experienced increased scrutiny from skeptical commissioners who associated their freedom with disloyalty. Commissioners were particularly reluctant to recognize free blacks who had owned extensive property, sometimes including slaves, as loyal. Believing a free black's sympathies and economic condition more akin to those of slave owners than other slaves, the SCC drew such distinctions not on skin color but on the status of slavery. "We do not understand that the legal implication of loyalty applies to color or complexion, but to status or condition of slavery," the SCC concluded after denying the claim of a free black man from Amelia County, Virginia, "and at all events a free man of color who is a slave owner must establish his loyalty by satisfactory evidence."[15]

As a result, free blacks were careful not to appear too affluent lest their property holdings cause doubt in the commissioners' minds as to their loyalty. Moses Hampton, a free black from Cherokee County, Alabama, reminded the commissioners that although free, his race had been a great political and economic liability. "Being a colored man, I had no vote," Hampton told the SCC, and as a result, "I was for the Union cause all the time." In his narrative of loyalty, Hampton stressed his poverty and commonality with the majority of slaves. In his words, his status as a free man was in many aspects only nominal. "I purchased my freedom from my old master about the year 1851 paying for it out of careful earnings made by hand and constant work, and have been free ever since," Hampton told the committee, highlighting his thrift and toil. Hampton continued:

> I had learned the cotton gin manufacturing business and earned a living and made a little property by working at the business and also renting land on

Coosa River and carrying on farming. I had owned horses cattle and hogs and other personal property for years. I owned no land in my own right till the close of the war. My old master had been dead years before the war and all his property distributed. I did not owe him anything at his death. I had lived where and as best I could—at different places for years before and during the war.[16]

Hampton emphasized his lack of property and landholdings and his subsistence lifestyle to distinguish himself from his former master and other white landowners, whose economic ties to slavery presupposed Southern independence in the minds of the claims commissioners. It helped that Hampton was known to be a lay preacher, which led the commissioners to conclude that he was a "truthful, pious man." They found him loyal and approved his claim but for considerably less than the loss he originally declared.[17]

Nonetheless, the SCC offered Hampton and other freedpeople a unique opportunity to express in public their new status as citizens and articulate their expectations of what that status entitled them to. Through the language of patriotism and loyalty, freedpeople staked their claim on American politics. Their love and dedication to the Union cause, they argued, proved their fitness for citizenship and their rightful claim to its material benefits. Whether arguing for their right to vote or for reimbursement for confiscated property, African Americans exposed the material connection between loyalty and citizenship.

Republicans hoped to exploit this connection to bring white Southerners into the reconstructed fold. Republicans used loyalty oaths to elicit cooperation through patronage and the threat of political exclusion. As such, loyalty oaths for white Southerners relied more on fear than love. While Democrats may have chided Radicals for believing that loyalty could be measured, supporters of the loyalty oath never presumed to make Southerners love them or Reconstruction. Radical firebrand Thaddeus Stevens doubted so deeply that Southern loyalty to the Union could be rekindled he advised the federal government to treat the former Confederacy as a "conquered province" and allow the military to guide Reconstruction. "This is not a 'white man's' Government!" he exclaimed upon hearing Southerner's reluctance to accept his terms of readmittance to the Union. "To say so is political blasphemy, for it violates the fundamental principles of our gospel of liberty," he pressed. He advised keeping former Rebels on a short leash to ensure that their disloyal sentiments did not find expression in the mistreatment of freedpeople or government officials. Fear and power, Stevens believed, were the twin motivators of white Southerners, and their unadulterated display was the only thing that could compel the

Rebels' submission, which in the Stevens's mind was the first step in reconstructing loyalty.[18]

Southerners' love for the Union was not at question in 1865. Most military leaders and government officials took it for granted that Confederate surrender had resulted from physical exhaustion rather than an abandonment of the ideological tenets of secession. "The loyalty of the masses and most of the leaders of the southern people consists in submission to necessity," General Carl Schurz explained.[19] The problem was how to continue to ensure their submission.

Schurz advised against test oaths and disfranchisement, which many Radicals favored, but the public sentiment in 1865 was anything but conciliatory toward the South. While President Johnson pondered the fate of Confederate leaders, the *National Anti-Slavery Standard* encouraged him to see that "they stand in the relation of pirates and murderers to the government" and "should be treated by the government in the same manner as it would treat criminals of that character named under other circumstances." Likewise, Stevens, whose fire-and-brimstone rhetoric made him more akin to a Great Awakening preacher than to Abraham Lincoln, spoke for many Northerners when he called for divine vengeance to punish the great sin of treason. "I am not fond of sanguinary punishments," Stevens told a crowd gathered in his hometown of Lancaster, Pennsylvania, "but surely some victims must be found to expiate the manes of our starved, slaughtered martyrs."[20]

Always polemical, Stevens nonetheless reflected the feeling of many Americans that Southerners must be shown a firm hand. Letters to the president from across the nation in 1865 echoed Stevens's and the *Standard*'s sentiments. Furious citizens demanded harsh punishment for Confederate leaders. "All leading and well informed rebels should be handled without gloves," Samuel Snyder wrote to Johnson. An Ohio businessman advised Johnson to seek Jefferson Davis's court martial for "crimes in violation to the laws of war," including the horrible conditions at Andersonville Prison, the massacre of black soldiers at Fort Pillow, and even the assassination of Lincoln, which many believed the Confederate president had instigated. Another Union man hoped the government would capture "Old Jeff" and "all of the rebells [sic] officer & slave holders" and "hang all of them 500 ft. high." One Andersonville survivor thought Confederate leaders should be confined in prisons "every bit as dirty and as lousy & as stinking as the Secesh Prisons were for us poor Union soldiers." Such advice from everyday Americans continued as Johnson's gestures toward the South became more conciliatory. Alexander Wilson warned that the talks of pardons and amnesty had "given the subdued Devil courage to show itself." Others warned that if severe punishments were not inflicted "we will neither be respected at hom [sic] or abroad & we will still be nursing a viper that will soon sting us again." Such harsh treatment would, according to Wilson, "teach these fellows, who think Heaven, Hell and all earth must bow to them, that there is power above them."[21]

The image of Jefferson Davis swinging from a sour apple tree, as the popular ditty went, indulged national cries for vengeance to be sure, but it also spoke to deeper concerns about the federal government's political legitimacy. Could Reconstruction succeed without displays of national authority strong enough to compel Southern respect and acquiescence? For those individuals who wrote to President Johnson advocating the execution or imprisonment of high-ranking Confederate leaders, loyalty was more a matter of submission than love. Southerners needed compelling reasons for laying down their arms for good and recognizing federal authority. It little mattered if they truly loved the Union or freedpeople, so long as they behaved. Eventually they might soften their views toward emancipation and black citizenship—Thaddeus Stevens predicted that it would take at least three generations of military occupation before white Southerners reached that turning point—but in the meantime, coercion and military force would guide them on the road to self-revelation.

Oaths worked best if issued on the point of a bayonet: This principle seemed too Machiavellian for some who decried oaths and oath-taking as "mediaeval" and "worn-out implements, taken from the old tool-house of European despotism and oligarchy."[22] Those who discounted the need for extensive military reconstruction that lay behind the quest for Southern loyalty failed to recognize that their belief in peaceful cooperation and the democratic process rested upon a foundation of coercive state power. The exceptional American heritage that critics called upon was not as unique as they would believe. The legitimacy of republican government derived from violence, beginning with a military victory over Great Britain and sustained by innumerable displays of violence and power, from Shays Rebellion to the Civil War itself. The romance of republicanism, with its talk of popular sovereignty and consent of the governed, was a political fiction hiding the realpolitik of American unity in the eighteenth and nineteenth centuries.[23]

As Edmund Morgan points out in his study of political storytelling in the United States, "government requires make-believe."[24] Political legitimacy cannot rest solely upon force but must also muster the active participation and cooperation of the governed. By creating stories of popular sovereignty and common political origins, both the governors and the governed cooperate in sustaining a political regime that often fell far short of true majority rule. Likewise, Reconstruction's officials utilized a language of national citizenship, universal political belonging, and emancipation to animate popular support for their programs. However, the language of loyalty not only spoke of love and devotion to the Union, it also informed Southerners of the repercussions of nonadherence: disfranchisement, military occupation, and the possibility of land confiscation, financial ruin, and (some Northerners hoped) physical punishment.

Democratic governments are in a constant, yet often hidden, state of war. Even in times of ostensible peace, states are required to honor Max Weber's dictum that they must monopolize the means of legitimate force.[25] Few, if any, other periods of American history exposed this facet of governance like Reconstruction. While Republican political legitimacy could not rely solely on force, it could not succeed without it. While African-Americans recounted their patriotism and spoke of their love and devotion to the Union to establish their political identity and (hopefully) a biracial nationalism, only the threat of force enabled them to act as citizens. Loyalty, the Janus of American political mythology, has two faces: one loving and hopeful, the other hard and unbelieving. In neither case does loyalty exist as a pure, altruistic emotion. It entails, indeed requires, material consequences for the person who swears allegiance, be they rewards for adherence or punishments for defiance. Republicans largely underestimated the warlike nature of the democratic revolution they attempted and put too much faith in the peacetime measures they hoped would accomplish it.

<table>
<tr><td>

11

</td><td>

Reconstructing the
Nation, Reconstructing
the Party: Postwar
Republicans and the
Evolution of a Party

MICHAEL GREEN

</td></tr>
</table>

O n April 14, 1865, Abraham Lincoln held what proved to be his last
Cabinet meeting. The meeting was unusual in several ways: The minister to whom Lincoln was closest personally, Secretary of State William Henry Seward, was absent, recovering from a fall from a carriage; it was
the first Cabinet meeting since Robert E. Lee had surrendered to Ulysses S.
Grant, effectively ending the major fighting in the Civil War; and, during his
first term, Lincoln had met with his Cabinet irregularly. That group originally
included four of his rivals for the Republican nomination in 1860—in other
words, a coalition Cabinet of fellow Republicans committed to the same cause
of Union but politically ambitious in their own right. As his second term began,
Lincoln's Cabinet included only two of its original members, Seward and Secretary of the Navy Gideon Welles, neither of whom was popular in the Republican Party. The rest included Secretary of War Edwin Stanton, whom Lincoln
had plucked from the opposition Democrats for the job; Attorney General
James Speed, the brother of his oldest friend; and Secretary of the Interior
James Harlan, a former senator from Iowa whose daughter was engaged to Lincoln's son. For the most part, the Cabinet members owed their jobs not to their
own party eminence, but to Lincoln, who had become his party's eminence.[1]

At that meeting, Lincoln suggested letting Jefferson Davis escape the country
and letting the Southern states try to govern themselves, "though I reckon that
at first some of them may do it badly." Speed told his fellow Radical, Salmon
P. Chase, that Lincoln "never seemed so near to our views." That night, John
Wilkes Booth crept into Lincoln's box at Ford's Theater. While Booth and his
coconspirators had discussed their plans for weeks, Lincoln had inspired Booth
to action during what turned out to be—thanks to Booth—Lincoln's last
speech. Addressing a group of serenaders from the White House window on
the evening of April 11, Lincoln suggested increasing acceptance of the radical
view of Reconstruction when he said, "It is also unsatisfactory to some that the
elective franchise is not given to the colored man. I would myself prefer that it
were now conferred on the very intelligent, and on those who serve our cause

as soldiers." Booth turned to a companion and said, "That means nigger citizenship. Now, by God, I'll put him through." Three nights later, he did. With Lincoln's death on April 15, 1865, Vice President Andrew Johnson became president.[2]

While any leadership change in the White House affects the country, the shift from Lincoln to Johnson could not have been more significant. Johnson had been the vice presidential nominee in 1864 despite spending his political career as a Democrat. His selection reflected the importance that the Union Party, the new look of the Republican Party, placed on national unity. It also demonstrated how little importance politicians attached to the vice presidency, despite the fact that the first two vice presidents to take office when the president died, John Tyler and Millard Fillmore, differed from their predecessors on important issues. Yet, despite or perhaps because of them, their political parties survived. Nominally a Whig, Tyler left office with that party intact; more conservative than many of his fellow Northern Whigs, Fillmore failed to win his party's nomination, and the Whig party eventually dissolved in the wake of the Kansas-Nebraska Act in 1854. But Johnson's impact proved far different. He hindered his adopted party's policies in ways that resonate to this day and forced the party to adopt a different mode of action in pursuit of its goals and policies. The results shaped not only the civil rights that Americans are supposed to enjoy but also the direction of American politics and government throughout Reconstruction and afterward—including after Johnson left office, replaced by Republican Ulysses S. Grant.[3]

Even before the Civil War ended, Republicans faced a series of adjustments. The party that won the White House in 1860 differed from the one that kept it in 1864. Not only had its name changed to the Union Party—at least for the purpose of its national campaign in 1864—but, more important, its beliefs and priorities also had changed. Before the war, Republicans had combined out of the ruins of the Whig Party, the ambitions of Free Soilers and some old Liberty Party men, the recruitment of recently arrived German voters, the acceptance of former Know-Nothings seeking a political home, and a Democratic Party divided over slavery—all to form a sectional party designed to stop the spread of the South's "peculiar institution" into the western territories. The party of "free soil, free labor, free men" then adjusted to the promise and peril of power and responsibility during the Civil War.[4]

As their earlier slogan made clear, Republicans could continue to emphasize freedom in its various forms. But they also stressed the importance of saving and preserving the Union. Doing that required them to figure out how to stay in control of the government under threats from the South and their Democratic opponents in the North, with the hope that they eventually would, like the Democrats and the Whigs, become a national party. Accordingly, they had to wield very different kinds of power: governmental, military, political, and electoral. Understanding their evolution requires an understanding of how Reconstruction evolved during the presidencies of Lincoln, a Republican who retained much of the ideology he had developed during his years as a Whig; Johnson, a Democrat who joined the Union Party but never became a Republican; and Grant, who belonged to the Republican Party only after the war had begun. They faced a varied set of issues, inside and outside of their parties.

For Lincoln, the question of Reconstruction required an answer from the moment he took the oath of office on March 4, 1861, and that fact helps explain the trajectory that Reconstruction would follow as an era and a policy. Historians usually trace the beginning of Reconstruction to Lincoln's signing of the Emancipation Proclamation on January 1, 1863, or to Lee's surrender to Grant on April 9, 1865. But when Lincoln took office, his first task was indeed to reconstruct a divided Union. Seven Southern states had seceded and formed the Confederate States of America. In his inaugural address, he sought to convince the South of his good intentions. He declared,

In view of the Constitution and the laws, the Union is unbroken; and, to the extent of my ability, I shall take care, as the Constitution itself expressly enjoins upon me, that the laws of the Union be faithfully executed in all the States. . . . I trust this will not be regarded as a menace, but only as the declared purpose of the Union that it will constitutionally defend, and maintain itself. In doing this there needs to be no bloodshed or violence; and there shall be none, unless it be forced upon the national authority.

His peroration repeated the point:

In *your* hands, my dissatisfied fellow countrymen, and not in *mine*, is the momentous issue of civil war. The government will not assail *you*. You can have no conflict, without being yourselves the aggressors. *You* have no oath registered in Heaven to destroy the government, while *I* shall have the most solemn one to 'preserve, protect and defend' it.[5]

Obviously, the South doubted his intentions. Four more states seceded after the firing on Fort Sumter on April 12, 1861. Four years and more than 600,000 dead later, the North had won the Civil War and the Thirteenth Amendment, outlawing slavery, was close to ratification. Along the way, Lincoln and his fellow Republicans renamed themselves the Union Party to signify their changed circumstances and, perhaps not coincidentally, paint their opponents as anti-Union. More significantly, they had to figure out how to govern not just the Union, but a divided United States. Making matters more difficult, Lincoln lacked experience in government, the Cabinet was convinced of his inferiority, and a newly Republican Congress had to acquaint itself with the requirements of chairing committees and managing legislation. And all of them were used to being in the opposition, which contributed to their tendency to squabble over large constitutional issues, such as the checks and balances between the executive and legislative branches, and smaller political and personal matters that ranged from patronage appointments to conflicts that had begun before the Republican Party existed and its members were Democrats, Whigs, or something else.[6]

Reconstructing the Union was at the heart of these debates. Lincoln's first approach to Reconstruction combined government and political policy with military action, such as calling up troops and ordering the Union Army forward to Bull Run. Militarily, the Union's actions resembled later debates among politicians who were divided over whether to restore the South to the Union or change it completely. From Lincoln and his generals to soldiers and civilians, one of the lengthier debates was over how hard the army fought. Generals who had been Democrats or showed sympathy for old army friends who had seceded with their states faced skepticism about their intentions (many Republicans found George McClellan especially obnoxious, but Radicals also were dubious at times about Grant and William T. Sherman, the generals ultimately responsible for winning the war). Radical Republicans in particular were a driving force behind forming the Joint Committee on the Conduct of the War, partly because they questioned the commitment of some military commanders—and by extension Lincoln—to taking the fight to the South with proper verve and passion.[7]

The key components of the Union's policy toward reconstructing the Union involved what to do about slavery and how quickly to do it. Lincoln originally refused to confiscate slaves and overruled emancipation orders issued by Generals John C. Frémont in 1861 and David Hunter in 1862. His reasons involved not his personal opposition to slavery, which he made clear, so much as his concern that the two generals claimed to have power that only he had the right to exercise and his concerns about whether the North would accept emancipation. He allowed General Benjamin Butler to treat slaves as contraband property, yet irked Congress by questioning legislation that approved the confiscation of Confederate slaves and by proposing the unpopular ideas of colonizing Africans and compensated emancipation. In each case, Lincoln wanted to keep the border slave states in the Union and dealt with these measures in ways designed to reassure them. But he also hoped that if he could reassure the Rebels that the Union was reasonable, they would stop fighting and return to the Union.[8]

The Emancipation Proclamation thus proved to be an end of one aspect of wartime "reconstruction"—the end of Lincoln's efforts to lure the South by dangling the carrot of continued slavery in front of it. The proclamation also was the beginning of the process of Reconstruction, as we now understand it, because the proclamation set slavery on the road to legal destruction. The proclamation also was part of a continuum of the policies Lincoln and the Republicans had been pursuing since the Preliminary Emancipation Proclamation of September 22, 1862, which warned the South that failing to lay down its arms in one hundred days would lead to the final proclamation. This warning provided another chance for the South to return to the Union; it was at the least a call to Southern slaveholding Unionists to come over to the Union side before it was too late. Following supposed constitutional strictures regarding his war powers in declaring for emancipation, Lincoln sweetened the pot for the South by applying the proclamation almost entirely outside of the unconquered Southern states, again showing his desire for restoration. When the South declined that opportunity, Lincoln issued the final proclamation and thereby changed the war's character, making it into the "remorseless revolutionary struggle" he had hoped to avoid when the war began.[9]

That some Republicans were dubious about the proclamation speaks to a problem that afflicted their party then and thereafter. Conservatives questioned the need for the proclamation and feared that the preliminary proclamation hurt them in the 1862 midterm election. In fact, they suffered what were actually the traditional losses that the party in power faces—except that Republicans never before had been in this position of power—and it happened at the height (or depth) of the Civil War. Radicals believed that the proclamation came too late, and some feared that Lincoln would back away from it. For his part, Lincoln doubted its efficacy and considered it a war measure that only his powers as commander-in-chief made possible.[10]

Lincoln was conscious of his war powers for constitutional reasons, but his powers also remained a thorny issue with his fellow Republicans. Thanks to Southern secession, Republicans controlled not only the White House but also Congress. Many Republican representatives and senators wanted a leader reminiscent of Andrew Jackson who would take the fight to the South. But whether they had been Democrats or members of the Whig Party that formed in response to Jackson's claims of presidential power, they also wanted the president to defer to the Congress on important issues, including (when Congress

deemed it necessary) military matters that might normally fall within the commander-in-chief's purview.[11]

The questions that congressional Republicans raised about Lincoln's powers
help explain the debate over Reconstruction that started during Lincoln's tenure and continued through Johnson's and Grant's presidencies. By December
1863, Lincoln was ready to propose a policy not to stop the fighting, although
he certainly would have welcomed that, but to reconstruct a Union that would
include a defeated South. His Proclamation of Amnesty and Reconstruction
consisted of what became known as the "10 Percent Plan." If the number of
otherwise eligible voters equal to ten percent of a Southern state's voters in the
1860 election took an oath of loyalty, that state began the process of being
restored to the Union. Lincoln concluded by noting that "while the mode presented is the best the Executive can suggest, with his present impressions, it
must not be understood that no other possible mode would be acceptable."[12]

But congressional Republicans, especially Radicals, considered Lincoln's
proposal too generous, as if he still expected the South to return willingly. The
Rebels might see such terms as proof that they really had not been defeated,
meaning that they would not have suffered—or suffered enough—for their
effort to destroy the Union. Worse, Lincoln's plan might preclude reordering
Southern society, which Radicals and many moderate Republicans deemed necessary for the sake of long-term stability (no more rebellions, they hoped), their
party, and the cause of human freedom. Radicals especially wanted to secure
emancipation, and suffrage would help protect the freedmen against their former masters and presumably help build the Republican Party in the South. But
they also opposed Lincoln taking the lead on the issue of Reconstruction, which
they saw as beyond the scope of his powers as commander-in-chief. Their
desire to assert legislative power and make greater demands to change Southern
society prompted Senator Benjamin Wade of Ohio and Representative Henry
Winter Davis of Maryland to introduce their own reconstruction bill. It
required 50 percent of the population of any state in rebellion against the
United States to take an "iron-clad" loyalty oath—swearing to never having
taken up arms against the Union or supported the rebellion—before a state
could petition for readmission.[13]

Lincoln responded by pocket-vetoing the bill as Congress finished its session, meaning that Wade and Davis had no chance to try to override him. Furthermore, Lincoln asserted that Southerners could choose either set of terms,
expecting that his more generous terms would gain more support than Congress's. Angry at their bill's fate and Lincoln's assertion of executive power,
Wade and Davis issued a manifesto in August 1864 that attacked his actions as
"a blow at the friends of his Administration, at the rights of humanity, and at

the principles of Republican Government." They also declared "that the authority of Congress is paramount and must be respected . . . and if he wishes our support, he must confine himself to his Executive duties—to obey and execute, not make the laws—to suppress by arms armed rebellion, and to leave political reorganization to Congress."[14]

While congressional Republicans shared many of the sentiments in the Wade-Davis manifesto, they were appalled at its timing, coming only three months before the 1864 election. If anything divided Republicans, it was whether to stake out the moral high ground, as Wade and Davis believed they were doing, or practice the art of the possible in hopes of winning elections and thereby being in a stronger position from which to pursue those moral policies. That anyone could have viewed the Wade-Davis manifesto favorably also reflected the differences between Lincoln and his fellow Republicans over who should control Reconstruction. As Lincoln told one of the bill's supporters, Radical Senator Zachariah Chandler of Michigan, "I conceive that I may in an emergency do things on military grounds which cannot be done constitutionally by Congress." Lincoln already had backed lopping off the Unionist portion of Virginia to create the new state of West Virginia and was nursing along governments in Tennessee, Louisiana, and Arkansas, where Union forces had triumphed and Radicals in Congress preferred to take the lead. None of the changes Lincoln wanted to make or did make would have been possible in a time of peace, and he questioned whether some of them were possible in time of war. His Cabinet was divided on the issue of West Virginia. Lincoln supported the new state's creation with more constitutional ambivalence than Republicans in Congress demonstrated on such issues as what powers a seceded state retained.[15]

Republicans in Congress also had strong feelings about Lincoln and his administration. Although they shared a variety of positions (though they expressed them differently) and often helped Lincoln force conservative Republicans closer to the middle, many Radicals simply had no faith in him. Their reasons were many: He was not one of them, he did not defer to them, and his Cabinet was too conservative, especially Seward, a onetime Radical whose old comrades saw him as too shifty and too willing to compromise. Furthermore, the Cabinet's only major Radical, Secretary of the Treasury Salmon P. Chase, often complained that Lincoln paid no attention to him. That Lincoln eventually pursued most of their policies, ultimately endorsing the end of slavery and cashiering poor generals, did nothing to mollify them. Not only did he take these actions long after they preferred, but he gave no sign that Radicals' importuning inspired them.[16]

Yet Lincoln proved to be a driving force behind the Thirteenth Amendment, which lay at the heart of Reconstruction. Its passage freed four million slaves and deprived the South and border states of more than one billion dollars worth of what slave owners considered their property. Lincoln pushed for the constitutional amendment in the Union Party platform and in Congress, which ultimately passed a short, watered-down version of what Radicals wanted. Radicals sought not only emancipation but also a clear statement of African American rights. But Lincoln's support for the amendment demonstrated his constitutional scruples. He realized that the Emancipation Proclamation was a war measure issued by the commander-in-chief under his war powers. Therefore it might not have survived constitutional scrutiny; even though Lincoln had appointed several Supreme Court justices, a future president might appoint justices who remained wedded to the *Dred Scott* decision. When the House added its approval to the Senate's on January 31, 1865, Lincoln proclaimed the amendment "a king's cure for all the evils. It winds the whole thing up." He also took the step of signing the congressional proclamation to send it to the states for ratification—inspiring several congressional Republicans to protest that as president, he had no right to do that.[17]

Little more than a month after this constitutional dustup came Lincoln's second inaugural address, in which he suggested the differences between wartime and postwar Reconstruction. The conclusion of the address talked about the need to show "malice toward none" and to "bind up the nation's wounds." But that paragraph can be parsed to show that first he wanted "to finish the work we are in," then "to care for him who shall have borne the battle"—the soldier who had come home from a completed war—and to "achieve and cherish a just, and a lasting peace, among ourselves, and with all nations." But in the previous paragraph Lincoln uttered what David Herbert Donald called "one of the most terrible statements ever made by an American public official": "If God wills that it continue, until all the wealth piled by the bond-man's two hundred and fifty years of unrequited toil shall be sunk, and until every drop of blood drawn with the lash, shall be paid by another drawn by the sword, as was said three thousand years ago, so still it must be said 'the judgments of the Lord, are true and righteous altogether.'" The struggle had indeed become "remorseless" and "revolutionary." Lincoln was prepared to fight to the finish and reconstruct the Union on the basis of eliminating what he described in the same speech as "somehow, the cause of the war": slavery.[18]

The Thirteenth Amendment's passage and Lincoln's second inaugural spoke volumes about Republican Reconstruction policies. Republicans were triumphant: Their party had guided the nation to victory and changed American society forever. But even the amendment ending slavery—certainly a moment of triumph for them—prompted a Republican debate over the freedpeople's rights and legislative and executive power. It followed nearly four years in which the president and Congress often squabbled over the power of their party and the government they were trying to preserve. The second inaugural address managed to capture the Radical view that the North needed to defeat the South and change Southern society while expressing Lincoln's older, often forlorn hope for a peaceful reunion.

As the war ended, Lincoln and his party were preparing to decide the fate of four million freedpeople and a defeated South, and whether the president or the Congress would have the most to say about it. At that final Cabinet meeting, Lincoln not only articulated some plans for the postwar South but also said, "If we were wise and discreet, we should reanimate the States and get their governments in successful operation, with order prevailing and the Union reestablished, before Congress came together in December. . . . We could do better, accomplish more without them." By December, Lincoln was dead. So was the Union Party they had formed during the Civil War and, in some ways, so was the Republican Party as they had known it, whether or not those involved realized it. The debates that sometimes had vexed Republicans during the Civil War had taken on a new cast. Lincoln's assassination would change not only the direction of Reconstruction but also the Republican Party.[19]

When Andrew Johnson took office as president, some Republicans were pleased, indeed to an unseemly degree, given the circumstances. Radical Representative George Julian of Indiana wrote, "Hostility towards Lincoln's policy of conciliation and contempt for his weakness were undisguised. The universal feeling among radical men here is that his death is a god-send." Wade, never noted for his subtlety, said, "Johnson, we have faith in you. By the gods, there will be no trouble now in running the government!" Wade may have meant that Radicals would be in charge or that Johnson would take a radical approach, but either way, he was wrong.[20]

Johnson's impact went beyond interfering with Republican plans for Reconstruction. He helped force another redefinition of the political system and of Republican ideology. Whether the Union Party was supposed to survive the Civil War is less certain than the willingness and desire of many Republicans to reconstitute party politics. Their feelings ranged from those of Charles Sumner, the Massachusetts Radical who always claimed to put principle ahead of partisanship, to Montgomery Blair, the Maryland conservative and scion of what may then have been the nation's leading political family, who wanted to unite Democrats with conservative and moderate Republicans, consigning "radicals" like Sumner to the political periphery. Not only did Johnson alter those plans, but he also ended up unintentionally lending aid and comfort to those Republicans who preferred to emphasize legislative power at the expense of executive power.[21]

At first, Republicans tried to reassure themselves of Johnson's loyalty to their cause and Johnson of their loyalty to him. Their early relationship reflected the fluidity of party politics. In little more than a decade (1854 to 1865), the Democratic Party had divided, the Whig Party had dissolved, the American (or Know-Nothing) Party and the Constitutional Union Party had been born and died, and the Republican Party had given way to the Union Party. As important as politics was to nineteenth-century society and culture, the party system was in such flux that Johnson, a lifelong Democrat who had owned slaves, had joined the Union Party, which was little more than the antislavery Republican Party under a different name. While he said all of the right things, at least as far as Republicans were concerned, what he failed to say was the problem—whether, like Lincoln, he shared their ideology of promoting freedom. The answer was no.[22]

Like Lincoln, Johnson preferred to operate with as little congressional oversight as possible and chose not to call a special session to deal with Reconstruction. At first Republicans were agreeable, since Johnson seemed to share their goals and plans. Some were skeptical because the war appeared to be over and they doubted his power to act without them. Thaddeus Stevens, the determined Radical who wielded considerable power in the House of Representatives, had never found Lincoln radical enough and suspected Johnson's heritage as a Southerner, slave owner, and Democrat would outweigh his more recent pronouncements attacking the South and defending the Union. By the end of Johnson's first month in office, Stevens suspected him of following the wrong path. Never noted for diplomacy, Stevens tried to reason tactfully with him. He wrote to Johnson, "Reconstruction is a very delicate question. The last Congress, (I expect the present) looked upon it as a question for the Legislative power exclusively. While I think we shall agree with you almost unanimously as to the main objects you have in view I fear we may differ as to the manner of effecting them." Stevens went on, "My only object now is to suggest the propriety of suspending further 'reconstruction' until the meeting of Congress." After Johnson issued his proclamation organizing North Carolina's government and began pardoning Confederates, Stevens wrote to him,

> I am sure you will pardon me for speaking to you with a candor to which men in high places are seldom accustomed. Among all the leading Union men of the North with whom I have had intercourse I do not find one who approves of your policy. They believe that 'Restoration' as announced by

you will destroy our party (which is of but little consequence) and will greatly injure the country. Can you not hold your hand and wait the action of Congress and in the mean time govern them by military rulers?[23]

Other Republicans also tried to influence Johnson. Radicals Salmon Chase and Carl Schurz toured the South and reported back to Johnson, who struck them as interested in and agreeing with what they had to say. But both left on their trips with agendas of their own. The *New York Herald*, whose conservative views proved far closer to Johnson's than did those of Republicans, reported that Chase, "the great negro-worshipper," was "in search of his old friends in the South" in hopes of achieving a political realignment that would help him run for president in 1868. Whatever his intentions (and Chase's panting after the presidency was well known), Chase did indeed hope for a party reorganization, including a return of the Democratic Party to what he considered its anti-slavery, Jeffersonian roots. Schurz also was ambitious, but he seemed to know in advance what he would find. "The Union must be reconstructed upon the basis of the results of the great social revolution brought about during the War in the South," he told a fellow German. Southern whites, however, were "thoroughly hostile to the tendencies of this revolution," especially the implications of a free labor system and race relations. A rapid restoration would soon leave the federal government powerless to intervene. Prompt action was required to ensure that Southerners would not attempt to repeal the results of the war in the future. In the meantime, he advised Johnson "not to have any elections held in the Southern States previous to the meeting of Congress." Charles Sumner reminded Schurz to emphasize that Southerners had to extend "complete justice to the negro. Preach this doctrine—talk it wherever you go." Like Johnson, Chase and Schurz would see what they wanted to see.[24]

What Chase and Schurz saw and said jibed with some of what their fellow Republicans wanted, but not entirely. While Stevens hoped that Johnson would defer to Congress, Chase told the president, "I have been careful to make them understand that the whole question of reorganization is in your hands." Schurz told Sumner that he was confident in Johnson and that it was his policy, "and in many respects a correct one, to bring about these results practically without making them the subject of popular discussion in the shape of an openly announced program"—a difference that reflected the continuing internal party debate over where power rested. But Chase remained ardently in favor of black suffrage, concluding that Southerners "would acquiesce in any mode of reorganization rather than see any more rebellion. You *can* do what you think right & do it *safely*," and that "I am anxious that *you* should have the honor of the lead in this work." Chase found "three classes," which he divided into "the old conservatives," "the acquiescents," and "the progressives," whom he called "the men of brains and energy; but they are few, & few of the few have been hertofore [sic] conspicuous. In the end, however, they will control." Yet he offered a news item that Republicans would have considered disquieting but probably appealed to Johnson: Some Southerners agreed to return to the Union without slavery but wanted "some mode of coercing labor," with Schurz chiming in that "they are as little as ever inclined to put in the place of slavery a bona fide system of free labor." Accordingly, Chase seemed surprised with "how little they seem to realize that any change in personal or political relations has been wrought by the war."[25]

Republicans soon began to include Johnson in that category. On May 29, 1865, he issued two proclamations that echoed the Lincoln who acted with the war still raging, not the Lincoln who had been shaping postwar policy. Johnson's first proclamation pardoned most Confederates who were willing to take a loyalty oath. He exempted those who owned more than $20,000 worth of land, requiring them to request a pardon personally—not to provide the freedpeople with forty acres and a mule, but to humble the aristocrats against whom Johnson had campaigned throughout his political career. The second proclamation set up North Carolina for readmission. It made the process even easier than Lincoln had contemplated and excluded from the process both African Americans and (not coincidentally) Congress, which remained out of session and largely unconsulted. Those men he did consult, such as Schurz, who called for black suffrage in some form, concluded that Johnson "listened so attentively that I was almost sure he would heed my advice." Chase and Sumner also listened to Johnson tell them that he agreed with them. With the May 29 proclamations, Schurz concluded, "I fear he has not that clearness of purpose and firmness of character he was supposed to have," and he warned Johnson that blocking black suffrage could force the legislative branch into "direct opposition."[26]

That is exactly what Johnson did, and the significance of his doing so was not limited to how he tried to shape Reconstruction to fit his racist views. He also claimed the power over Reconstruction that Lincoln had wielded more carefully and by referring to his war powers as commander-in-chief. Johnson hoped to use that power to reconstruct both the United States and the Union Party. Schurz wrote to Johnson, "I presume it is the desire of the Administration to build up a Union party in the Southern States; but I apprehend this object cannot be attained if the power and patronage connected with federal offices are placed into the hands of late rebels to the discouragement of the true Union element."[27] Johnson wanted to build the Union Party just as Schurz and other Republicans feared. Johnson's inclinations and interests proved crucial to the Republican Party's immediate and long-term future, for Republicans now confronted still another problem: trying to rebuild their party when its presumed titular leader subscribed to an almost completely different ideology.

As Stevens had anticipated, Johnson's actions drove Republicans into the opposition, despite being the clear majority party, because they no longer controlled the White House. When the war ended, those who had called themselves Republicans were not wholly united, but most of them agreed that the defeated South required change and the newly freed slaves needed protection to secure the fruits of their labor. One of the obvious problems was that Johnson saw the required change as bringing the planters to heel for the sake of poor whites, not to help African Americans in the process. And protecting the slaves would demand federal intervention in the South on a scale that a onetime Democrat like Johnson would find constitutionally, politically, and ideologically unacceptable. This forced Republicans to oppose the president they had been responsible for installing into office—the same situation the Whigs encountered when John Tyler became president.[28]

The Whigs had proved unable to pass the legislation they wanted, but their party survived, albeit with divisions between North and South over slavery. Almost completely united against Johnson, Republicans went through three distinct phases in their opposition that demonstrated both the power they retained and its limitations. The first phase lasted until Johnson's veto of the Civil Rights Act of 1866. Although Johnson had vetoed the bill to extend the life of the Freedmen's Bureau, which offended his states' rights and racist sensibilities by involving the federal government in helping the freedpeople, Republicans thought that they still could work with him. Senator Lyman Trumbull of Illinois, the guiding force behind the civil rights measure and the chairman of the Judiciary Committee, thought that he had Johnson's agreement not to veto his bill. But Johnson vetoed it, adding that the legislation to protect the freedmen's rights exceeded constitutional limits. It was a measure of how out of touch Johnson was with Northern sentiment that Republicans had so little trouble overriding his vetoes. And it was a measure of the popularity of Republican ideas with Northerners who wanted at least some degree of change in the South. They were able to pass legislation that directly aided the freedmen, reflecting their commitment to freedom, even though many Northern states had long since passed laws that distinguished between the races and sought to discourage blacks from even residing within their borders.[29]

The second phase of the relationship between Johnson and the Republicans extended from the Civil Rights Act veto until his impeachment in February 1868. Johnson did his best to end Republican control of Congress in what became known as his "Swing 'Round the Circle" during the midterm election campaign in 1866. It was the first time a president campaigned as a stump speaker directly to the people. Other politicians commonly faced the people in this fashion, but at that time it was considered beneath the dignity expected of a president, especially when Johnson responded to hecklers by likening himself to Jesus and Radicals like Stevens to Judas. Republicans actually increased their congressional majorities, which would have been a departure for the majority party in off-year elections if they still could have claimed the executive branch as their own. With even greater control of the Fortieth Congress pending, Republicans in the Thirty-Ninth Congress passed the Military Reconstruction Act, dividing the Southern states into a series of military commands, and the Tenure of Office Act, to keep Johnson from ejecting anyone from his Cabinet and thereby protecting Secretary of War Stanton, the last connection between Radicals and the administration. Possibly the former act and probably the latter went beyond what the Constitution intended, but Republicans were more committed to saving the freedpeople from the almost slave-like fate that Johnson had chosen for them, and perhaps to defanging Johnson, than to fretting about constitutionality.[30]

The third phase extended from Johnson's impeachment until he left office a year later on March 4, 1869. When House Republicans passed eleven articles of impeachment, Johnson's advisers and allies prevailed upon him to avoid the limelight and took steps to assure Republicans of Johnson's reasonableness. The belief among Radical and some moderate Republicans that ends mattered more than means proved problematic when their impeachment articles were too general and political to muster the votes to remove Johnson. The Senate acquitted him that May, falling one vote short of the required two-thirds to convict him thanks to seven moderate Republicans who joined conservatives and Democrats. The moderates feared the effects of Johnson's removal more than his continued presence in the White House for less than a year, especially when he was sure to be less obnoxious and with Grant likely to win the presidency that fall anyway. Johnson would do little damage in the remaining months of his presidency; besides, he already had done enough damage to Congressional Reconstruction and black civil rights.[31]

All three phases of this relationship had something in common: Republicans could legislate their views, but not enforce them. Those views evolved partly in response to the South's treatment of the former slaves and partly in response to Johnson's policies. The party's outlook shifted more toward Radical views than it had in the past, just as belonging to the opposition affected their words and deeds in the 1850s and led to a difficult adjustment when they gained power in 1861. Another factor was the Republicans themselves and the combination of time and circumstance. The Civil War was over, but in many ways the South redirected its violent response to slavery from Northerners to former slaves. Republicans kept legislating on issues related to slavery and freedom, but with almost no army to enforce them in the South and without a president to assure that enforcement. Thus, even with a congressional majority, they spent the Johnson administration in the minority.[32]

Their evolving relationship with Johnson also highlighted that Republicans were changing. As his term ended, several of the party's early leaders were gone or going, literally and figuratively. Stevens died soon after prosecuting Johnson's impeachment. William Pitt Fessenden, one of the seven Republican senators voting for acquittal and long the party's Senate leader, died not long after Johnson left office, as did Stanton, who may never have officially been a Republican but joined their cause. James Grimes, one of Fessenden's colleagues, had suffered a major stroke even before the vote, removing him from high-level involvement. Sitting as chief justice of the Supreme Court, Chase still wobbled between whichever interests might support him for the presidency, and his even-handed handling of the evidence in Johnson's impeachment trial angered his old Radical friends; health problems also helped sideline him. The Blair family returned to their Democratic roots. By remaining in Johnson's White House, Seward effectively ended his influence with the Republican Party. Politics in their states had all but assured Trumbull and Wade would be defeated for reelection, eliminating both a leading Radical and a leading moderate.[33]

Tellingly, one of the reasons moderate and conservative Republicans felt uneasy about convicting and removing Johnson was that Wade, as Senate president pro tempore, would succeed him. While they may have appreciated his radicalism on race, his views of the tariff made him anathema to some Republicans who feared that his presence in the White House would make it impossible to elect their candidate in the 1868 election. Thus, by then, most first-generation Republicans and the issues that brought them together were fading from the scene or changing. Some of the old guard obviously remained, committed to the principles upon which the party had been founded and those it evolved when faced with civil war. But another generation was coming to the fore. This group of Republicans was newer to the party and the issues. Their presence helps explain how the party—and Reconstruction—would evolve.

The party's evolution began with Grant's presidency. When Grant was dying of throat cancer and trying desperately to finish his memoirs, Mark Twain helped him obtain a publisher. Ironically, a Twain novel gave the late nineteenth century the name of the Gilded Age, and Grant often has been considered one of its examples. Grant never achieved the financial eminence of industrialists such as Andrew Carnegie and John D. Rockefeller, but his administration's policies contributed to the rise of late-nineteenth-century big business and political corruption. That rise was due in part to the economic and industrial expansion fostered by the Civil War, which propelled Grant from obscurity to international fame.[34]

Whatever the merits of that argument, Grant ascended to the presidency at a difficult time. As if the four years of hard fighting were not enough, the issues involved in the Civil War had long preceded the attack on Fort Sumter. By 1868 the Civil War was over—at least its military phase ostensibly was over—and slavery was dead, leaving the question of how much American society would change as a result. How long the nation would be willing to sustain so great an effort at reforming itself was open to question, especially when no comparable revolutionary change had happened in the nineteenth century.

Grant had been part of the military end of that reform but had little to do with policymaking. During the war he concentrated on what he did best: making war. Yet he also demonstrated political subtlety and shrewdness in turning Lincoln's orders and wishes into reality, dealing with the interplay of the political and the military and avoiding too much involvement in elective politics. Unlike generals like McClellan, Grant refrained from dictating policy on such issues as slavery. But he did advise Johnson after visiting the postwar South, "Four years of War during which law was executed only at the point of the bayonet, throughout the states in rebellion, has left the people possibly in a condition not to yield that ready obedience to civil authority the American people have generally been in the habit of yielding. . . . The white and the black mutually require the protection of the General Government." While he painted a rosier picture of Southern acceptance of defeat than reality suggested, Grant clearly sought a middle ground:

> The presence of black troops, lately slaves, demoralizes labor both by their advice and furnishing in their camps a resort for the Freedmen for long distances around. White troops generally excited no opposition and therefore a small number of them can maintain order in a given district. Colored troops must be kept in sufficient bodies to defend themselves. It is not the thinking man who would use violence towards any class of troops, sent among them by the General Government, but the ignorant in some places might, and the late slave seems to be imbued with the idea that the property of his late master should by right belong to him, or at least should have no protection from the colored soldier. There is danger of collisions being brought on by such causes.[35]

By the time he won the Republican presidential nomination in 1868, Grant knew plenty about political collisions. He had served as Secretary of War the first time Johnson tried to oust Stanton from the Cabinet (the second time inspired the impeachment). As general-in-chief, he worked with Johnson but managed to distance himself from him as the president grew more isolated. But despite his popularity as the winning general, he faced two problems as he entered the White House. One, he had declared, "Let us have peace." While that suggested a desire to end the violence that kept African Americans from enjoying their freedom in the South, it also reflected Northern weariness with fighting against white Southerners and for black people many still viewed with prejudice. Two, while Grant won a significant victory in the Electoral College— 214–60—over the Democratic ticket of Horatio Seymour and Frank Blair, Seymour had run stronger than Republicans could have anticipated in the popular vote, especially in the North. That, in turn, underscored the first problem.[36]

Grant's ascent also marked the second Republican generation's introduction to power. Unlike Lincoln, Seward, and Sumner, he had had nothing to do with the party's origins in the wake of the Kansas-Nebraska Act, nor did he engage in debates about slavery, the tariff, or any of the other Republican arguments, partly because he had been a prewar Democrat with little interest in politics. Also, historians differ about his approach to the presidency, disagreeing over whether he saw it as a reward for his service or as a position similar to being in the army, complete with chains of command. Accordingly, Republicans still debated whether the executive or legislative branch would drive Reconstruction.[37]

What made this debate different was that while Republicans again controlled both the White House and Congress, they were not the same Republicans as before and during the Civil War. Even if his political abilities were greater than many believed, Grant was no Lincoln and would inevitably have more trouble steering between Radicals out to reverse Johnson's racist policies and conservatives who wanted to move on to other topics. Also, while Lincoln started out with a Cabinet consisting of party leaders who were better known than he was, Grant surrounded himself with a largely mediocre group who generated less respect and leadership than Lincoln's controversial yet extraordinarily able set of ministers—and Grant inevitably would suffer in comparison, too. Lincoln's Cabinet, for all its failings, appealed to all wings of the Republican party; Grant's more closely resembled the kind of staff he might have assembled as a general.

Another factor in determining Republican ideas and policies during Grant's administration was what Lincoln and the Republican Congresses during the Civil War had accomplished on other fronts. Hoping to build "the greatest nation of the earth," Republicans approved such far-reaching measures as the Pacific Railroad Act and the Legal Tender Act. Both would affect Grant's administration in ways that reflected the Republican Party's wartime and post-war evolution. The legislation to build the transcontinental railroad set up what was essentially a public–private partnership to build the Union Pacific. Although Republicans could hardly have known what was to come, the Union Pacific's creation helped lead to the Crédit Mobilier scandal when the financial interest members of Congress held in it came to light. The series of subsidies for the construction of the Central Pacific prompted its owners to use their railroad's power to elect lawmakers who would block disagreeable taxes and regulation. The Legal Tender Act allowed the printing of paper money and showed the problems that Republicans faced in gaining and holding power: Chase, who supported the measure in 1863 as treasury secretary, later ruled against it as chief justice, which prompted Congress to create two new seats on the Court and Grant to appoint two new justices who proceeded to overrule Chase's decision. Republicans had learned, if they had not already known it, not just how to win office, but how to use that office to win political battles.[38]

Thus the Republican split in the election of 1872 reflected the evolution of the party and the issues it confronted. The reasons for the division and the rise of the Liberal Republicans varied from state to state and person to person—from Sumner breaking with Grant to Horace Greeley, the editor of the *New York Tribune*, believing that Radical Reconstruction had run its course and that this was his long-awaited opportunity to institute the policies he long had advocated as perhaps the nation's most influential newspaperman. Some Liberal Republicans hoped to go back to those halcyon days when Republicans seemed to stand more strongly for reform and honesty—not exactly the freedom the party advocated for African Americans, but they too would benefit from the change. They certainly believed that the party's desire to retain power had corrupted it, and they resented their lack of power in the process. By dividing the party and refocusing the issues, Liberal Republicans did a great deal to turn the attention of the party and the country away from Reconstruction and to the other problems that had to be confronted.[39]

The third factor determining Republican ideas and policies during Reconstruction was that the threat to the Union's survival was gone by 1868. The Civil War Republican or Union Party members who addressed slavery and Reconstruction did so with the nation's existence in the balance. Postwar Republicans, without the uniting force of the nation's potential demise, had difficulty agreeing on the definition of freedom and how much of it former slaves should have. The war also seemed to have settled whether a state could leave the Union. Therefore, for Republicans, the stakes in Reconstruction involved not the Union's survival so much as their political survival. If extending the vote and other rights to blacks would help them stay in power, they would do it. But

Radical Reconstruction would grow harder to pursue under Grant for a variety of reasons.

The first obstacle to Radical Reconstruction might be called a Republican return to the idea of free labor that had been central to the party's antebellum ideology, but with a revision. As early as 1866, Radical George Washington Julian pinpointed the South's problem with black suffrage:

> The leaders of Southern opinion openly declare that they would rather die than give the ballot to their former slaves. While it would give their section an increased representation in Congress, that representation would be secured by the votes of negroes and abolitionists, whose darling purpose would be to Yankeeize and abolitionize the entire South, and put the old slave dynasty hopelessly under their feet. And the old slave dynasty understands this perfectly. They know that negro suffrage, by checking rebel rapacity and restoring order, and thus rendering emigration from the North and from Europe a safe and practicable thing, will reorganize the whole structure of society in their region, and thus doom their pride and sloth to a hopeless conflict with the energy and enterprise of free labor.[40]

Julian's heart was in the right place, but the rise of the Black Codes that governed and limited former slaves, and the violence inflicted by the Ku Klux Klan and similar groups, made clear that simply putting the ballot into the freedmen's hands would not protect them. Whether they suffered from racism or war weariness, many Northerners believed that they had done their part for the cause of human freedom by fighting what ultimately became a war of emancipation and passing legislation that would protect the freedpeople.[41]

While Grant and other Republicans empathized with the freedpeople, they also suffered from the naiveté inherent in their ideology. Before the war, their belief in free labor suggested, as Julian did, that the South need only remove slavery and its economy would respond accordingly. A free-labor economy would translate into social benefits once Southerners grasped it would help white and black, rich and poor. Southerners surely would accept that fact because the Northern free-labor economy had defeated their way of life. Given abolitionist leader William Lloyd Garrison's decision to shutter the American Anti-Slavery Society in response to the Thirteenth Amendment's passage, it was understandable for Republicans with a more conservative view of the antislavery cause to think they had done enough and all would be well.

Ironically, the Republican Party's ideological shift during wartime to an understanding and appreciation of power and responsibility, which required a certain degree of cunning or shrewdness, also was related in part to that naiveté.

Republicans knew that their success demanded the retention of power; those who were not convinced of this fact were certainly persuaded by Johnson's presence in the White House. Accomplishing their agenda required them to win elections, which demanded they appeal more to the voters than did their Democratic counterparts. It was one thing to argue before the war that Southern society was either decrepit or benefiting from an unfair political or economic advantage through slavery and to argue during the war that the South's slave society was trying to destroy the republic. But to argue after the war that Northerners still had a moral obligation to go south and fight for the freedom they thought they already had won might be riskier and less likely to succeed, thereby leaving not only the freedpeople but also the rest of the country to a Democratic Party whose loyalty Republicans had openly and unsubtly questioned. Nor would that position attract Southern voters, who would be unlikely to vote for those who insulted them. Republicans also grasped the limits of continued action. As Grant said, "The whole subject of Executive interference with the affairs of a state is repugnant to public opinion. . . . Unless most clearly on the side of the law, such interference becomes a crime; with the law to support it, it is condemned without a hearing." That statement captured the Southern mentality, but it also did a great deal to explain Northern attitudes.[42]

Worse, emancipation and enlisting black soldiers, followed by Reconstruction and blacks taking advantage of newly available opportunities, had not eradicated racism—it had only reduced it. No Republican had more ardently supported ending slavery and spreading civil rights than Sumner, but his arrogance and holier-than-thou attitude had long since worn thin, especially when he challenged Grant over his plans to annex Santo Domingo. In the process, Sumner lost his chairmanship of the Senate Foreign Relations Committee in 1871—a far more dire fate than previous administration critics like Wade and Davis had met—and provided a warning to other Republicans that to get along, they needed to go along. Even then, Sumner always had been more of a moral leader than a practical one. The duty of real party leadership in Congress had fallen to the Radical but highly partisan and shrewd Stevens in the House and the moderate but bluntly pragmatic Fessenden in the Senate. They were now dead, and their successors included Republicans who had been less committed to Radical views, less determined to protect the freedpeople, and less supportive of the type of federal involvement in state affairs that Radical Reconstruction required.[43]

Further, Grant and his fellow Republicans wanted to turn their sectional party into a national one. This required them to resolve a conundrum: Could they accomplish this if they concentrated on protecting black civil rights in the

South? Their views on increasing the protective tariff and encouraging industri-
alization remained more popular in the North but might gain acceptance in the
South if they aided that region's economy. Recently freed African Americans
were less likely to enjoy the benefits of those policies, and white Southerners
were even less likely to support the Republicans advocating them if they saw
them as part of a plan to change the South not only economically, but also
racially. Samuel Bowles, the moderate editor of the *Republican* of Springfield,
Massachusetts, offered an observation that was not unique: "The Republican
party cannot long maintain its supremacy in the South by negro votes alone."[44]

A related problem for Republicans was how willing they were to fight to
protect black voters and workers against white intimidation and violence, and
how willing their constituents were to support them in that fight. In 1875, Grant
wrote, "The whole public are tired out with these annual, autumnal outbreaks
in the South." While Grant wanted to assure fair and free elections, he and
other Republicans saw a limit to Northern patience. They had other policies to
pursue. Although they would keep trying to help African Americans exercise
their rights as citizens, the benefits of doing so and their ability to do it might
prove limited. Republicans had to decide whether becoming the national party
they truly wanted to be was possible if they committed themselves to African
Americans over whites, which the situation in the South required them to do.[45]

Thus Republicans made a difficult choice. Retaining power to give them the
chance to do what they now deemed necessary for the country also required
them to sacrifice Southern blacks, not that they fully intended to do so. When
Rutherford B. Hayes took office in 1877 after the disputed election against Democrat Samuel Tilden, he hoped Southerners would accord some protection to
black rights. Hayes's policies would promote reconciliation rather than
violence.[46]

Republicans entered the Civil War with a belief in freedom that they perpetuated in wartime. After the war, they were successful to the extent that they
forced through constitutional amendments that gave freedom and the rights of
citizenship to African Americans. But protecting those rights required more
power and patience than Republicans were prepared to expend and white
Americans were prepared to accept. Instead, as Eric Foner wrote, "The dark
night of injustice settled over the South." And, in the process, it engulfed the
nation.[47]

Notes

Introduction: An Unfinished War / G. Ward Hubbs

1. Horace Porter, "The Surrender at Appomattox Court House," *Battles and Leaders*, ed. Ned Bradford (New York: Appleton-Century-Crofts, 1956), 615.

2. My study of Civil War diarists found none that continued once they returned home. See G. Ward Hubbs, *Voices from Company D: Diaries by the Greensboro Guards, Fifth Alabama Infantry Regiment, Army of Northern Virginia* (Athens: University of Georgia Press, 2003), xviii.

3. William Faulkner, *The Unvanquished* (New York: Random House, 1938), 229, quoted in George C. Rable, *But There Was No Peace: The Role of Violence in the Politics of Reconstruction* (Athens: University of Georgia Press, 1984), 32.

4. Among the few earlier historians to buck the trend was Avery Craven, who decided to treat "the so-called Reconstruction as the final phase of the American Civil War" in his *Reconstruction: The Ending of the Civil War* (New York: Holt, Rinehart, and Winston, 1969), iv. Extending the Blundering Generations thesis, Craven argued that the politicians of the 1850s and early '60s led the country into the horrors of Sharpsburg and Cold Harbor by their failure to resolve their differences by discourse and compromise. The post-Appomattox politicians continued their irresponsibility, albeit without resorting to massed armies, by deferring solutions to future generations. Craven thus saw continuity across the Civil War and Reconstruction where others saw only discontinuity (iv–v). Others who sought to extend the periodization included Rembert Wallace Patrick, whose *The Reconstruction of the Nation* (New York: Oxford University Press, 1967) emphasized economics and moved the end of Reconstruction up to the turn of the century. Herman Belz argued in *Reconstructing the Union: Theory and Policy during the Civil War* (Ithaca, N.Y.: Cornell University Press, 1969) that the beginning of Reconstruction must be moved back to before Fort Sumter, as politicians tried to avert division.

5. Benjamin H. Severance has just published a new book on the Tennessee state guard, *Tennessee's Radical Army: The State Guard and Its Role in Reconstruction, 1867–1869* (Knoxville: University of Tennessee Press, 2005), which argues that the guard should have been used more forcefully.

6. Rable, *But There Was No Peace*, 15. Gary W. Gallagher succinctly argues that Rable's exploration of violence in Reconstruction argues against continuity in *The Confederate War* (Cambridge, Mass.: Harvard University Press, 1997), 206–7n1.

7. The phrase may have been usd first by Allen W. Trelease in his *White Terror: The Ku Klux Klan Conspiracy and Southern Reconstruction* (New York: Harper & Row, 1970), xlvii.

8. I am currently completing a book about an 1868 encounter among the carpetbagger Lakin, a scalawag, a freedman, and a klansman in Tuscaloosa, Alabama.

9. C. Vann Woodward, introduction to *Rehearsal for Reconstruction: The Port Royal Experiment*, by Willie Lee Rose (New York: Bobbs-Merrill, 1964), xv.

10. G. Ward Hubbs, *Guarding Greensboro: A Confederate Company in the Making of a Southern Community* (Athens: University of Georgia Press, 2003).

11. Despite titles that claim otherwise, I have yet to find an adequate study of the effects of the Civil War on a Northern town.

12. David M. Potter, "The Historian's Use of Nationalism and Vice Versa," in *History and American Society: Essays of David M. Potter*, ed. Don E. Fehrenbacher (New York: Oxford University Press, 1973), 60–108. The better works looking at Confederate nationalism include Drew Gilpin Faust, *The Creation of Confederate Nationalism: Ideology and Identity in the Civil War South* (Baton Rouge: Louisiana State University Press, 1988); and Anne Sarah Rubin, *A Shattered Nation: The Rise and Fall of the Confederacy, 1861– 1868* (Chapel Hill: University of North Carolina Press, 2006).

13. Some recent works by historians have not been constrained by conventional periodization. David W. Blight, in his *Race and Reunion: The Civil War in American Memory* (Cambridge, Mass.: Belknap Press of Harvard University Press, 2001) focuses on historical memory, which cuts through traditional categories. And in her recently published study, *A Shattered Nation: The Rise and Fall of the Confederacy, 1861–1868*, Anne Sarah Rubin argues that the identity of those white Southerners who supported the war was not destroyed by the war. Indeed, even as former Confederates sought to accommodate themselves to Union victory, they intensified their identity as former Confederates by continuing their campaign of violence and resistance and by elevating Confederate symbols and rituals. Applying David Potter's understanding of nationalism, Rubin insists that the defeat of the armies may have meant the end of a nation, but it also marked the creation of a lasting identity. "It sometimes seems," she begins her book, "that the Confederacy is more alive today than it was in the 1860s" (*Shattered Nation*, 1). Also look at Nicholas Lemann, *Redemption: The Last Battle of the Civil War* (New York: Farrar, Straus, and Giroux, 2006). In studying Mississippi after the war by focusing on provisional Governor Adelbert Ames, Lemann, like the authors in this book, portrays Reconstruction as an extension of the war. This raised the ire of Sean Wilentz, whose examination of *Redemption* was published in the *New York Times Book Review*, Sept. 10, 2006. "By depicting Reconstruction as the final phase of the Civil War," writes Wilentz, "he suggests that the Confederates actually won, which diminishes the epochal importance of emancipation and secession's defeat." Wilentz's criticism is instructive, because it represents as clear a case of imposing a presentist agenda on the past as we will ever read. Some will always find an unfinished war either inconvenient or disturbing or both.

14. Robert Penn Warren, *The Legacy of the Civil War* (New York: Random House, 1961), 15.

1. A Victory Spoiled: West Tennessee Unionists during Reconstruction / Derek W. Frisby

1. LeRoy Graf et al., eds., *The Papers of Andrew Johnson*, 16 vols. (Knoxville: University of Tennessee Press, 1967–2000), 6:xxviii–xlii (hereinafter cited as the *Johnson Papers*); James Bingham to Andrew Johnson, Nov. 25, 1864, *Johnson Papers*, 6:314–16; Thomas Alexander, *Political Reconstruction in Tennessee* (Nashville: Vanderbilt University Press, 1950), 16–17. A group of prominent Tennessee Unionists, composed primarily of Johnson's close friends and supporters, tried to spur him into action, or failing that, to seize the initiative themselves. Nine representatives, three from each of the state's three Grand Divisions, met in Nashville in early September 1864 to press Johnson for the quick reestablishment of civilian government through a constitutional convention and the abolition of slavery. The Unionists also hoped to participate in the upcoming presidential election and to mobilize a new state militia. Although he refused to provide a written endorsement or accept an invitation to speak at their meeting, Johnson did issue a series of vague proclamations aimed at fulfilling some of the convention's demands.

In September 1864, Johnson issued three proclamations. The first, the Proclamation Concerning the Restoration of Civil Government, offered little more than advice and assurance to Tennesseans. Continued guerilla violence prompted the September 13 proclamation demanding all able-bodied males, white and black, enroll for the militia. This militia enrollment, however, was widely ignored. Finally, the September 30 proclamation established a process for holding the upcoming presidential elections, but Congress ultimately rejected Tennessee's returns.

2. *Johnson Papers*, 6:xxxiv–xxxv; Alexander, *Political Reconstruction in Tennessee*, 26–28. East Tennessee Unionists had issued a statewide call in November 1864 for delegates to a "preliminary State convention" to be held in Nashville on December 19 for the purpose of electing delegates and setting an agenda for a future constitutional convention. James Bingham, Johnson's chief advisor for West Tennessee, and the rest of West Tennessee's Unionist delegation were "a little taken back" by this unilateral call to action when military operations were still ongoing in East and Middle Tennessee; however, they pledged to send "good, true, and able men." Because of inclement weather and the battle of Nashville raging around the state capital during mid-December, Unionists delayed the "Liberty and Union Convention" until January 9, 1865. James Bingham to Andrew Johnson, Nov. 25, 1864, 7:314–16.

3. Alexander, *Political Reconstruction in Tennessee*, 26–28.

4. Ibid., 28–32; *Johnson Papers*, 6:xxxiv–xxxvii; "Proclamation Ordering Elections," Jan. 26, 1865, *Johnson Papers*, 6:436–38. A schedule to the state constitution generally provides for temporary measures for the transition from the previous constitution to the new one. The 1865 schedule contained several "substantive provisions of lasting effect," according to Tennessee constitutional scholar Lewis Laska. The 1865 schedule nullified the secession acts and subsequent acts of the Confederate Tennessee legislature, voided all debts incurred by the Confederate state government, and set voter qualifications, including provisions effectively disfranchising a majority of state voters. Lewis Laska, *The Tennessee State Constitution: A Reference Guide*, (Westport, Conn.: Greenwood Press, 1990), 159–60.

5. *Memphis Bulletin*, Mar. (n.d.) and Nov. 21, 1863.

6. Alexander, *Political Reconstruction in Tennessee*, 36–42. Secessionists had imprisoned Brownlow for his Unionism early in the war. He witnessed the torture and execution of Unionists and contracted a chronic illness during his imprisonment. Following his release, a very bitter Brownlow became a minor celebrity by using his background as a pastor and a reporter to rail against his former captors in books and Northern speaking tours about his experiences. In Tennessee, the term *Conservative* referred to opponents of the expedited constitutional revision measure and later opponents of the Brownlow policies of punishing and disfranchising former Confederates and the institution of freedmen suffrage. Radicals in Tennessee generally supported Brownlow's policies, but a sizable number of them became concerned over his tactics to accomplish them.

7. Bingham to Johnson, Dec. 23, 1864, *Johnson Papers*, 6:351–54. Johnson had appointed an executive committee for each Grand Division to keep him informed, and West Tennessee's committee consisted of James Bingham, William Hall, James Tomeny, Alvin Hawkins, and James Merriman. Bingham harbored a misplaced faith in Johnson's radicalism, telling the governor that Lincoln's plan to win the former Rebels back through "kindness" and leniency was doomed to fail, and that congressional Radicals' current dissatisfaction with Lincoln would eventually place Johnson in the Oval Office. "Lincoln's star will wane," Bingham predicted, "and just so as surely as you shall strike out boldly and fearlessly for the most rigorous measures and the most complete extinguishment of the rebels, just so surely your star will grow into the first magnitude."

8. Alexander, *Political Reconstruction in Tennessee*, 36–42.

9. Richard N. Current, *Lincoln's Loyalists: Union Soldiers from the Confederacy* (Boston: Northeastern University Press, 1992), 200; West Tennessee Refugees, letter to Johnson, Feb. 11, 1865, *Johnson Papers*, 7:470–71.

10. Fielding Hurst to William G. Brownlow, July 26, 1865, Andrew Johnson Papers, Library of Congress, Washington, D.C.; Brownlow to Johnson, July 30, 1865, William G. Brownlow Papers, Tennessee State Library and Archives, Nashville.

11. Alexander, *Political Reconstruction in Tennessee*, 72–75.

12. Ibid., 79–97.

13. Lonnie Maness, "Emerson Etheridge and the Union," *Tennessee Historical Quarterly* 48 (Summer 1989): 104–5. Etheridge denied statements attributed to him calling for violence against the white officers of United States Colored Troops (USCT) regiments as well as tax collectors.

14. Ibid.; Emerson Etheridge to Johnson, July 13, 1865, *Johnson Papers*, 8:394–403; Alexander, *Political Reconstruction in Tennessee*, 89–91. Etheridge's arbitrary arrest was one of as many as 38,000 made on civilian members of the loyal opposition since President Lincoln's suspension of *habeas corpus* during the Civil War. See Mark Neely Jr., *The Fate of Liberty: Abraham Lincoln and Civil Liberties* (New York: Oxford University Press, 1991). Neely's book focuses on the Lincoln administration's civil liberties policies rather than Tennessee's military occupation government under Andrew Johnson, and thus ignores Etheridge's unique predicament as an active candidate arrested during a campaign.

15. Alexander, *Political Reconstruction in Tennessee*, 98–112. Tensions increased in July 1866 as Tennessee prepared to ratify the Fourteenth Amendment in order to be readmitted into the Union. Many Tennesseans expressed their dissatisfaction with the amendment and urged their representatives to defeat it. When the General Assembly convened for a vote, Conservatives in the lower house managed to stage another boycott to prevent a quorum. Brownlow, fearing violence, requested assistance from federal authorities to maintain the peace; his request was denied. Brownlow then ordered the arrest of two Conservative legislators, who were apprehended, brought to the Capitol, and held in an antechamber off the House floor. The Speaker declared the two representatives "present, not voting," giving the House a quorum to ratify the Fourteenth Amendment, making Tennessee the first Southern state to meet Congress's qualifications for readmission to the Union. Brownlow, who suspected President Johnson had instigated opposition to the amendment, sent notification of the results to Congress: "We have fought the battle and won it. . . . 43–11 against [the amendment], two of Andrew Johnson's tools not voting. Give my regards to the dead dog in the White House." William Brownlow to James Folney, July 19, 1866 in *Knoxville Whig*, July 25, 1866. Tennessee ratification of the Fourteenth Amendment exempted it from the Reconstruction Acts and allowed the state's congressional delegation, including West Tennessean Isaac Hawkins, to take their seats in December 1866.

16. Charles Lufkin, "A Forgotten Controversy: The Assassination of Senator Almon Case of Tennessee," *West Tennessee Historical Society Papers* 39 (1985): 37–50. Case's other son, Alden, had served with the Seventh Tennessee Cavalry and had died at Andersonville in 1865.

17. *Nashville Daily Press and Times*, Feb. 5, 1867; Lufkin, "A Forgotten Controversy," 37–50.

18. Alexander, *Political Reconstruction in Tennessee*, 149–52; Benjamin H. Severance, *Tennessee's Radical Army: The State Guard and Its Role in Reconstruction, 1867–1869* (Knoxville: University of Tennessee Press, 2005), 11–21.

19. Jonesboro *Union Flag*, Apr. 5, 1867; Lonnie Maness, "Henry Emerson Etheridge and the Gubernatorial Elections of 1867: A Study in Futility," *West Tennessee Historical Society Papers* (1993): 17–49; Alexander, *Political Reconstruction in Tennessee*, 141–45. See also Rosalyn Smith, "Emerson Etheridge as a Candidate in the Tennessee Gubernatorial Election of 1867" (master's thesis, University of Tennessee, 1969).

20. *Nashville Daily Press and Times*, Apr. 17, 1867; Maness, "Henry Emerson Etheridge," 42.

21. C. V. Underwood to Brownlow, Mar. 29, 1867, and Apr. 15, 1867, Brownlow Papers; Alexander, *Political Reconstruction in Tennessee*, 150–51; Severance, *Tennessee's Radical Army*, 26, 36–38, 235–37.

22. Alexander, *Political Reconstruction in Tennessee*, 153–54; Maness, "Henry Emerson Etheridge," 47–48; Severance, *Tennessee's Radical Army*, 169–72.

23. Alexander, *Political Reconstruction in Tennessee*, 152–54; Maness, "Henry Emerson Etheridge," 43–49.

24. Alexander, *Political Reconstruction in Tennessee*, 156–62; Maness, "Henry Emerson Etheridge," 47–49; Severance, *Tennessee's Radical Army*, 61–144.

25. Alexander, *Political Reconstruction in Tennessee*, 195–99; Severance, *Tennessee's Radical Army*, 188.

26. Alexander, *Political Reconstruction in Tennessee*, 212–13; Severance, *Tennessee's Radical Army*, 206, 211–214. According to provisions within the state constitution, DeWitt Senter, speaker of the state senate, became Tennessee's governor to serve out the remainder of Brownlow's term when the legislature named Brownlow to a seat in the U.S. Senate in February 1869.

27. Alexander, *Political Reconstruction in Tennessee*, 212–13, 215–38.

28. Ibid.

29. W. H. Stillwell to Brownlow, Apr. 18, 1870, Brownlow Papers; Current, *Lincoln's Loyalists*, 204; Peggy Scott Holley, "The Seventh Tennessee Volunteer Cavalry: West Tennessee Unionists in Andersonville Prison," *West Tennessee Historical Society Papers* 42 (1988): 58.

30. Gary Blankenship, "Fielding Hurst: Tennessee Tory: A Study of a West Tennessee Unionist of the American Civil War" (master's thesis, Memphis State University, 1977), 121–35; Kevin D. McCann, *Hurst's Wurst: Colonel Fielding Hurst and the Sixth Tennessee Cavalry U.S.A.* (1995, reprint ed., n.p.: McCann Publishing, 2007), i–ii, 58–63; Lufkin, "West Tennessee Unionists in the Civil War," 33–42; W. Clay Crook, "Hurst!" *Confederate Veteran* (Mar./Apr. 1992): 20–23.

31. Isaac Hawkins, "Rights of Citizens," speech, *Congressional Globe* (Jan. 25, 1868): 759–64.

32. Ibid., 763.

33. "The Commissioners of Claims appointed under Act of Congress, March 3, 1871," appendix in Frank Klingberg, *The Southern Claims Commission* (Berkeley: University of California Press, 1955), 16–18, 56–156. For additional insight into the operation of the commission, see Klingberg, "The Southern Claims Commission: A Post War Agency in Operation," *Mississippi Valley Historical Review* 32 (Sept. 1945): 195–214. For an excellent account of Alabama Unionists from the Southern Claims Commission records, see Margaret Storey, *Loyalty and Loss: Alabama's Unionists in the Civil War and Reconstruction* (Baton Rouge: Louisiana State University Press, 2004).

34. Klingberg, *Southern Claims Commission*, 16–37, 56–156.

35. John Edwards, letters to Charles Benjamin, July 13, 1874, roll 5, and Mar. 20, 1875, roll 11, Records of the Commissioner of Claims (Southern Claims Commission), 1871–81, National Archives Microfilm Publication M87, National Archives and Records Administration (hereinafter cited as Southern Claims Commission, M87); Claim 10270, Mary E. Allen, Carroll County, Settled Case Files for Claims Allowed by the Southern Claims Commissions, 1871–1880, Records of the Accounting Officers of the Department of the Treasury, Record Group 217, National Archives Building, Washington, D.C. (hereinafter cited as Allowed Claims, SCC, RG 217).

36. Claim # 10378, William T. Dickens, Gibson County; Claim 21935, William Jones, Hardeman County; Claim 14183, William Stringfellow, Hardeman County, Barred and Disallowed Case Files of the Southern Claims Commission, 1871–1880, National Archives

Microfilm Publication M1407, National Archives and Records Administration, Washington, D.C. (hereinafter cited as Disallowed Cases, SCC, M1407).

37. Claim 10287, Sarah Anne Stailey, Shelby County; Claim 10341, Nathaniel Brewer, Carroll County, Disallowed Cases, SCC, M1407.

38. Claim 9119, W. H. Allen, Carroll County; Claim 9121, A. D. Bennett, Carroll County, Disallowed Cases, SCC, M1407.

39. Thomas Bond, Claim 19890, Haywood County, Allowed Claims, SCC, RG 217.

40. Studies of Southern Unionism during the Civil War concentrate almost exclusively on the East Tennessee Unionists. See Current, *Lincoln's Loyalists*, and Carl Degler, *The Other South: Southern Dissenters in the Nineteenth Century* (Gainesville: University Press of Florida, 2000). Some research on wartime occupation and Reconstruction has provided some insights on the problems Southern Unionists encountered during Reconstruction. Peter Maslowski's *Treason Must Be Made Odious: Military Occupation and Wartime Reconstruction in Nashville, Tennessee, 1862–1865* (Millwood, N.Y.: KTO Press, 1978) discusses the consequences of the improvised and inconsistent Union occupation and Reconstruction strategies in hindering the assertion of Southern Unionists in the postwar state government. Steven Ash's *When the Yankees Came: Conflict and Chaos in the Occupied South, 1861–1865* (Chapel Hill: University of North Carolina Press, 1995) casts a wider net on the problems of federal occupation policies, and it highlights the struggles Southern Unionists faced within their communities and the obstacles to success placed in their way by Union leaders.

41. Robert E. Park, "Human Migration and the Marginal Man," *American Journal of Sociology* 23 (1928): 881–93.

2. "I Wanted a Gun": Black Soldiers and White Violence in Civil War and Postwar Kentucky and Missouri / Aaron Astor

1. H. A. Cook, Capt., Ninth Missouri Cavalry to Lieut., Feb. 22, 1865, Letters Received, box 16, series 3537, District of North Missouri, United States Army Continental Commands, 1821–1920, Record Group 393/2 (hereinafter cited as RG 393/2), National Archives, Washington, D.C. It is unclear whether the spelling of "knot" in reference to a lynched man was intended to further intimidate African Americans with the threat of the noose, or if Jim Jackson simply could not spell. His misspelling of "army" as "arma" leads to the more innocent explanation.

2. By "conservative Unionist," I refer to the mass of white people of both Whig and Democratic orientation who supported the Union and slavery. Though they supported the Union war effort to the end, they bitterly opposed all efforts to radicalize the war through emancipation and the enlistment of black soldiers. Some conservative Unionists reluctantly accepted black enlistment in the war's final months as a measure to relieve the draft quota, or to end the war. Many more conservative Unionists, within the border states and the free North, abandoned their conservative interpretation of Union war aims and supported a more radical course as necessary and moral for the destruction of the Confederacy. For purposes of this essay, however, I refer to conservative Unionists as those who maintained a conservative posture regarding the Union war effort to the very end, and not those who came around to accept emancipation and black enlistment in the latter years of the war.

3. *Danville Central Kentucky Gazette*, Dec. 26, 1866.

4. David Rice founded the First Presbyterian Church at Danville when the town served as Kentucky's first capital. Rice advocated the prohibition of slavery in Kentucky's founding 1792 constitution. For his opinions regarding slavery at the Kentucky Constitutional Convention, see David Rice, *Slavery Inconsistent with Justice and Good Policy Proved by a Speech Delivered in the Convention, Held at Danville, Kentucky* (New York: Isaac Collins, 1804).

5. Geographers disagree on the precise boundaries of Little Dixie and the Bluegrass. For purposes of this essay, I include the Missouri River counties of Lafayette, Saline, Chariton, Cooper, Howard, Boone, and Callaway as composing Little Dixie. The term "Little Dixie" is of unknown origin, but it gained wide currency after the war because of the region's propensity to support the Democratic Party and because of its relatively pro-Confederate outlook. Antebellum Missourians often referred to the region as the "Boonslick" because of a famous salt lick that drew some of Missouri's earliest white settlers to the area in the 1810s. The most distinctive trait of Little Dixie before the Civil War, however, was the high proportion of slaves in the region. For the Bluegrass of Kentucky, I include Bourbon, Fayette, Woodford, Mercer, Jessamine, Garrard, Boyle, and Marion counties. Like Little Dixie, the Bluegrass included the most heavily enslaved region of Kentucky. For more on antebellum Little Dixie and the importance of slavery to the region, see R. Douglas Hurt, *Agriculture and Slavery in Missouri's Little Dixie* (Columbia: University of Missouri Press, 1992). There are few remarkable studies of the antebellum Bluegrass, but the classic work by the late-nineteenth-century writer James Lane Allen offers a keen insight into the society, culture, and economy of the region. See James Lane Allen, *The Blue Grass Region of Kentucky* (New York: Harper & Brothers, 1899). Maryland and Delaware, the other slaveholding Union border states, experienced some of the same phenomena as Kentucky and Missouri. But the more formidable presence of the Union Army in the vicinity of the nation's capital helped reduce racial violence in the eastern border states. Moreover, the shock of military-based emancipation affected Delaware and Maryland less because a majority of African Americans in those states were already free by 1860.

6. There were, in effect, two stages of secessionism in the border states, as in the South. When Abraham Lincoln was elected president in November 1860, a small handful of Missourians and Kentuckians supported secession. The rest supported the Union because of decades of compromise over the slavery question, which convinced border conservatives that the Union would continue to protect the institution of slavery as in the past. After the war broke out, however, many Missourians and Kentuckians abandoned this view, seeing the Union as effectively destroyed with Lincoln's troop call-up. For the remaining conservative Unionists, the Confederate cause still appeared foolish and counterproductive as a measure to protect the slave-based social order. Moreover, conservative Unionists never believed that the war itself, as defined early on by Lincoln, would result in the destruction of slavery. Radicalism would eventually emerge among some elements in Missouri, and to a lesser extent in Kentucky, though it remained largely unpopular and ever at odds with conservative Unionism. For a discussion of internal Unionist politics in a Deep South Confederate state, see Margaret M. Storey, *Loyalty and Loss: Alabama's Unionists in the Civil War and Reconstruction* (Baton Rouge: Louisiana State University Press, 2004).

7. Linda Kerber, *No Constitutional Right to be Ladies* (New York: Hill & Wang, 1998), 241.

8. On postwar racial violence, see especially George C. Rable, *But There Was No Peace: The Role of Violence in the Politics of Reconstruction* (Athens: University of Georgia Press, 1984). He discusses the Memphis and New Orleans riots of 1866, among other acts of violence, both of which involved partisan politics and working-class tensions between blacks and Irish. On postwar black life and ambitions, see Leon Litwack, *Been in the Storm So Long* (New York: Vintage, 1979). See also Allen W. Trelease, *White Terror: The Ku Klux Klan Conspiracy and Southern Reconstruction* (Baton Rouge: Louisiana State University Press, 1971); and Scott Reynolds Nelson, *Iron Confederacies: Southern Railways, Klan Violence, and Reconstruction* (Chapel Hill: University of North Carolina Press, 1999). On racial violence in postwar Kentucky, see George C. Wright, *Racial Violence in Kentucky: Lynchings, Mob Rule, and "Legal Lynchings," 1865–1940* (Baton Rouge:

Louisiana State University Press, 1990), 19–60; and J. Michael Rhyne, " 'The Whole Family Driven Away': Regulators, Politics, and the Assault on Black Households in Post-Emancipation Kentucky" (paper presented at the Southern Historical Association Annual Conference, Baltimore, 2002).

9. In accordance with the Military Reconstruction Act of 1867, each of the eleven states of the former Confederacy held multiracial elections for state constitutional conventions as early as 1867. Neither Kentucky nor Missouri were subject to the new law.

10. The best discussion of Missouri's Radical regime between the Drake Constitution of 1865 and the election of the Democratic Woodson administration in 1872 is William Parrish, *Missouri Under Radical Rule, 1865–1870* (Columbia: University of Missouri Press, 1965). Charles Drake chaired the constitutional committee that drafted the strict 1865 constitution barring all Rebels and Rebel sympathizers from voting, holding office, or even performing significant civilian services like teaching, preaching the Gospel, or practicing law. In 1870, with the anger of guerrilla war fading into distant memory and the state entering a more vigorous period of capitalist expansion, Liberal Republican dissidents under B. Gratz Brown and Carl Schurz successfully pushed for a general enfranchisement amendment to the constitution in 1870. With Brown elected governor in 1870, the Radical period effectively came to an end, though many Liberals hoped that newly enfranchised former Rebels would reward their new benefactors in their more conservative wing of the Republican Party. Sadly for the Liberals, rebels turned immediately to the old Democratic Party and elected Silas Woodson to the governor's mansion in 1872. Democrats proceeded to dominate the state's political scene for the next 100 years, placing Missouri squarely in the Solid South.

11. Ironically, a state constitutional amendment in 1870, pushed by dissident Liberal Republicans, was passed that enfranchised both African Americans and former Rebels, thus equating both blacks and ex-rebels as equally unacceptable elements in the postwar political order. Not surprisingly, the number of re-enfranchised whites vastly outnumbered the new black voters, thus establishing Democratic Party hegemony in Missouri for a century. On black political campaigns for enfranchisement, see Gary Kremer, *James Milton Turner and the Promise of America: The Public Life of a Post–Civil War Black Leader* (Columbia: University of Missouri Press, 1991).

12. On civil and legal rights for blacks in Kentucky, see Victor B. Howard, *Black Liberation in Kentucky: Emancipation and Freedom, 1862–1884* (Lexington: University Press of Kentucky, 1983), 130–76. Howard notes that African Americans appealed for civil and legal rights immediately after emancipation, but the conservative Kentucky government utterly ignored their demands.

13. United States Census Office, *Eighth Census of the Population of the United States* (Washington, D.C.: Government Printing Office , 1864). In the Deep South, slaveholdings averaged 12.7 slaves per holding.

14. On the declining hemp industry after the Civil War, see James F. Hopkins, *A History of the Hemp Industry in Kentucky* (Lexington: University Press of Kentucky, 1951), 193–219.

15. This is not to suggest that there were no violent conflicts in postwar Kentucky and Missouri over farm discipline or the demands of freedpeople to own their land. There were dozens of cases reported to the Freedmen's Bureau of black families pressured to make onerous sharecropping arrangements with white landowners. But the degree to which this occurred paled in comparison to the Deep South, where such disputes over labor relations on cotton plantations roiled the countryside for years.

16. On gender relations within the slave household, see Stephanie McCurry, *Masters of Small Worlds: Yeoman Households, Gender Relations, and the Political Culture of the Antebellum South Carolina Low Country* (New York: Oxford University Press, 1995),

208–38; and Elizabeth Fox-Genovese, *Within the Plantation Household: Black and White Women of the Old South* (Chapel Hill: University of North Carolina Press, 1988), 192–241.

17. By contrast, slavery in the eastern border states of Maryland and Delaware was in decline; half of Maryland's black population was free in 1860, as was 90 percent of Delaware's. Surplus slaves in Kentucky and Missouri were sent *en masse* to the Deep South in the lucrative Mississippi River slave trade.

18. Peter Bruner, *A Slave's Adventures Toward Freedom. Not Fiction, but the True Story of a Struggle* (Chapel Hill: University of North Carolina Press, 2000), 33, 43. Camp Nelson was situated along the Kentucky River in southern Jessamine County, about twenty miles south of Lexington.

19. For an excellent documentary history of Camp Nelson, see Richard D. Sears, *Camp Nelson, Kentucky: A Civil War History* (Lexington: University Press of Kentucky, 2002).

20. Elijah P. Marrs, *Life and History of the Rev. Elijah P. Marrs, First Pastor of Beargrass Baptist Church* (Louisville: Bradley and Gilbert Co., 1885), 22.

21. The Militia Act, passed on July 17, 1862, "authorized to receive into the service of the United States, for the purpose of constructing intrenchments, or performing camp service or any other labor, or any military or naval service for which they may be found competent, persons of African descent." See *U.S. Statutes at Large* (Washington, D.C.: General Printing Office, 1937). "Treaties, and Proclamations of the United States of America, vol. 12" (Boston: Little Brown and Company, 1863), 597–600. While free blacks joined the U.S. military in the latter part of 1862, slaves did not really join the military *en masse* until after the Emancipation Proclamation. Still, some slaves did enter military service before that time, even if they were mostly used for labor and construction purposes. See Ira Berlin et al., *Slaves No More: Three Essays on Emancipation and the Civil War* (New York: Cambridge University Press, 1992), 189–233.

22. See U.S. War Department, *The War of the Rebellion: A Compilation of the Official Records of the Union and Confederate Armies* (Washington, D.C.: Government Printing Office, 1880–1901; hereinafter cited as *Official Records*), series 3, 5:138. For a full tabulation of enlistment rates see Berlin et al., *Slaves No More*, 203. In Tennessee, 39 percent of the eligible slave population also joined the military, though at a rate a few tenths of a percent less than Missouri. The state with the highest raw total of black recruits was Louisiana, with 24,052, which made up 31 percent of the state's eligible black male population.

23. The recruitment totals listed in the Bureau of Colored Troops only reflect those "credited" to each state, not necessarily the number actually emerging from those states. The Bureau of Colored Troops was created in May 1863 to handle all administrative responsibilities relating to the recruitment and organization of black soldiers. Bureau of Colored Troops, Adjutant General's Office, War Department of the United States, Record Group 94, National Archives Building, Washington, D.C.

24. Berlin et al., *Slaves No More*, 203. This is especially probable because the 1860 census only counted 126 black people in Kansas.

25. Out of 930 eligible recruits, 600 joined the Union Army. *History of Howard and Cooper County, Missouri* (St. Louis: Missouri Historical Co., 1883), 278–82. Howard County's slave enlistment percentage (37 percent) was the highest in the state; the highest number of enlistments was in Lafayette County, to the west.

26. Only 4.5 percent of all black Kentuckians were free in 1860; in Missouri, only 3 percent were free. *Eighth Census* Population Statistics, 1860: 181, 285.

27. O'Connor to Comm. Gen. John Schofield, Dec. 7, 1863, Letters Received, box 10, O-111, series 2593, Dept. of the Missouri, RG 393/2.

28. Howard County (Mo.) *Advertiser*, Jan.15, 1864.

29. According to the slave census, John R. White owned seventy-six slaves in 1860. See *Eighth Census*, Slave Schedules, 1860.

30. Fulton *Missouri Telegraph*, Feb. 26, 1864.

31. Paris *Western Citizen*, Mar. 11, 1864.

32. General Order 34, *Official Records*, series 3, 4:233–34, issued by Thomas Fairleigh, acting assistant adjutant-general on behalf of Gen. Stephen Burbridge.

33. C. Dickson to W. H. Sidell, May 26, 1864, Letters Received, box 2, series 3967, Assistant Adjutant Provost Marshal General for Kentucky (hereinafter KY AAPMG), RG 110, National Archives, Washington D.C.

34. It is possible that an official in Boyle County notified slaves that all could enlist even though official restrictions were not removed until early June 1864. In this case, the rumor of unrestricted slave enlistment mattered more than the actual change in policy.

35. General Order Number 20, *Official Records*, series 3, 4:429–30.

36. Sears, *Camp Nelson, Kentucky*, xxxviii–xxxix.

37. Danville *Tribune*, Aug. 4, 1864, reprinted in the Lexington *National Unionist*, Aug. 9, 1864.

38. Boyle County had 3,714 total black inhabitants in 1860. Using the same ratio of black males of military age to the total population of blacks—as in Berlin et al., *Slaves No More*—(17.7 percent), the number of militarily eligible African Americans in Boyle County was 659. Of these, the 275 enlistees make up 42 percent.

39. In 1860, 95.5 percent of all African Americans were enslaved in Kentucky. In Missouri, 97 percent of all African Americans were enslaved. *Eighth Census*, Population and Slave Schedules, 1860.

40. Mass slave escapes were not unknown in antebellum Kentucky.

41. Henry Clay Bruce, *The New Man: Twenty-Nine Years a Slave, Twenty-Nine Years a Free Man* (York, Pa.: P. Anstadt and Sons, 1895), 99–100.

42. Paris (Ky.) *Western Citizen*, June 16, 1865.

43. Ibid., Oct. 27, 1865. Many black soldiers were removed to Texas as a way to placate white conservatives.

44. *History of Lafayette County, Missouri* (St. Louis: Missouri Historical Co., 1881), 294.

45. For a discussion of Missouri Provisional Governor Hamilton Gamble's view of the war and the Union cause, see William Parrish, *Turbulent Partnership: Missouri and the Union, 1861–1865* (Columbia: University of Missouri Press, 1963). Gamble was never actually elected governor, but was assigned to the position by a state convention after the elected governor, Claiborne Fox Jackson, attempted to take the state out of the Union in 1861. Another conservative, William P. Hall, succeeded Gamble upon his death in 1864. Following passage of the new radical constitution, Thomas Fletcher was elected in 1865. For Kentucky, the best account of Governor Thomas Bramlette's views of the war remains E. Merton Coulter, *Civil War and Readjustment in Kentucky* (Chapel Hill: University of North Carolina Press, 1926), 189–214. Bramlette was elected governor in 1863 and served until 1867. Two secessionists had governed the state prior to Bramlette's administration: Beriah Magoffin (1859–62) and James F. Robinson (1862–63).

46. In the Cuban wars of independence, particularly the Ten Years War between 1868 and 1878, slaves in the eastern Santiago de Cuba province regularly fought alongside slaveholders for Cuban independence. However, white insurgent leaders differed over the propriety of emancipation. Early insurgents supported emancipation as the best tool to gain soldiers for the cause. But as the Spanish colonial administration successfully deployed the discourse of race war and the specter of Saint Domingue, later insurgents distanced themselves from both general emancipation and the use of Afro-Cubans as soldiers. For an excellent discussion of this case, see Ada Ferrer, *Insurgent Cuba: Race, Nation, and Revolution, 1868–1898* (Chapel Hill: University of North Carolina Press,

1999). In central Missouri and Kentucky, virtually no white Unionists embraced general emancipation or slave soldiers as a means to put down the rebellion until several years into the Civil War. Even then, support for such revolutionary measures remained tepid at best.

47. The current narrative painting black soldiery as a fight against the master class begins with Dudley Cornish, *The Sable Arm: Negro Troops in the Union Army, 1861–1865* (New York: Longmans, Green, and Co., 1956) and continues with Ira Berlin et al., *Slaves No More*, and John David Smith, ed., *Black Soldiers in Blue: African American Soldiers in the Civil War Era* (Chapel Hill: University of North Carolina Press, 2002). Black soldiers' accounts portray black enlistment in a similar light.

48. *Advertiser*, Jan. 29, 1864.

49. Bruce, *The New Man*, 103.

50. See Robert Durden, *The Gray and the Black: The Confederate Debate on Emancipation* (Baton Rouge: Louisiana State University Press, 1972); and James McPherson, *Battle Cry of Freedom* (New York: Ballantine, 1988), 831–38. While some Confederate commanders, such as General Patrick Cleburne, openly floated the possibility of arming slaves for the Confederacy, Confederate civilian leaders were aghast at the prospect. Most famously, Georgian Howell Cobb remarked that slaves could not become good soldiers because if they did, "our whole theory of slavery is wrong." *Official Records*, series 4, 3:1009–10. By the time the Confederate Congress ultimately authorized the employment of black soldiers, the war was in its closing hour.

51. On Midwestern acquiescence to black enlistment, see V. Jacque Voegeli, *Free But Not Equal: The Midwest and the Negro During the Civil War* (Chicago: University of Chicago Press, 1967). On the postwar assessment of black troop performance and support for Radical Republicanism in Iowa, see Robert Dykstra, *Bright Radical Star: Black Freedom and White Supremacy on the Hawkeye Frontier* (Cambridge, Mass.: Harvard University Press, 1993).

52. W. S. King, Lt. Col., 35th Mass. Infantry to Wm. Whiting, Solicitor, War Dept., Mar. 12, 1864, Lexington, Ky., Letters Received, K-66, Provost Marshal General Office, RG 110.

53. *Western Citizen*, Mar. 18, 1864.

54. Lexington *Observer and Reporter*, Mar. 11, 1864, reprinted in the *Western Citizen*, Mar. 18, 1864. There is no extant copy of Wolford's complete speech.

55. *Western Citizen*, Mar. 18, 1864.

56. Bramlette himself had been one of the most outspoken critics of black enlistments and had even the fanned the flames of violent resistance to it. In January 1864 he wrote to General Boyle regarding black recruiting: "No such recruiting will be tolerated here. Summary justice will be inflicted upon any who attempt such unlawful purpose." *Western Citizen*, Jan. 29, 1864.

57. W. S. King, Lt. Col. 35th MA Infantry, to Wm. Whiting, Solicitor War Dept, March 12, 1864, Lexington, KY, Letters Received, K-66, Provost Marshal General Office, RG 110.

58. Ibid.

59. James Fidler to Sidell, June 9, 1864, Letters Received, box 2 F-178, series 3967, KY AAPMG, RG 110.

60. Ibid. The letter describes James and Jasper Edwards as "boys," though it is unclear if the term refers to actual children or the standard, diminutive term used by white Kentuckians to refer to all black men.

61. J. Winston Coleman, *Slavery Times in Kentucky* (Chapel Hill: University of North Carolina Press, 1940), 247. Coleman cites a Boyle County slave with "both ears slightly cropped." The citation comes from a runaway advertisement and suggests that the ear cropping was a result of an earlier runaway attempt.

NOTES

62. Neither McMann nor Burns appear in the 1860 census. If they lived in the area for any considerable time they would have been required to serve as patrollers. James Fidler, Union Army official at Lebanon, believed that McMann was the only assailant, even though Burns was arrested too. Fidler to Sidell, June 9, 1864. Regarding Kentucky slave patrol law, custom, and social makeup see Coleman, *Slavery Times in Kentucky*, 96–97. The slave code neither demanded nor prohibited bodily mutilation in the enforcement of runaway laws. Patrollers maintained full authority to exact whatever punishment they deemed necessary, as long as they did not materially diminish the value of the slave.

63. Hiram Cornel to J. P. Sanderson, Mar. 28, 1864, Letters Received, box 1, C-258, series 2786, Office of Provost Marshal General, Dept. of the Missouri, RG 393/2.

64. Lexington *National Unionist*, Oct. 4, 1864.

65. The 1860 census lists a man from Midway, Woodford County, named Joseph Maddox. He was a wagon maker and a relatively small property holder. He did not own any slaves, according to the slave schedules. There are no other entries for the name "Maddox" in Woodford County. *Eighth Census*, Population Schedules, 1860; *Eighth Census*, Slave Schedules, 1860.

66. The Missouri constitutional convention formally abolished slavery in the state on January 11, 1865.

67. F. Russell to C. B. Fisk, Feb. 21, 1865, Letters Received, box 16, series 3537, Dist. of North Missouri, 393/2.

68. Maj. A. H. Bowen, letter to Brig. Gen. J. S. Brisbin, Sept. 25, 1865, Letters Received, B-549 1865, series 2173, Dept. of Kentucky, RG 393/2, [C-4336].

69. Ibid.

70. Paris *True Kentuckian*, Sept. 1865, reprinted the article from the *Observer and Reporter*, Sept. 1865.

71. The most powerful quote comes from General George H. Thomas, a conservative Unionist from Virginia and commander of the Army of the Cumberland, who declared, "Gentlemen, the question is settled; negroes will fight." Thomas long doubted the propriety of black soldiers. Cornish, *Sable Arm*, 261.

72. Evidence from dozens of such attacks in the postwar period demonstrates that the Union military's perception of ex-Rebel leadership in racial violence largely matched reality. For a claim that ex-Rebels led most antiblack mobs, see, for example, Lt. Col. R. E. Johnston to Bvt. Brig. Gen. John Ely, Sept. 30, 1867, Lexington, Ky., Letters Sent 2:123, Kentucky Assistant Commissioner, Record Group 105, Bureau of Refugees, Freedmen, and Abandoned Lands, National Archives Microfilm Publication M1904, roll 98.

73. A. H. Bowen, the officer who reported the Danville Shooting Affray, was the superintendent for recruitment of Colored Troops in central Kentucky. It is not clear where Bowen originated from, though the 1860 census lists a twenty-five-year-old A. H. Bowen from Cerro Gordo, Iowa. Tellingly, he trusted the word of a black man as equal to that of a white. See *Eighth Census*, Manuscript Census, 1860.

74. Lt. Col. R. E. Johnston to Bvt. Brig. Gen. John Ely, Sept. 5, 1866, Lexington, Ky., Letters Sent 1:122, Kentucky Assist. Com., BRFAL, RG 105, M1904, roll 98. The Freedmen's Bureau established a presence in Kentucky, but not in Missouri. The Bureau justified its operations in Kentucky because of the state's refusal to accept black testimony in courts. On the role of the Freedmen's Bureau in Kentucky, see Howard, *Black Liberation in Kentucky*.

75. *Central Kentucky Gazette*, Oct. 31, 1866, reprinted from the Lebanon *Kentuckian*.

76. Between 1864 and 1867, a handful of newspapers in central Kentucky advanced the cause of Radical Reconstruction, supporting the Freedmen's Bureau and the Civil Rights Act as well as the Congressional Reconstruction Acts (even though they did not apply in Kentucky). The *Central Kentucky Gazette*, Lexington *National Unionist*, and

Lebanon Kentuckian fit this mold. By mid-1867, all remaining Radical newspapers disappeared, replaced entirely with conservative newspapers like the Danville *Advocate* (which still exists today) and the Lexington *Gazette*. For more on Southern Republican newspapers, see Richard Abbott, *For Free Press and Equal Rights: Republican Newspapers in the Reconstruction South*, ed. John W. Quist (Athens: University of Georgia Press, 2004).

77. *Gazette*, July 11, 1866.

78. Mid–nineteenth-century lynching apologists did not employ the same language of "white womanhood" used by lynching advocates at the turn of the twentieth century. But the sentiment offered by conservative newspapers unmistakably suggests protection of white women as a legitimate cause for mob violence. In one telling example, a Fulton *Missouri Telegraph* article defends mob law against a black man accused of raping a white woman as "deserving." But in reference to a different incident, the newspaper excuses the lack of mob law against a white man accused of raping a black woman because the victim was a "strumpet" and the assailant was "just drunk." Still, Kentuckians and Missourians did not employ generalized terms like "white womanhood" the way that lynching apologists later did. *Missouri Telegraph*, Sept. 10, 1869. On lynching and gender in late-nineteenth-century America, see Jane Dailey, Glenda Gilmore, and Bryant Simon, eds., *Jumpin' Jim Crow: Southern Politics from Civil War to Civil Rights* (Princeton: Princeton University Press, 2001), 140–61.

79. *True Kentuckian*, Apr. 5, 1866.

80. Ibid.

81. *Weekly Brunswicker*, Mar. 30, 1867.

82. In addition to the *Weekly Brunswicker*, the Saline *Progress* described the incident, which was reprinted in the Lexington *Caucasian and Express*, Mar. 30, 1867.

83. For an example of conservative Unionists' rejection of postwar Radicalism, see the *Weekly Brunswicker*, Mar. 23, 1867. In response to the recent Military Reconstruction Act, the newspaper proclaimed itself opposed to "corrupt and unscrupulous assumptions of power exercised by the dominant party in this State; the implacable enemy of the new Dogmas of the Radical Party, as represented by the tyrannical majority in Congress."

84. Lexington (Mo.) *Caucasian*, Apr. 25, 1866.

85. Ibid., Sept. 26, 1866. J. M. Allen, editor of the *Caucasian*, was not a Union supporter during the war. In a bid to draw support from the large base of disaffected conservative Unionists in central Missouri, however, he portrayed himself and his allies as "conservative Union" men in the war's aftermath.

86. A Radical editor in 1868 observed the editor of the *Caucasian* returning from the site of a lynching of a white man. The victim had been a Rebel soldier, but had vowed to bear witness against fellow Rebels who tried to vote illegally in Missouri elections. Worse than a Radical, or even a black man, the victim was a turncoat. Still, the presence of the *Caucasian* editor at the lynching suggests his approbation of mob violence to solve "community" problems. See the Boonville *Weekly Eagle*, Aug. 1, 1868, reprinting a story from the Lexington *Register*.

87. *Caucasian*, May 16, 1866.

88. As historian George C. Rable notes in his analysis of the 1866 riot in Memphis, the newspapers played a significant role in instigating racial tension, with a particular emphasis on the problem of black soldiers. See Rable, *But There Was No Peace*, 37, citing the Memphis *Daily Avalanche*, Jan. 4, 1866.

89. See Bertram Wyatt-Brown, *Southern Honor: Ethics and Behavior in the Old South* (New York: Oxford University Press, 1982).

90. As Steven Hahn points out, the fear of "Negro rule" in the Reconstruction era was not unwarranted in much of the South, especially in states and localities where African Americans made up a majority. See Hahn, *A Nation Under Our Feet: Black Political*

Struggles in the Rural South from Slavery to the Great Migration (Cambridge, Mass.: Belknap Press, 2003), 237–49. But in Kentucky and Missouri, the black percentage never approached the size of such Deep South centers of slavery as the Mississippi Delta or the South Carolina Low Country. Kentucky's Woodford County was the only county in either Kentucky or Missouri to have a slave majority in 1860, and even there the percentage of the population enslaved was only 52 percent. With no chance to form a black political majority at the county level within the Bluegrass and Little Dixie, "Negro rule" would have been virtually impossible in the border states.

91. White mobs often cloaked their extra-legal activities with pseudo-legalisms and "solemn" regard for an alternative form of due process. A series of letters appeared in various Kentucky newspapers in late 1866 from "Judge Lynch," which detailed meticulous proceedings prior to the hanging of blacks and white Union men. See "Judge Lynch" to J. R. King, Dec. 8, 1866, copied verbatim in letter from J. R. King to Bat. Lt. Col. W. F. Drum, Dec 14, 1866, Letters Received, box 6, series 2173, Dept. of Kentucky, RG 393/2.

92. Kentucky contributed fewer white troops to either side of the Civil War than any other state. With the draft in full effect, and no option for emancipation available, African Americans filled the state's quota at a higher rate than elsewhere. William Freehling, *The South vs. the South: How Anti-Confederate Southerners Shaped the Course of the Civil War* (New York: Oxford University Press, 2001).

93. Violence was not the only motivation for black emigration. Many African Americans sought better economic opportunities in Northern cities like Cincinnati and Chicago and land in states like Kansas. But the violence undoubtedly encouraged mass emigration just as it did in the Deep South in the 1910s and 1920s. James R. Grossman, *Land of Hope: Chicago, Black Southerners, and the Great Migration* (Chicago: University of Chicago Press, 1989).

94. Virginia's black population also dropped, but the census data for 1860 includes the region that became West Virginia in 1863.

95. *Ninth Census*, Population Statistics, 1870. Note that the white population of Kentucky and Missouri continued to rise between 1860 and 1870, including in the central counties of the Bluegrass and Little Dixie.

96. The data for Kansas City is actually Jackson County, which was increasingly dominated by Kansas City. St. Louis City and St. Louis County were part of the same administrative district until 1876. The higher rate of black emigration from Missouri's central counties may be a reflection of the chaotic nature of guerrilla war in that region. The rapid rise of guerrilla activity across central Missouri in late 1861 drove a significant portion of blacks and whites to flee the region. However, by the end of the war most whites returned to their Little Dixie homes as new immigrants from Northern states and from Germany arrived *en masse* to settle in Radicalized Missouri. African Americans who fled to Kansas, Iowa, Kansas City, and St. Louis had little incentive to return to central Missouri. On social changes and Northern immigration in postwar Missouri, see David Thelen, *Paths of Resistance: Tradition and Dignity in Industrializing Missouri* (New York: Oxford University Press, 1986).

97. *Eighth Census and Ninth Census of Population and Housing.*

98. Many blacks in the border states moved to the larger towns and cities within those states, like Lexington, Louisville, St. Louis, and Kansas City. Fayette County, Kentucky, home of the city of Lexington, was the only Bluegrass county to experience a sizable increase in its black population between 1860 and 1870. On black movement into and around the South after emancipation, see Litwack, *Been in the Storm So Long*, 292–335.

99. Kentucky experienced nothing resembling Radical Reconstruction. Missouri's Radical Reconstruction government from 1865 to 1870 did little to grant political rights to African Americans, though it did provide more legal protection against mob violence.

Blacks did not obtain the right to vote in Missouri until 1870. For more on black suffrage and Radical Reconstruction in Missouri see William E. Parrish, *Missouri under Radical Rule, 1865–1870* (Columbia: University of Missouri Press, 1965).

100. *Weekly Caucasian and Express*, Aug. 24, 1867.

101. For bushwhackers returning runaway slaves to their owners, see General Orders Apr. 25, 1865, General Orders vol. 383–942, series 3367, Dist. of Central Missouri RG 393/ 2. In response, Major Davis issued General Order 7 declaring that any ex-slaveholder who threatens his former slaves will be charged with aiding the bushwhackers.

102. The "Proclamations of Judge Lynch" appeared in numerous Kentucky newspapers from late 1866 until 1868. See, for example, *Danville Central Kentucky Gazette*, Feb. 27, 1867; and *Lexington Kentucky Gazette*, Nov. 24, 1866.

103. The Freedmen's Bureau in Kentucky operated criminal courts to prosecute whites guilty of abusing ex-slaves. The excuse for the Bureau's presence in a Union state was Kentucky's refusal to admit black testimony in court. With civil courts in suspension on matters involving African Americans, white conservatives bitterly complained that the federal government had "usurped" the proper state authority. See Victor Howard, "The Black Testimony Controversy in Kentucky, 1866–1872," *Journal of Negro History*, 58 (April 1973): 140–65.

3. "The Rebel Spirit in Kentucky": The Politics of Readjustment in a Border State, 1865–1868 / Anne E. Marshall

1. Lowell H. Harrison and James C. Klotter, *A New History of Kentucky* (Lexington: University Press of Kentucky, 1997), 234–35; Whitelaw Reid, *After the War: A Tour of the Southern States, 1865–1866* (New York: Harper Torch, 1966), 294.

2. Harrison and Klotter, *A New History of Kentucky*, 234–35. For a detailed account of emancipation in Kentucky, see Victor Howard, *Black Liberation in Kentucky: Emancipation and Freedom, 1862–1884* (Lexington: University Press of Kentucky, 1983).

3. The subject of Kentucky's post–Civil War turn has been explored extensively. See for example, Anne E. Marshall, " 'A Strange Conclusion to a Triumphant War:' Memory, Identity, and the Creation of a Confederate Kentucky" (PhD diss., University of Georgia, 2004); E. Merton Coulter, *The Civil War and Readjustment in Kentucky* (Chapel Hill: University of North Carolina Press, 1926); Ross Webb, "Kentucky: Pariah Among the Elect," in *Radicalism, Racism, and Party Realignment: The Border States During Reconstruction*, ed. Richard O. Curry (Baltimore: Johns Hopkins University Press, 1969), 105–45; Thomas Connelly, "Neo-Confederatism or Power Vacuum? Post-War Kentucky Politics Reappraised," *Register of the Kentucky Historical Society* 64 (Oct. 1966): 257–69; Michael Flannery, "Kentucky History Revisited: The Role of the Civil War in Shaping Kentucky's Collective Consciousness," *Filson Club Historical Quarterly* 71 (Jan. 1997): 27–51; and James C. Klotter, *Kentucky Justice, Southern Honor, and American Manhood: Understanding the Life and Death of Richard Reid* (Lexington: University Press of Kentucky, 2003). For more information on the subject of Civil War memory, see David Blight, *Race and Reunion: The Civil War in American Memory* (Cambridge, Mass.: Belknap Press, 2001); W. Fitzhugh Brundage, ed., *Where These Memories Grow: History, Memory, and Southern Identity* (Chapel Hill: University of North Carolina Press, 2001); W. Fitzhugh Brundage, *The Southern Past: A Clash of Race and Memory* (New York: Belknap Press, 2005); James C. Cobb, *Away Down South: A History of Southern Identity* (New York: Oxford University Press, 2005); Karen Cox, *Dixie's Daughters: The United Daughters of the Confederacy and the Preservation of Confederate Culture* (Gainesville: University Press of Florida, 2003); Gaines Foster, *Ghosts of the Confederacy: Defeat, The Lost Cause, and the Emergence of the New South* (New York: Oxford University Press, 1987); and Nina Silber, *The Romance of Reunion: Northerners and the South, 1865–1900* (Chapel Hill: University of North Carolina Press, 1993).

4. Coulter, *The Civil War and Readjustment in Kentucky*, 439; Lexington *Observer and Reporter*, May 22, 1867.

5. Elizabeth Hardin, diary entry, July 25, 1865, in *The Private War of Lizzie Hardin: A Kentucky Confederate Girl's Diary of the Civil War in Kentucky, Virginia, Tennessee, Alabama, and Georgia*, ed. G. Glenn Clift (Frankfort: The Kentucky Historical Society, 1963), 284.

6. Ibid., Aug. 2, 1865, 286.

7. Lewis Collins and Richard Collins, *Collins' Historical Sketches of Kentucky*, rev. ed. (Covington, Ky., 1882), 1:163–64.

8. *Cincinnati Gazette*, Jan. 12, 1865; July 28, 1865.

9. Ibid.

10. *New York Times*, Aug. 27, 1868; *Observer and Reporter* (semiweekly edition), Oct. 5, 1867.

11. Eric Foner succinctly explains the difference between Kentucky and other border states: "The elements that would transform Kentucky's neighbors were either weak or absent. Although loyal to the Union, the state's mountain region was politically inactive; there was no major city (like Baltimore or St. Louis) with an anti-slavery cadre ready to lead in reconstructing the state; and the traditional leadership retained sufficient unity to fend off challenges of authority." Foner, *Reconstruction: America's Unfinished Revolution, 1863–1877* (New York: Harper & Row, 1988), 38. For a more detailed account of Reconstruction-era politics in the Southern border states, see Harold B. Hancock, "Reconstruction in Delaware"; William E. Parrish, "Reconstruction Politics in Missouri, 1865–1870"; and Charles L. Wagandt, "Redemption or Reaction?—Maryland in the Post–Civil War Years," in *Radicalism, Racism, and Party Realignment*, ed. Curry.

12. For a detailed account of the complicated shifts of political factions in postwar Kentucky, see Klotter and Harrison, *A New History of Kentucky*, 239–44; Ross A. Webb, *Kentucky in the Reconstruction Era* (Lexington: University Press of Kentucky, 1978), 12–35; and Webb, "Kentucky: Pariah Among the Elect," 107–45.

13. C. Vann Woodward, *Origins of the New South* (Baton Rouge: Louisiana State University Press, 1951), 6.

14. *Cincinnati Gazette*, Nov. 4, 1865.

15. The state legislature had first rejected the Thirteenth Amendment in February 1865 by a vote of 56–18 in the House and 23–10 in the Senate. Coulter, *Civil War and Readjustment in Kentucky*, 261, 281–82; Harrison and Klotter, *A New History of Kentucky*, 240; Webb, *Kentucky in the Reconstruction Era*, 15; Collins, *Historical Sketches*, 1:176; *Observer and Reporter*, Jan. 10, 1866; *New York Times*, Feb. 15, 1866.

16. James Speed, *James Speed: A Personality* (Louisville, Ky.: John P. Morton and Company, 1914), 77–78.

17. *Cincinnati Gazette*, June 23, 1865; Nov. 4, 1865. For examples of blended Democratic and Confederate rhetoric, see the *Cincinnati Gazette*, July 29, 1865; and July 4, 1866.

18. Webb, *Kentucky in the Reconstruction Era*, 21; Frankfort *Daily Kentucky Yeoman*, July 26, 1866, quoted in Webb, "Kentucky: 'Pariah among the Elect,'" 121; *Louisville Daily Journal*, quoted in Webb, *Kentucky in the Reconstruction Era*, 22; *Cincinnati Gazette*, June 22, 1866; July 29, 1866.

19. *Louisville Courier*, quoted in the *Cincinnati Gazette*, July 29, 1866; *Louisville Daily Journal*, quoted in the *Cincinnati Gazette*, June 29, 1866.

20. *Frankfort Commonwealth* quoted in Harrison and Klotter, *A New History of Kentucky*, 241.

21. *Cincinnati Gazette*, Aug. 10, 1866.

22. *Frankfort Commonwealth*, Jan. 8, 1867.

23. *Cincinnati Commercial*, May 13, 1867.

24. Harrison and Klotter, *A New History of Kentucky*, 241–42; Frankfort *Kentucky Statesman* (semiweekly edition), Aug. 9, 1867.

25. Frankfort *Tri-Weekly Yeoman*, May 30, 1867.

26. Lexington *Observer and Reporter*, May 22, 1867.

27. The list of "rebel" officeholders originated in the *Frankfort Commonwealth*, Aug. 9, 1867, and was reprinted by the *New York Times*, Aug. 18, 1867. For information on Kentucky's "rebel" governors John Stevenson, James B. McCreary, Luke Blackburn, John Knott, and Simon Bolivar Buckner, see Harrison and Klotter, *A New History of Kentucky*, 243–48, 257–63, 447–48.

28. *New York Times*, Dec. 25, 1866; Tapp and Klotter, *Decades of Discord*, 14; *Louisville Courier-Journal*, Apr. 9, 1866; *Cincinnati Gazette*, Apr. 21, 1866.

29. *Cincinnati Gazette*, Feb. 2, 1866, Mar. 13, 1866, Aug. 16, 1866; Aug. 21, 1866.

30. For more on African Americans' symbolism and ordering of parades and memorial activity, see Kathleen Clark, *Defining Moments: African American Commemoration and Political Culture in the South, 1863–1913* (Chapel Hill: University of North Carolina Press, 2006); Clark, "Celebrating Freedom: Emancipation Day Celebrations and African American Memory in the Early Reconstruction South," in Brundage, ed., *Where These Memories Grow*, 119–23; Clark, "Making History: African American Commemorative Celebrations in Augusta, Georgia, 1865–1913," in Cynthia Mills and Pamela H. Simpson, eds., *Monuments to the Lost Cause: Women, Art, and the Landscapes of Southern Memory* (Knoxville: University of Tennessee Press, 2003), 46–63; Mitch Kachun, *Festivals of Freedom: Memory and Meaning in African American Emancipation Celebrations, 1808–1915* (Amherst: University of Massachusetts Press, 2003); William H. Wiggins Jr., *O Freedom!: Afro-American Emancipation Celebrations* (Knoxville: University of Tennessee Press, 1987); Elsa Barkley Brown and Gregg Kimball, "Mapping the Terrain of Black Richmond," in *The New African American Urban History*, ed. Kenneth W. Goings and Raymond A. Mohl (Thousand Oaks, Calif.: Sage, 1996), 66–115.

31. *Cincinnati Commercial*, Jan. 3, 1866; Coulter, *Civil War and Readjustment in Kentucky*, 350. For other examples of African American political meetings in Kentucky, see the *Cincinnati Commercial*, Sept. 20; May 13, 1867; and the *New York Times*, Aug. 18, 1867.

32. *Cincinnati Commercial*, Jan. 2, 1867; Howard, *Black Liberation in Kentucky*, 146.

33. *Cincinnati Commercial*, Sept. 20, 1867; *Observer and Reporter* (semiweekly edition), Oct. 5, 1867; Coulter, *Civil War and Readjustment*, 350–51.

34. *Kentucky's Black Heritage: The Role of Black People in the History of Kentucky from the Pioneer Days to the Present* (Frankfort: Kentucky Commission on Human Rights, 1971), 45; *Lexington Observer and Reporter* (semiweekly edition), Oct. 5, 1867.

35. David Ross Locke, *Ekkoes From Kentucky, by Petroleum V. Nasby, P.M. at Confedrit X Roads (which is in the State uv Kentucky), and perfesser uv Biblikle Polity in the Southern Military and Classikle Instytoot. Bein a perfect Record uv the ups and Downs and Experiences uv the Democrisy, Doorin the eventful year 1867, ez seen by a Naturalized Kentuckian* (Boston: Lee and Shepard, 1868).

36. Ibid., 96, 273, 14–15.

37. Ibid., 23, 166, 251–52; James C. Austin, *Petroleum V. Nasby (David Ross Locke)* (New York: Twayne, 1965), 77–79.

38. For more on Watterson's political influence and voice in Kentucky, the South, and the nation, see Daniel Margolies, *Henry Watterson and the New South: The Politics of Empire, Free Trade, and Globalization* (Lexington: University Press of Kentucky, 2006); Joseph Wall, *Henry Watterson: Reconstructed Rebel* (New York: Oxford University Press, 1956); Henry Watterson, *"Marse Henry," An Autobiography* (New York: George H. Doran Co., 1919), 1:240, 176, 241.

39. I discuss the long, complicated process by which white Kentuckians created a Confederate identity for their state through cultural and memorial activities in "'A Strange Conclusion to a Triumphant War.'"

4. The Crucible of Reconstruction: Unionists and the Struggle for Alabama's Postwar Home Front / Margaret M. Storey

1. This essay is based on the author's book *Loyalty and Loss: Alabama's Unionists in the Civil War and Reconstruction* (Baton Rouge: Louisiana State University Press, 2004). Reprinted by permission of Louisiana State University Press from *Loyalty and Loss: Alabama's Unionists in the Civil War and Reconstruction* by Margaret M. Storey. Copyright © 2004 by Louisiana State University Press.

2. Claim 6791, Ebenezer Leath, Cherokee County, July 2, 1875, in Settled Case Files for Claims Approved by the Southern Claims Commission, 1871–1880, Records of the Accounting Officers of the Department of the Treasury, Record Group 217, National Archives, Washington, D.C. (hereinafter cited as SCC). Wilkes was thirty-three years old, married, and the father of two small children in 1860. His census record lists farming as his profession and shows him to be a man of some means in the rather poor Cherokee County, owning real estate worth $1,200 and a personal estate of $1,500 (slave ownership could not be confirmed). Wilkes lived in the same neighborhood as the men he targeted for mob action. His most ferocious enemy, Ebenezer Leath, was younger than Wilkes (only 20 in 1860), but he also was the head of a new household with a young wife and baby. Leath was a considerably less well-off farmer, owning only $400 of personal estate. Leath also avoided Confederate service by obtaining an exemption, and, like Wilkes, seemed to have gotten it through some measure of subterfuge: "I . . . underwent an examination in which my uncle, Dr. George W. Lawrence figured considerably and got me discharged and I got back home and they never got me in." (Though by all accounts Leath was able enough to fight well and to lie out during the entire war, he nonetheless obtained a second disability discharge when he was arrested by the local conscript officer and sent to the enrollment camps at Talladega.) United States Census Office, *Eighth Census of the United States, 1860*: Alabama Free and Slave Populations, Manuscript returns, NAMS-M653 (hereinafter cited as *Eigth Census*); Testimony of R. W. Wilkes, Claim 6791, Ebenezer Leath, Cherokee County, July 2, 1875, SCC.

3. Testimony of Joseph Baker and James Davis, Claim 6791, Ebenezer Leath, Cherokee County, July 2, 1875, SCC.

4. Claim 6791, Ebenezer Leath, Cherokee County, July 2, 1875, SCC. The term *Ku Klux Klan* was used by Leath and his friends to describe their enemies, but we should be careful to note that this was a catchall term for vigilantes rather than a descriptor of formal, organized membership in a given group. See note 67 for more on this question.

5. Testimony of Joseph Baker, Claim 6791, Ebenezer Leath, Cherokee County, July 2, 1875, SCC.

6. Ibid.

7. Claim 6837, John Smith, Cherokee County, May 13, 1874, SCC.

8. Ibid.

9. Claim 6791, Ebenezer Leath, Cherokee County, July 2, 1875, SCC.

10. Claim 7252, Joseph Stricklin, Cherokee County, May 30, 1875, SCC.

11. As historians of the period are increasingly apt to point out, the boundary between the wartime home front and the actual battlefield was highly permeable in many parts of the South. Soldiers from both armies moved through, lived off, and fought on the home front; guerrilla warfare, a significant aspect of the war strategically and tactically, was by definition a home front activity. Indeed, for most Southern Unionists, the home front was always the premier site of violent and sometimes deadly conflict—there, behind Confederate lines, they resisted conscription and suffered persecution at the

hands of secessionist neighbors and the Rebel army. There they conspired with slaves to spy for the Union. There they enlisted as soldiers and guerrilla fighters for the Union Army. See Daniel E. Sutherland, *A Savage Conflict: The Decisive Role of Guerillas in the American Civil War* (Chapel Hill: University of North Carolina Press, 2009); Margaret M. Storey, *Loyalty and Loss: Alabama's Unionists in the Civil War and Reconstruction* (Baton Rouge: Louisiana State University Press, 2004), chapters 3 and 4; Kenneth W. Noe, "Who Were the Bushwhackers? Age, Class, Kin and Western Virginia's Confederate Guerrillas, 1861–1862," *Civil War History* 49 (Mar. 2003): 5–26; Martin Crawford, *Ashe County's Civil War: Community and Society in the Appalachian South* (Charlottesville: University Press of Virginia, 2001); Victoria E. Bynum, *The Free State of Jones: Mississippi's Longest Civil War* (Chapel Hill: University of North Carolina Press, 2001); William W. Freehling, *The South vs. the South: How Anti-Confederate Southerners Shaped the Course of the Civil War* (New York: Oxford University Press, 2001); Sutherland, "Guerrilla Warfare in the Confederacy," *Journal of Southern History* 68 (May 2002): 259–92; Daniel E. Sutherland and Anne J. Bailey, eds., *Civil War Arkansas: Beyond Battles and Leaders* (Fayetteville: University of Arkansas Press, 2000); Sutherland, ed., *Guerrillas, Unionists, and Violence on the Confederate Home Front* (Fayetteville: University of Arkansas Press, 1999); David Williams, *Rich Man's War: Class, Caste, and Confederate Defeat in the Lower Chattahoochee Valley* (Athens: University of Georgia Press, 1998); Noel C. Fisher, *War at Every Door: Partisan Politics and Guerrilla Violence in East Tennessee, 1860–1869* (Chapel Hill: University of North Carolina Press, 1997); Steven V. Ash, *When the Yankees Came: Conflict and Chaos in the Occupied South, 1861–1865* (Chapel Hill: University of North Carolina Press, 1995); and Mark Grimsley, *The Hard Hand of War: Union Military Policy toward Southern Civilians, 1861–1865* (Cambridge: Cambridge University Press, 1995).

12. Few loyalists lived in the Black Belt region that straddled the center and southern part of the state, though there were loyalists who lived along Gulf Coast in the wiregrass counties of the southeast and a few settlements along the eastern side of Mobile Bay. Storey, *Loyalty and Loss*, 4.

13. Though there is no reliable "census" of Unionists in the state, it is most likely that in 1861 the loyalist population never exceeded 15 percent of the adult white population, and was likely closer to 10 percent. For a complete discussion of the size of the population, as well as the socioeconomic status of loyalists, see Storey, *Loyalty and Loss*, 15–17. Also note that slaves and free blacks, though not included here as Unionists, also petitioned the SCC. For a complete discussion of black resistance to the Confederacy and support of the Union war effort, see ibid., chapters 4 and 5.

14. Claim 21220, Creed Lewis Taylor, Marshall County, Feb. 28, 1874, SCC.

15. Testimony of Archibald Steele, *Testimony Taken by the Joint Select Committee to Inquire into the Condition of Affairs in the Late Insurrectionary States* (Washington, D.C.: GPO, 1872), 9:944. See also Claim 2652, Archibald J. Steele, Madison County, Aug. 1, 1872, SCC.

16. Claim 4190, Jasper Harper, Marshall County, Apr. 24, 1874, SCC.

17. Daniel Sutherland, "The Absence of Violence: Confederates and Unionists in Culpeper County, Virginia," in Sutherland, ed., *Guerrillas, Unionists and Violence*, 79; Carl Degler, *The Other South: Southern Dissenters in the Nineteenth Century* (New York: Harper & Row, 1974), 182–84; Clarence Denman, *The Secession Movement in Alabama* (Montgomery: Alabama State Department of Archives and History, 1933), 61–64, 94; William L. Barney, *The Secessionist Impulse: Alabama and Mississippi in 1860* (Princeton: Princeton University Press, 1974), 279–81; William K. Scarborough, *Masters of the Big House: Elite Slaveholders of the Mid-Nineteenth-Century South* (Baton Rouge: Louisiana State University Press, 2003), 307, 342–45.

18. Testimony of John C. Berry, Claim 20979, John Morgan Brown, Estate, et al., Mobile County, Jan. 30, 1874; Claim 2656, John G. Winston, Marshall County, Feb. 16, 1874; Claim 12231, Thomas E. Potts, Bibb County, Dec. 7, 1872; Claim 36834, Thomas Nation, Blount County, July 17, 1873; all in SCC.

19. Claim 36834, Thomas Nation, Blount County, July 17, 1873, SCC.

20. Claim 20979, John Morgan Brown, Estate, et al., Mobile County, Jan. 30, 1874, SCC.

21. Barney, *The Secessionist Impulse*, 54–60; Daniel W. Crofts has ably outlined these moderate positions as they took shape in the Upper South in *Reluctant Confederates: Upper South Unionists in the Secession Crisis* (Chapel Hill: University of North Carolina Press, 1989), 106–125.

22. Degler, *The Other South*, 120.

23. Testimony of John Terry, Claim 6813, Aquilla Ferguson, Cherokee County, May 14, 1874, SCC.

24. Mark E. Neely Jr., *Southern Rights: Political Prisoners and the Myth of Confederate Constitutionalism* (Charlottesville: University of Virginia Press, 1999), 88–89; William M. Robinson Jr., *Justice in Grey: A History of the Judicial System of the Confederate States of America* (Cambridge, Mass.: Harvard University Press, 1941), 383–86, 389–90, 393–95, 452; Curtis Arthur Amlund, *Federalism in the Southern Confederacy* (Washington, D.C.: Public Affairs Press, 1966), 106–7.

25. Claim 3128, Robert Guttery Sr., Walker County, Jan. 17, 1872, SCC.

26. Noel C. Fisher, *War at Every Door: Partisan Politics and Guerrilla Violence in East Tennessee, 1860–1869* (Chapel Hill: University of North Carolina Press 1997), 62–63.

27. Daniel E. Sutherland, "Guerrillas: The Real War in Arkansas," in *Civil War Arkansas*, ed. Sutherland and Bailey, 136–37.

28. Wade H. Richardson, *How I Reached the Union Lines* (Milwaukee, Wisc.: Milwaukee Telegraph Publishing Co., 1896), 24. The injustice of this wartime abuse burned red-hot in the minds of Unionists long after the war. Mial Abernathy of Cherokee County, for instance, yearned to punish the local Confederate who had revealed Abernathy's whereabouts to the conscript cavalry. Soldiers had then come to his home, arrested him, and stolen nearly every item he owned down to the clothes and shoes he and his family were wearing. "I know who told them I was at home," he hotly exclaimed to the SCC in 1875, "and Damn him, I ought to kill him for it." Claim 4806, Mial S. Abernathy, Limestone County, July 23, 1875, SCC.

29. William Blair, "The Use of Military Force to Protect the Gains of Reconstruction," in "Reconstruction as It Should Have Been: An Exercise in Counterfactual History," special issue, *Civil War History* 51 (Dec. 2005): 388–402. Blair offers an excellent discussion of this problem of military presence. He suggests that ten to twenty thousand soldiers should have been stationed in the South during the entirety of Reconstruction but argues that a policy of robust military occupation was "unthinkable for practical, economic, and political-ideological reasons" (398). I would add that the interests and fears of white Unionists figured little in the bigger discussions of military occupation policies, which were usually concerned with the protection of black political and civil rights.

30. Dan T. Carter, *When the War Was Over: The Failure of Self Reconstruction in the South, 1865–1867* (Baton Rouge: Louisiana State University Press, 1987), 8–12.

31. George W. Howard to Brig. Gen. R. S. Granger, July 1, 1865, War Department, *The War of the Rebellion: A Compilation of the Official Records of the Union and Confederate Armies* (Washington, D.C.: GPO, 1880–1901), series 1, vol. 49, part 2, 1057.

32. J. A. Hammond et al. to Gov. Lewis E. Parsons, Oct. 9, 1865, in "State Militia of Alabama During the Administration of Lewis E. Parsons, Provisional Governor June 21st 1865 to December 18th, 1865," by Clyde E. Wilson, *Alabama Historical Quarterly* 14

(1952): 313–14. Ridge and his fellow petitioners were refused permission to organize a militia by Provisional Governor Lewis Parsons. Evidence suggests that Parsons may have been encouraged not to use Unionists in militias by President Andrew Johnson or his advisors. Brooks D. Simpson, LeRoy P. Graf, and John Muldowny, eds., *Advice After Appomattox: Letters to Andrew Johnson, 1865–1866* (Knoxville: University of Tennessee Press, 1987), 111.

33. J[oseph]. H. Davis to Gen. Wager Swayne, June 20, 1866, Records of the Assistant Commissioner, State of Alabama, Bureau of Refugees, Freedmen and Abandoned Lands, National Archives Microfilm Publication M809, roll 8 (hereinafter cited as BRFAL-AL [M809]).

34. Ibid.

35. Michael Perman, *Reunion Without Compromise: The South and Reconstruction, 1865–1868* (Cambridge: Cambridge University Press, 1973), 7, 69. See also 11–12, 68–70.

36. Carl Schurz to Andrew Johnson, Nov. 1865, in *Advice After Appomattox*, 75.

37. William Miller to Alexander Boyd, Sept. 5, 1866, Alexander Boyd Papers, Birmingham (Ala.) Public Library.

38. Perman, *Reunion without Compromise*, 5–10.

39. Richard H. Abbott, *The Republican Party and the South, 1855–1877: The First Southern Strategy* (Chapel Hill: University of North Carolina Press, 1986), x–xi, 49–52, 187–91. In "The Use of Military Force to Protect the Gains of Reconstruction," William Blair concludes that, though an expansive military occupation force might have helped African Americans defend themselves and their freedom during Reconstruction, such a plan "had little chance of ever coming about. Nineteenth-century attitudes about race, a desire for reunion with the white people who resisted granting power to black people, and the practical problems of paying for this intervention in the face of economic problems worked against extended occupation by the army in the South" (401).

40. Abbott, *The Republican Party and the South*, 22, 28–29.

41. Ibid., x–xii, 43–60.

42. H. W. McVay to Brig. Gen. Wager Swayne, Mar. 11, 1866, BRFAL-AL (M809), roll 8.

43. "Late Officers in the U.S.A. and loyal citizens of Morgan Co." to Brig. Gen. Swayne, June 8, 1866, BRFAL-AL (M809), roll 7.

44. "Petition to [Congress] of George White and 90 Other Loyal Citizens of Blount County, Alabama," Nov. 21, 1866, Records of the Committee on the Judiciary, Thirty-Ninth Cong., HR 39A-H14.10, Record Group 233, National Archives, Washington, D.C.

45. General John Pope was appointed to take military control of the Third Military District, of which Alabama was a part.

46. Sarah Woolfolk Wiggins, *The Scalawag in Alabama Politics, 1865–1881* (Tuscaloosa: University of Alabama Press, 1977), 19–20; Eric Foner, *Reconstruction: America's Unfinished Revolution* (New York: Harper & Row, 1988), 275–76. The Reconstruction Acts took much of their language regarding voter proscription from the Fourteenth Amendment, which in 1866 had been soundly rejected by all the Southern states but Tennessee. Their rejection of the amendment, in fact, was one of the acts precipitating Congress's decision to take control of Reconstruction; each state had to ratify the Fourteenth Amendment to regain representation in Congress.

47. Abbott, *The Republican Party and the South*, 70.

48. For a deeper discussion of the wartime alliances between slaves, free blacks, and white Unionists, see Storey, *Loyalty and Loss*, chapters 3 and 4.

49. Montgomery *Mail*, Apr. 17, 1867. See also Foner, *Reconstruction*, 259–261; and Malcolm C. McMillan, *Constitutional Development in Alabama, 1798–1901: A Study in Politics, the Negro, and Sectionalism* (Tuscaloosa: University of Alabama Press, 1992), 131.

50. See Richard L. Hume, "The 'Black and Tan' Constitutional Conventions of 1867–1869 in Ten Former Confederate States: A Study of Their Membership" (PhD diss., Johns Hopkins University, 1972), 52–68.

51. McMillan, *Constitutional Development*, 119–122n41, n60, n63, 114, 121–22n60; Foner, *Reconstruction*, 317; Thomas McAdory Owen and Marie Bankhead Owen, *History of Alabama and Dictionary of Alabama Biography*, 4 vols. (Chicago: S. J. Clarke, 1921), 13, 69, 463, 525, 556, 964 1165, 1372, 1412, 1567; Hume, "The 'Black and Tan' Constitutional Conventions of 1867–1869," 52–68. See also Claims 1343, 1346, and 1348, William A. Austin, Jackson County, 1871, 1873, and 1878; Claim 5517, Alfred Collins, DeKalb County, 1873; Claim 2493, Joseph H. Davis Jr., Randolph County, 1878; Claim 6678, George J. Dykes, Floyd County, Georgia, 1872; Claim 5514, Charles A. Clayton (for reference to W. T. Ewing), Etowah County, Jan. 9, 1879; Claim 1, J. J. Martin, Macon County, Apr. 12, 1871; Claim 129, Sarah A. Goins (for reference to William Skinner), Franklin County, July 28, 1875; Claim 3970, John B. Penn (for reference to John Wilhite), Morgan County, Jan. 29, 1879; all in SCC.

Refugees included William A. Austin of DeKalb County; Arthur Bingham of Talladega County; W. T. Ewing of Etowah County; William C. Garrison of Blount County; and Benjamin Saffold of Dallas County. Those who joined the federal army upon fleeing their homes included Joseph H. Davis of Randolph County; Thomas Haughey of Morgan County, an officer from 1862 to 1865; S. F. Kennamer of Marshall County, leader of a group of Union independent scouts from 1863 to 1865; Henry J. Springfield of St. Clair County, head of a similar group of Union scouts from 1864 to 1865; J. R. Walker of Shelby County, Union soldier from 1862 to 1865; and John W. Wilhite of Winston County, who, after being arrested for treason in 1861, escaped north in 1862 and enlisted in the federal army, where he remained until 1865.

Other native white delegates to the 1867 convention had stayed the Union course, including Thomas Adams of Clay County; James H. Autrey of Calhoun County; 1865 constitutional convention delegates Alfred Collins of Jackson County and Early Greathouse of Tallapoosa County; George J. Dykes of Cherokee County; Gustavus Horton of Mobile County; John J. Martin of Macon County; Byron O. Masterson and Thomas M. Peters of Lawrence County; William S. Skinner of Franklin County; and Benjamin L. Whelan of Hale County. Even the president of the convention, New York–born Elisha Woolsey Peck of Tuscaloosa, had been a steadfast opponent of the Confederacy, denouncing "secession at the first, in the middle, and at the end" (quoted in McMillan, *Constitutional Development*, 123). He had moved to Rockford, Illinois, after the war, but returned to Alabama to preside over the convention.

Of the one hundred delegates, all but four were Republicans, eighteen of which were African Americans. Of these eighteen African American delegates, thirteen were elected from Black Belt counties, where black voters held a majority. See William Warren Rogers Jr. et al., *Alabama: The History of a Deep South State* (Tuscaloosa: University of Alabama Press, 1994), 245; *Official Journal of the Constitutional Convention of the State of Alabama, Held in the City of Montgomery, Commencing on Tuesday, November 5, A.D. 1867* (Montgomery: Barrett & Brown, Binders and Printers, 1868), II–III; McMillan, *Constitutional Development*, 116–19, n32, n33; Owen and Owen, *Dictionary of Alabama Biography*, 375; Claim 11501, James T. Rapier, Montgomery County, 1874, SCC; Foner, *Reconstruction*, 318.

52. Michael W. Fitzgerald, *The Union League Movement in the Deep South: Politics and Agricultural Change during Reconstruction* (Baton Rouge: Louisiana State University Press, 1989), 122; Testimony of John G. Stoke, Claim 14, Robert Heflin, Randolph County, Apr. 18, 1871, SCC.

53. Fitzgerald, *Union League Movement*, 122–24.

54. Foner, *Reconstruction*, 309–11.

55. Ibid., 235; Fitzgerald, *Union League Movement*, 117–25.

56. Quoted in McMillan, *Constitutional Development*, 128; Michael W. Fitzgerald, "Radical Republicanism and the White Yeomanry during Reconstruction, 1865–1868," *Journal of Southern History* 54 (Nov. 1988): 579–80.

57. McMillan, *Constitutional Development*, 12; Fitzgerald, "Alabama Yeomanry during Reconstruction," 580.

58. *Official Journal of the Constitutional Convention of the State of Alabama Held in the City of Montgomery Commencing on Tuesday, November 5th A.D. 1867*. (Montgomery, Ala: Barrett and Brown, 1868), 530.

59. Ibid., 42, 129. McMillan presents Haughey as a carpetbagger, which is incorrect. Haughey was a native of Scotland but had lived in Alabama since the 1840s.

60. Quoted in McMillan, *Constitutional Development*.

61. Abbott, *The Republican Party and the South*, 138–39.

62. Ibid., 140–41, quotation on 140.

63. Alabama Constitution of 1868, Article VII, Section 3. Furthermore, the new constitution created two enormous loopholes through which even the status quo might be undone, revealing the extent to which the Republican Party continued to tolerate, even to advocate, "reconstruction through reconciliation." Anyone who "aided in the reconstruction proposed by Congress and accepted the political equality of all men before the law" would be absolved of any franchise restrictions. The convention further provided that "the General Assembly shall have power to remove the disabilities" incurred through the Reconstruction Acts or the Fourteenth Amendment. Anyone with influence with the state legislature could reverse the proscription, given sufficient majorities willing to approve the pardon. McMillan, *Constitutional Development*, 131; Hume, "The 'Black and Tan' Constitutional Conventions of 1867–1869," 20–21n18; *Official Journal of the Constitutional Convention*, 95; Abbott, *The Republican Party and the South*, 140–41.

64. Allen W. Trelease, *White Terror: The Ku Klux Klan Conspiracy and Southern Reconstruction* (New York: Harper & Row, 1971), 87.

65. For an excellent recent reconsideration of the origins and purposes of the Klan, as well as the problem with identifying the vigilantes as a single "organization," see Edward John Harcourt, "Who Were the Pale Faces? New Perspectives on the Tennessee Ku Klux," *Civil War History* 51 (Mar. 2005): 23–66.

66. *Testimony Taken by the Joint Select Committee*, 8:77, 9:750.

67. William Powell to Governor W. H. Smith, Oct. 1870, Alabama Governors' Papers, W. H. Smith, 1867–1870, Alabama Department of Archives and History, Montgomery, Alabama (hereinafter cited as ADAH).

68. S. S. Plowman, letter to W. H. Smith, July 12, 1868; T. C. Brannon to Smith, Aug. 29, 1870; C. P. Simmons to Smith, Sept. 3, 1868; C. P. Simmons to Smith, Jan. 11, 1869; all in Alabama Governors' Papers, W. H. Smith, 1867–1870, ADAH.

69. M. Frank Gallagher to Lieut. James Miller, July 12, 1870, Alabama Governors' Papers, W. H. Smith, 1867–1870, ADAH.

70. A Duke University Special Collections librarian first alerted me to the byname "Republican Methodist Church," by which the Jefferson County church he attended as a child in the 1950s was commonly known. See also William W. Sweet, "Methodist Church Influence in Southern Politics," *Mississippi Valley Historical Review* 1 (Mar. 1915): 548.

71. Ibid., 548, 551–57; Fitzgerald, "Alabama Yeomanry During Reconstruction," 571; Trelease, *White Terror*, 254; Daniel W. Stowell, *Rebuilding Zion: The Religious Reconstruction of the South, 1863–1877* (New York: Oxford University Press, 1998), 134–35.

72. Cincinnati *Western Christian Advocate*, Nov. 8, 1865.

73. "Church Reconstruction in Rebeldom," *Christian Advocate and Journal* (Feb. 9, 1865), quoted in Stowell, *Rebuilding Zion*, 57.

74. Sweet, "Methodist Church Influence in Southern Politics," 522.

75. J. Lawrence Brasher, *The Sanctified South: John Lakin Brasher and the Holiness Movement* (Urbana; Chicago: University of Illinois Press, 1994), 9–10; Marion Ellis Lazenby, *History of Methodism in Alabama and West Florida: Being an Account of the Amazing March of Methodism through Alabama and West Florida* (n.p.: North Alabama Conference and Alabama–West Florida Conference of the Methodist Church, 1960), 362–69. Lakin had served as chaplain for the 39th Regiment Indiana Volunteers, later reorganized as the 8th Indiana Cavalry, which spent a good bit of time in and around northern Alabama from 1862 to 1864. See "Rev. Arad S. Lakin, D. D.," in *The Minutes of the Fourteenth Annual Session of the Central Alabama Conference, of the Methodist Episcopal Church, held in Mobile, Ala., January 30 to February 3, 1890* (Nashville, Tenn.: Ligon & Co., 1890). Thanks to Guy Hubbs for photocopying the latter from the North Alabama Conference Archives at Birmingham-Southern College Library in Birmingham, Alabama.

76. Cincinnati *Western Christian Advocate*, Oct. 30, 1867.

77. Ibid.; John Lakin Brasher, "History of the Alabama Conference Methodist Episcopal Church," typescript, John Lakin Brasher Papers, Library, Duke University, Durham, North Carolina.

78. Sweet, "Methodist Church Influence in Southern Politics," 549.

79. *Testimony Taken by the Joint Select Committee*, 9:776.

80. *Fifth Annual Report of the Church Extension Society of the Methodist Episcopal Church for the Year 1870* (New York: Printed for the Society, [1871?]), 32.

81. U.S. District Court Records, Northern District of Alabama, Northeastern Division, Huntsville, Criminal Case Files, 1865–1877, Record Group 21, Box 1, Case Number 67, Location: B/22/14/G, National Archives and Records Administration, Atlanta Branch, East Point, Georgia.

82. "Rev. Arad S. Lakin, D. D.," *The Minutes of the Fourteenth Annual Session of the Central Alabama Conference*, 39. This biographical essay mentions, and probably relied in part on, Lakin's testimony before the congressional committee investigating political violence during Reconstruction. It also notes that "the half was never told."

83. Testimony of John Helms, Claim 6785, Levin A. Clifton, Cherokee County, Nov. 18, 1874, SCC; "Minutes of the Alabama Mission Conference Held in Talladega, Alabama, Oct. 17–20, 1867" in *Annual Conferences of the Methodist Episcopal Church for the Year 1866* (New York: Carlton & Lanahan, 1868), 271.

84. *Journal of the Alabama Annual Conference of the Methodist Episcopal Church* (1924), 44.

85. Claim 6701, Ebenezer Leath, Cherokee County, July 2, 1875, SCC. As was the case during the war, Leath continued to have a reputation as a fighter. The reason he wasn't harmed, at least according to him, was that he "would kill the first man that touched the door." Apparently, his opponents took him seriously.

86. Letter of M. B. Sullivan, *The Nationalist* (Mobile), June 11, 1869.

87. Ibid. See also mention of Sullivan's beating in A. S. Lakin to Gov. W. H. Smith, July 27, 1869, Alabama Governors' Papers, W. H. Smith, 1867–1870, ADAH.

88. Trelease, *White Terror*, xxxiv; James E. Sefton, *The United States Army and Reconstruction, 1865–1877* (Baton Rouge: Louisiana State University Press, 1967), appendix B: "Numbers and Locations of Troops, 260–62."

89. W. J. Haralson and G. W. Moore to Gov. W. H. Smith, Aug. 16, 1869, Alabama Governors' Papers, W. H. Smith, 1867–1870, ADAH; Claim 14463-A, James Copeland, DeKalb County, Mar. 22, 1875, SCC.

90. J. F. Morton and J. Pinkney Whitehead and Many Citizens to Gov. W. H. Smith, June 10, 1870, Alabama Governors' Papers, W. H. Smith, 1867–1870, ADAH.

91. Trelease, *White Terror*, xxxiv; Abbott, *The Republican Party and the South*, 189.

92. *Testimony Taken by the Joint Select Committee*, 9:775.

93. W. J. Haralson and G. W. Moore to Governor W. H. Smith, Aug. 16, 1869, Alabama Governors' Papers, W. H. Smith, 1867–1870, ADAH.

94. Ibid.

95. William Powell to Gov. W. H. Smith, Oct. 1870, Alabama Governors' Papers, W. H. Smith, 1867–1870, ADAH.

96. W. T. Beard to Gov. W. H. Smith, July 23, 1869, Alabama Governors' Papers, W. H. Smith, 1867–1870, ADAH.

97. Ibid.

98. For his wartime record, see Testimony of Henry H. Smith, Claim 4194, John Barnes, DeKalb County, May 26, 1875, SCC. Smith, although a refugee who claimed to have served in the Union Army, was denied his claim before the SCC. Claim 6237, Henry H. Smith, DeKalb County, Office Number 80, Report Number 6, 1876; NAMS-M1407, Disallowed Claims, SCC.

99. *Nationalist*, June 11, 1869.

100. Foner, *Reconstruction*, 442, 553; Allen Johnston Going, *Bourbon Democracy in Alabama, 1874–1890* (Tuscaloosa: University of Alabama Press, 1951, reprint 1992), 50–54. In Alabama's Morgan County, Unionist C. C. Sheets stood for governor as a Republican in 1876; a decade later, Arthur Bingham, prominent Union Leaguer and radical, did the same; and W. T. Ewing, also a wartime Unionist and 1867 Constitutional Convention delegate, followed suit in 1888. The adherence of some white Unionists to the Republican Party does not change our picture of Alabama politics after 1870. In none of these above cases did a Republican come close to winning the governorship; moreover, in 1886 and 1888 the Republicans won no legislative seats at all.

5. "A New Field of Labor": Antislavery Women, Freedmen's Aid, and Political Power / Carol Faulkner

1. For a comprehensive analysis of white and black women's activism in the freedmen's aid movement, see Carol Faulkner, *Women's Radical Reconstruction: The Freedmen's Aid Movement* (Philadelphia: University of Pennsylvania Press, 2004), on which this essay is based. Copyright © 2004 University of Pennsylvania Press. Reprinted by permission of the University of Pennsylvania Press.

2. Lyde Cullen Sizer, *The Political Work of Northern Women Writers and the Civil War, 1850–1872* (Chapel Hill: University of North Carolina Press, 2000), 4. See also Wendy Hamand Venet, *Neither Ballots Nor Bullets: Women Abolitionists and the Civil War* (Charlottesville: University Press of Virginia, 1991); Elizabeth Leonard, *Yankee Women: Gender Battles in the Civil War* (New York: Norton, 1994); Jeanie Attie, *Patriotic Toil: Northern Women and the American Civil War* (Ithaca, N.Y.: Cornell University Press, 1998); Judith Ann Giesberg, *Civil War Sisterhood: The U.S. Sanitary Commission and Women's Politics in Transition* (Boston: Northeastern University Press, 2000); and Nina Silber, *Daughters of the Union: Northern Women Fight the Civil War* (Cambridge, Mass.: Harvard University Press, 2005).

3. Jacqueline Jones, *Soldiers of Light and Love: Northern Teachers and Georgia Blacks, 1865–1873* (Athens: University of Georgia Press, 1980, 1992); Julie Roy Jeffrey, *The Great Silent Army of Abolitionism: Ordinary Women in the Antislavery Movement* (Chapel Hill: University of North Carolina Press, 1998), chapter 6; Ellen Carol DuBois, *Feminism and Suffrage: The Emergence of an Independent Women's Movement in America, 1848–1869* (Ithaca, N.Y.: Cornell University Press, 1978).

4. Though the federal government expanded permanently during the Civil War, this expansion was not without tensions. Subsequently, the government scaled back as its interest in Reconstruction receded. Michael Les Benedict, "Preserving the Constitution: The Conservative Basis of Radical Reconstruction," *Journal of American History* 61 (June 1974): 65–90; Morton Keller, *Affairs of State: Public Life in the Late Nineteenth Century*

(Cambridge, Mass.: Belknap Press, 1977); Richard F. Bensel, *Yankee Leviathan: The Origins of Central State Authority in America, 1859–1877* (New York: Cambridge University Press, 1991).

5. Similarly, historian Elizabeth Leonard describes the hostility to women's leadership among the male officials of the Sanitary Commission, particularly in war relief efforts. See Leonard, *Yankee Women*, 81.

6. *Twelfth Annual Report of the Rochester Ladies' Anti-Slavery Society* (Rochester, N.Y.: A. Strong, 1863), 3.

7. Julia A. Wilbur to Anna M. C. Barnes, Nov. 12, 13, 26, 1862, Rochester Ladies' Anti-Slavery Society Papers, William L. Clements Library, University of Michigan (hereinafter RLASS); Lucretia Mott, letter to Martha Coffin Wright, Dec. 27, 1862, Mott Manuscripts, Friends Historical Library, Swarthmore College. On women's voluntarism in an earlier period, see especially Anne M. Boylan, *The Origins of Women's Activism: New York and Boston, 1797–1840* (Chapel Hill: University of North Carolina Press, 2002).

8. Testimony of the Ladies' Contraband Relief Society, American Freedmen's Inquiry Commission Papers, file 7, roll 21, National Archives Microfilm Publication M69, Record Group 94, National Archives, Washington, D.C.; Leslie Schwalm, "Encountering Emancipation: Slave Migration to the Midwest During the Civil War" (paper presented at the Southern Historical Association 65th Annual Meeting, Fort Worth, Texas, Nov. 3–6, 1999).

9. For the racial and class tensions in women's benevolence, see Jones, *Soldiers of Light and Love*, 144–153; Peggy Pascoe, *Relations of Rescue: The Search for Female Moral Authority in the American West, 1874–1939* (New York: Oxford University Press, 1990); Louise Michele Newman, *White Women's Rights: The Racial Origins of Feminism in the United States* (New York: Oxford University Press, 1999).

10. Josephine Griffing, petition presented May 9, 1864, Records of the House of Representatives, HR38A-G10.5, National Archives, Washington, D.C.; Elizabeth Cady Stanton, Susan B. Anthony, and Matilda Joslyn Gage, eds., *History of Woman Suffrage* (1881; repr., New York: Source Book, 1970), 1:110.

11. Emily Howland to Slocum Howland, Apr. 29, 1866, Emily Howland Papers, Friends Historical Library, Swarthmore College, read on microfilm at the Rare Books and Manuscripts Division, Kroch Library, Cornell University, Ithaca, New York. For similar views, see Hannah Stevenson to J. Miller McKim, July 16, 1866, July 20, 1866, Samuel J. May Anti-Slavery Collection, Cornell University.

12. Wilbur to Edwin M. Stanton, Mar. 24, 1863, quoted in Ira Berlin et al., eds., *Freedom: A Documentary History of Emancipation, 1861–1867*, series 1, vol. 2: *The Wartime Genesis of Free Labor: The Upper South* (New York: Cambridge University Press, 1993), 280–82.

13. Wilbur to Anna M. C. Barnes, Feb. 27, 1863, RLASS.

14. Lt. Col. H. H. Wells to Brig. Gen. J. P. Slough, Apr. 23, 1863, quoted in Berlin et al., eds., *Freedom*, 286.

15. Amy Dru Stanley, *From Bondage to Contract: Wage Labor, Marriage, and the Market in the Age of Emancipation* (New York: Cambridge University Press, 1998), chapter 3; Nancy Fraser and Linda Gordon, "A Genealogy of Dependency: Tracing a Keyword of the U.S. Welfare State," *Signs* 19 (Winter 1994): 309–36.

16. Josephine Griffing to William Lloyd Garrison, Mar. 24, 1864, Ms.A.1.2.v.33 p. 32b, Boston Public Library. See also Henrietta S. Jacquette, ed., *South after Gettysburg: Letters from Cornelia Hancock of the Army of the Potomac, 1863–65* (Philadelphia: University of Pennsylvania Press, 1937), 42–43. During the Civil War, government agencies offered new employment opportunities for middle-class women. See Cindy Sondik Aron, *Ladies and Gentlemen of the Civil Service: Middle-Class Workers in Victorian America* (New York: Oxford University Press, 1987).

17. Elizabeth C. Stanton, Susan B. Anthony, and Matilda J. Gage, eds., *History of Woman Suffrage*, 6 vols. (New York: Arno Press, 1969), 2:37, 29. See also Griffing to Gen. Oliver Otis Howard, May 8, 1865, Officer of the Commissioner, Letters Received, National Archives Microfilm Publication M752, Bureau of Refugees, Freedmen, and Abandoned Lands (BRFAL), Record Group 105, National Archives, Washington, D.C.

18. *Fourteenth Annual Report of the Rochester Ladies' Anti-Slavery Society* (Rochester, N.Y.: Wm. S. Falls, 1865), 13; *Fifteenth Annual Report of the Rochester Ladies' Anti-Slavery Society* (Rochester, N.Y.: Wm. S. Falls, 1866), 17.

19. *Fourteenth Annual Report*, 16–17.

20. *Fourteenth Annual Report*, 25–26; Mary J. Farmer, "'Because They Are Women': Gender and the Virginia Freedmen's Bureau's 'War on Dependency,'" in *The Freedmen's Bureau and Reconstruction: Reconsiderations*, ed., Paul A. Cimbala and Randall M. Miller (New York: Fordham University Press, 1999), 161–92. For freedwomen's struggle against the apprenticeship of their children, see Karin L. Zipf, "Reconstructing 'Free Woman': African-American Women, Apprenticeship, and Custody Rights during Reconstruction," *Journal of Women's History* 12 (Spring 2000): 8–31.

21. Emma V. Brown to Emily Howland, Jan. 20, no year, Box 10, Emily Howland Papers.

22. *Liberator*, Nov. 3, 1865.

23. On Rachel Moore, see Minutes, Oct. 9, 1862, Philadelphia Female Anti-Slavery Society, Reel 30, Pennsylvania Abolition Society Papers, Historical Society of Pennsylvania; *Revolution*, Apr. 7, 1870. Mary Farmer argues that local officials of the Freedmen's Bureau were often willing to extend material aid to women and children, but women's labors in Washington provoked a different response from officials. Farmer, "'Because They Are Women,'" 161–192. See also Mary Farmer-Kaiser, *Freedwomen and the Freedmen's Bureau: Race, Gender, and Public Policy in the Age of Emancipation* (New York: Fordham University Press, 2010).

24. James M. McPherson, *Struggle for Equality: Abolitionists and the Negro in the Civil War and Reconstruction* (Princeton: Princeton University Press, 1964), 389–92; Keith Melder, "Angel of Mercy in Washington: Josephine Griffing and the Freedmen, 1864–1872," *Records of the Columbia Historical Society of the District of Columbia* 45 (1965), 259.

25. Sojourner Truth to Amy Post, July 3, 1866, Isaac and Amy Post Papers, Rush Rhees Library, University of Rochester (N.Y.).

26. J. C. Thayer to Truth, Mar. 15, 1867; Theodore Backus to Truth, Feb. 22, 1867; Davis Carpenter to Isaac Post, Mar. 14, 1867; Mrs. James Annin to Truth, Mar. 15, 1867; Griffing to Truth and Post, Mar. 26, 1867, all in Post Papers. See also Nell Irvin Painter, *Sojourner Truth: A Life, A Symbol* (New York: Norton, 1996), 217–19; Carleton Mabee, "Sojourner Truth Fights Dependence on Government: Moves Freed Slaves Off Welfare in Washington to Jobs in Upstate New York," *Afro-Americans in New York Life and History* 14 (Jan. 1990): 7–26; and "A Noble Charity," newspaper clipping with letter of A. F. Williams to S. N. Clark, Feb. 13, 1867, Letters Received, Assistant Commissioner for the District of Columbia, National Archives Microfilm Publication M1055 (ACDC), BRFAL, National Archives Building, Washington, D.C.

27. Stephanie McCurry discusses gender and race relations in yeomen farm families in the antebellum South in *Masters of Small Worlds: Yeomen Households, Gender Relations, and the Political Culture of the Antebellum South Carolina Low Country* (New York: Oxford University Press, 1997).

28. Griffing to Truth and Post, Mar. 26, 1867; Truth to Griffing, Mar. 30, 1867, both in Post Papers.

29. Anna Lowell to Gen. C. H. Howard, Dec. 4, 1866, Letters Received, ACDC, BRFAL. Anna Lowell did not identify with radical abolitionists but rather with moderate antislavery Republicans. *Reports of the Soldiers' Memorial Society Presented at its Third*

Annual Meeting, June 11, 1867 (Boston: Soldiers' Memorial Society, 1867), 3, 12–13; Faye Dudden, *Serving Women: Household Service in Nineteenth-Century America* (Middletown, Conn.: Wesleyan University Press, 1983).

30. Anna Lowell to Gen. C. H. Howard, Sept. 1, 1867, Letters Received, ACDC, BRFAL.

31. Anna Lowell to C. H. Howard, Dec. 4, 1866, Jan. 13, 1867, Feb. 6, Feb. 27. See also ibid., Oct. 25, 1866, and Nov. 1, 1866.

32. Anna Lowell to C. H. Howard, Jan. 13, 1867.

33. Anna Earle to Gen. C. H. Howard, Oct. 12, 1867; Jan. 24, 1868, Letters Received, ACDC, BRFAL.

34. Frederick Douglass to McKim, May 1865, Box 13, Samuel J. May Anti-Slavery Collection, Cornell University, Ithaca, New York; Jones, *Soldiers of Light and Love*, 148; Newman, *White Women's Rights*, 12.

35. Griffing to Eliphalet Whittlesey, Aug. 29, 1868, Letters Received, Office of the Commissioner, BRFAL. For more on Williams and Griffing, see Faulkner, *Women's Radical Reconstruction*, 129.

36. *Autobiography of Oliver Otis Howard* (New York: Baker & Taylor, 1907), 2:213–14. See also Farmer-Kaiser, *Freedwomen and the Freedmen's Bureau*.

37. S. N. Clark to Mr. E. Carpenter, Dec. 5, 1865, Letters Sent, ACDC, BRFAL.

38. Lucretia Mott to Martha Coffin Wright and Anna Temple Brown, Apr. 10, 1865, *The Selected Letters of Lucretia Coffin Mott*, ed. Beverly Wilson Palmer (Urbana: University of Illinois Press, 2002), 357.

39. Jacob R. Shipherd to Gen. O. O. Howard, Oct. 30, 1865, Letters Received, Office of the Commissioner, BRFAL.

40. Ibid. See also McKim to Shipherd, Jan.10, 1866, McKim Letterbooks, Samuel J. May Anti-Slavery Collection, Cornell University, Ithaca, New York. For examples of Freedmen's Bureau agents attacking Griffing and other female reformers, see W. F. Spurgin to S. N. Clark, Nov. 1, 1865, and Jan. 1, 1866; Will Coulter to Gen. C. H. Howard, Nov. 5, 6, and 7, 1867; Maj. Vandenburgh to Coulter, Nov. 7, 1867; all in Letters Received, ACDC, BRFAL. See also Faulkner, *Women's Radical Reconstruction*, chapter 5 and passim.

41. *Fifteenth Annual Report*, 16.

42. *National Anti-Slavery Standard*, Feb. 20, 1869.

43. Griffing to Gen. O. O. Howard, Nov. 22, 1869, Letters Received by the Commissioner, BRFAL.

44. *Sixteenth Annual Report of the Rochester Ladies' Anti-Slavery Society* (Rochester, N.Y.: William S. Falls, 1867), 22; *National Anti-Slavery Standard*, May 1, 1869.

45. Stanton, Anthony, and Gage, eds., *History of Woman Suffrage*, 2:89; Newman, *White Women's Rights*.

46. Griffing to Elizabeth Cady Stanton, Dec. 27, 1870, in *The Selected Papers of Elizabeth Cady Stanton and Susan B. Anthony*, vol. 2: *Against an Aristocracy of Sex, 1866–1873*, ed. Ann Gordon (New Brunswick, N.J.: Rutgers University Press, 2000), 390–91.

6. "Objects of Humanity": The White Poor in Civil War and Reconstruction Georgia / Denise E. Wright

1. Registers of Letters Received by the Commissioner of the Bureau of Refugees, Freedmen, and Abandoned Lands, 1865–1872, roll 23, Record Group 105, National Archives Microfilm Publication M752.

2. The terms *planters, yeomen, poor whites, plain folk,* and *common folk* used here are based on those found in David Williams, *Rich Man's War: Class, Caste, and Confederate Defeat in the Lower Chattahoochee Valley* (Athens: University of Georgia Press, 1998), 211n15. Williams's definitions are standard, but they concisely describe commonly used

terms: "Planters are defined by their ownership of twenty slaves or more . . . *yeomen* here refers to small farmers and herdsmen ranging from those who owned at least three acres of land and no slaves to those who held up to four slaves. Tenants, sharecroppers, and farm laborers, generally referred to (along with unskilled urban workers) as poor whites, worked land owned by someone else. The designation plain folk or common folk when used in this study generally means *yeomen* and *poor whites*, although most often it includes small merchants and skilled artisans (mechanics) as well." With those definitions in mind, the term used here, "white poor," refers to whites who received aid from any source. As discussed throughout this study, the requirements for aid did not depend upon a recipient's class identification (such as landowner or non-landowner) but on their current state of need. Therefore the use of *poor white* in this case would be inaccurate. For more discussion of the subtleties of and complications that arise from these definitions, see Stephen V. Ash, "Poor Whites in the Occupied South, 1861–1865," *Journal of Southern History* 57 (Feb. 1991): 39–62. A classic study of poor whites in Georgia is found in Steven Hahn, *The Roots of Southern Populism: Yeoman Farmers and the Transformation of the Georgia Upcountry, 1850–1890* (New York: Oxford University Press, 1983).

3. John Hope Franklin, "Public Welfare in the South during the Reconstruction Era, 1865–1880," *Social Service Review* 44 (Dec. 1970): 379–92. Franklin examined the South as a whole, but most of his data came from North Carolina.

4. Elna C. Green, *This Business of Relief: Confronting Poverty in a Southern City, 1740–1940* (Athens: University of Georgia Press, 2003). Interestingly, Green's edited collection *Before the New Deal: Social Welfare in the South, 1830–1930* (Athens: University of Georgia Press, 1999) does not address the role of the Freedmen's Bureau in great detail. For more on the ever-evolving roles of the Freedmen's Bureau and its agents in Georgia, see Paul A. Cimbala, *Under the Guardianship of the Nation: The Freedmen's Bureau and the Reconstruction of Georgia, 1865–1870* (Athens: University of Georgia Press, 1997). Robert H. Bremner's *The Public Good: Philanthropy and Welfare in the Civil War Era* (New York: Knopf, 1980) and his article "The Impact of the Civil War on Philanthropy and Social Welfare," *Civil War History* 12 (Dec. 1966): 294–98, are excellent resources for understanding the ideology behind welfare in the era. For more on the evolution of the role of welfare in Civil War and Reconstruction historiography, see Denise Wright, "Civil War and Reconstruction Welfare Programs for Georgia's White Poor: The State, the Freedmen's Bureau, and Northern Charity, 1863–1868" (PhD diss., University of Georgia, 2005), 19–35.

5. Peter Wallenstein, *From Slave South to New South: Public Policy in Nineteenth-Century Georgia* (Chapel Hill: University of North Carolina Press, 1987), 30; Emory M. Thomas, *The Confederacy as a Revolutionary Experience* (Englewood Cliffs, N.J.: Prentice Hall, 1971; Columbia: University of South Carolina Press, 1991), 86. The drought and military activities in Georgia are best described in Lee Kennett, *Marching Through Georgia: The Story of Soldiers and Civilians During Sherman's Campaign* (New York: Harper-Collins, 1995). For interesting details of the shortages people faced throughout the Confederacy, see Mary Elizabeth Massey, *Ersatz in the Confederacy* (Columbia: University of South Carolina Press, 1952). For one of the few book-length accounts of life as a refugee, see Massey, *Refugee Life in the Confederacy*, with a new introduction by George C. Rable (Baton Rouge: Louisiana State University Press, 1964, 2001). The summer droughts also are discussed in a series of letters from Governor Joseph E. Brown contained in Allen D. Candler, comp., *The Confederate Records of the State of Georgia* (Atlanta: C.P. Byrd, State Printer, 1910–41), 3:328–29, 501–3.

6. These acts and expenditures are detailed in Wallenstein, *From Slave South to New South*, 99–109; and *Acts of the General Assembly of the State of Georgia, Passed in Milledgeville at an Annual Session in November and December, 1863; also Extra Session of*

1864, part I: *Public Laws*, title I: *Appropriations*, section XII: *Passed November and December 1863* (Milledgeville: Boughton, Nisbet, Barnes, & Moore, State Printers [hereinafter cited as BNB&M], 1864), 8. This section includes both the $500,000 salt appropriation as well as the $200,000 appropriation for cotton and wool cards. By the time the comptroller general issued his 1865 report, salt distribution had become part of the larger Indigent Soldiers' Families Fund, discussed below. For cotton card legislation, see *Journal of the Senate of the State of Georgia, 1862* (Milledgeville: BNB&M, 1862), 58; and *Annual Report of the Comptroller General of the State of Georgia Made to the Governor, October 16, 1865* (Milledgeville: BNB&M, 1865), 54–66. All government publications are available online from Documenting the American South, http://docsouth.unc.edu.

   7. Joseph E. Brown, "Relief to the People," *Journal of the Senate, 1861*, 22–23. Brown noted that "in this state of things it is the duty of the Government to do all that can be done, to afford relief." The advances on crops would be overseen by a single state officer who would be solely devoted to the job. By mid-November, the Georgia Senate responded with a proposal to incorporate the Cotton Planters' Bank to exchange the treasury notes for cotton (77). On December 14, the proposal became law. See "An Act to Incorporate the Cotton Planters Bank of Georgia," *Acts of the General Assembly, 1861*, 20–22. The fund was sometimes referred to as the "Soldiers' Families Fund" in legislative documents and state reports.

   8. Brown, "Governor's Message," *Journal of the Senate, 1862*, 19–20. The bounty was available to families with a soldier in the field, widows of soldiers, and widows who had at least one son in service. Funding from the railroad would be increased by a 25 percent hike in freight rates and a 33.3 percent tax on income from "speculation." Initial monies would be procured by a short-term loan. It is worth noting that in the fall of 1862, the discussion of salt took up more of Governor Brown's annual message than other relief efforts. For more on the problems of speculation, even from within the Confederate War Department, see Williams, *Rich Man's War, Poor Man's Fight*, chapter 4.

   9. *Journal of the Senate, Extra Session, March 1863*, 124–25. See also Wallenstein, *From Slave South to New South*, 102; and Williams, *Rich Man's War, Poor Man's Fight*, 110. According to the comptroller general's 1864 report, $809,569.75 of this fund remained "undrawn" as of October 15, 1863—the end of the fiscal year.

   10. Brown, "Governor's Message," *Journal of the Senate, 1863*, 19–20, 218. One of Brown's reasons for the larger request was because of "depreciation" and scarcity of supplies. He even proposed that the funds be raised "if it takes an annual tax of ten per cent" (20). Kennett describes Georgia's welfare expenditures in 1863 as "in a sense class legislation, destined for members of the class that was at once most loyal to Brown and most vulnerable to the wrenching economic changes the state was undergoing" (*Marching Through Georgia*, 31). This description is accurate, and it is interesting to note that Brown's home county of Cherokee received the largest disbursements from the Indigent Soldiers' Families Fund for the fiscal years 1863–64 and 1864–65.

   11. "An Act to provide for raising a revenue for the political year 1864," *Acts of the General Assembly, 1863; also Extra Session of 1864*, part I: *Public Laws*, title I: *Appropriations*, section XVI, 8.

   12. "An Act to appropriate money for the support of indigent families of Soldiers," *Acts of the General Assembly, 1863; also Extra Session of 1864*, part I: *Appropriations*, title XVIII: *Soldiers and Soldiers Families*, section I, 70. Additional funding for the bill came from taxing bank stock (74).

   13. Ibid., 70–73. As with other appropriations, the state comptroller general would disburse the funds to the inferior court representatives and also was responsible for keeping records. For more on Confederate widows, see Lee Ann Whites, *The Civil War as a Crisis in Gender: Augusta, Georgia, 1860–1890* (Athens: University of Georgia Press,

1995); and Jennifer Lynn Gross, "'Good Angels': Confederate Widowhood and the Reassurance of Patriarchy in the Post-Bellum South" (PhD diss., University of Georgia, 2001).

14. Massey, *Refugee Life in the Confederacy*, 244–46. Massey details the complexities of distributing aid to refugee populations throughout the Confederacy. In Massey's comparison, Georgia's laws concerning refugees were more liberal than most Confederate states.

15. *Annual Report of the Comptroller General, 1864*. The three counties who made no returns for the Soldiers' Families Fund were Catoosa, Chattooga, and Dade. Murray and Walker Counties, also in northwestern Georgia, made their returns sometime between late March and October. Further evidence of the disruptions of war is found in Thweatt's enumeration of income tax returns by county. Nineteen counties (Catoosa, Charlton, Chattooga, Cherokee, Cobb, Dade, Fannin, Floyd, Forsyth, Gilmer, Gordon, Milton, Monroe, Murray, Paulding, Pickens, Pierce, Polk, and Walker) filed no income tax returns whatsoever for the tax year 1863–64 (April to April). Of those nineteen, sixteen are in northwestern Georgia. Pierce and Charlton Counties are in far southeastern Georgia, but their returns were missing because the office of "Receiver of Tax Returns" is reported as vacant in the report. Regarding Monroe County, just north of Macon in the center of the state, the report informs us that the return was "so deficient" that the governor asked to have it reformulated and resubmitted. It is interesting to note that far more northern counties made their returns for the Soldiers' Families Funds than their income tax returns, implying that they perceived the former to be more crucial, or at least filled a more immediate demand, than the latter. For more on the Fosterville settlement in Terrell County, see Massey, *Refugee Life in the Confederacy*, 246; and *Acts of the General Assembly*, Mar. 11, 1865, 81–82. Kennett, *Marching Through Georgia*, supplies the most detailed description of the exiles, white Confederates who were expelled from the city of Atlanta by an order from General Sherman on September 5, 1864. Kennett identifies the location of the exiles' destination as Dawson, the county seat of Terrell County, and notes that Brown "bent the rules" to use military funds to support the exiles (207–12).

16. *Annual Report of the Comptroller General, 1865*, 54–66. "Indigent Soldiers' Families Fund" and "Soldiers Families Fund" are used interchangeably in various reports.

17. Ibid., 20–22. Thweatt was in the unenviable position of attempting to reconcile prewar and wartime debts amid discussion of repudiating the Confederate debt, which he vehemently opposed. Part of his argument against repudiation was the fact that there was a "morality" to the debts incurred to assist soldiers' families.

18. "An Act for raising a Revenue for the political year eighteen hundred and sixty-six," *Acts of the General Assembly*, Dec. 1865 and Jan.–Mar. 1866, part I: *Public Laws*, title III: *Appropriations, &c.*, vol. I, section XI, 12–13; "An Act for raising a Revenue for the political year eighteen hundred and sixty-seven," *Acts of the General Assembly*, 1866, part I: *Public Laws*, title II: *Appropriations, &c.*, vol. I, section XXXV, Dec. 13, 1866, 11; both at "Georgia's Acts and Resolutions from 1799–1999," Georgia Legislative Documents Project, presented in the Digital Library of Georgia, http://neptune3.galib.uga.edu/ssp/cgi-bin/legis-idx.pl?sessionid=7f000001&type=law&byte=38189857. Section XXVIII of the December 1866 appropriation also provided $20,000 for transportation of "corn and other supplies donated by the people of Kentucky and benevolent societies of other States, to the destitute of Georgia," which is examined in detail below. Former Comptroller General Peterson Thweatt, who so dramatically argued against repudiating the state's debt, was the state agent in charge of distributing this fund. It also is notable that once the war was over, the "aged and infirm persons" who were eligible for aid were specifically described as "white."

19. *Congressional Globe*, 39th Congress, First Session (Jan. 30, 1866), 516. Congressman Eliot also stated that in a case where one was not comparing freedmen and refugees, it was possible to use refugee to apply to a black person if that person had not been enslaved. In short, it was possible for a black refugee to exist, but because most discussion centered on freedmen and refugees, as is obvious from the title of the Bureau, most of the time refugee meant white. For further analysis of the racial equity of the original Freedmen's Bureau legislation, including the House and Senate debates, see Paul Moreno, "Racial Classifications and Reconstruction Legislation," *Journal of Southern History* 61 (May 1995): 271–304. Moreno does not limit his examination to this bill, but also includes analysis of subsequent legislation to determine whether "the new American citizenship [of the freedpeople], constitutionally and legally defined, [was] to be colorblind or color conscious" (27).

20. Office of the Commissioner, *Reports*, Entry 33, Box 6, Record Group 105, National Archives, Washington, D.C. (hereinafter cited as BRFAL). This untitled, fourteen-page report is not part of the microfilmed records of the Freedmen's Bureau. The statistics it contains were compiled from each state's and the District of Columbia's monthly reports, which were filed by assistant commissioners.

21. Ibid. The four states that distributed more rations than Georgia were Virginia, Alabama, South Carolina, and North Carolina. The four states that issued a greater percentage of rations to whites were Arkansas, Alabama, Kentucky, and Maryland. The assistant commissioners submitted their data on folio-sized, preprinted report forms, found in *Monthly Reports of the Assistant Commissioner of the Bureau of Refugees, Freedmen, and Abandoned Lands (BRFAL) for the State of Georgia*, Dec. 1865–Dec. 1867, Entry 33, BRFAL. The Georgia commissioners submitted separate sheets clearly labeled "Freedmen" and "Refugees." The reports identify the number of rations issued rather than the number of people who received rations, which precludes determining the number of people who received the enumerated rations. Ration distribution is subdivided by gender and age (adult or child under fourteen); "First Class," which included "Dependents," both "Well" and "Sick"; "Second Class," defined as "In Government Employ"; and "Third Class," defined as "Receiving Rations and Giving Lien on Crop." Unfortunately, the narrative reports that originally accompanied these statistical reports were separated after receipt in Washington and are no longer part of this entry.

22. *Monthly Reports of the Assistant Commissioner*, Dec. 1865–Dec. 1867, BRFAL. A "ration" was far from standardized. Officially, a ration should include enough food—primarily corn—to feed one person for one week. In reality, one ration was often whatever food the agent could procure, divided between the most desperate citizens. Corn, corn meal, bacon, salt pork, and flour are listed in various agents' records. The original monthly reports use a combination of descriptors for distribution points. Most often, the "station" identified is a city, which is presumably the location of the Freedmen's Bureau agent in that county. Generally, it is the county seat, but there are exceptions. In some cases, the station is identified as a county, and in even fewer cases, counties are combined as a single station. For example, a single monthly report could contain a combination of city stations (Savannah), county stations (Morgan), and multi-county stations (Henry and Newton).

23. Walton County, which is just north of the boundary separating the upcountry from the eastern Black Belt, had a slave population in 1860 of 4,621, or 41 percent of the total county population. Gilmer County, in the mountains, was a ration distribution station, but ranked last in Georgia's slave population in 1860 with 167, 2 percent of a total population of 6,724. University of Virginia Library, Historical Census Browser, 1860.

24. *Monthly Reports of the Assistant Commissioner*, Dec. 1865–Dec. 1867, BRFAL.

25. The use of inferior court judges to administer welfare after the war's end is confirmed in a letter, dated Feb. 6, 1867, found in Anne Middleton Holmes, *The New York Ladies' Southern Relief Association, 1866–1867: An Account of the Relief Furnished by Citizens of New York City to the Inhabitants of the Devastated Regions of ht South Immediately After the Civil War* (New York: The Mary Mildred Sullivan Chapter, United Daughters of the Confederacy, 1926), 31–33. Signed by W. B. Johnston, whose title and position are not identified, the letter states that the author had recently spoken to Georgia Governor Jenkins and found "that there is an organization of Agents under the supervision of the Inferior Courts of each County in the State for distributing contributions. All that is sent in money, provisions, & clothing is properly distributed to the poor" (31).

26. Holmes, *The New York Ladies' Southern Relief Association*. The pamphlet includes a narrative introduction by the author as well as transcripts of letters received. The final report is accompanied by a list of subscribers and their donations as well as brief information concerning the Brooklyn auxiliary. This pamphlet is by no means an unbiased source. The narrative is clearly supportive of the Dunning School of Reconstruction history, which is unsurprising given its publication date and connection to the United Daughters of the Confederacy. It also is possible that the letters published in the pamphlet were edited to include only those that supported Holmes's ideology. This does not, however, compromise their worth as sources. The original records are housed in the Brockenbrough Library at the Museum of the Confederacy in Richmond, Virginia.

27. Holmes, *The New York Ladies' Southern Relief Association*, 7, 21. Holmes's pamphlet is careful to point out that Mrs. Sullivan never offered aid of which the federal government would disapprove. The Sullivans' Southern connections continued after their deaths. Their son founded the Algernon Sydney Sullivan Foundation in 1934. It took over the responsibility of awarding the Algernon Sydney Sullivan Award from the New York Southern Society, now defunct but which had given the award since the 1890s. The foundation, now based in Oxford, Mississippi, continues today and awards more than $1 million in grants to thirty private Appalachian colleges. They also continue to award the Algernon Sydney Sullivan and Mary Mildred Sullivan Awards, both based upon criteria including philanthropy and humanitarianism, annually at those colleges and another twenty-five southeastern colleges. Details are found at www.sullivanfdn.org. Holmes also wrote *Algernon Sydney Sullivan* (New York: New York Southern Society, 1929), and *Mary Mildred Sullivan (Mrs. Algernon Sydney Sullivan): A Biography* (Concord, N.H.: Rumford Press, 1924), which notes it was "written for the records of The Mary Mildred Sullivan Chapter of the United Daughters of the Confederacy, New York City. Printed by the Chapter for private circulation" (i).

28. Holmes, *The New York Ladies' Southern Relief Association*, 111–13, 83. There were three officers and thirty-two executive committee members. Leary is identified in Holmes's pamphlet narrative as "brother of Countess Annie Leary." Annie and Arthur's father was a wealthy New York merchant. Arthur once served as the excise commissioner for the city, and Annie was a philanthropist noted for her work with the Catholic Church and with immigrant women and children. One result of this work was the granting of the title of papal countess in 1901, the first woman in the United States to receive this recognition. For a detailed biography, see the searchable online version of the *Biographical Cyclopedia of U.S. Women*, vols. I–II (New York: Halvord Publishers, 1924–25), www.ancestry.com/search/db.aspx?dbid = 2018 (accessed June 24, 2006). All the executive committee members except two were married. Holmes's pamphlet refers to Mrs. J. I. Roosevelt, "wife of the distinguished Judge of that name." Presumably, this was James I. Roosevelt, who served on the New York State Supreme Court and in congress, and was related to the future president, Teddy Roosevelt. The listing of officers on page 111 includes "Mrs. J. J. Roosevelt," which is likely a typographical error. J. C. Frémont was, among other things, Union Army general and the first Republican candidate for

president. Cyrus McCormick invented the mechanical reaper. George Ticknor Curtis was a noted attorney and served on the defense team in the *Dred Scott* case, and was a presidential biographer. Egbert Viele was the engineer who proposed and executed the construction of New York's Central Park, one among many notable accomplishments. E. W. Stoughton was presumably Edwin Wallace Stoughton, noted New York attorney who had defended Charles Goodyear in an early patent case and was one of the attorneys for the Electoral Commission in the 1876 election. Arguing for Rutherford B. Hayes paid off, as Stoughton was appointed minister to Russia in 1878.

29. Holmes, "Report," "Receipts," and "Statement," *The New York Ladies' Southern Relief Association* 83–110. Miscellaneous expenses included "rent, freight, stationery, advertising & printing, express charges, &c" (110). The exact amounts were $7,114.81 for provisions and $3,527.99 for expenses.

30. Ibid. See page 103 for the disbursement to Rev. Coley. On page 106, on May 6, an entry notes that $104.00 was sent to Opelika, but there is no Georgia town of that name. It is likely that this was sent to Opelika, Alabama, which is immediately across the Chattahoochee River from Columbus, Georgia. Periodically, the NYLSRA publicized their disbursements in newspapers, as evidenced by clippings found in the Records of the Southern Famine Relief Commission, New-York Historical Society, "Newspaper Abstracts," microfilm roll 4. The SFRC, established a bit later than the NYLSRA, was a larger organization, but there was considerable interaction between the two. For more on the SFRC, see Wright, "Civil War and Reconstruction Welfare Programs for Georgia's White Poor." The complete records of the commission are housed at the New-York Historical Society, but many have been included on four rolls of microfilm housed at the University of Georgia library. The microfilmed records include "Correspondence and Papers" on rolls 1 and 2; "Minutes of the Executive Committee (Loose)," on roll 3; and "Cash Book," "Subscription Books," "Telegrams Received," and "Newspaper Abstracts" on roll 4. There also is an immensely detailed finding aid describing the full contents of the records, which is available online from the New-York Historical Society, http://dlib.nyu.edu/findingaids/html/nyhs/southernfamrelief.html [accessed Dec. 18, 2009].

31. Ibid. Further research is required to determine why Columbus, though a major city, received so little aid from the NYLSRA. As the city is on the border with Alabama, it is possible that aid to Columbus was combined with aid to another Alabama city, but a thorough examination of patterns in Alabama is beyond the scope of this work.

32. Holmes, *The New York Ladies' Southern Relief Association*, 29. This is the only letter from a Freedmen's Bureau representative in Holmes's pamphlet, though further research may discover additional interaction between the two groups.

33. Ibid., 46–48. In the first letter, Mrs. Bachman is identified as "Mrs. S.W. Bachman," but in the second she is identified as "Mrs. T.W. Bachman." As the distribution of goods is not detailed in Holmes's pamphlet, it cannot be determined if the counties received any material aid from the NYLSRA. It is notable that neither of the men Mrs. Bachman listed as willing to distribute aid was specifically identified as a minister (one had no title, the other was a judge). This may have been the reason those counties received no cash, as there was no known minister to distribute it. The "Bureau" reference is presumably to the Freedmen's Bureau. The first of Mrs. Bachman's letters was reprinted verbatim in the New York *Sun*, dated April 30, and is part of the Records of the Southern Famine Relief Commission, New-York Historical Society, "Newspaper Abstracts," microfilm roll 4. One of the eight letters, dated February 6, 1867, from Macon, Georgia, describes conditions in the state and the poor relief agents who were supervised by the county inferior courts, as described above.

34. Ibid., 77–78. It is not impossible that women in similar circumstances received direct assistance from the NYLSRA. The report of cash distributions includes six notations of "Donated to a Southern Lady per Committee" in amounts ranging from $25 to $100. Only one specifically notes a destination city and state.

35. Ibid., 48–49. A total of $200 was sent to Decatur during 1867.

36. Ibid., 60. George's letter highlights one of the pitfalls in using the detailed "Statement of money distributed," as the only disbursement to "Rev. Mr. George" before mid-May was presumably sent to Lafayette, Georgia, not La Grange. La Grange is in Troup County, in the western Black Belt, and Lafayette is in Walker County, in the mountains. If this donation did go to La Grange, it would reduce the total amount of cash sent to Walker County to $50.00, reducing the total cash distribution to the mountains to $350.00. This would, of course, increase the amount to Troup County to $100.00, increasing the total to the western Black Belt to $550.00.

37. Ibid., 72.

38. Brooklyn *Daily Union*, March 12 and 14, 1867, Records of the Southern Famine Relief Commission, Newspaper Abstracts, microfilm roll 4 (hereinafter cited as SFNC Records). This file contains individual newspaper clippings, primarily though not exclusively from New York papers, with publication names and dates handwritten in the margins. A comparison to the online database of the *New York Times*, available through ProQuest.umi.com, confirms the handwritten dates as publication dates; therefore the handwritten dates are presumed to be publication dates for all other referenced newspapers. It cannot be determined if the pseudonymous "Inkgall of Andersonville" was an intentional reference to the infamous Georgia prison. For an interesting discussion of the role of women in late-nineteenth-century charitable associations, see John T. Cumbler, "The Politics of Charity: Gender and Class in Late 19th Century Charity Policy," *Journal of Social History* 14 (Fall 1980): 99–111.

39. *Congressional Globe*, 40th Cong., 1st sess., Mar. 9, 1867, 39. Howard's letter and "tabular statement" are reprinted here in full. A clipping from the *New York Post*, dated March 9, 1867, which reprinted Howard's letter as well as the statistical table, is included in the newspaper clippings found in the Records of the Southern Famine Relief Commission, "Newspaper Abstracts." The states, in order of total numbers of destitute people, were Alabama (10,500); South Carolina (10,000); Georgia (8,000); Virginia and North Carolina (5,000 each); Mississippi (3,900); Tennessee (2,000); Florida and Arkansas (1,500 each); Louisiana (500); and Texas (0). In his letter Howard included a postscript that he had since made his report: The Bureau assistant commissioner and the governor of Georgia had written with an estimate of numbers of destitute persons which far exceeded Howard's estimate of 7,500 whites and 5,000 freedpeople. He noted, however, that he was "unwilling to recommend a larger appropriation for Georgia before another estimate shall be made based on a thorough inspection." The question of whom the Bureau was assisting, or would assist with this new appropriation, would find its way into the House debate of the bill. On March 13, Representative Logan noted that during the war he had witnessed the wives and children of Confederate soldiers lining up "at the doors of the commissary department at different posts receiving food, while we were fighting their husbands and friends at the front. They were not then above asking us to feed them, while they despised us and our cause, and I have no doubt the same class are now to be fed under this appropriation" (88). On March 20, Representative Stevens posed the question, "Have the officers of the b[u]reau, in relieving destitution, ever made any distinction between the poor loyalist and the poor disloyalist?" Representative Stevens (Pennsylvania), responded, "All I can say is that nine out of ten of those who have been fed by the Freedmen's Bureau have been disloyal men who had become poor" (236).

40. *Congressional Globe*, 40th Cong., 1st sess., Mar. 13, 1867, 83–87; Mar. 20, 1867, 235. In his argument of March 13, Butler also mentioned that the state of Mississippi had allotted $20,000 not to feed the poor, but to defend Jefferson Davis, and that "ladies in Texas" had raised funds by selling Confederate uniforms, which they then sent to endow "the college in Virginia over which the rebel General Robert E. Lee presides." Fernando Wood, Democratic Representative of New York, expressed his concerns about the bill multiple times. On March 13, he stated that he was "opposed to the government of the United States distributing alms under any circumstances whatever, and in direction whatever." Additionally, he felt what the South needed (and he had recently traveled there) was capital, not charity. On March 20, he expanded his reasons for opposition to six. They were: Congress had no power to spend public money for charity; the South had not applied for aid; that the bill itself was "derogatory and insulting" to the Southern people; the Freedmen's Bureau agents were prejudiced against white Southerners and would not distribute the aid equitably; he suspected political motivations as the bill was offered just before Southern elections; and because the Bureau had $2.1 million "unexpended."

41. SFRC Records. These are only the papers whose clippings are found in the SFRC records. A more thorough examination of papers beyond New York would likely unearth additional editorials and letters.

42. *Congressional Globe*, 40th Cong., 1st sess., Mar. 13, 1867, 85, 282, 260. Boyer also argued that the Freedmen's Bureau was the best agency for distribution because it already existed and was organized. He felt the great need required expediency rather than arguments over the possibility of misappropriation. The congressional debates were lengthy and revisited many of the central issues surrounding the original legislation, including whether Congress had the power to provide charity at all. The final joint resolution (S 16) was enrolled on March 25. Representative Lawrence detailed in his floor speech his estimate of $2.1 million of unexpended Bureau funds. He estimated that this amount remained from both the "appropriation act of July 18, 1866," which totaled $4,770,250, and the "'deficiency appropriation act' of March 2, 1867," which totaled $1.5 million (SFRC Records, roll 4). The resulting joint resolution, and the final vote, was printed in the March 23 issue of the New York *Tribune*.

43. *New York Times*; New York *Herald*, Mar. 25, 1887; both in SFRC Records. Howard also urged the various charitable organizations to send their own representatives to the South to ascertain the situation. These, too, were published. *New York Post*, Mar. 26, 1867. A relief committee in Boston followed Howard's advice, and on May 14, 1867, published an account in the Boston *Transcript* describing their agent's trip south and the disbursement of funds to various states. Georgia received $9,000, the largest amount given to a single state.

44. "An Act for raising a Revenue for the political year eighteen hundred and sixty-seven," section XXVIII, approved Dec. 13, 1866, 11 "Georgia's Acts and Resolutions from 1799–1999," The Georgia Legislative Documents Project, presented in the Digital Library of Georgia.; *New York Times*, May 25, 1867, SFRC Records. Jenkins was elected governor in late 1865, replacing James Johnson, who had been appointed provisional governor in June. Joseph E. Brown, the previous governor, had been arrested in May. Jenkins had been a Whig before the war and then switched to the Democratic Party. Jenkins was forcibly removed from office by General George G. Meade in January 1868 after Jenkins, who had refused to recognize the legality of Congressional Reconstruction, repeatedly refused to pay the expenses of the required convention. For more on the complexities of these maneuvers, see Elizabeth Studley Nathans, *Losing the Peace: Georgia Republicans and Reconstruction, 1865–1871* (Baton Rouge: Louisiana State University Press, 1968), 56–78.

45. Clipping from *New York Times*, hand-dated May 25., SFRC Records, roll 4.

46. Alice B. Keith, "White Relief in North Carolina, 1865–1867," *Social Forces* 17 (Mar. 1939): 337, 345. At the time of her research, Keith could not locate the records or even confirm the existence of the SFRC, but she did discover many other private charitable organizations, as well as state appropriations, devoted to Southern poor relief. She quoted from a September 5, 1867, Raleigh *Sentinel* article titled "Our Best Friends," which stated, "The entire Southern Relief Fund amounts to $2,876,809. Of this $500,000 comes from Louisville; $321,000 from New York; $1,000,000 from the State of Maryland; from Boston $49,127; from Saint Louis $347,375." Keith noted that "the Southern Famine Commission is puzzling. There is the intimation that there was an attempt to consolidate the work for the famine relief in a central committee in New York City, but no description of such an organization has been discovered." She was, however, intimately familiar with the ladies' organization, thanks to Anne Middleton Holmes' publication.

47. Ibid., 337.

7. Racial Identity and Reconstruction: New Orleans's Free People of Color and the Dilemma of Emancipation / Justin A. Nystrom

This chapter is derived in part from Chapters 3, 6, and 9 in Justin A. Nystrom, *New Orleans after the Civil War: Race, Politics, and a New Birth of Freedom* (Baltimore: Johns Hopkins University Press, 2010). The material is used with the permission of the Johns Hopkins University Press.

1. Rodolphe Lucien Desdunes, *Nos Hommes et Notre Histoire—Our People and Our History: Fifty Creole Portraits*, trans. Sister Dorothea Olga McCants, (1911; Baton Rouge: Louisiana State University Press, 1973), 18; Charles Barthelemy Roussève, *The Negro in Louisiana: Aspects of His History and His Literature* (New Orleans: Xavier University Press, 1937), 99–100. When discussing Creole New Orleans, it is important to define what one means by the potentially contentious term *Creole*. I defer to the judgment of Joseph G. Tregle, who applies the definition to all individuals of any race born in Louisiana and of Latin ancestry. "Creoles and Americans," in *Creole New Orleans: Race and Americanization*, ed. Arnold R. Hirsch and Joseph Logsdon (Baton Rouge: Louisiana State University Press, 1992), 140. For a discussion of the variant definitions of Creole, particularly in Afro-Creole terms, see Sybil Kein, ed., *Creole: The History and Legacy of Louisiana's Free People of Color* (Baton Rouge: Louisiana State University Press, 2000), xiii–xvii; Gwendolyn Midlo Hall, "The Formation of Afro-Creole Culture," in *Creole New Orleans*, 60–61.

2. David Rankin, "The Impact of the Civil War on the Free Colored Community in New Orleans," *Perspectives in American History*, 13 (1977–1978): 401; Roussève, *The Negro in Louisiana*, 99. For an excellent study of the legal aspects of racial "passing" in Louisiana, see Virginia R. Domínguez, *White By Definition: Social Classification in Louisiana* (New Brunswick, N.J.: Rutgers University Press, 1986).

3. For one of the earliest key works in whiteness studies, see David R. Roediger, *The Wages of Whiteness: Race and the Making of the American Working Class* (London, New York: Verso, 1991); for a work focused specifically on the American South, see Grace Elizabeth Hale, *Making Whiteness: The Culture of Segregation in the South, 1890–1940* (New York: Pantheon, 1998). Toni Morrison has used the phrase "master narrative" or referred to the same in many of her works. See, for example, *Beloved: A Novel* (New York: Plume, 1988).

4. David Rankin, "The Politics of Caste: Free Colored Leadership in New Orleans During the Civil War," in Robert R. Macdonald, John R. Kemp, and Edward F. Haas, eds., *Louisiana's Black Heritage* (New Orleans: Louisiana State Museum, 1979), 107–46; Joseph Logsdon and Caryn Cossé Bell, "The Americanization of Black New Orleans," in *Creole New Orleans*, 201–61; Shirley Elizabeth Thompson, " '*Ah Toucoutou, ye conin vous*': History and Memory in Creole New Orleans," *American Quarterly* 53 (June 2001):

235. Whereas literary critics have written much about racial passing in popular fiction, the historical literature on the topic is relatively thin. The principal synthesis in this regard is Joel Williamson, *New People: Miscegenation and Mulattos in the United States* (New York: Free Press, 1980). See also Stephan Talty, *Mulatto America: At the Crossroads of Black and White Culture, A Social History* (New York: HarperCollins, 2003). For works that take a similar approach to investigating Afro-Creoles, see Frances Jerome Woods, *Marginality and Identity: A Colored Creole Family through Ten Generations* (Baton Rouge: Louisiana State University Press, 1972); and Gary B. Mills, *The Forgotton People: Cane River's Creoles of Color* (Baton Rouge: Louisiana State University Press, 1977).

5. For a discussion of antebellum New Orleans's three-tiered racial caste system, see Kimberly S. Hangar, "Origins of New Orleans's Free Creoles of Color," in *Creoles of Color of the Gulf South*, ed., James H. Dormon (Knoxville: University of Tennessee Press, 1996), 22–23; Jerah Johnson, "Colonial New Orleans" in *Creole New Orleans*, 53–55; Desdunes, *Our People and Our History*, 3–9, 111, 134–35; Logsdon and Bell, "The Americanization of Black New Orleans," 207–11; Judith Kelleher Schafer, *Becoming Free, Remaining Free: Manumission and Enslavement in New Orleans, 1846–1862* (Baton Rouge: Louisiana State University Press, 2003), xiv–xvi, 1.

6. John W. Blassingame, *Black New Orleans, 1860–1880* (Chicago: University of Chicago Press, 1973), 25–77; Domínguez, *White By Definition*, 133–36.

7. This is the central narrative of both Desdunes and Rousséve. For a more contemporary narrative of the role played by New Orleans's free black community in the Civil War, see Stephen J. Ochs, *A Black Patriot and a White Priest: André Cailloux and Claude Paschal Maistre in Civil War New Orleans* (Baton Rouge: Louisiana State University Press, 2000); James G. Hollandsworth Jr., *The Louisiana Native Guards: The Black Military Experience during the Civil War* (Baton Rouge: Louisiana State University Press, 1995); and Caryn Cossé Bell, *Revolution, Romanticism, and the Afro-Creole Protest Tradition in Louisiana, 1718–1868* (Baton Rouge: Louisiana State University Press, 1997), 222–75.

8. Fee services such as Ancestry.com as well as the Louisiana death, birth, and marriage indexes have sped up this research an immeasurable amount.

9. A large number of white and black slaveholding Creole refugees came to New Orleans in 1809, bolstering the population, wealth, and Creole attributes of the city's free black population. See Nathalie Dessens, *From Saint-Domingue to New Orleans: Migration and Influences* (Gainesville: University Press of Florida, 2007); and *1860 U.S. Federal Census*, National Archives Microfilm Publication M653, roll 418, p. 363. A search of the 1850 and 1860 census slave schedules produced no details of the Raynals, though this may be an issue of indexing. Auguste Raynal was born in 1796 in New Orleans. Auguste Raynal and his son appear in postbellum city directories as planters living at 338 Main St. d 2. *Gardner's New Orleans Directory for 1866* (New Orleans: Charles Gardner, 1866); *Gardner's New Orleans Directory for 1867* (New Orleans: Charles Gardner, 1867); Andrew B. Booth, *Records of Louisiana Confederate Soldiers & Confederate Commands* (New Orleans: [—], 1920) 3:258.

10. Joseph Raynal, Complied Service Records, Record Group 94 (RG94), National Archives Building, Washington, D.C.; *Report of the Adjutant General, Louisiana State Militia, 1870*, Jackson Barracks Military Archives, Chalmette, Louisiana; *Edwards' Annual Directory to the Inhabitants, Institutions, Incorporated Companies, Manufacturers, Establishments, Businesses, Business Firms, etc., etc., in the City of New Orleans for 1870* (St. Louis & New York: Edwards & Co., 1870); Dennis C. Rousey, *Policing the Southern City: New Orleans, 1805–1889* (Baton Rouge: Louisiana State University Press, 1996), 126–58.

11. Birth Certificate, Marie Ella Raynal, Orleans Parish Birth Records (OPBR), Louisiana State Archives, Baton Rouge, 47:91; Death Certificate, Olympe Raynal, Louisiana Death Records Index (LDRI), Louisiana State Archives, Baton Rouge, 46:840.

12. *1850 U.S. Federal Census*, National Archives Microfilm Publication M432, roll 238, p. 28; Eric Foner, *Freedom's Lawmakers: A Directory of Black Officeholders during Reconstruction* (New York: Oxford University Press, 1993), 71; David Rankin, "Origins of the Black Leadership Class in New Orleans During Reconstruction," *Journal of Southern History* 40 (Aug. 1974): 425, 428.

13. See the testimony of Mme J. B. Esnard in *Succession of Pierre Dejean (Jules, Victor J, and Arthur Dejean vs. Mrs. Josephine Schaeffer, Widow of Pierre Dejean)*, no. 19588, June 24, 1887, Division A Orleans Parish Civil District Court. Josephine Schaeffer, the mother of Josephine Krach, possibly had ties to this parish through her first husband.

14. Birth Certificate, Louis Aristide Summers, OPBR 103:799; Birth Certificate, Charles Henry Summers, OPBR 112:142; *1900 U.S. Federal Census*, National Archives Microfilm Publication T623, roll 572, p. 1B; *1920 U.S. Federal Census*, National Archives Microfilm Publication T625, roll 620, p. 9B. There is some question as to the ethnic background of August Summers. His death certificate bears the racial description of "white or Mexican." Death Certificate, August J. Summers, LDRI, July 5, 1948.

15. *1900 U.S. Federal Census*, National Archives Microfilm Publication T623, roll 572, pp. 5A, 7B; Birth Certificates for Marie Louise Esnard, 91:518, Marie Josephine Esnard, 86:276, and Marie Florentine Esnard, 87:752, all in OPBR; *1910 U.S. Federal Census*, National Archives Microfilm Publication T624, roll 521, pp. 67B, 129B; *1920 U.S. Federal Census*, National Archives Microfilm Publication T625, roll 112, p. 12A.

16. The Louisiana State Museum possesses an 1832 portrait of Sauvinet's white father, Joseph Sauvinet, by Jean Joseph Vaudechamp. *Sauvinet v. Walker*, no. 3513, 27 La. Ann. 14, (1875).

17. *Sauvinet v. Walker*; Foner, *Freedom's Lawmakers*, 190; *1870 U.S. Federal Census*, National Archives Microfilm Publication 593, roll 522, p. 583.

18. *Sauvinet v. Walker*; *New Orleans Louisianian*, Mar. 2, 1871.

19. Ibid.

20. Birth Certificates for James Nelson Sauvinet, 34:442, Charles Silas Sauvinet, 34:443, and Marie Clothilde Sauvinet, 34:443, all in OPBR. These three offspring appear to have been registered on the same day, Feb. 18, 1863; Death Certificate, Charles S. Sauvinet Jr., LDRI 71:573; *New Orleans Times*, July 26, 1868; *New Orleans Times*, July 24, 1878; *Daily Picayune*, Aug. 11, 1878; *Houston Directory, 1889–1890* (Houston: Morrison & Fourmy, 1889); *1910 U.S. Federal Census*, National Archives Microfilm Publication T624, roll 1519, p. 317B; *1920 U.S. Federal Census*, National Archives Microfilm Publication T625, roll 1763, p. 8B (James N. Sauvinet). A wealth of genealogical data on the Sauvinets descended from Angela C. Sauvinet D'Arpa had been placed online by Rosemary DeFiglio, a great-granddaughter of C. S. Sauvinet. Formerly posted at http://rand.pratt.edu/~defiglio/tree.html, the link is no longer active. A hardcopy of this site in the author's possession.

21. *1850 U.S. Federal Census*, National Archives Microfilm Publication M432, roll 235, p. 15; *1850 U.S. Federal Census—Slave Schedules*, National Archives Microfilm Publication M432; *Gardner's New Orleans Directory for 1861* (New Orleans: Charles Gardner, 1861). C. S. Sauvinet also lacked any denotation of color in antebellum city directories. *New Orleans Directory for 1841* (New Orleans: J. L. Sollee & Co, 1840). City directory entries for the free black branches of the Esnard or Raynal clans do not bear racial designations either. *Michel & Co. New Orleans Directory and Commercial Register for 1846* (New Orleans: Michel & Co, 1846); Death Certificate, William F. Vigers, LDRI 17:338; Foner, *Freedom's Lawmakers*, 219.

22. Foner, *Freedom's Lawmakers*, 219; *New Orleans Weekly Louisianian*, Apr. 14, 1872; *New Orleans Weekly Pelican*, Aug. 20, 1887; *Charles Gardner's Directory for New Orleans, 1866, 1867, 1868, 1869* (New Orleans: Charles Gardner, 1866–69). William Vigers first appears as "(col'd)" in 1870. *Edwards' Annual Directory* (New Orleans: Edwards & Co.,

1870); *Weekly Pelican*, Oct. 1, 1887; *Soards New Orleans Directory* (New Orleans: Soards, 1890); *1910 U.S. Federal Census*, National Archives Microfilm Publication T624, roll 520, p. 10B. Caryn Cossé Bell relates an antebellum equivalent of this dynamic in *Revolution, Romanticism, and Afro-Creole Protest*, 128–29.

23. Peter Joseph, Compiled Service Record, National Archives RG 94; *Report of the Adjutant General, Louisiana State Militia, 1870*; *Peter Joseph v. David Bidwell*, 28 La. Ann. 382 (1876); Justin A. Nystrom, "Redeemer's Carnival: The Urban Drama of Reconstruction in New Orleans" (PhD diss., University of Georgia, 2004), 155–56.

24. Applications for Appointments as Customs Service Officers, box 17, Record Group 56–246, National Archives Building Washington, D.C.; Appointment Registers of Customs Service Employees 11:365–421, Record Group 56–241, National Archives Building Washington, D.C. Like John Benjamin Esnard, Arnold Bertonneau moved to California around the turn of the century, where he and his descendants successfully crossed the color line. Foner, *Freedom's Lawmakers*, 18; *1920 U.S. Federal Census*, National Archives Microfilm Publication T625, roll 117, p. 12A; *1880 U.S. Federal Census*, National Archives Microfilm Publication T9, roll 464; *1900 U.S. Federal Census*, National Archives Microfilm Publication T623, roll 118, p. 9A; World War I Draft Registration Cards, M1509 (online database), National Archives Building Washington, D.C. Sumner Geddes Joseph passed as white the rest of his life. *1930 U.S. Federal Census*, National Archives Microfilm Publication T626M, roll 2578, p. 9A.

25. Unless otherwise noted, personal information about Louise Drouet and Sylvanie Morgan comes from *Louise Drouet vs. the Succession of L. F. Drouet*, no. 4800, 26 La. Ann. 323 (1874). For a discussion of the custom of *plaçage*, see Violet Harrington Bryan, "Marcus Christian's Treatment of *Les Gens de Coleur Libre*," in *Creole*, 50–53; Joan M. Martin, "*Plaçage* and the Louisiana *Gens de Coleur Libre*: How Race and Sex Defined the Lifestyles of Free Women of Color," in *Creole*, 65–68; M. Boniface Adams, "The Gift of Religious Leadership: Henriette Delille and the Foundation of the Holy Family Sisters," in *Cross, Crozier, and Crucible: A Volume Celebrating the Bicentennial of a Catholic Diocese in Louisiana*, ed. Glen R. Conrad (New Orleans: Archdiocese of New Orleans, 1993), 370–73.

26. *Drouet vs. the Succession of Drouet*.

27. *1870 U.S. Federal Census*, National Archives Microfilm Publication 593, roll 519, p. 350.

28. The children of Sylvanie Morgan and Eugene Duvernay received a variety of classifications on their birth certificates: Elizabeth Duvernay (1868) 47:283—white; Eugene A. Duvernay (1869) 53:283—no color recorded; Sylvania Duvernay (1872) 60:59—no color recorded; Adelaide Duvernay (1877) 71:652—colored; Samuel George Duvernay (1880) 104:138—no color recorded; Frederick Allen Duvernay (1883) 104:203—no color recorded; Maria Leado Duvernay (1884) 104:407—white; all in Louisiana Birth Records Index, Vital Records Collection Louisiana State Archives, Baton Rouge, La.

29. *Drouet vs. the Succession of Drouet*; Louisiana Marriage Records Index, Louisiana State Archives, Baton Rouge 6:590. Edouard Phillipe Ducloslange had been a delegate to the 1872 Republican state convention from the same ward as Governor Henry Clay Warmoth. *New Orleans Weekly Louisianian*, July 1, 1872; *1900 U.S. Federal Census*, National Archives Microfilm Publication T623, roll 574, p. 3A.

30. *1910 U.S. Federal Census*, National Archives Microfilm Publication T624, roll 27, part 2; *1920 U.S. Federal Census*, National Archives Microfilm Publication T625, roll 35, p. 27A; *1930 U.S. Federal Census*, National Archives Microfilm Publication T626I, roll 1775, p. 16B; Rebecca Darling to author, Mar. 21, 2003.

31. Blanche Penn is registered as "colored" on her birth certificate. Birth Certificate, Blanche Penn, OPBR 6:383; *1860 U.S. Federal Census*, National Archives Microfilm Publication M653, roll 256, p. 296; Death Certificate, Josephine Keating (July 7, 1868), LDRI

43:18; *1870 U.S. Federal Census*, National Archives Microfilm Publication M593, roll 520, p. 712; *1870 U.S. Federal Census*, National Archives Microfilm Publication M593, roll 520, p. 667; Birth Certificate, Alfred Hugh Wright, OPBR 72:410; *1880 U.S. Federal Census*, National Archives Microfilm Publication T9, roll 459, p. 226.4. In a twist of irony, Davidson Bradfute Penn married the sister of Charles Conrad Jr., one of the attorneys who represented Louise Drouet in her suit against her father's estate. *Drouet vs. the Succession of Drouet*; Domínguez, *White By Definition*, 161.

8. "My Children on the Field": Wade Hampton, Biography, and the Roots of the Lost Cause / Rod Andrew Jr.

1. Much of this material appears in the author's book *Wade Hampton: Confederate Warrior to Southern Redeemer* (Chapel Hill: University of North Carolina Press, 2008). Copyright © 2008 by The University of North Carolina Press. Used by permission of the publisher. www.uncpress.unc.edu

2. Ulysses R. Brooks, ed., *Butler and His Cavalry in the War of Secession* (Columbia, S.C.: The State Co., 1909), 352–54, 358–59; Edward L. Wells, *Hampton and his Cavalry in '64* (Richmond, Va.: B. F. Johnson Publishing Co., 1899), 345–46; Wells, *Hampton and Reconstruction* (Columbia, S.C.: The State Co., 1909), 59; Mary Boykin Chesnut, *Mary Chesnut's Civil War*, ed. C. Vann Woodward (New Haven, Conn.: Yale University Press, 1981), 665. The fight at the Boydton Plank Road, also known as the battle of Burgess Mill, was a Confederate tactical victory—the federals withdrew and made no more attempts to cut the railroad until the following spring. Wells, *Hampton and his Cavalry*, 334–35; Brooks, *Butler and His Cavalry*, 354; J. Tracy Power, *Lee's Miserables: Life in the Army of Northern Virginia from the Wilderness to Appomattox* (Chapel Hill: University of North Carolina Press, 1998), 211.

3. Clipping in box 1, folder 98, Virginia Gurley Meynard Papers, South Caroliniana Library, University of South Carolina, Columbia (hereinafter cited as SCL-USC); *New York Times*, Dec. 23, 1876, and Sept. 22, 1877.

4. Unless otherwise noted, biographical material on Hampton comes from Manly Wade Wellman, *Giant in Gray: A Biography of Wade Hampton of South Carolina* (New York: Scribner's, 1949); Virginia G. Meynard, *The Venturers: The Hampton, Harrison and Earle Families of Virginia, South Carolina, and Texas* (Greenwood, S.C.: Southern Historical Press, 1980); Edward G. Longacre, *Gentleman and Soldier: The Extraordinary Life of General Wade Hampton* (Nashville, Tenn.: Rutledge Hill Press, 2003); Walter Brian Cisco, *Wade Hampton: Confederate Warrior, Conservative Statesman* (Washington, D.C.: Brassey's, 2004); and Rod Andrew Jr., *Wade Hampton: Confederate Warrior to Southern Redeemer* (Chapel Hill: University of North Carolina Press, 2008). Glenn W. LaFantasie skillfully uses a biographical approach to understand the postwar positions of an ex-Confederate officer in *Gettysburg Requiem: The Life and Lost Causes of Confederate Colonel William C. Oates* (New York: Oxford University Press, 2006), though he does not explicitly make the same argument about Oates and the Lost Cause that I make about Hampton.

5. Wade Hampton (WH) to Mary Fisher Hampton (MFH), Sept. 2, 1855, Wade Hampton Papers, Southern Historical Collection, University of North Carolina, Chapel Hill.

6. Manisha Sinha, *The Counter-revolution of Slavery: Politics and Ideology in Antebellum South Carolina* (Chapel Hill: University of North Carolina Press, 2000), 129–32, 145–49, 173–79; "Speech of Hon. Wade Hampton on the Constitutionality of the Slave Trade Laws. Delivered in the Senate of South Carolina, December 10th, 1859," Hampton Family Papers (HFP), SCL-USC.

7. WH to MFH, May 21, 1862, box 3, Hampton Family Papers (HFP), SCL, USC); ibid., Oct. 11, 1864, box 3, folder 64a, HFP, SCL-USC.

8. WH to MFH, June 3, 1862, box 3, HFP, SCL-USC.

9. WH to MFH, Oct. 5, 1862, box 2, folder 64a, HFP, SCL-USC.

10. Brooks, *Butler and His Cavalry*, 165–68; *New York Times*, June 27, 1897.

11. WH to MFH, Nov. 14, 1864, box 2, folder 64a, HFP, SCL-USC.

12. U. R. Brooks, in Brooks, *Butler and his Cavalry*, 359.

13. Cisco, *Wade Hampton*, 146; Brooks, *Butler and his Cavalry*, 354, 359.

14. *Mary Chesnut's Civil War*, 665.

15. Ibid., 666.

16. Gen. Braxton Bragg to WH, Nov. 2, 1864, box 3, HFP, SCL-USC; Meynard, *The Venturers*, 236.

17. *Mary Chesnut's Civil War*, 665.

18. WH to MFH, Nov. 20, 1864, box 2, folder 64a, HFP, SCL-USC.

19. David W. Blight, *Race and Reunion: The Civil War in American Memory* (Cambridge, Mass.: Harvard University Press, 2001), 282; Catherine Clinton, *Tara Revisited: Women, War, and the Plantation Legend* (New York: Abbeville Press, 1995), 19. Fred Arthur Bailey, in his studies of Redeemer-era textbooks, argues that the myth of the Lost Cause represented a deliberate effort to justify continued dominance by Southern elites in the postwar era. See, for example, "The Textbooks of the Lost Cause: Censorship and the Creation of Southern State Histories," *Georgia Historical Quarterly* 75 (Fall 1991): 507–33. Though the works cited here are only a small sample that claim the Lost Cause was a cover for the reinstatement of white supremacy, much of the older Lost Cause historiography does not focus heavily on that aspect of the myth. Gaines Foster's *Ghost of the Confederacy: Defeat, the Lost Cause, and the Emergence of the New South* (New York: Oxford University Press, 1987) argues that the Lost Cause mediated a postwar struggle between Old South conservatives and New South boosters after the war over many issues, of which race was only one. Charles Reagan Wilson treats the Lost Cause as a "civil religion" with religious motifs and elements in *Baptized in Blood: The Religion of the Lost Cause, 1865–1920* (Athens: University of Georgia Press, 1980). W. Scott Poole's more recent *Never Surrender: Confederate Memory and Conservatism in the South Carolina Upcountry* (Athens: University of Georgia Press, 2004) argues that the Lost Cause was, at least initially, part of a larger struggle by nineteenth-century Southern conservatives against the forces of modernity, and not simply a political weapon in the hands of cynical politicians; only later would it become that.

20. War Department, *The War of the Rebellion: A Compilation of the Official Records of the Union and Confederate Armies* (hereinafter cited as *Official Records*), 70 vols. in 128 (Washington, D.C.: Government Printing Office, 1880–1901), series 1, vol. 42, part 1, p. 949; Wade Hampton, "Hampton's War Reminiscences," HFP, SCL-USC, 101. The latter source is a long account compiled by Hampton for Robert E. Lee after the war. Both a manuscript and a typescript copy are in HFP, SCL-USC; the page number here refers to the typescript.

21. "Hampton's War Reminiscences," 103–4.

22. Ibid., 104.

23. WH to Lee, July 21, 1866 and Nov. 11, 1866, box 3, HFP, SCL; copy of letter from Lee to Gen. P. T. Beauregard, July 31, 1865, forwarded to Hampton, in box 3, HFP, SCL-USC.

24. "Hampton's War Reminiscences," 104, 105.

25. Rollin G. Osterweis, *Romanticism and Nationalism in the Old South* (New Haven, Conn.: Yale University Press, 1949).

26. Undated Obituary, Preston Hampton, newspaper clipping, box 3, HFP, SCL-USC. The verse is paraphrased from English poet Thomas Babington, Lord Macaulay (1800–1859), "Lays of Ancient Rome."

27. "Constitution of the Survivors' Association of the State of South Carolina," Survivors' Association Papers, 11–481–2, South Carolina Historical Society, Charleston.

28. WH to James Conner, Apr. 11, 1869, box 3, HFP, SCL-USC; "Minutes of the Proceedings of the Reunion of the Hampton Legion held in Columbia, South Carolina, July 21, 1875" (Charleston, S.C.: Walker, Evans, & Cogswell, 1875), 3; *The (Columbia) State*, May 25, 1895, May 10, 11, 1901; *Charleston News & Courier*, May 10, 11, 12, 1899.

29. WH, to MFH, May 21, 1862, box 2, folder 64a, HFP, SCL-USC.

30. *Official Records*, series 1, vol. 47, part 2, p. 547.

31. Andrew, *Wade Hampton*, 259–63, 317–20; Marion B. Lucas, *Sherman and the Burning of Columbia* (College Station: Texas A & M University Press, 1976); transcript of article from *New York Day Book*, July 15, 1865, transcript, box 3, HFP, SCL-USC, 15–16; *Official Records*, series 1, vol. 47, part 1, pp. 21–22; James McCarter, "The Burning of Columbia Again," *Harper's New Monthly Magazine* 33, no. 197 (Oct. 1866): 642–47; D. Z. Daniel H. Trezevant, "The Burning of Columbia, South Carolina: A Review of Northern Assertions and Southern Facts," (Columbia, S.C., 1866), Huntington Library; Agnes Law, "The Burning of Columbia—Affidavit of Mrs. Agnes Law," *Southern Historical Society Papers* 12 (1884): 234; William T. Sherman, *Memoirs of General William T. Sherman* (1875; Bloomington: Indiana University Press, 1957), 287; C. M. Calhoun, *Liberty Dethroned. A Concise History of Some of the Most Startling Events Before, During, and Since the Civil War* (n.p., 1903), 290. For other contemporary articles on this controversy, see "The Burning of Columbia," (Charleston, S.C., 1888), Huntington Library; *New York World*, June 17, 1875; *The Land We Love* 4, no. 5 (Mar. 1868): 361–69; WH, letter to the *Baltimore Enquirer*, July 1, 1873; "'Burning of Columbia,' A Collection of Pamphlets," Huntington Library; Edwin J. Scott, *Random Recollections of a Long Life, 1806–1876* (Columbia, S.C.: C. A. Calvo Jr., 1884), 175–92; "The Burning of Columbia," pamphlet containing Hampton's 1873 letter to the *Baltimore Enquirer* (Charleston, S.C.: Walker, Evans, and Cogswell, 1888), 12; Meynard, *The Venturers*, 247; *Testimony Taken Before the Mixed Commission on American and British Claims*, Dec. 10, 1872, 18–20, in Nichols, ed., "Burning of Columbia." Hampton complained of Sherman's "lies" in letters to Jefferson Davis, Robert E. Lee, P. G. T. Beauregard, and many others.

32. Washington Light Infantry, "Proceedings on the Occasion of Unveiling the Monument Erected in Memory of Their Comrades who Died in the Service of the State, June 16, 1870," Perkins Library, Duke University, Durham, North Carolina, 14.

33. Ibid., 19. Paraphrased from 2 Samuel 18:33 and Shakespeare's *Macbeth*, act V, scene 8. Hampton obviously borrowed King David's words from Scripture but ignored much of the context, since Absalom had been fighting against his father David. For other speeches documenting Hampton's insistence that the South must accept federal authority but never dishonor their Confederate dead, see, for example, *Columbia Daily Phoenix*, Nov. 15, 1865; *Charleston Daily Courier*, Oct. 10, 1866.

34. "Proceedings of the Joint Meeting of Camp Moultrie, Sons of Confederate Veterans and the Daughters of the Confederacy held on Tuesday Evening May 14th, 1895, at the Academy of Music, Charleston, South Carolina," in Theodore D. Jervey Papers, South Carolina Historical Society, Charleston, 28–291–13, p. 30.

35. Traditional sources state that Hampton appointed 86 blacks to office, based on a survey by the South Carolina Historical Commission in the mid-twentieth century. A more recent tabulation shows the figure of 116, with four names added afterward. George B. Tindall, *South Carolina Negroes, 1877–1900* (Columbia: University of South Carolina Press, 1952), 22, 22n28; "Negroes Appointed to Public Office by Gov. Wade Hampton," folder 48, Governor Wade Hampton Miscellaneous Papers, South Carolina Department of Archives and History.

36. WH to James Conner, Mar. 24, 1867, folder 8, box 181, Conner Family Papers, South Carolina Historical Society, Charleston; WH to Andrew Johnson, clipping in *Metropolitan Record and New York Vindicator*, Aug, 1866, box 3, HFP, SCL-USC.

37. U.S. Congress, *Congressional Record* 9, 46th Cong., 1st sess., vol. 9 (1881).

38. For a few other examples of Hampton's appeals to veterans, see *Edgefield Daily Advertiser*, Sept. 16, 1868; *Columbia Daily Phoenix*, Jan. 21, 1866; and the *Charleston Daily Courier*, Oct. 10, 1866.

39. *Charleston Daily Courier*, Oct. 10, 1866.

40. See the *Columbia Daily Phoenix*, Jan. 21, 1866; *Charleston Daily Courier*, Oct. 10, 1866; and "Ought the Negro to be Disfranchised? Ought He to have been Enfranchised?" *North American Review* 128, no. 268 (Mar. 1879): 239–44.

41. Wellman, *Giant in Gray*, 257.

42. *Charleston Daily Courier*, Mar. 23, 1867; Meynard, *The Venturers*, 190, 227, 236, 245–46; Wellman, *Giant in Gray*, 52, 218, 325; Wells, *Hampton and Reconstruction*, 228–29. For examples of Hampton family members writing about their slaves, see WH II to MFH, Nov. 17, 1855; WH III to MFH, Feb. 14 and Aug. 26, 1857; all in box 3, HFP, SCL-USC.

43. Jefferson Davis, *The Rise and Fall of the Confederate Government* (New York: D. Appleton, 1881); Jubal Early, *A Memoir of the Last Year of the War for Independence in the Confederate States of America*, ed. Gary Gallagher (Columbia: University of South Carolina Press, 2001).

44. Alfred Hampton, "Last Words of Father. Gen. Wade Hampton," folder 5, Wade Hampton Family Papers, Library of Congress, Washington, D.C.

9. Rebels in War and Peace: Their Ethos and Its Impact / Jason Phillips

1. John M. Schofield, *Forty-Six Years in the Army* (New York: The Century Co., 1897), 248. See also Shelby Foote, *The Civil War: A Narrative*, vol. 3: *Red River to Appomattox* (New York: Random House, 1974), 669, 675–81; and James M. McPherson, *Battle Cry of Freedom: The Civil War Era* (New York: Oxford University Press, 1988), 812–15. This essay is based on Chapters 1 and 2 and the Conclusion of Jason Phillips, *Diehard Rebels: The Confederate Culture of Invincibility* (Athens: University of Georgia Press, 2007). The material is used with the permission of the University of Georgia Press.

2. George Knox Miller, letter to his wife, July 12, 1864, George Knox Miller Papers, Southern Historical Collection, University of North Carolina, Chapel Hill (hereinafter cited as SHC-UNC); J. Frederick Waring, diary entries, Sept. 9, 10, 1864, Joseph Frederick Waring Papers, Georgia Historical Society, Savannah (hereinafter cited as GHS); John William McLure to his wife, Feb. 6, 1865, McLure Family Papers, 1845–1922, South Caroliniana Library, University of South Carolina, Columbia (hereinafter cited as SCL-USC).

3. For examples of scholars' rushing to judgment, see Reid Mitchell, *Civil War Soldiers* (New York: Viking, 1988), 191; Richard E. Beringer et al., *Why the South Lost the Civil War* (Athens: University of Georgia Press, 1986), 87.

4. Scholarship on Southern intellectual life offers Civil War historians excellent examples of how to avoid judgment. Michael O'Brien permits Southern culture "to define its own terms" without favoring or castigating it. Drew Faust has noted, "The judgmental—even condemnatory—approach in many earlier explorations of Southern thought has been replaced by an effort to trace the connections between expressed beliefs and the regional way of life." Michael O'Brien, ed., *All Clever Men Who Make Their Way: Critical Discourse in the Old South* (Fayetteville: University of Arkansas Press, 1982), 11; Drew Gilpin Faust, "The Peculiar South Revisited: White Society, Culture, and Politics in the Antebellum Period, 1800–1860," in *Interpreting Southern History: Historiographical Essays in Honor of Sanford W. Higginbotham*, ed. John B. Boles and Evelyn Thomas Nolen (Baton Rouge: Louisiana State University Press, 1987), 99.

5. Peter S. Carmichael, *The Last Generation: Young Virginians in Peace, War, and Reunion* (Chapel Hill: University of North Carolina Press, 2006). Carmichael's work

examines how a group of young, elite Virginians maintained confidence in Confederate victory to the end of the war. A number of factors, including class, religion, military service, and place of origin, affected soldiers' diehard sentiments. My work shows how such expressions belonged to a widespread ethos that transcended the views of privileged Virginians who fought with Robert E. Lee.

6. Paul D. Escott, *After Secession: Jefferson Davis and the Failure of Confederate Nationalism* (Baton Rouge: Louisiana State University Press, 1978).

7. W. J. Cash, *The Mind of the South* (New York: Knopf, 1941), 103–4.

8. This essay relies on the diaries and letters of hundreds of Confederates who wrote after the war intensified in 1863. The hard war changed these men, but my research does not confirm Gerald F. Linderman's assertion that the conflict undermined Victorian conceptions of courage and honor. These men sustained their ideals and grew bitter at civilians, shirkers, and politicians who seemed to lack sufficient devotion. See Gerald F. Linderman, *Embattled Courage: The Experience of Combat in the American Civil War* (New York: Free Press, 1987).

9. Gary W. Gallagher, *The Confederate War* (Cambridge, Mass.: Harvard University Press, 1997); Anne Sarah Rubin, *A Shattered Nation: The Rise and Fall of the Confederacy, 1861–1868* (Chapel Hill: University of North Carolina Press, 2005). It is worth noting that research on diehard Rebels does not endorse the Lost Cause excuse for defeat. The persistence of a group of extremists does not prove that the Confederacy was overwhelmed by Union numbers and industry. Historians have been arguing the relative significance of internal and external causes of defeat for years. But that is an old debate, and we should shift our focus away from it. Instead of exploring how scholars explain defeat to each other, this essay considers how Confederates explained the war's outcome to themselves.

10. For more on the connections between religion and persistence, see my essay "Religious Belief and Troop Motivation: 'For the Smiles of My Blessed Saviour,'" in *Virginia's Civil War*, ed. Peter Wallenstein and Bertram Wyatt-Brown (Charlottesville: University of Virginia Press 2005), 101–13.

11. John McCorkle to his wife, July 15, 1864, John McCorkle Papers, GHS.

12. John Francis Shaffner to his wife, Oct. 12, 1864, Fries and Shaffner Papers, SHC-UNC; George Knox Miller to his wife, Nov. 15 1864, George Knox Miller Papers, SHC-UNC.

13. Thomas Hampton to his wife, Feb. 26, 1865, Thomas B. Hampton Letters, Center for American History, University of Texas, Austin (hereinafter cited as UTA); William W. Heartsill, diary entry, Apr. 19, 1865, in Bell. I. Wiley, ed., *Fourteen Hundred and 91 Days in the Confederate Army* (Jackson, Tenn.: McCowat-Mercer Press, 1954), 238–39. It is worth noting that Heartsill did not know of Lee's surrender at the time.

14. John B. Boles explained how similar ideas animated earlier evangelicalism. Like their predecessors, devout Rebels preached that "out of disappointment and pain came patience and strength—lessons long taught by Christianity." Boles, *The Great Revival, 1787–1805: The Origins of the Southern Evangelical Mind* (Lexington: University Press of Kentucky, 1972), 30. Charles Royster argues that Americans on both sides expected, even demanded, the war's destructive nature because they thought a great effusion of blood would purge America of its sins. Royster, *The Destructive War: William Tecumseh Sherman, Stonewall Jackson, and the Americans* (New York: Knopf, 1991). In the war's final period, death challenged Rebels' convictions in many ways: Not only did theodicy have to calm their fears of mortality, it also had to convince them that dying for their country was still a sacred act. This challenge was critical after Spotsylvania Court House and Franklin. As the war worsened, Rebel theodicy had to consecrate increasingly futile sacrifices. But they might not have seemed futile or tragic to soldiers who were still confident of victory.

15. Reuben Pierson, letter to his father, Aug. 22, 1863, in Thomas W. Cutrer and T. Michael Parrish, eds., *Brothers in Gray: The Civil War Letters of the Pierson Family* (Baton Rouge: Louisiana State University Press, 1997), 210. For a soldier's use of this Scripture, see Rawleigh Downman to his wife, June 20, 1864, Downman Family Papers, Virginia Historical Society, Richmond (hereinafter cited as VHS).

16. Joshua Callaway to his wife, July 19, 1863, in Judith Lee Hancock, ed., *The Civil War Letters of Joshua K. Callaway* (Athens: University of Georgia Press, 1997), 114; Pierson to his father, July 19, 1863, in Cutrer and Parish, eds., *Brothers in Gray*, 204; Tally Simpson to his cousin, July 18, 1863, in Guy R. Everson and Edward H. Simpson Jr., eds., *"Far, Far from Home": The Wartime Letters of Dick and Tally Simpson, Third South Carolina Volunteers* (New York: Oxford University Press, 1994), 257–58.

17. William Casey to his mother, June 19 1864, William Thomas Casey Papers, VHS; John William McLure to his wife, Sept. 5, 1864, McLure Family Papers, 1845–1922, SHC-USC; Henry Alexander Chambers to his wife, Sept. 6, 1864, Henry Alexander Chambers Papers, 1832–1925, SHC-UNC. Future scholarship should compare how the belligerents envisioned God's plan for them. As Protestants, Confederates and federals had much in common, but they related to God in different ways. See Randall M. Miller, Harry S. Stout, and Charles Reagan Wilson, eds., *Religion and the American Civil War* (New York: Oxford University Press, 1998); and Steven E. Woodworth, *While God Is Marching On: The Religious World of Civil War Soldiers* (Lawrence: University Press of Kansas, 2001).

18. James Drayton Nance to his wife, Jan. 1, 1865; Nance to Mr. Brantly, Jan. 12, 1864, both in James Drayton Nance Letters, SCL-USC; John Francis Shaffner to his wife, Nov. 21, 1864, Fries and Shaffner Papers, SHC-UNC; John William McLure to his wife, Sept. 20, 1864, John William McLure Papers, 1845–1922, SCL-USC; James Blackman Ligon to his mother, Aug. 25, 1864, James Blackman Ligon Letters, SCL-USC.

19. Joseph Frederick Waring, diary entry, Jan. 1, 1865, Joseph Frederick Waring Papers, GHS.

20. Henry Calvin Conner to his wife, July 28 and Dec. 14, 1864, both in Henry Calvin Conner Papers, SCL-USC; Rev. J. L. Burrows, D. D., *Nationality Insured!: Notes of A Sermon Delivered at the First Baptist Church, Augusta, Ga., September 11th, 1864* (Augusta,1864), 6.

21. As James McPherson put it, "If soldiers' letters and diaries are an accurate indication, bitterness and hatred were more prevalent than kindness and sociability." McPherson, *For Cause and Comrades: Why Men Fought in the Civil War* (New York: Oxford University Press, 1998), 152. See also Thomas J. Newberry to his father, Nov. 19, 1863, in Enoch L. Mitchell, ed., "The Civil War Letters of Thomas Jefferson Newberry" *Journal of Mississippi History* 10 (Jan. 1948): 74; and Randall C. Jimerson, *The Private Civil War: Popular Thought during the Sectional Conflict* (Baton Rouge: Louisiana State University Press, 1988), 175.

22. Robert Stiles to Rosa Stiles, June 15, 1864, Robert Augustus Stiles Papers, VHS; William Casey to his mother, Feb. 14, 1864, William Thomas Casey Papers, VHS; Urban G. Owen to his wife, June 2, 1864, in Enoch L. Mitchell, ed., "Letters of a Confederate Surgeon in the Army of Tennessee to His Wife" *Tennessee Historical Quarterly* (June 1946): 169; Samuel T. Foster, diary entry, July 23, 1864, in Norman D. Brown, ed., *One of Cleburne's Command: The Civil War Reminiscences and Diary of Capt. Samuel T. Foster, Granbury's Texas Brigade, CSA* (Austin: University of Texas Press, 1980), 115. For similar impressions of the enemy dead, see John Walters, *Norfolk Blues: The Civil War Diary of the Norfolk Light Artillery Blues*, ed. Kenneth Wiley (Shippensburg, Pa.: Burd Street, 1997), 123, 140; and Spencer Glasgow Welch, *A Confederate Surgeon's Letters to His Wife* (Marietta, Ga.: Continental, 1954), 94–95, 98. For similar treatments of dead enemies in other wars, see Paul Fussell, *The Great War and Modern Memory* (New York: Oxford University Press, 1975), 77. Hiram Williams, an engineer in the Army of Tennessee,

expressed empathy for the fallen foe on a number of occasions: "Poor fellows! I would
pity the untimely death of the bitterest foe I have on Earth," diary entry, in Lewis N.
Wynne and Robert A. Taylor, eds., *This War So Horrible: The Civil War Diary of Hiram
Smith Williams* (Tuscaloosa: University of Alabama Press 1993), 68; see also 32–33. In
contrast, when Edwin Fay helped bury enemy bodies, he "printed Abolitionist on a Oak
Board and stuck it at his head for the Yanks to see if they should come after we left."
Bell I. Wiley, ed., *"This Infernal War": The Confederate Letters of Srgt. Edwin H. Fay*
(Austin: University of Texas Press, 1958), 180.

23. Urban G. Owen to his wife, May 28 and June 2, 1864, in "Letters of a Confederate
Surgeon," 167, 169; Edwin Fay to his wife, Oct. 8, 1863, in *"This Infernal War,"* 342.

24. Richard Launcelot Maury, diary entry, Mar. 28, 1865, VHS (emphasis added);
Edmund T. Eggleston, diary entry, Nov. 28, 1864, in Edward Noyes, ed., "Excerpts from
the Civil War Diary of E. T. Eggleston," *Tennessee Historical Quarterly* 17 (Dec. 1958): 354;
Sam Pickens, diary entry, Nov. 15, 1864, in G. Ward Hubbs, ed., *Voices from Company D:
Diaries by the Greensboro Guards, Fifth Alabama Infantry Regiment, Army of Northern
Virginia* (Athens: University of Georgia Press, 2003), 325; Richard Stanford Webb to his
cousin, Nov. 3, 1864, Webb Family Papers, UNC-SHC; David Crawford to his mother,
May 12, 1864, Crawford Family Letters, USC; Leonidas Polk to his wife, June 9, 1864,
Leonidas Lafayette Polk Papers, UNC-SHC; W. R. Redding to his wife, n.d., W. R. Redd-
ing Papers, UNC-SHC. I added the emphasis to Maury's text because Creed Davis used
the same word when describing prisoners in June 1864: "Some prisoners captured to
day. Good specimens of the New England Yankees." Creed Thomas Davis, diary entry,
June 4, 1864, VHS.

25. Creed Thomas Davis, diary entry, May 18, 1864, VHS; Reuben Pierson to David
Pierson, May 22, 1864, in Cutrer and Parish, eds., *Brothers in Gray*, 237; John Cotton to
his wife, June 9, 1864, in Lucille Griffith, ed., *Yours Till Death: The Civil War Letters of
John W. Cotton* (Birmingham: University of Alabama Press, 1951), 112; George Knox
Miller to his wife, July 1, 1864, George Knox Miller Papers, UNC-SHC; Abe G. Jones to
his mother, Oct. 28, 1864, Jones Family Papers, UNC-SHC. See also John Walters, diary
entry, Oct. 10, 30, 1864, in *Norfolk Blues*, 162–63, 170; J. Tracy Power, *Lee's Miserables:
Life in the Army of Northern Virginia from the Wilderness to Appomattox* (Chapel Hill:
University of North Carolina Press, 1998), 77.

26. Mark Grimsley, *The Hard Hand of War: Union Military Policy toward Southern
Civilians, 1861–1865* (New York: Cambridge University Press, 1995); William Blair, *Vir-
ginia's Private War: Feeding Body and Soul in the Confederacy, 1861–1865* (New York:
Oxford University Press, 1998); Jacqueline Glass Campbell, *When Sherman Marched
North from the Sea: Resistance on the Confederate Home Front* (Chapel Hill: University
of North Carolina Press, 2003); Jared Y. Saunders II to "Bessie," May 11, 1865, Jared Y.
Saunders and Family Papers, Hill Memorial Library, Louisiana State University (hereinafter cited as LSU).

27. Edgeworth Bird to Wilson Bird, Jan. 17, 1865, in John Rozier, ed., *The Granite
Farm Letters: The Civil War Correspondence of Edgeworth & Sallie Bird* (Athens: University of Georgia Press, 1988), 236–37.

28. Parents to Fred Fleet, June 12, 1864, in Betsy Fleet and John D. P. Fuller, eds.,
*Green Mount: A Virginia Plantation Family during the Civil War: Being the Journal of
Benjamin Robert Fleet and Letters of His Family* (Lexington: University Press of Kentucky, 1962), 332. As the war intensified, even religious propaganda told soldiers to grasp
independence or expect colonization, miscegenation, or even extermination at the hands
of the brutal North. James W. Silver, *Confederate Morale and Church Propaganda* (Tuscaloosa, Ala.: Confederate Press, 1957), 82–84, 90–91.

29. James Madison Brannock to his wife, Mar. 29, 1864, James Madison Brannock
Papers, VHS; "Georgia," "Call All!, Call All!" in Frank Moore, ed., *Songs and Ballads of*

the Southern People. 1861–1865 (New York: Appleton, 1886), 30–33; Charles Fenton James to Emma A. James, Feb. 7, 1865, Charles Fenton James Letters, VHS.

30. McPherson, *For Cause and Comrades*.

31. Robert E. Park, diary entry, Apr. 10, 1865, in "Diary of Captain Robert E. Park, Twelfth Alabama Regiment," *Southern Historical Society Papers* 3 (Jan.–June, 1877): 244; David Gregg McIntosh, diary entry, Apr. 9, 1865, in David Gregg McIntosh Papers, VHS; Ham Chamberlayne to Lucy Parke (Chamberlayne) Bagby, Apr. 21, 1865, in C. G. Chamberlayne, ed., *Ham Chamberlayne—Virginian: Letters and Papers of an Artillery Officer in the War for Southern Independence, 1861–1865* (Richmond, Va.: Dietz Printing Co., 1932), 325.

32. Robert Park, diary entry, Apr. 10, 1865, "Diary of Captain Robert E. Park," 244; Henry Chambers, diary entry, Apr. 9, 1865, Henry Alexander Chambers Papers, 1832–1925, SHC-UNC; Reuben Wilson to his aunt, May 13, 1865, Jones Family Papers, SHC-UNC.

33. Junius Newport Bragg to his wife, May 20, 1865, in Mrs. T. J. Gaughan, ed., *Letters of a Confederate Surgeon, 1861–65* (Camden, Ark.: Hurley, 1960), 276; William H. Ellis, diary entry, Apr. 10, 1865, LSU; Johnny Jackman, diary entry, May 8, 1865, in William C. Davis, ed., *Diary of a Confederate Soldier: John S. Jackman of the Orphan Brigade* (Columbia: University of South Carolina Press, 1990), 168; Whitelaw Reid, *After the War: A Southern Tour. May 1, 1865, to May 1, 1866* (New York: Moore, Wilstach, and Baldwin, 1866), 360.

34. David McIntosh, diary entry, Apr. 23, 1865, David Gregg McIntosh Papers, VHS; Henry Robinson Berkeley, diary entry, June 24, 1865, in William H. Runge, ed., *Four Years in the Confederate Artillery: The Diary of Private Henry Robinson Berkeley* (Chapel Hill: University of North Carolina Press, 1961), 144; Kena King Chapman, diary entry, Apr. 16, 19 1865, SHC-UNC.

35. Henry Berkeley, diary entry, Apr. 26, 1865, in *Four Years in the Confederate Artillery*, 135; Sam Pickens, diary entry, June 16, 1865, in *Voices from Company D*, 386; Rubin, *Shattered Nation*, 165; George Mercer, diary entry, Aug. 8, 1865, in Mills Lane, ed., *Times that Prove People's Principles: Civil War in Georgia* (Savannah, Ga.: Beehive Press, 1993), 256; Henry Conner, letter to his mother, sisters, and brothers, Aug. 11, 1865, Henry Calvin Conner Papers, SCL-USC; unknown friend to John Bratton, Nov. 20, 1865, John Bratton Papers, SCL-USC.

36. David W. Blight, *Race and Reunion: The Civil War in American Memory* (Cambridge, Mass.: Harvard University Press, 2001), 259; Jubal A. Early, *A Memoir of the Last Year of the War for Independence, in the Confederate States of America, Containing an Account of the Operations of His Commands in the Years 1864 and 1865*, introduction by Gary Gallagher (Columbia: University of South Carolina Press, 2001), xiv (Gallagher quotation), xxv, 71, 142; William Faulkner, *Absalom, Absalom!* (New York: Random House, 1936), 11.

37. Edmund Jones, letter to "Editor," n.d., ; Memorial Day Address delivered in Raleigh, North Carolina, May 11, 1896; both in Edmund Walter Jones Papers, SHC-UNC.

38. William W. Bennett, *A Narrative of the Great Revival which Prevailed in the Southern Armies during the Late Civil War between the States of the Federal Union* (Philadelphia: Claxton, Remsen, and Haffelfinger, 1877), 416; J. William Jones, *Christ in Camp or Religion in Lee's Army* (Richmond, Va.: B. F. Johnson & Co., 1887), 353.

39. David Goldfield, *Still Fighting the Civil War: The American South and Southern History* (Baton Rouge: Louisiana State University Press, 2004), 19.

40. Charles Fenton James, "Address to the Hollywood Memorial Association," May 30, 1901, Charles Fenton James Papers, SHC-UNC; John Shaffner, "Memorial Day Speech," 1902, Fries and Shaffner Papers, SHC-UNC. For more on the connections

between wartime identity and the postwar lives of white Southerners, see Rubin, *A Shattered Nation*. My work supports Rubin's in many ways, though some important differences are worth noting. Rubin attempts to connect wartime mentalities and postwar culture through the prism of nationalism. I think nationalism is the wrong paradigm for exploring white Southern defiance. By concentrating on nationalism, Rubin finds herself arguing that the war generation maintained its values but changed its self-identity from Americans to Confederates to Southerners. I think unreconstructed Rebels were Southerners first and last. Moreover, a sense of superiority, not separateness, distinguished them.

41. Charles Reagan Wilson, *Baptized in Blood: The Religion of the Lost Cause, 1865–1920* (Athens: University of Georgia Press, 1980); Gaines M. Foster, *Ghosts of the Confederacy: Defeat, the Lost Cause and the Emergence of the New South* (New York: Oxford University Press, 1987); W. Scott Poole, *Never Surrender: Confederate Memory and Conservatism in the South Carolina Upcountry* (Athens: University of Georgia Press, 2004).

42. C. Vann Woodward, *American Counterpoint: Slavery and Racism in the North–South Dialogue* (Boston: Little, Brown, 1964), 276.

43. Cash, *The Mind of the South*, 103.

44. Jay Winik, *April 1865: The Month that Saved America* (New York: HarperCollins, 2001).

45. Robert Penn Warren, *The Legacy of the Civil War: Meditations on the Centennial* (New York: Random House, 1961), 15.

46. Shelby Foote, *The Civil War: A Narrative*, 3 vols. (New York: Random House, 1958–1974); Michael Shaara, *The Killer Angels* (New York: Random House, 1974); McPherson, *Battle Cry of Freedom*; *The Civil War*, DVD, directed by Ken Burns (New York: PBS, 1990).

47. Faulkner, *Absalom, Absalom!*, 11.

48. Royster, *The Destructive War*; Blight, *Race and Reunion*. Gary Gallagher called for a more complex study of white Southern intransigence in *The Confederate War*.

49. Edward L. Ayers, "Worrying about the Civil War" in *Moral Problems in American Life: New Perspectives on Cultural History*, ed. Karen Halttunen and Lewis Perry (Ithaca, N.Y.: Cornell University Press, 1998), 165.

10. Reconstructing Loyalty: Love, Fear, and Power in the Postwar South / Carole Emberton

1. Charles Eliot Norton, "American Political Ideas," *North American Review* 101 (Oct. 1865): 564; Hezekiah S. Bundy, "Loyal Men Must Rule, Traiters Must Take Back Seats," speech to Congress, 39th Cong., 1st sess., May 5, 1866 (n.p.), 206–9. "Speech of Garrett Davis," March 3, 1873, *Congressional Globe*, 41st Cong., 3rd Sess., 1971.

2. Harold M. Hyman, *Era of the Oath: Northern Loyalty Tests During the Civil War and Reconstruction* (Philadelphia: University of Pennsylvania Press, 1954), 35. Recent work, most notably Margaret M. Storey's study of Alabama Unionists, follows the contested meanings of loyalty and argues that there was no single meaning for it or how to achieve it. Storey, *Loyalty and Loss: Alabama's Unionists in the Civil War and Reconstruction* (Baton Rouge: Louisiana State University Press, 2004).

3. Hyman, *Era of the Oath*, 156; Hyman, *To Try Men's Souls: Loyalty Tests in American History* (Berkeley: University of California Press, 1960), 266.

4. Merle Curti describes patriotism's more ephemeral qualities in *The Roots of American Loyalty* (New York: Columbia University Press, 1946), 179. Benedict Anderson discusses imagined communities in *Imagined Communities: Reflection on the Origins and Spread of Nationalism*, rev. ed. (London: Verso, 1991).

5. For more on race and postwar nationalism, see Edward J. Blum, *Reforging the White Republic: Race, Religion, and American Nationalism, 1865–1898* (Baton Rouge: Louisiana State University Press, 2005).

6. On South Carolina's violent struggle against white supremacy, see Otis Singletary, *Negro Militia and Reconstruction* (New York: McGraw Hill, 1959); Melinda Meek Hennessey, "Racial Violence During Reconstruction: The 1876 Riots in Charleston and Cainhoy," *South Carolina Historical Magazine* 86 (Apr. 1985): 100–112; Richard Zuczek, *State of Rebellion: Reconstruction in South Carolina* (Columbia: University of South Carolina Press, 1996); and Stephen Kantrowitz, "One Man's Mob is Another Man's Militia: Violence, Manhood, and Authority in Reconstruction South Carolina," in *Jumpin' Jim Crow: Southern Politics from Civil War to Civil Rights*, ed. Jane Dailey, Glenda Gilmore, and Bryant Simon (Princeton: Princeton University Press, 2000), 67–87. Recent work on Reconstruction stresses the paramilitary nature of grassroots politics in the South. See Steven Hahn, *A Nation Under Our Feet: Black Political Struggles in the Rural South from Slavery to the Great Migration* (Cambridge, Mass.: Harvard University Press, 2003), 265–316. See also my own essay, "The Limits of Incorporation: Violence, Gun Rights, and Gun Regulation in the Reconstruction South," *Stanford Law & Policy Review* 17, 3 (2006): 615–33; and James K. Hogue, *Uncivil War: Five New Orleans Street Battles and the Rise and Fall of Radical Reconstruction* (Baton Rouge: Louisiana State University Press, 2006).

7. Sylvia R. Frey, *Water from the Rock: Black Resistance in a Revolutionary Age* (Princeton: Princeton University Press, 1991), 57. See also Sidney Kaplan and Emma Nogrady Kaplan, *The Black Presence in the Era of the American Revolution* (Amherst: University of Massachusetts Press, 1989); Philip S. Foner, *Blacks in the American Revolution* (Westport, Conn.: Greenwood Press, 1975); and Benjamin Quarles, *The Negro in the American Revolution* (New York: Norton, 1973).

8. William C. Nell, *The Colored Patriots of the American Revolution . . . With an Introduction by Harriet Beecher Stowe* (Boston: Robert F. Wallcut, 1855), 19.

9. Frederick Douglass, *The Frederick Douglass Papers*, series 1: *Speeches, Debates and Interviews*, vol. 3: *1855–63*, ed. John W. Blassingame (New Haven, Conn.: Yale University Press, 1986), 596.

10. For his bravery, Carney was the first African American awarded the Congressional Medal of Honor, in 1900. See Hondon B. Hargrove, *Black Union Soldiers in the Civil War* (Jefferson, N.C.: McFarland, 1988), 156. See also Luis F. Emilio, *A Brave Black Regiment* (New York: Bantam, 1992), 81, 84, 90.

11. Philip S. Foner and George E. Walker, eds., *Proceedings of the Black National and State Conventions, 1865–1900* (Philadelphia: Temple University Press, 1986), 61, 160, 250.

12. Ibid. Black veterans in the North also pushed for an end to segregation and voting restrictions outside the South. For more on the struggles of black veterans, see Paul A. Cimbala and Randall M. Miller, eds., *Union Soldiers and the Northern Home Front: Wartime Experiences, Postwar Adjustments* (New York: Fordham University Press, 2002); and Donald Robert Shaffer, *After the Glory: The Struggles of Black Civil War Veterans* (Lawrence: University Press of Kansas, 2004).

13. Stephanie McCurry takes up the question of slaves' political subjectivity in the South in her essay "Citizens, Soldiers' Wives, and 'Hiley Hope Up Slaves': The Problem of Political Obligation in the Civil War South," in *Gender and the Southern Body Politic*, ed. Nancy Bercaw (Jackson: University of Mississippi Press, 2000), 95–130.

14. On slave property and ownership, see Dylan C. Penningroth, *The Claims of Kinfolk: African American Property and Community in the Nineteenth-Century South* (Chapel Hill: University of North Carolina Press, 2003).

15. Reginald Washington, "Geneology Notes: The Southern Claims Commission, a Source for African-American Roots," *Negro History Bulletin* 59 (1996): 15. See also Frank Wysor Klingberg, *The Southern Claims Commission* (Berkeley: University of California Press, 1955).

16. Testimony of Moses Hampton, Claim 14476, *Southern Claims Commission, Approved Claims, 1871–1880: Alabama*, roll 1, National Archives Microfilm Publication M2062 (Washington, D.C.: National Archives and Records Administration, 1999).

17. Ibid.

18. Stevens quoted in Hans L. Trefousse, *Thaddeus Stevens: Nineteenth-Century Egalitarian* (Chapel Hill: University of North Carolina Press, 1997), 172.

19. Carl Schurz, *Report on the Condition of the South*, Senate Executive Document no. 2, 39th Cong., 1st sess., Dec. 19, 1865.

20. *National Anti-Slavery Standard* (New York), June 10, 1865; Trefousse, *Thaddeus Stevens*, 170–71. See also David Blight's excellent discussion of Stevens's use of "bloody shirt rhetoric" in *Race and Reunion: The Civil War in American Memory* (Cambridge, Mass.: Harvard University Press, 2001), 50–52.

21. Samuel R. Snyder to Andrew Johnson, June 5, 1865, in LeRoy Graf et al., eds., *The Papers of Andrew Johnson*, 16 vols. (Knoxville: University of Tennessee Press, 1967–2000), 8:184–86 (hereinafter cited as *Johnson Papers*); E. D. Morgan to Johnson, May 29, 1865, *Johnson Papers*, 134–35; E. A. Thomas to Johnson, May 19, 1865, *Johnson Papers*, 90–91; "An Ever Union Soldier" to Johnson, Nov. 25, 1865, *Johnson Papers*, 431–32; Alex N. Wilson to Andrew Johnson, Oct. 25, 1865, *Johnson Papers*, 286.

22. *The Nation* (New York), July 13, 1865, 37.

23. On the role of violence in American political culture, see, among others, Richard Slotkin, *Regeneration Through Violence: The Mythology of the American Frontier, 1600– 1800* (Middletown, Conn.: Wesleyan University Press, 1973); and Richard Maxwell Brown, *Strain of Violence: Historical Studies of American Violence and Vigilantism* (New York: Oxford University Press, 1975). More recently, scholars have begun to explore the interdependence of state-sanctioned violence with methods of extralegal control, such as lynching. On this issue, see Christopher Waldrep, *The Many Faces of Judge Lynch: Extralegal Violence and Punishment in America* (New York: Palgrave, 2002); and Michael J. Pfeifer, *Rough Justice: Lynching and American Society, 1874–1947* (Urbana: University of Illinois Press, 2004).

24. Edmund S. Morgan, *Inventing the People: The Rise of Popular Sovereignty in England and America* (New York: Norton, 1988), 13.

25. Max Weber, *The Theory of Social and Economic Organization* (New York: Free Press, 1964), 156.

11. Reconstructing the Nation, Reconstructing the Party: Postwar Republicans and the Evolution of a Party / Michael Green

1. The most recent study of this often-fractious group is Doris Kearns Goodwin, *Team of Rivals: The Political Genius of Abraham Lincoln* (New York: Simon & Schuster, 2005). See also Michael S. Green, *Freedom, Union, and Power: Lincoln and His Party During the Civil War* (New York: Fordham University Press, 2004); and Burton J. Hendrick, *Lincoln's War Cabinet* (Boston: Little, Brown, 1946).

2. Gideon Welles to Andrew Johnson, July 27, 1869, cited in Brooks D. Simpson, *The Reconstruction Presidents* (Lawrence: University Press of Kansas, 1998), 62; Salmon P. Chase, diary entry, Apr. 15, 1865, in David H. Donald, ed., *Inside Lincoln's Cabinet: The Civil War Diaries of Salmon P. Chase* (New York: Knopf, 1954), 268; Roy P. Basler, ed., *The Collected Works of Abraham Lincoln*, 9 vols. (New Brunswick, N.J.: Rutgers University Press, 1953–55), 8:403 (hereinafter cited as *Collected Works*); William Hanchett, *The Lincoln Murder Conspiracies* (Urbana: University of Illinois Press, 1983), 37.

3. On the Whig Party and the impact of Tyler and Fillmore, see Michael F. Holt, *The Rise and Fall of the American Whig Party: Jacksonian Politics and the Onset of the Civil War* (New York: Oxford University Press, 1999); and Sean Wilentz, *The Rise of*

American Democracy: Jefferson to Lincoln (New York: Norton, 2005). On the vice presidency and its problems, see Arthur M. Schlesinger Jr., *The Cycles of American History* (Boston: Houghton Mifflin, 1986), 337–72.

4. Eric Foner, *Free Soil, Free Labor, Free Men: The Ideology of the Republican Party Before the Civil War* (New York: Oxford University Press, 1970).

5. Lincoln, "First Inaugural Address—Final Text," Mar. 4, 1861, *Collected Works*, 4:265–66, 271. For a discussion of when the era began and ended, see Eric Foner, *Reconstruction: America's Unfinished Revolution, 1863–1877* (New York: Harper & Row, 1988), xvii, xxvii. On Lincoln and wartime Reconstruction, see William C. Harris, *With Charity for All: Lincoln and the Restoration of the Union* (Lexington: University Press of Kentucky, 1997). I have relied heavily upon both of these books for the details of Reconstruction.

6. The outstanding one-volume history of the era is James M. McPherson, *Battle Cry of Freedom: The Civil War Era, 1848–1865* (New York: Oxford University Press, 1988). On Civil War politics, see Mark E. Neely Jr., *The Union Divided: Party Conflict in the Civil War North* (Cambridge, Mass.: Harvard University Press, 2002); Joel H. Silbey, *A Respectable Minority: The Democratic Party in the Civil War Era, 1860–1868* (New York: Norton, 1977); and Adam I. P. Smith, *No Party Now: Politics in the Civil War North* (New York: Oxford University Press, 2006).

7. See T. Harry Williams, *Lincoln and His Generals* (New York: Knopf, 1952); and Bruce Tap, *Over Lincoln's Shoulder: The Committee on the Conduct of the War* (Lawrence: University Press of Kansas, 1998).

8. David Herbert Donald traces Lincoln's actions in *Lincoln* (New York: Simon & Schuster, 1995). So does Phillip Shaw Paludan in *The Presidency of Abraham Lincoln* (Lawrence: University Press of Kansas, 1994).

9. Lincoln, "Annual Message to Congress," Dec. 3, 1861, *Collected Works*, 5:49; Allen C. Guelzo, *Lincoln's Emancipation Proclamation: The End of Slavery in America* (New York: Simon & Schuster, 2004); John Hope Franklin, *The Emancipation Proclamation* (Garden City, N.Y.: Doubleday, 1963).

10. See Guelzo, *Lincoln's Emancipation Proclamation*. An excellent study of Radical Republican attitudes is Hans L. Trefousse, *The Radical Republicans: Lincoln's Vanguard for Racial Justice, 1863–1869* (New York: Knopf, 1969).

11. The outstanding studies on constitutional questions in the Civil War are James G. Randall, *Constitutional Problems Under Lincoln* (Urbana: University of Illinois Press, 1951); and Harold M. Hyman, *A More Perfect Union: The Impact of the Civil War and Reconstruction on the Constitution* (New York: Knopf, 1973).

12. "Proclamation of Amnesty and Reconstruction," Dec. 8, 1863, *Collected Works*, 7: 53–56.

13. Foner, *Reconstruction*, 61–62. See also Richard H. Abbott, *The Republican Party and the South, 1855–1877: The First Southern Strategy* (Chapel Hill: University of North Carolina Press, 1986).

14. *New York Tribune*, Aug. 5, 1864; Herman Belz, *Reconstructing the Union: Theory and Policy During the Civil War* (Ithaca, N.Y.: Cornell University Press, 1969), 227–31; *The New York Times*, Aug. 9, 1864.

15. John Hay, diary entry, July 4, 1864, in Tyler Dennett, ed., *Lincoln and the Civil War in the Diary of John Hay* (New York: Dodd, Mead, 1939), 204; Lincoln, "To Members of the Cabinet," Dec. 23, 1862, *Collected Works*, 6:17; Lincoln, "Opinion on the Admission of West Virginia into the Union," Dec. 31, 1862, *Collected Works*, 6:26–28; LaWanda Cox, *Lincoln and Black Freedom: A Study in Presidential Leadership* (Columbia: University of South Carolina Press, 1981); Peyton McCrary, *Abraham Lincoln and Reconstruction: The Louisiana Experiment* (Princeton: Princeton University Press, 1978).

16. On Lincoln's relationship with the radicals, see especially Trefousse, *Radical Republicans*. See also Hendrick, *Lincoln's War Cabinet*, and Goodwin, *Team of Rivals*.

17. On the Thirteenth Amendment, see Michael Vorenberg, *Final Freedom: The Civil War, the Abolition of Slavery, and the Thirteenth Amendment* (Cambridge: Cambridge University Press, 2001).

18. Lincoln, "Second Inaugural Address," Mar. 4, 1865, *Collected Works*, 8:332–33; Donald, *Lincoln*, 566–68; Paludan, *The Presidency of Abraham Lincoln*, 304–5; Ronald C. White Jr., *Lincoln's Greatest Speech: The Second Inaugural* (New York: Simon & Schuster, 2002).

19. Donald, *Lincoln*, 589–92; Foner, *Reconstruction*, 74–75.

20. Trefousse, *Radical Republicans*, 307; George W. Julian, *Political Recollections, 1840–1872* (Chicago: Jansen, McClurg & Co., 1884).

21. David H. Donald, *Charles Sumner and the Rights of Man* (New York: Knopf, 1970). Many of Blair's ideas about reconstituting the party system may be found in the S. L. M. Barlow Papers, Huntington Library, San Marino, California. See also LaWanda Cox and John H. Cox, *Politics, Principle, and Prejudice, 1865–1866: Dilemma of Reconstruction America* (New York: Free Press of Glencoe, 1963).

22. Smith, *No Party Now*, argues for the lack of loyalty to party. See also Green, *Freedom, Union, and Power*, 253–99. On the dissolution of the old party system, see William E. Gienapp, *The Origins of the Republican Party, 1852–1856* (New York: Oxford University Press, 1987); and Michael F. Holt, *The Fate of Their Country: Politicians, Slavery Extension, and the Coming of the Civil War* (New York: Hill & Wang, 2004).

23. Thaddeus Stevens to Johnson, Caledonia Iron Works, May 16, 1865, in Beverly Wilson Palmer, ed., *The Selected Papers of Thaddeus Stevens*, vol. 2: *April 1865–August 1868* (Pittsburgh: University of Pittsburgh Press, 1998), 5; Stevens to Johnson, Philadelphia, July 6, 1865, in ibid., 7. See also Stevens to Charles Sumner, Philadelphia, May 10, 1865, in ibid., 4; Stevens to Sumner, Caledonia Iron Works, May 17, 1865, in ibid., 6; and Stevens to William D. Kelley, Caledonia, May 30, 1865, in ibid., 6. See also Hans L. Trefousse, *Thaddeus Stevens: Nineteenth Century Egalitarian* (Chapel Hill: University of North Carolina Press, 1997).

24. *New York Herald*, May 20, 22, and 24, 1865, in Brooks D. Simpson, Leroy P. Graf, and John Muldowny, eds., *Advice After Appomattox: Letters to Andrew Johnson, 1865–1866* (Knoxville: University of Tennessee Press, 1987), 32n11, 67–68; John Niven, *Salmon P. Chase: A Biography* (New York: Oxford University Press, 1995); Frederick J. Blue, *Salmon P. Chase: A Life in Politics* (Kent, Ohio: Kent State University Press, 1987); Hans L. Trefousse, *Carl Schurz* (Knoxville: University of Tennessee Press, 1982).

25. Salmon P. Chase to Johnson, Hilton Head, May 17, 1865, *Advice After Appomattox*, 26; Chase to Johnson, Beaufort, May 4, 1865, in ibid., 18; Chase to Johnson, Beaufort Harbor, May 7, 1865, in ibid., 20; Chase to Johnson, Charleston, May 12, 1865, in ibid., 23; Chase to Johnson, Fernandina, Florida, May 21, 1865, in ibid., 35; Chase to Johnson, Key West, May 23, 1865, in ibid., 37, 62; Carl Schurz to Johnson, Hilton Head, July 28, 1865, in ibid., 80.

26. Simpson, Graf, and Muldowny, eds., *Advice After Appomattox*, 62–63; Foner, *Reconstruction*, 176–227; Simpson, *The Reconstruction Presidents*, 67–132.

27. Schurz to Johnson, Vicksburg, Mississippi, Aug. 29, 1865, in *Advice After Appomattox*, 112.

28. Hans L. Trefousse, *Andrew Johnson: A Biography* (New York: Norton, 1989), 214–310.

29. Foner, *Reconstruction*, 77–260. On Trumbull, see Ralph J. Roske, *His Own Counsel: The Life and Times of Lyman Trumbull* (Reno: University of Nevada Press, 1979). On the evolution of Republicans in Congress and their relations with Johnson, see Michael

Les Benedict, *A Compromise of Principle: Congressional Republicans and Reconstruction, 1863–1869* (New York: Norton, 1974).

30. Foner, *Reconstruction*, 261–332; Simpson, *The Reconstruction Presidents*, 67–132.

31. Foner, *Reconstruction*, 333–411; Michael Les Benedict, *The Impeachment and Trial of Andrew Johnson* (New York: Norton, 1973); Hans L. Trefousse, *Impeachment of a President: Andrew Johnson, the Blacks, and Reconstruction* (Knoxville: University of Tennessee Press, 1975).

32. George C. Rable, *But There Was No Peace: The Role of Violence in the Politics of Reconstruction* (Athens: University of Georgia Press, 1984).

33. See Glyndon G. Van Deusen, *William Henry Seward* (New York: Oxford University Press, 1967); William E. Smith, *The Francis Preston Blair Family in Politics*, 2 vols. (New York: Macmillan, 1933); Charles A. Jellison, *Fessenden of Maine: Civil War Senator* (Syracuse, N.Y.: Syracuse University Press, 1962).

34. Mark Perry, *Grant and Twain: The Story of a Friendship That Changed America* (New York: Random House, 2004); Mark Twain and Charles Dudley Warner, *The Gilded Age* (reprint ed., New York: Oxford University Press, 1996); Mark Wahlgren Summers, *The Gilded Age, Or, The Hazard of New Functions* (Upper Saddle River, N.J.: Prentice Hall, 1997).

35. Ulysses S. Grant to Johnson, Washington, D.C., Dec. 18, 1865, in John Y. Simon, ed., *The Papers of Ulysses S. Grant*, vol. 15: *May 1–December 31, 1865* (Carbondale: Southern Illinois University Press, 1988), 434–36. See also Brooks D. Simpson, *Let Us Have Peace: Ulysses S. Grant and the Politics of War and Reconstruction* (Chapel Hill: University of North Carolina Press, 1991); and William S. McFeely, *Grant: A Biography* (New York: Norton, 1981).

36. Simpson, *Let Us Have Peace*, deals amply with this subject.

37. A less favorable view of Grant's attitudes about his role as president is McFeely, *Grant*. See also Benedict, *A Compromise of Principle*.

38. Heather Cox Richardson, *The Greatest Nation of the Earth: Republican Economic Policies during the Civil War* (Cambridge, Mass.: Harvard University Press, 1997).

39. Foner, *Reconstruction*, 488–511. See also Andrew L. Slap, *The Doom of Reconstruction: The Liberal Republicans in the Civil War Era* (New York: Fordham University Press, 2006).

40. George W. Julian, "Amendment of the Constitution," speech, House of Representatives, Jan. 29, 1866, in *Speeches on Political Questions* (New York: Negro University Press, 1970), 316.

41. For more on the struggle over black suffrage, see Xi Wang, *The Trial of Democracy: Black Suffrage and Northern Republicans, 1860–1910* (Athens: University of Georgia Press, 1997).

42. Simpson, *The Reconstruction Presidents*, 175.

43. Although I do diverge from their interpretations, my thinking here owes much to Slap, *The Doom of Reconstruction* and Heather Cox Richardson, *The Death of Reconstruction: Race, Labor, and Politics in the Post–Civil War North, 1865–1901* (Cambridge, Mass.: Harvard University Press, 2001).

44. George S. Merriam, *The Life and Times of Samuel Bowles*, 2 vols. (New York: Classic Books, 1885), 2:125.

45. Grant to Edwards Pierrepont, Washington, D.C., Sept. 13, 1875, Pierrepont Papers, Beinecke Library, Yale University, New Haven, Connecticut.

46. Ari Hoogenboom, *Rutherford B. Hayes: Warrior and President* (Lawrence: University of Kansas Press, 1995).

47. Foner, *Reconstruction*, 612.

Contributors

Rod Andrew Jr. is a professor of history at Clemson University in South Carolina. He is the author of *Long Gray Lines: The Southern Military School Tradition, 1839–1915* and most recently *Wade Hampton: Confederate Warrior to Southern Redeemer.*

Aaron Astor is an assistant professor of history at Maryville College in Maryville, Tennessee. He is completing the revisions for his book *Belated Confederates: Black Politics, White Guerillas, and the Collapse of Conservative Unionism in Kentucky and Missouri, 1860–1870.*

Paul A. Cimbala is a professor of history at Fordham University in the Bronx, New York. His most recent publication is *American Soldiers' Lives: The Civil War.* He is completing *Soldiering on the Home Front: The United States Army's Veteran Reserve Corps during the Civil War and Reconstruction.*

Carole Emberton is an assistant professor of history at the University of Buffalo, The State University of New York. She is revising for publication her dissertation "The Politics of Protection: Violence and the Political Culture of Reconstruction."

Carol Faulkner is an associate professor of history at Syracuse University. She is the author of *Women's Radical Reconstruction: The Freedmen's Aid Movement.*

Derek W. Frisby is an assistant professor of history at Middle Tennessee State University in Murfreesboro. He is the editor of the *West Tennessee Historical Society Papers* and is completing his book manuscript *Homemade Yankees: West Tennessee Unionists in the Civil War Era.*

Michael Green is a professor of history at the College of Southern Nevada. He is the author of *Freedom, Union, and Power: Lincoln and His Party During the Civil War.* He is writing a history of the politics of the 1850s.

G. Ward Hubbs is an associate professor of history and archivist at Birmingham-Southern College in Alabama. He is the editor of *Voices of Company D: Diaries by the Greensboro Guards, Fifth Alabama Infantry Regiment,*

Army of Northern Virginia and the author of *Guarding Greensboro: A Confederate Company in the Making of a Southern Community.*

Anne E. Marshall is an assistant professor of history at Mississippi State University. She is presently completing her book manuscript *Lost Cause, Gained
Identity: History, Memory, and the Creation of a Confederate Kentucky.*

Randall M. Miller is the William Dirk Warren '50 Sesquicentennial Chair and
Professor of History at Saint Joseph's University. His most recent book, as co-
author, is *Unto a Good Land: A History of the American People.* He is collaborat-
ing, again, with Paul A. Cimbala on a new book about the Northern home front
during the Civil War.

Justin A. Nystrom is an assistant professor of history at Loyola University of
New Orleans. He is the author of the forthcoming *New Orleans after the Civil
War: Race, Politics, and a New Birth of Freedom.* His new work explores the
impact of emancipation on racial self-determination among free people of
color and immigrants in the urban South.

Jason Phillips is an assistant professor of history at Mississippi State University.
He is the author of *Diehard Rebels: The Confederate Culture of Invincibility.*

Margaret M. Storey is an associate professor of history at DePaul University
and the author of *Loyalty and Loss: Alabama's Unionists in the Civil War and
Reconstruction.* She is currently at work on a study of Civil War Memphis.

Denise E. Wright is a managing partner in a consulting firm that specializes in
educational publications. She is revising for publication her 2005 University of
Georgia doctoral dissertation, "Civil War and Reconstruction Welfare Programs for Georgia's White Poor: The State, the Freedmen's Bureau, and Northern Charity, 1863–1868," and is continuing her research into Northern
charitable agencies' roles in Reconstruction.

Index

abolitionists: African American, 94, 96, 176–77; female, 88–96, 98; male, 89, 96–98, 176–77, 201; white, 88–89, 201
African American soldiers: families of, 42, 90, 93; in Kentucky, 34–43, 50, 52–54, 56, 66; in Louisiana, 128–29, 131, 134; in Missouri, 34–36, 38–43, 52; significance of, 31, 33, 38, 49, 176–77; in Tennessee, 19–20; violence against, 31, 44–46, 198. *See also* Danville Shooting Affray; Fort Pillow Massacre; Louisiana Native Guards
African Americans: citizenship of, 31, 33, 96, 182, 184, 203; enfranchisement of, 99, 183–84, 188, 194, 200–1; enfranchisement of in particular states, 32, 65–66, 77; lynching of, 30, 46–47, 49; migration of, 50–51, 56, 127, 130, 134, 136; patriotic loyalty of, 174–79, 182; poor people among, 93–94, 106–7, 109–10, 117; violence against in border states, 30–32, 41–42, 45–53; violence against in former Confederate states, 80, 177, 197, 203. *See also* African American soldiers; Afro-Creoles; emancipation, social consequences of; free people of color; free women of color; freedmen; freedpeople; freedwomen; *and under names of particular states*
Afro-Creoles, 4, 122–26, 128–29, 131, 134–36
Alabama: African Americans in, 79–80, 84; during the Civil War, 69–73, 87; Freedmen's Bureau in, 76, 78–79, 81, 85, 108; post–Civil War era in, 3, 5–6, 69–70, 74, 78–87; white Unionists in, 3, 5–6, 69–74, 78–87
Andersonville Prison, 22, 117–18, 180

Berkeley, Henry R., 166, 167
Black Codes, 177, 201

blacks. *See* African American soldiers; African Americans; Afro-Creoles; free people of color; free women of color; freedmen; freedpeople; freedwomen
Blight, David, 144, 167, 172
border states, 32; Lincoln and, 186–87; emancipation in, 31, 33–35, 52, 55, 190; slavery in, 56–59, 66, 74, 106; social upheaval in, 31, 33, 37–39, 52; white Unionists in, 2–3, 31, 39. *See also* Kentucky; Missouri
Bramlette, Thomas, 40–41
Brownlow, William G., 12–21
Bruce, Henry Clay, 37–38, 39
Bruner, Peter, 34, 39
Bureau of Refugees, Freedmen and Abandoned Lands. *See* Freedmen's Bureau
Burns, Ken, 171–72
Butler, Benjamin F., 117, 131, 186

Case, Almon, 16–17
Casey, William, 159, 162
Cash, W. J., 156, 171
Caucasian (Lexington, Missouri, newspaper), 48–49, 50, 52
Chambers, Henry, 159, 165
Chase, Salmon P., 183, 189, 193–94, 197, 200
Chesnut, Mary Boykin, 144
Civil Rights Act (1866), 195
Civil War: Lincoln and, 7–8, 185–87, 190–91; military conduct of, 186. *See also* African American soldiers; Confederates; *and under names of particular states*
Clinton, Catherine, 144
Compromise of 1877, 1, 7, 129, 133, 203
Confederates: characterizations of Union soldiers by, 22, 147–48, 150, 161–65, 167–69; diehards among, 142–43, 154–56, 164–72, 198; disfranchisement of in Alabama, 77, 79–80; disfranchisement

of in Kentucky, 56, 58; disfranchise-
ment of in Missouri, 32, 48; disfran-
chisement of in Tennessee, 14–16,
20–21; invincibility ethos of, 155–61,
168, 171; nationalism of, 6, 156; post–
Civil War loyalty of, 6, 165–68, 173–75,
179–82; and white supremacism, 156.
See also Lost Cause narrative
Connor, Henry Calvin, 160, 167
Coulter, E. Merton, 55
Crédit Mobilier scandal, 200
Creoles of color, 4, 122–24, 126, 129, 137

Danville Shooting Affray, 44–46
Daughters of the Confederacy, United,
111, 149, 168
Davis, Jefferson, 144, 152, 180–81, 183
Desdunes, Rodolphe, 122–23
Douglass, Frederick, 96, 176
Drouet, Louise, 135–36
Duvernay, Sylvanie Morgan, 135–36

Early, Jubal, 152, 167–68
emancipation, social consequences of: in
border states, 31, 33, 52; in Kentucky,
30, 32, 55–59, 61–62; in Missouri, 32,
43; in New Orleans, 125–28, 134–35,
137; in Tennessee, 28
Emancipation Proclamation: Lincoln
and, 187, 190; and border states, 34–35,
52; political consequences of, 11, 58, 62,
187
Esnard, Siméon, 129; descendants of, 127–
30, 133
Etheridge, Emerson, 12, 15–16, 18–21

Farris, Frank, 16–17
Fifteenth Amendment, 32, 99–100
Foner, Eric, 203
Foote, Shelby, 171–72
Fort Pillow Massacre, 12, 176, 180
Fourteenth Amendment, 18, 62, 79, 80
Franklin, John Hope, 102
free people of color, 122–27, 132, 137,
178–79
free women of color, 134–36
freedmen: enfranchisement of, 17–18, 20,
76, 99, 188, 201; in Tennessee State
Guard, 19–20. *See also* freedpeople
freedmen's aid movement: emphasis of,
94, 96, 97; women in, 88–100

Freedmen's Bureau: in Alabama, 76, 78–
79, 81, 85, 108; Johnson and, 195; focus
of, 64, 93–94, 97–98, 177; in Georgia,
101, 107–10, 112–13; in Kentucky, 46, 52,
59, 65; migration network of, 94–95;
and private charities, 97–98, 110, 112–
13, 119; white poor aided by, 101–2,
107–10, 112–13, 117–19; women and, 88–
89, 92–93, 96–100
freedpeople: aid to, 90–94, 96–100, 107,
109–10, 195–96, 202–3; army's treatment of, 90–92; Creoles of color and,
126, 129; employment for, 94–95, 100;
migration of, 94, 126; patriotic loyalty
of, 175, 177–79; relocation of, 94–95;
rights of, 178–79, 191; violence against,
17, 19, 80, 177, 197; in Washington area,
89–91, 93–94
freedwomen, 89–97

Gallagher, Gary, 156, 167
Georgia: during the Civil War and its
aftermath, 101, 103–10, 112–16, 120;
Freedmen's Bureau in, 101, 107–10,
112–13; poor African Americans in,
106–7, 109–10; poor whites in, 4, 101,
103–10, 112–16, 120; white Unionists in,
101
German Americans, 13, 32, 49, 135, 184
Goldfield, David, 169–70
Goodwyn, Kit, 144, 152
Grant, Ulysses S.: and Andrew Johnson,
198–99; during the Civil War, 198;
presidency of, 197–203; and Republican Party, 185–86, 196–97, 199–202;
views on Reconstruction of, 198, 201,
203
Greeley, Horace, 200
Green, Elna C., 102
Griffing, Josephine, 90–100
Grinnell, Josiah, 64

Hampton, Moses, 178–79
Hampton, Preston, 139–46, 152–53
Hampton, Wade, III: before the Civil
War, 140–41, 151–53; during the Civil
War, 139–45, 147–48, 151, 153; and the
Lost Cause, 139–40, 142, 145–53; in the
post–Civil War era, 140, 145–53; racial
views of, 150–53
Hampton, Wade, IV, 139–40, 142, 144–45,
153

Hawkins, Alvin, 12–13, 21, 23
Hawkins, Isaac, 12, 20–21, 23–24, 27
Hayes, Rutherford B., 203
Howard, Oliver Otis, 59, 92, 97–98, 110, 117, 119
Hurst, Fielding, 14, 17, 22–23
Hyman, Harold, 173–74

Irish Americans, 13, 42, 47
"iron-clad oath," 11, 78, 173, 188
Italian Americans, 132

Jackson, Jim, 30, 43, 51
James, Charles Fenton, 164, 170
James-Younger gang, 50
Johnson, Andrew: impeachment of, 195–97; lenient Reconstruction policy of, 15, 74–75, 83, 173, 180, 192–95; and Republican Party, 184, 191–97, 201; and Tennessee, 9–14; and Grant, 198–99; and Union Party, 192, 194
Jones, Edmund, 168–69, 170
Joseph, Peter, 134
Julian, George Washington, 201

Keith, Alice B., 120–21
Kentucky: African Americans in, 30–48, 50–61, 65–66; during the Civil War and its aftermath, 2, 30–48, 50–67; white Unionists in, 36, 39–42, 44–45, 55, 58–64
Kerber, Linda, 31
Ku Klux Klan, 3, 31, 201; in Alabama, 3, 5, 69–70, 80–81, 84–87; in Tennessee, 2, 16, 21

Lakin, Arad, 3, 83, 84
Leath, Ebenezer, 69–70, 85
Legal Tender Act, 199–200
Liberal Republicans, 137, 200
Lincoln, Abraham: assassination of, 14, 180, 183–84, 191; cabinet of, 183, 186, 189, 199; and the Civil War, 7–8, 185–87, 190–91; and Emancipation Proclamation, 8, 186–87, 189–90; presidential election of, 72, 141; Radical Republicans and, 183, 188–89, 191; and Reconstruction, 183–91, 194
Locke, David Ross, 66–67
Lost Cause narrative, 140, 144, 148, 152, 167–71; Hampton family and, 139–40, 144–53; Jubal Early and, 152, 167–68; in

Kentucky, 55, 68; and white supremacism, 140, 144, 149, 151
Louisiana: laws affecting races in, 125, 131–32, 134; Republican Party in, 128, 129, 133, 137. See also New Orleans
Louisiana Native Guards, 126, 128, 131
Lowell, Anna, 95
loyalty, patriotic, 174; African Americans and, 174–79, 182; of Confederates, 6, 165–68, 173–75, 179–82; military enforcement of, 173–75, 179, 181; oaths of, 165, 167, 173–75, 179, 181–82, 188; political uses of, 174–75, 179. See also "iron-clad oath"
lynching, 30, 46, 47, 49

McKim, J. Miller, 97–98
McLure, John, 155, 159
McPherson, James, 171–72
Methodist Episcopal Church, 3, 69, 82–85
Military Reconstruction Acts, 77–79, 86, 196
Missouri: African Americans in, 30–41, 43, 46–52; Civil War era in, 30–31, 37–41, 43, 50–52, post–Civil War era in, 2, 32–36, 40–42, 46–52; Radical Republicans in, 32, 50; white Unionists on, 2, 30, 32, 39–41, 50
Mott, Lucretia, 98

Nasby, Petroleum V. (fictional character), 66–67
Nell, William C., 176
New Orleans, 4, 123; antebellum, 125, 128–29, 132, 137; during the Civil War, 125–29, 131–33; post–Civil War era in, 122, 127–28, 130–37
New York Ladies' Southern Relief Association (NYLSRA), 111–16
New York Southern Society, 111
Norton, Charles Eliot, 173, 175

Pacific Railroad Act, 199–200
Palmer, John, 56, 65
passing (racial), 122–38
patriotism. See loyalty, patriotic
Penn, Blanche, 137
Pickens, Samuel, 162, 167
Plessy v. Ferguson, 134
poor people: African American, 93–94, 106–7; 109–10, 117; relief to, 92–93, 96–121; white, 78, 101–10, 112–20
Pope, John, 79, 173–74

Rable, George C., 2
Radical Republicans: and Lincoln, 183,
    188–89, 191–92; and Johnson, 191–93,
    196, 199; and conduct of the Civil War,
    186; and emancipation, 187–90; in
    Missouri, 32, 49–50; and post–Civil
    War Southern loyalty, 173, 179–80
Rankin, David, 122, 124, 125
Raynal, Auguste, 128; descendants of, 127–
    28, 130, 133
Reconstruction: Lincoln and, 183–91, 194;
    in Alabama, 70, 77–78; Johnson and,
    15, 74–75, 83, 173, 180, 191–95; begin-
    nings of, 3, 185, 187; border states and,
    57; Confederate intransigence toward,
    171, 179, 193, 197–98; ending of, 7, 53,
    200–3; racial politics of, 76–77, 80,
    126–28, 133; Radical, 51–53, 77–78, 102,
    168, 196; Republican views on, 75–76,
    80, 185, 188–202; in Tennessee, 14;
    Grant and, 190, 200; white Unionists
    and, 9, 29, 75–80; women's vision for,
    88, 96, 99
Redemption, 28–29, 53, 134, 139, 150, 175
Regulators, 46–47, 49–50, 52
republican government, violence and,
    181–82
Republican Party: and aid to freedpeople,
    93, 191, 195, 200, 202–3; Johnson and,
    184, 191–97, 201; and Emancipation
    Proclamation, 187; evolution of, 184–
    87, 191, 196–97, 199–203; in Louisiana,
    128–29, 133–34; and post–Civil War
    nation-building, 174, 179, 181–82, 188,
    193; Grant and, 185–86, 196–97, 199–
    202; views on Reconstruction in, 75–
    80, 185, 188–97, 199–202; white
    Unionists and, 76. See also Radical
    Republicans
Rousseau, Lovell, 64
Rousseve, Charles Barthelemy, 122–23
Rubin, Anne Sarah, 156, 167

Sauvinet, Charles St. Albin, 130–33;
    descendants of, 132–33
Schurz, Carl, 180, 193–94
Seward, William Henry, 183, 189, 197
Shaffner, John, 157, 159, 170
Sherman, William T., 140, 147–48, 150,
    186
Smith, William H., 148, 153

Southern Claims Commission (SCC), 23–
    27, 69–71, 178–79
Southern Famine Relief Commission, 116
Southern Historical Society, 146
Southerners, white, culture of, 5–6, 123,
    155–56, 170–71; and religion, 157–60,
    164. See also Confederates; Lost Cause
    narrative; white supremacism
Stanton, Edwin, 183, 196, 197
Stevens, Thaddeus, 179–81, 192–93, 195–
    97, 202
Sullivan, Algernon Sydney, 111
Sullivan, Mary Mildred Hamilton, 111
Sumner, Charles, 64, 188, 193–94, 200,
    202
Sweet, William W., 83

Tennessee: Johnson and, 9–14; Civil War
    era in, 9–14, 25–28; East, 10–12, 15, 19,
    21, 28; Middle, 10–11, 13, 15, 18, 20, 28;
    post–Civil War era in, 2, 14–29;
    Reconstruction in, 14; Redemption of,
    28–29; West, 2, 9, 11–29; white Union-
    ists in, 2, 9–29
Tenure of Office Act, 196
Thirteenth Amendment, 43, 59, 190–91,
    201
Tillman, Benjamin R., 139, 151
Truth, Sojourner, 94–95

Union Leagues, 18–20, 77–81, 87
Union Party, 184–85, 190–92, 194
Unionists, white: in Alabama, 3, 6, 69–74,
    78–87; in border states, 2, 31, 52–53;
    during the Civil War, 12, 23–28, 69–71;
    in Georgia, 101; in Kentucky, 36, 39–
    42, 44–45, 55, 58–64; in Missouri, 2,
    30, 32, 39–41, 50; and Reconstruction,
    9, 29, 75–80; and Republican Party, 76;
    in South Carolina, 150; and Southern
    Claims Commission, 23–27, 69–71; in
    Tennessee, 2, 9–17, 19, 21–29; violence
    against in Alabama, 69–70, 72–74, 80–
    82, 84–87; violence against in Ken-
    tucky, 64; violence against in
    Tennessee, 2, 13–14, 16–17, 21
United Daughters of the Confederacy, 111,
    149, 168

vagrancy laws, 57
Vigers, William H., 132–33, 134

Wade, Benjamin, 188–89, 191, 197, 202
Wade-Davis bill, 188–89
Waring, J. Frederick, 155, 160
Washington, D.C., freedpeople in and near, 89, 90–91, 93–94
Waterson, Henry, 67–68
white supremacism, 48–50, 68, 156; Lost Cause and, 140, 144, 149, 151. *See also* Ku Klux Klan; Regulators
whiteness, 123. *See also* Southerners, white, culture of

Wilbur, Julia, 89–99
Williams, Diana, 96–97
Wolford, Frank, 40–41, 53
women, actions and roles of: in aiding white Southerners, 111, 116; in freedmen's aid movement, 3, 88–100; men's opposition to, 88–89, 91, 98, 100, 116; for women's rights, 88–90, 90–100. *See also* free women of color; freedwomen
Woodward, C. Vann, 3, 58, 171

Reconstructing America
Paul A. Cimbala, series editor

1. Hans L. Trefousse, *Impeachment of a President: Andrew Johnson, the Blacks, and Reconstruction.*

2. Richard Paul Fuke, *Imperfect Equality: African Americans and the Confines of White Ideology in Post-Emancipation Maryland.*

3. Ruth Currie-McDaniel, *Carpetbagger of Conscience: A Biography of John Emory Bryant.*

4. Paul A. Cimbala and Randall M. Miller, eds., *The Freedmen's Bureau and Reconstruction: Reconsiderations.*

5. Herman Belz, *A New Birth of Freedom: The Republican Party and Freedmen's Rights, 1861 to 1866.*

6. Robert Michael Goldman, *"A Free Ballot and a Fair Count": The Department of Justice and the Enforcement of Voting Rights in the South, 1877–1893.*

7. Ruth Douglas Currie, ed., *Emma Spaulding Bryant: Civil War Bride, Carpetbagger's Wife, Ardent Feminist—Letters, 1860–1900.*

8. Robert Francis Engs, *Freedom's First Generation: Black Hampton, Virginia, 1861–1890.*

9. Robert F. Kaczorowski, *The Politics of Judicial Interpretation: The Federal Courts, Department of Justice, and Civil Rights, 1866–1876.*

10. John Syrett, *The Civil War Confiscation Acts: Failing to Reconstruct the South.*

11. Michael Les Benedict, *Preserving the Constitution: Essays on Politics and the Constitution in the Reconstruction Era.*

12. Andrew L. Slap, *The Doom of Reconstruction: The Liberal Republicans in the Civil War Era.*

13. Edmund L. Drago, *Confederate Phoenix: Rebel Children and Their Families in South Carolina.*

14. Mary Farmer-Kaiser, *Freedwomen and the Freedmen's Bureau: Race, Gender, and Public Policy in the Age of Emancipation.*